MW00652902

SPARTAN SEASONS II

OTHER LYNN HENNING BOOKS:

Spartan Seasons:
The Triumphs and Turmoil of Michigan State Sports
Published by Momentum Publishing, 1987

Bottom of the Ninth, by Kirk Gibson, with Lynn Henning
Published by Thomson Gale, 1997

SPARTAN SEASONS II

More Triumphs and Turmoil
of Michigan State Sports

LYNN HENNING

Sports Seasons Publishing

Spartan Seasons II:
More Triumphs and Turmoil of Michigan State Sports

Copyright © 2006 by Sports Seasons Publishing LLC
First Edition 2006

Sports Seasons Publishing books are available
for special promotions and charitable fund-raisers
and for use as premiums.
For details, contact the publisher,
attention Special Markets.

Jacket design by Image Graphics & Design
Photography editor: Stan Stein
Interior design by Jacinta Calcut and Bill Haney

Printed in the United States of America

Sports Seasons Publishing
1947 Long Lake Shores
Bloomfield Hills, MI 48302
email: sportsseasonspublishing@comcast.net

ISBN 0-9787195-1-4

TO SUSIE
Whose love is always patient

It was vintage Michigan State. The pattern had long since been chronicled; it would be repeated in years to come. Act impulsively or reflexively when selecting or retaining a coach. Be over-generous when restraint was needed; be tight-fisted when a bold and extravagant decision could lead to years of success.

FOREWORD

THIS BOOK IS FOR THAT MOST CURSED, MOST BLESSED of creatures: the devoted follower of Michigan State Spartans sports teams.

I rejoice with them, I have pity for them.

It's easy enough for me to do that because I admit to being one of them.

There are few highs in life more glorious than the afterglow of a victory over the University of Michigan Wolverines. And there are few lows more dismal than the depths the Spartan fan is plunged into by yet another clock malfunction or blocked field goal that snatches defeat from the jaws of seemingly certain victory.

Devoted Spartan fans have known it all, being jerked up and down like a Yo-Yo, usually several times a season and sometimes within the same week.

So this book is for them, the lifelong loyalists of the Green and White, through good days and bad, and everything in between.

More than twenty years ago, I got the bright idea of publishing a book on the triumphs and turmoils of Michigan State sports. Teaming with sports- and books-savvy Bill Haney (ironically a very unbiased UM grad), we enlisted Lynn Henning, one of the best sports writers anywhere—and an MSU sports expert who doesn't wear green-tinted glasses—and brought out the original *Spartan Seasons.*

Our timing, fall of 1987, was fortuitous, to say the least.

With the cooperation of George Perles' talented Lorenzo White,

Andre Rison, and the Gang Green defense, State won the Big Ten title and capped off a super season with a victory over Southern Cal's Trojans, 20-17, in the 1988 Rose Bowl.

Ah, those were the days.

Little did we know that a seemingly endless gridiron desert with few oases lay just over the horizon.

But we also couldn't see into a rosier future that was in store under the guidance and inspiration of a basketball genius named Tom Izzo. There was indeed life after Magic and Special K. Once again, the excitement and glory would return to the hardcourt, stamping MSU as an elite basketball program for the first time in school history.

And there would be other delightful surprises, such as the rise to prominence of the hockey program under one of the game's greatest coaches ever, Ron Mason. Or that the women's basketballers would surge to the forefront with their great run in the NCAA tournament.

Many exciting, surprising and triumphant moments on the Spartans' fields of sports. And, as we have discovered and recount in these pages, many fascinating, untold stories.

So, it is no accident that we bring out *Spartan Seasons II* exactly twenty years after we launched the original. Planning for the current book began more than three years ago. There was already plenty to cover even before the tumultuous events of the last three years. The question was this: could Bill Haney and I convince Henning—whose stature had grown to place him among the premier sports writers in America—to take on the grueling task yet again? We were asking a distinguished writer with an already full plate to subject himself one more time to the burden of all the researching and interviewing, the reliving that must be done, the confirmation of facts with unimpeachable sources, before he could tell the story of this turbulent, tempestuous college sports program.

But we wanted the most definitive, thorough and insightful book that could be done on the subject, as well as the most compelling to read. So great is his knowledge of the subject and so special is Henning's access to the people who know the story behind the story, that had he not accepted the challenge, there was no Plan B and there would be no *Spartans Season II*.

So this has been a book a long while in the making. We hope our soul-mates among the legions of MSU and college sports followers find it worth the wait. In these pages, you will find new wrinkles on events already familiar to you. You will also find many provocative—even stunning—revelations never before reported.

By the time you turn the last page, you will have lived yet again through the roller-coaster emotions of the true Spartans fan. And you will have learned something new about a storied college sports program.

Perhaps that will make it easier to cope for the next twenty years with the triumphs and turmoils of Michigan State sports.

Stan Stein
August 22, 2006

PREFACE

ONE AFTERNOON IN MAY OF 1986, while working on a story for *The Detroit News*, there came a phone call requesting that I have lunch in Bloomfield Hills with Bill Haney and Stan Stein to discuss a book project they had been mulling. Their idea was that the modern-day stories of Michigan State's news-provoking sports program and major teams needed to be told in a behind-the-scenes fashion—the goal was to illuminate one of the more fascinating major-college athletic programs in America.

Their idea made sense. MSU had for decades been home to a university sports program that was endlessly making news, good and not so good, in a manner fairly disproportionate to other major universities. For example, a Rose Bowl trip (the 1965 national-championship team) and an epic Game of the Century event (MSU-Notre Dame, 1966) might be followed a decade later by one of the harshest NCAA probation sentences in collegiate history.

Through the years there had been grand hirings and ignominious firings spanning each of the two high-profile sports, football and basketball. In that context, an NCAA basketball championship (1979) lighted up East Lansing four years after a pre-game walkout by Spartan basketball players had helped pave the way for a coach's dismissal. Meanwhile, athletic directors of all flavors were leaving their particular impressions upon a Big Ten athletic department, as had been the case since Biggie Munn departed after suffering a stroke in October of 1971.

A decision was made to do the book: *Spartan Seasons, The Triumphs and Turmoil of Michigan State Sports*, which was released in July 1987, published by Haney—who has produced more than four hundred books during his career—in conjunction with Stein, an MSU alum and long-time active observer of the Michigan State sports scene, as Haney's associate.

Almost twenty years later, it became apparent that the essential purpose and value of the first *Spartan Seasons*—that a major-college sports program needed to be chronicled and revealed for more than the fate of its teams—warranted a twenty-year revisit.

There had been four head football coaches since the first *Spartan Seasons.* There had been five athletic directors. A new basketball coach by the name of Tom Izzo had arrived to build something of a dynasty in East Lansing.

It was time to do *Spartan Seasons II.*

This particular effort began in June 2003 with long interviews at the homes of two football coaches profiled in this book: George Perles and Nick Saban. In the ensuing three years, dozens more coaches, executives, administrators, and athletes have been interviewed—and, in some cases, repeatedly—in an effort to glean the fullest possible story of how Michigan State's indefatigable efforts toward building a prestigious sports program have succeeded, failed, been debated, or have been fought over.

The stories of how men and women were hired, and fired, are often dramatic, and many times instructive. There are moments of conviction throughout MSU sports history just as there have been exercises in conformity. There are portraits of courage and perhaps a few instances of desertion. There have been acts of political expediency and, at times, singular displays of statesmanship.

There have been sports other than football and basketball where additional color and news have become part of MSU's overall athletics mosaic. MSU hockey history was detailed in the first *Spartan Seasons.* Its story picks up in *Spartan Seasons II.* The Spartan women's basketball team, which has risen to stunning prominence during the past decade, is profiled in this book's final chapter.

Michigan State University's abiding strength, and its legacy, is that it is an eminently human community, flowing with the virtue and foibles shared by all of humankind. It is, in that sense, an expression of this very world, a reminder of who we are and, more important, who we are forever trying to be.

Lynn Henning
August 9, 2006

CONTENTS

CHAPTER 1

PERLES GOES FOR TWO

RECRUITING HIGH-OCTANE FOOTBALL PLAYERS had been the fuel powering George Perles and his five-year plan to put Michigan State into a Rose Bowl. Recruiting—and another Perles staple, tough defense—had taken the Spartans to Pasadena on January 1, 1988, when MSU did its best to make up for a twenty-two-year hiatus by stuffing Southern Cal, 20-17.

Perles stepped into a mess when he arrived in December of 1982. Michigan State under Muddy Waters had slid into irrelevance. Bad teams (2-9 in '82) and Division II-quality recruiting had left the Spartans in a bind that would be fixed only by new energy in the Duffy Daugherty Football Building and better talent on State's roster.

Perles made inroads in 1983 at 4-6-1, and likely would have been better if quarterback Dave Yarema had not been injured. In 1984, State posted a 6-5 mark and played in the Cherry Bowl. Halfway through Perles' second season, there was buzz that two of the state's best high-school players, Andre Rison of Flint Northwestern and John Miller of Farmington Hills Harrison, had all but committed to play football in East Lansing.

Rison would be the billboard catch, no question. He was a superstar prep athlete who figured to be a game-changer. Football quarterback, basketball standout, state-champion trackman. He was also the kind of player who always seemed to end up at Michigan. Bo Schembechler had no problem with tradition there. In the Field Marshal's mind, there was no way a new guy in East Lansing would step into Michigan's territory and shanghai prep talent Schembechler had decided should belong to U-M.

Perles had parceled MSU's recruiting turf into multi-state assignments. Charlie Baggett was in charge of Flint, Detroit and Florida. Nick Saban had Lansing, part of Ohio, and West Virginia. Morris Watts, when he hired on in 1986, was to oversee Indiana, etc. Steve Beckholt was recruiting coordinator and doing a nice job of identifying impact players MSU had been losing out on and perhaps overlooking for too many years.

Two heavily recruited players in January 1984 were Florida kids from Fort Lauderdale: Lorenzo White, a running back from Dillard High, and a wide receiver from St. Thomas Aquinas High named Michael Irvin.

White had been coaxed into visiting MSU, even if there were only two high-powered football schools he was seriously considering: Michigan and Tennessee. It had not been easy getting White to put MSU on his shopping list. He budged only after one of Baggett's old Spartan teammates from the early '70s, Greg Brewton, who lived in Fort Lauderdale, pressed White's mother to have her son at least take a peek at life in East Lansing.

Irvin seemed the better bet for MSU. He was a spectacularly talented wide receiver, one of seventeen kids from a single family whom Baggett figured might warm up to Perles and his father-figure persona. If Baggett knew anything about high school players and their tendencies deep into a recruiting process, he could see Irvin was headed for Michigan State.

White and Irvin visited on the same weekend in January, one of those red-carpet stay-overs when everything had gone smoothly for a school trying to convince warm-weather kids to come north. At mid-day Sunday, when players were chauffeured to the airport for their trips back home, Baggett was at the wheel as White and Irvin sat in the back seat talking about Michigan State and their futures.

"Lorenzo, this ain't the place for me," Irvin said. "But it's the place for you."

Irvin had deduced a George Perles offense would be the wrong match for a man who needed to catch passes, lots of them, to maximize his skills and NFL value. White, on the other hand, was made for Perles and for a power running game that needed a standout feature back.

Irvin decided on Miami. White opted for a school he never considered until his mother got a sales pitch from Spartan alum Brewton. MSU, he concluded, presented a better shot than he might get at Michigan or Tennessee, where running backs were in surplus and a guy, no matter how talented, could get buried.

Rison was another challenge altogether. Years later Baggett would call him the toughest recruiting project he had ever tackled. By autumn of his senior year, Rison was headed to Michigan State, in great part because Andre's grandfather was the household boss and had his grandson's respect. Baggett and grandpa had gotten close in a way recruiters and family members typically form a bond ahead of a high school kid's decision to follow suit. MSU figured to benefit.

If there was a problem securing Rison—separate from Schembechler's tenacity—and there was, it came in the person of Rison's high-school coach, Glenn Kelly. Kelly had sent star receiver Mark Ingram to MSU and figured it was Michigan's turn to grab Flint's premier high-school hotshot. Schembechler tended to see it that way, as well. He had touched down, dramatically, at Flint Northwestern in Tom Monaghan's Domino's Pizza corporate helicopter to tell a blue-ribbon recruit he needed to end this nonsense and commit to the place where he belonged: Michigan. Ann Arbor. It was Anthony Carter's school, after all, where Rison could expect the same cover-boy career.

Baggett had been tipped off about Schembechler's recruiting mission, a visit akin to the president arriving in Air Force One. By the time Baggett got through the door at Northwestern, Schembechler was gone and Kelly was delivering a news bulletin:

"Andre said he's 95 percent sure he's going to Michigan."

Later that week Rison was working at point guard for Northwestern's basketball team and two Big Ten schools' recruiting reps were in the stands. Harlan Huckleby, a musically named, prime-time running back at Michigan a decade earlier, was also on hand to tell a state prep star Michigan was his school.

Baggett had calmed down since Kelly had dropped the "95 percent" bomb. Ingram was close with Rison and had been telling him to stick with his earlier plan. More important, grandpa had repeated that Andre was going nowhere but to Michigan State. Grandpa was right—Rison signed with MSU.

Perles was predictable in most aspects of his life and his coaching. Recruiting was no different. He and an assistant coach would sit with a recruit and his family, in the living room or at a kitchen table for recruiting season's main act: the in-home visit.

"The most important thing is your family and your religion," George would say as his mental CD played the first track. "Next is academics. Third is social life. Fourth is football.

"If one of those things doesn't jibe, you're not going to be happy."

He was never a hard-seller, never an arm-twister. He refused to talk disparagingly about his imperious rival seventy miles away, the University of Michigan.

"Michigan is a great school," he would say, genuinely. "Jerry Hanlon (longtime offensive line coach) is a great friend of mine. Michigan State is just different. It all depends on what you're looking for."

Sometimes what the recruit was looking for was a Super Bowl ring. Perles owned four of them and always wore one. That wowed recruits, who would ask the coach if they could see his souvenir from Pittsburgh Steelers days, fingering it and studying it with the awe an art major might hold for a gallery piece.

Perles tried to make recruiting trips for himself and for his staff more than late hotel check-ins and too-early flights the next morning. If he were in South Florida there would be a stop at the restaurant owned by his old friend and Spartan teammate, Franny O'Brien.

O'Brien had opened a top-shelf seafood restaurant in Washington, D.C., after his Redskins playing days, and later retired before starting another seafood haven near Miami. Perles loved the logistics. He would stop in with a coach and four or five friends and Franny would begin a long night of waiting on his buddy's table.

Bucket after bucket of stone crabs would arrive amid a blizzard of side dishes and drinks.

"Hey, Franny," George would yell, his face aglow, "we need more stone crabs."

"I don't have enough for my customers," O'Brien would bark, one more jab at an old teammate with whom he had traded plenty over the years.

Perles, loving it: "I don't care. We've got to have enough for us."

Back in East Lansing, on the football field, life was less giddy. Perles and his staff were still fighting to turn Michigan State into a consistent Big Ten contender. It was an up-and-down effort as exemplified by the 1986-88 seasons. MSU won six games and missed a bowl trip in '86 before punching its ticket to Pasadena in '87 with an 8-2-1 record. In 1988, coming off the Rose Bowl victory, and with enough returning talent to make the Spartans a contender again, Perles' team started 0-4-1 and had to win its final six games to sneak into a Gator Bowl game MSU lost to Georgia.

There was sentiment that Perles might have been wise to have taken the Green Bay job he nearly grabbed a few weeks after the Rose Bowl. He had reached his goal in East Lansing, getting Michigan State to Pasadena within the five years he had long said would be needed. No one had a deeper understanding than Perles of how difficult it had been–or how much luck had been required–to put Michigan State into that Rose Bowl.

MSU's breakthrough had, in fact, come by way of things Perles directly influenced, whether it was players he recruited or coaches he had hired.

Nick Saban, who by 1988 had moved on as an assistant coach with the NFL Houston Oilers, was the architect of an MSU defense in 1987 that allowed only 61 points in eight Big Ten games, and only 22 in MSU's final four conference games. The Perles-Saban relationship was a pristine example of how natural passion for one's work and getting to know the right people pay off down the line for both parties.

Perles had met Saban during his Steelers days when, as a young assistant coach from Navy, Saban would stop by to pick brains and absorb what he could. Saban had a glossy resume and all the necessary skills by the time Perles was looking to fill out his MSU staff. He hired Saban away from Ohio State, which was also courting him.

Norm Parker, MSU's linebacker coach and defensive coordinator after Saban departed, knew Perles and was a friend of Tom Moore, who had coached with Perles at Pittsburgh. Parker was hired in the fashion Perles preferred: Come in for an interview. I may decide to offer you a job. Accept or decline at that time. Don't string me out.

Charlie Baggett was an ex-Spartan quarterback and Perles friend who had burnished his reputation as a strong recruiter and solid assistant during a stint at Minnesota. He would work ten seasons as a Perles assistant. It was the kind of longevity a Perles staffer could count on. After Sally and the kids, the people who meant most to George Perles were his assistants.

"You'll never be fired," he would tell them. "I may move you to another position. But I will never put you and your kids on the street."

Charlie Baggett's playing and coaching career at MSU spanned three different decades.

Perles thought loyalty was especially important when his coaches were anything but overpaid. Without knowing for sure, he had always figured MSU's staff to be middle of the pack in Big Ten coaching salaries.

When the conference's coaches showed up in Chicago for July's Big Ten Kickoff Luncheon, Perles did a little research. At a head coaches' meeting he asked his counterparts to write out the salaries of their assistants, one through nine.

He wondered about other issues, as well.

"What do you make on your radio show? What about your clothes deals?"

Perles was stunned. Michigan State was anything but mid-level. MSU was, in fact, near the bottom. The coach himself didn't necessarily have to be first in staff compensation, but he certainly didn't want to be last. Soon after, Perles huddled with athletic director Doug Weaver on boosts in salaries and perks that put his staff closer to the Big Ten's upper tier.

Upgrading player talent was another issue. Perles knew Michigan would get its annual haul, just as Ohio State and Notre Dame would recruit nothing but thoroughbreds. The trick for MSU was to get just enough blue-chip personnel to equip the Spartans with game-breakers a team had to have if it expected to contend in a tough conference and play in bowl games every year.

Next came the dicey part. State had to be smart about signing kids who weren't lighting up the recruiting boards but who had upside and could be molded into skilled Big Ten players. That required that you sign Lorenzo White and then score with a walk-on like Bobby Morse. You needed to bring in a linebacker of Percy Snow's speed and strength–he could win big ballgames for you–just as you had to hit it lucky on a lightly recruited offensive lineman who would win four letters: Vince Tata.

Bobby McAllister had the kind of panache top recruits flash when he was signed out of Ely High in Pompano Beach, Florida, just as it appeared he was heading to Boston College. Dan Enos, who followed McAllister as State's starting quarterback, might have been headed to a Mid-American Conference school until Perles decided the kid from Dearborn had what it took to play in East Lansing, even if his arm was light by Big Ten standards.

It was the game you had to play at Michigan State. Recruit, develop and count on some luck along the way. Michigan State had enough campus pluses to get its share of Grade A recruits. It was how you fared with the rest of the crop that would, most years, tell the story.

For years, Perles had tied his coaching identity to basic football values: You run the football. You play rock-solid defense. Perles would flash a grin as wide as a hash-mark and say to friends: "My goal is to have a 300-pound fullback, a 300-pound tight end, and run the ball."

However, by 1986, well after Jim Young at Purdue and Mike White at Illinois had been stretching fields and winning games MSU seemed many Saturdays to be losing, Perles got bold. He wanted a coordinator who would jazz up State's offense and give the Spartans a pass attack built to take advantage of NFL-bound receivers like Ingram and Rison.

Perles called his buddy Rollie Dotsch, another old Spartan who had coached with Perles at Pittsburgh. Dotsch was wrapping up a stint as head coach in the soon-to-be defunct United States Football League and had just the guy George needed: Morris Watts, a Missouri-born running back at Tulsa who had blueprinted big-show offenses at a host of colleges in his long coaching career.

Watts' problem was that he had already interviewed with Danny Ford at Clemson and had an offer there. Dotsch suggested he talk with Perles and opt for the security Michigan State and Perles would provide if George was interested. There would be only one proviso: If Dotsch were to get another head coaching job, Watts would rejoin him. Sadly for three men and their friendships, Dotsch developed pancreatic cancer and died within a year.

Watts liked what he saw when he pulled into East Lansing in 1986. There was skilled young talent, a good-looking defense, and a quarterback MSU could win with, Dave Yarema, who that season would set an MSU record for pass-completion percentage (67 percent).

Four three-point losses—mostly because of ill-timed interceptions and a knee injury to White—ruined what could have been a bust-out season in '86, Year Four of the George Perles era. Nothing, though, changed in Perles' view about Michigan State's offense or the need to match Lorenzo White's and Blake Ezor's ball-hauling styles with a downfield pass attack.

Rather, what changed in 1987 was MSU's new quarterback. Bobby McAllister had a good arm and excellent feet. He had mobility Yarema dreamed about. It was a perfect set of skills to meet the needs of a suddenly sophisticated conference.

It was the speed at which defenses changed in major-college football that baffled McAllister. A computer science major with mainstream skills, McAllister was hardly the first quarterback who got flustered when defensive sets and pass-catchers merged in such chaotic ways, as if spun in a kaleidoscope. It could be overwhelming for kids new to a position so demanding. So it was, in those early weeks of '87, with a junior who was MSU's Number 1 quarterback whether the Spartans liked it or not.

McAllister survived Michigan State's opener against Southern Cal at Spartan Stadium, a 27-13 victory on a gorgeous Labor Day evening in East

Lansing. It was a night when neither team was looking ahead to a chance for an MSU-USC rematch in four months at a venue called the Rose Bowl.

Not so promising were Michigan State's and McAllister's next two games: a 31-8 loss at Notre Dame followed by Florida State's 31-3 wipeout of the Spartans at East Lansing. McAllister had taken such a pounding that Perles and Watts threw away the playbook State had incorporated in '86 with a standard drop-back passer like Yarema.

McAllister would never be a classic drop-and-wing-it quarterback. Michigan State could forget about those three-receiver sets Perles and Watts ideally wanted to use as they had in '86 or during their pro-football coaching days. Forget about pass progressions, about initial reads off your wide receivers with a third-receiver dump-off option.

What they would do with McAllister is give him a single edge-receiver in pass situations—Rison—or let him use his feet if he had room to run. It was pared-down football, crude by contemporary standards, but there was no practical choice. Perles knew MSU's defense was good enough to win most games in 1987 as long as the offense didn't botch things.

McAllister was not pleased. He was a quarterback with an arm who wanted to throw the football.

Perles understood. Football, that is.

When McAllister got overly rambunctious at practice or in a game, Perles would say, "You know, Bobby, my favorite play is when the quarterback takes a knee. My second favorite play is the quarterback sweep."

McAllister had help, of course, beginning with White, who was on his way to contending for a Heisman Trophy. He was the hop-scotching power back who could carry forty times a game for 200 yards and a week later do it all over again.

Ezor gave defenses a different look: straight-ahead speed. He was a wiry kid with blonde hair and a touch of Dennis the Menace about him. Appropriate, given that Ezor had taken a wild route to East Lansing.

When Perles was with Pittsburgh, it was traditional for Steelers owner Art Rooney to send the team on a post-season vacation to Las Vegas. They would check into The Dunes Hotel, which was owned by a Rooney friend who was only too happy to have the Steelers with their

Super Bowl rings roaming the casino.

The team would be taken care of royally by a Pittsburgh native who ran the baccarat table, Bernie Ezor. A decade later Bernie called Perles to tell him his son was a speedster and definite college prospect who might interest Michigan State.

Perles had heard this one before. He asked Ted Guthard, the lone assistant George had kept from Muddy Waters' staff, to take a look at some film and at least give Bernie the courtesy of a critique.

Guthard called back with a one-word scouting report: "Wow."

Guthard's response was typical of how it went between Perles and his staffers. Life in the Duffy Daugherty Building was never formal or official. Relationships were relaxed, coaches' families were held in esteem. It helped explain why Perles had the distinction, remarkable by today's measure, of never having lost an assistant coach to another school.

Work schedules followed a comfortable routine. Perles would be in the office by 7 a.m. and would greet his staffers at 8 for a meeting that could last five minutes, or much longer, depending upon day and season.

There would be practice-schedule adjustments, game-plan discussions, personnel updates, and general administration. Most of the staff would burrow into game film and more meetings before lunch, which Perles always had delivered into the office, the better to keep a staff on hand. Menu items were standard and always donated: Little Caesar's pizza one day, sub sandwiches another, take-out from Pistachio's (Perles friend and restaurateur Ron Gibson was the benefactor there), Dmitri's hot dogs another.

Game-week Fridays were particularly special. There would be bagels and cream cheese, fruit, pastries, coffee—a Sunday-brunch kind of spread—as Perles opened up the office and got MSU Football Weekend rolling. It was an atmosphere folksy and friendly, a mandatory stop-over for AD Weaver, an ex-coach and old Spartan who loved reconnecting with his football days.

Fridays were sometimes more fun than Saturdays. Michigan State's Rose Bowl stupor had begun to wear off as quickly as Perles had his January romance with Green Bay. Shifting in a few days from Pasadena's bliss to the reality of a Rose Bowl coach bolting for Green Bay was an unsettling episode for fans and for a university too familiar with East Lansing's pogo-sticking highs and lows.

MSU's 1988 football season would be another jolt. The Spartans lost their opener to Rutgers at home, then got pounded by Notre Dame and Florida State ahead of a tie with Iowa and another loss at Michigan. The Rose Bowl champions were eight months removed from Pasadena and suddenly floundering at 0-4-1. A big reason was that hole in the offensive line. Tony Mandarich, a 6-foot-5, 315-pound bulldozer of a tackle who was months from becoming the second overall pick in 1989's NFL draft, was on a three-game NCAA suspension for having flirted with an agent before the '88 draft. Bob Kula, who lined up next to Mandarich, was hit with a two-game team suspension. Coupled with White's graduation to the NFL, Michigan State had lost a ton of offensive muscle that might have made a difference in the Rutgers and Iowa games.

MSU's Gang Green defense of '87 had also dropped a tick. After that season, Nick Saban had split for the Houston Oilers once discovering he was at the bottom of Big Ten salaries for defensive coordinators. Only the promotion of a rock-solid defensive coach, Norm Parker, offset Saban's departure for Jerry Glanville's staff at Houston.

Perles had final say over everything that happened on the field, but in 1987 he had mostly deferred to his coordinators, Watts, and Saban, who because of his age (Saban turned thirty-six in October

George Perles (right) enjoyed his best days at Michigan State when Nick Saban served as defensive coordinator, before Saban left to become an NFL assistant at Houston.

1987) had been reluctant to stray too far from Perles' philosophy.

Sitting in the coaches' booth in Spartan Stadium or at a road game, Saban would check with Perles via sideline phone if he were mulling a blitz. It was unnecessary deference as far as the head coach was concerned. After all, he had never advised Chuck Noll before any gambits when Perles was defensive coordinator at Pittsburgh.

Parker was older, and was happy with the latitude in his new job running MSU's defense. A man who disliked all the public-relations and administrative chores that went with head coaching was in his realm as a coordinator. If he wanted to blitz, he blitzed. Never did Perles interfere.

As bad as 1988 had started for Michigan State, the regular-season finish would be brilliant, thanks to a six-game winning streak. MSU beat its final three regular-season teams—Purdue, Indiana and Wisconsin—by a combined score of 122-15. That monster run put Big Ten commissioner Wayne Duke on a safari to find MSU and its 6-4-1 record a bowl-game slot.

Final destination: Jacksonville, Florida, and the New Year's Day Gator Bowl against Vince Dooley's Georgia Bulldogs. Dooley had decided on an obvious strategy in getting ready for Perles and the Spartans. Georgia would load up the line of scrimmage and shut down Michigan State's running game. It would leave McAllister with no option but to throw the football against a Bulldogs team that had better speed on defense than any of the teams Michigan State had pulverized at the end of the season.

What Georgia didn't count on was Rison playing his way into the NFL draft's first round. As those who had seen him play understood, Rison had first-round skills. He would have unveiled them at the NFL Combine scouting camp in March in the event a pro team hungry for a receiver had not taken close notice of his repertoire, which, given MSU's no-frills offense, was conceivable.

Rison had chafed under McAllister's straitjacket the past two seasons. Shutting down MSU's passing game had been solitary confinement for a receiver who had skills so exceptional he could have been a Biletnikoff Award winner, a deserving successor to Tim Brown, who had won the Heisman Trophy at Notre Dame a year earlier.

It didn't change Rison's status as a two-edged sword at Michigan State. He was a high-maintenance pain in the butt for Perles. Rison's mouth ran as fast as his legs, never more than when he was on the field lining up against defenders.

"You can't cover me," he would bark at an opposing cornerback. "No one can cover 'Dre Rison. No one can check 'Dre Rison."

Most of the time, they couldn't. Rison burned defenders, in games, or in practice, where he might spike a ball in the face of a corner or safety he had just torched.

On balance, teammates found him an amusing, harmless entertainer who spiced up practices and drove his coaches nuts. One afternoon at practice after Rison had seen far too few passes from McAllister the previous Saturday, he showed up wearing a fullback-style neck roll. It was his not-so-subtle way of saying a he had been doing too much blocking and not enough pass-catching.

Andre Rison's combination of speed, agility and great hands helped make him one of MSU's best receivers of all time.

He was a lot busier at the Gator Bowl. Rison caught nine passes for 252 yards and three touchdowns in the kind of game ESPN SportsCenter can't wait to highlight. Rison's show was a spectacular act of one-man athleticism–leaping catches in the end zone, tumbling grabs of 50-yard bombs from McAllister—in a game where the Spartans had trailed 17-0 and 24-7 before finally losing, 34-27. In fact, if MSU had figured out Georgia couldn't cover Rison before the second half rolled around, the Spartans may have won.

Such performances weren't lost on pro scouts; four years after he signed with MSU, Andre Rison joined Indianapolis as the twenty-second player picked in the 1989 NFL draft.

Over a four-year stretch from 1987-90, the loss to Georgia would be Michigan State's only football defeat spanning a stretch from the final week of October through four post-season bowl games. A key reason for the slow-start, sizzling-finish, pattern had to do with schedules. Michigan State's autumn lineup for so many years had been front-loaded with heavyweights: Notre Dame, Michigan, and the Iowa Hawkeyes after Hayden Fry had turned an old doormat into a mean and bruising Big Ten contender.

A Spartans team that for so long had been in a rebuilding phase, struggling to carry late-season momentum into the next year (1987 to '88 was a perfect example) too many times faced the wrong types of teams at the worst stages of a season.

Perles had to wonder if 1989 would be a repeat. After winning the home opener against Miami (Ohio), 49-0, the Spartans fixed bayonets and attacked, in order, Notre Dame, Miami (Florida), Iowa, Michigan and Illinois, every one of them tough, nasty, difficult to beat no matter where they had been planted on the schedule.

The Spartans were also breaking in a new quarterback, which might or might not signal a step up from the McAllister era. Dan Enos had made his way into the pilot's seat after a long and fervid mission to turn himself into a Big Ten quarterback.

He had not been a prized recruit out of Dearborn High, drawing serious interest only from Indiana, Colorado and Michigan State. Neither his arm nor his size was overwhelming. What Perles liked about Enos was his athleticism and make-up. You could turn those components into a Big Ten football player if a kid had the kind of moxie Perles sensed Enos would bring to East Lansing.

On an afternoon recruiting visit at Dearborn High, Perles and Guthard found Enos playing ping-pong during a free hour, and ushered him toward the high school's library for a chat. Perles noticed a student passing by who had something in his ear. It was January of 1986 and a male fashion trend was beginning.

"Dan, did you see that guy?" Perles asked, astonished. "He had a ring in his ear. Ted, did you see that guy had an earring on?"

Perles soon amended one of his enduring rules: Not only hats, but earrings also had to be removed before a player walked into the Duffy Daugherty Football Building.

Enos had broken in during McAllister's reign, and by the end of his freshman year was trying to separate himself from a phalanx of would-be quarterbacks: John Gieselman, Antonio Merritt and Mario Bongiorni. He needed to know if he had a future at MSU or should plan on a transfer. Enos walked into Watts' office and asked his quarterbacks coach to level with him.

"Can I play here?"

Watts paused, forming thoughts that needed to be direct yet diplomatic.

"I'm not sure," he said. "I think you've got a lot of intangibles to play here. But, physically, your arm strength isn't sufficient to play at the Big Ten level."

Watts also mentioned that Enos had a hitch in his delivery. In other words, he had more against him than for him as MSU began thinking about McAllister's replacement.

Quarterback Dan Enos started at State in 1989 and 1990 and produced two bowl victories.

It was all Enos

needed to hear. He bored into a daily regimen at the Duffy Daugherty Building's indoor field. He would throw passes into a net, two hundred to three hundred a day, often recruiting a receiver or two—Courtney Hawkins, another Flint star, or perhaps James Bradley or tight end Duane Young—to catch balls until Enos risked wearing them out. Then it would be back to the net for another sequence.

When he wasn't throwing to strengthen his arm he was watching film. In meetings, he was insatiable when it came to information and strategy, asking so many questions during quarterback meetings Watts pondered the relative joys of becoming a line coach. Watts was impressed nonetheless. Here was a kid whose work ethic and insistence on being prepared for any situation was slowly turning him into a starting quarterback.

It showed quickly as he moved in as starter in '89. Enos knew when to throw, when to pull down the ball and run. He compensated for an arm that would never be a downfield howitzer by running an offense with such precision he became, very quickly in the eyes of teammates, a quarterback to trust, a leader.

Watts learned, as well, the dividend from those streams of questions Enos unleashed during meetings. Enos might step under center and have four run-pass options depending upon the defense. Rarely did he miss on a check-off.

Neither was he asked to beat a team with his arm. Michigan State was keeping the heat off his quarterback all because the Spartans had reacquainted themselves with two Perles trademarks in 1989: a running game and a punishing defense. While Ezor ran for 1,299 yards, linebacker Percy Snow ran all over opposing offenses en route to winning the Butkus Award as America's top college linebacker, and the Lombardi Award, the first player in NCAA history to win both.

Snow was an awesome mix of ferocity and speed. MSU had stolen Snow from the usual array of high-powered schools when they signed him out of Canton (Ohio) McKinley High. He was tough, a natural leader, and closed on a running back like something fired from the gun of a fighter plane.

Snow was so innately aggressive that Perles had thrown him out of

Tailback Blake Ezor had many multiple-touchdown games, including six against Northwestern and three in the 1988 Aloha Bowl. Coach George Perles recruited the Las Vegas speedster through his relationship with Ezor's father, a casino worker.

practice a time or two for mashing players who weren't supposed to be hit in non-contact drills. Snow joined Carlos Jenkins and a lightly recruited linebacker who morphed into a first-round draft pick, Dixon Edwards, to become one of the most menacing defenses Perles had ever melded at Michigan State.

The Bash Brothers linebacker corps had allies up front—Travis Davis, Tim Ridinger, Matt Vanderbeek, Chris Willertz—and hammerers in the secondary: Harlon ("Da Bang Stick") Barnett, Alan Haller, Ventson Donelson, Mike Iaquaniello.

Until a 1989 investigation by *The Detroit News* changed a football team's monitoring systems, some wondered if State had been building its he-man reputation for physical football in illicit ways: through steroids.

The News had questioned players and arranged polygraph tests in an effort to trace steroid use dating to MSU's 1987 Rose Bowl team. Evidence painted the picture of a quiet culture where steroids, while not widespread, had become the fast-track path to 300-pound bodies brimming with muscle.

Most players and coaches had a hunch that steroids were part of the body-building regimen for a specific few. The hang-up was trying to prove steroid use. Artful evasion during drug tests had made it a tough case to nail down. Not wanting to find anything wrong might have been another motivation for coaches being less probing than FBI agents.

It was also difficult to draw lines between those who might be using "juice" and those who were beefing up by way of a hyper-intense weight-lifting frenzy at the Duffy Daugherty Football Building.

There were twenty-five players bench-pressing 400 pounds even after the steroids crackdown had given way to tougher testing. Ezor, all 175 pounds of him, was bench-pressing 405 pounds. No wonder, his teammates thought, that a running back could get slammed by linebackers 50 pounds bigger and get up as if he had fallen down playing a game of school-yard tag.

Peer pressure in the weight room was relentless as "Guns 'N Roses" CDs blared over the stereo. A player who was perceived to be lifting less than 100 percent was going to be ridiculed, and not in a playful way.

Watts was trying to pump some of the same pugnacity into his offense as the '89 season wore on. He was particularly hard on rookie quarterback Enos. Watts wanted perfection. He demanded urgency in every aspect of MSU's offense.

"Man," Enos would say when Watts had taken him to the brink. "What's this guy want?"

It hardly mattered to Watts that Enos was undergoing a crash course in quarterbacking. The coach's assignment was to toughen an offense and a quarterback who was already a junior. What most grated on Enos was when defensive players implied he was a sissy for wearing the tomato-colored Do Not Tackle jersey coaches mandated for a starting quarter-back. They never understood, Enos said to himself, the abuse he was taking from Watts on the other side of the practice field.

"Hey, it's not personal," Watts would say to Enos after one more practice when the coach had raked him particularly hard. "I'm just trying to make you better."

Enos knew it, appreciated it. Besides, it was all you could do not to bust out laughing when Watts launched into one of his Ozark Mountain diatribes that almost always included his trademark epithet, "shitfire."

"Shitfire, son, you throw that pass Saturday against Troy Vincent (Wisconsin cornerback) and he's gonna take it to the house," Watts would say in his one-of-a-kind twang.

He had endless pet expressions, each of them worth a grin if players could manage during practice to crimp their homicidal thoughts:

"You look like a cow on ice, son."

"You look like you're runnin' in mud."

Michigan State was stuck in the mud six games into its 1989 season. The Spartans were 2-4 after cruel losses to Notre Dame (21-13), Miami (Florida), (26-20), Michigan (10-7), and Illinois (14-10). All MSU had on the plus side were victories over Iowa, 17-14, at Iowa City, as well as an opening-game rout of Miami (Ohio). In the 10-7 U-M loss, Blake Ezor was stopped on fourth-and-goal at the one. In the Illinois game Hyland Hickson fumbled deep in MSU territory late in the game while MSU was attempting to run out the clock against the Jeff George-led Illini.

Naturally, a team that never seemed to warm up until Halloween closed with a five-game winning streak (combined score: MSU 207, Opponents 65) to win a ticket to Hawaii for the Christmas Day Aloha Bowl against the University of Hawaii and a near-sellout crowd of Rainbow rooters.

The Aloha Bowl was over quickly as State's offensive front began an Oahu earth-moving project that unleashed Ezor for 179 yards and three touchdowns. Final score: MSU 33, Hawaii 13.

Michigan State finished 8-4 with its only two Big Ten losses by a total of seven points. It had been a nice comeback after the miserable '88 falloff, more akin, it seemed, to the kind of year Perles and Michigan State could expect most seasons without anything exceptional happening.

There had been only one unsettling wrinkle to a Perles program wrapping up its seventh season. The previous February's recruiting crop had fallen off. One year removed from the Rose Bowl, and Perles was trying to pretty up the ugliest recruiting class he had ever assembled at MSU.

"This is the kind of goddam program we've got now when Charlie Baggett doesn't get anybody," Perles had harrumphed to his staff after the '89 list was in.

Much of the change had to do with Michigan. Schembechler had turned up the heat at U-M: "This better not ever happen again," he had been heard to say to his own staff when State stole a kid who in earlier years would have been a lock for Ann Arbor.

Another shift in East Lansing's football climate was also evolving. Perles was about to leap into a maelstrom of university politics and distractions that would have permanent, and perilous, effects on his ability to coach football with the same energy and focus he had shown during the '80s.

Now, in a power move Perles wanted to match, he was going to add "athletic director" to his duties, just as Schembechler had done at Ann Arbor.

Michigan State's 1990 season was the last big season for Perles. It was yet another up-and-down trip spanning a football season's polar extremes. It began with an opening-game tie at Syracuse, followed by a gut-ripping 20-19 loss at home against Notre Dame when a late Rick Mirer pass caromed off cornerback Todd Murray's chest and bounced into the hands of Irish receiver Lake Dawson to set up Notre Dame's winning touchdown. A big win against Rutgers followed, but at a great cost— Courtney Hawkins was lost to a broken collarbone. Then State lost another groaner at Spartan Stadium, 12-7, to Iowa. That game ended up sending the Hawkeyes to Pasadena over Michigan State and the Big Ten's two other "quad-champions."

Perles had gotten credit for the turnaround. Players were still heartsick three days after the loss to Iowa when Michigan State began getting ready for a trip to Ann Arbor on Saturday for a lovely get-together with Michigan.

"Hey, guys, this could get ugly," a player or two had been heard to murmur to teammates as Michigan Week began in an air of utter despondency.

Perles knew they were hurting and issued a simple order at Sunday's team meeting: "Guys, you've got to forget about that one. Get ready for Michigan."

What surprised the players at Wednesday's practice was how they were responding. For some it was the best week of practice they remembered at any point in their MSU careers.

Perles had been working on their psyches, suffusing the Iowa defeat's self-pity with a massive dose of kill-Michigan rage.

The coach would stand amid his players circled around him after practice.

"Hey," he would say to a particular MSU player. "That guy you're going against Saturday (Perles would provide the name). I know him. I was in his home. He's from (whatever) high school.

"If you got into a fight with him, do you think you could kick his ass?"

It was a personal, one-on-one challenge that grabbed kids who had only begun to leave adolescence in their rear-view mirrors. State's players and coaches realized how close they had come to having the national ranking Michigan was taking into Saturday's game: Number 1. The bizarre one-point loss to Notre Dame; the 12-7 strangulation against Iowa; a tough tie at the Carrier Dome against a quality Syracuse team playing in the single noisiest place in college football. This was a good football team that had missed by a sliver having a record to match.

Perles and his coaches were planning on an upset Saturday. So, by mid-week, were MSU's players. Saturday's pre-game hours were more an experience in hysteria. Players had not remembered ever being so revved. It was a psychotic kind of energy, so intense Perles gave up trying to hold his team in the locker room ahead of the National Anthem. Not so honorably, State charged onto the field as 106,000 people stood for the last civilized moment of a long football afternoon and evening.

The game became in many ways a repeat of the Notre Dame squeaker that would join 2004 MSU-Michigan as one of those rotational features rolled out on ESPN Classic.

It was punishing, relentless and dramatic. Michigan State took a late 21-14 lead, and seconds later watched Desmond Howard take the kickoff to the house in the Big House to tie it. Now it was Michigan State's turn.

The Spartans plowed down the field on a drive so in-the-trenches tough and impressive it was more like an excavation, finally scoring on a run by Hyland Hickson. State had the lead again, 28-21. Michigan answered yet again with a touchdown in the waning seconds to make it 28-27. The Wolverines lined up for two points to win.

Everyone knew Elvis Grbac's pass was headed for Howard, who, a year later, would be carting around a Heisman Trophy. Eddie Brown, a junior-college transfer cornerback from Grand Rapids, had the same notion. He broke for Howard, grabbed his foot as Howard cut to the inside to catch a pass that was already on its way, and spilled Howard as the ball bounced against his chest and out of Desmond's hands.

Incomplete pass, game over, Michigan State wins, 28-27, at least as far as the officials were concerned. Everyone else in Michigan Stadium had seen Brown hogtie Howard. One of the more outrageous acts of pass interference in big-game history was never called.

Perles wasn't apologizing. He was still steamed over Schembechler's remark after Michigan had beaten State in the '89 game at East Lansing: "The better team won." Now, Perles was ready with his own zinger.

"The tougher team won," he said.

Anyone who knew Perles would have grinned. There were many aspects to a man and coach of such colorful composition, none of them more overwhelming, perhaps, than George Julius Perles' power for remembering.

CHAPTER 2

PARADISE LOST

FOOTBALL LIFE AT MICHIGAN STATE had settled into a kind of quiet rhythm by the final week of November 1989. George Perles and the Spartans hadn't over-achieved, but hadn't necessarily under-accomplished in putting together a 7-4 season that would send them to an Aloha Bowl date on Christmas Day against the University of Hawaii.

This was more the way it should work in most seasons at East Lansing, fans were inclined to say. Rose Bowl trips as dreamy as the one that followed MSU's 1987 season weren't going to be the norm. Follow-up seasons as tense as 1988, when State had to win its final five games to finish 6-4-1 and slip into the Gator Bowl, were at the lower end of a prime-time Big Ten school's football capabilities.

At long last, there was stability in the eyes of fans who had wondered why a school with MSU's charms had such ongoing difficulties forging a half-decent football program. Perles was central to this new sense of serenity. He had been on the job for seven seasons, the longest stint by a Spartans coach since Duffy Daugherty.

He had a solid staff, a deep friendship with his boss, Doug Weaver, rapport with MSU's administration and—most pleasing to Perles—community affection. He was tight with governor James Blanchard, and with attorney general Frank Kelley. Two years after Daugherty's death, Perles had supplanted his old coach and boss as Michigan State's football ambassador. Perles was loving life and was only too happy he had turned down the Green Bay Packers job twenty-two months earlier.

Weaver, who was a few weeks away from ten years as Michigan State's athletic director, was one more reason why a battle-fatigued Michigan State sports culture had entered into an era of relative peace and prosperity. In Weaver, the Spartans had an effective AD who cared about his alma mater and who had the respect of Big Ten colleagues, not the least of whom was Don Canham, Michigan's retired AD who had long regarded Weaver as a conference crackerjack.

No one was more satisfied than MSU president John DiBiaggio, who had been in his position for almost five years. The University was growing and moving ahead at a time when state-budget cutbacks were making it hard for universities to be as progressive and as ambitious as they had been during the '50s, '60s, and even '70s, when Michigan State had evolved into a collegiate giant, on the football field and off.

It would explain DiBiaggio's surprise when his athletic director late that November dropped into the president's office.

"John," Weaver said, solemnly, "I want to step aside as athletic director."

Doug Weaver's sudden departure as AD in 1990 led to arguably the highest-profile power grab in MSU history, forcing the board of trustees to choose between president John DiBiaggio and football coach George Perles.

DiBiaggio might as well have been told the governor was resigning. Why, the president wondered, would a man at the top of his game, fifty-nine years old, want to leave Michigan State?

The president was baffled. Weaver seemed so morose.

"I just want to step aside," Weaver said, making clear that, whatever his motivations, they would remain private.

DiBiaggio could see by the man's expression and tone of his words that Weaver was serious. The president began conjuring hurry-up plans and thoughts as he sat in his office in the John A. Hannah Administration Building.

"I'll honor your request," DiBiaggio said, almost sympathetically. "But would you at least wait until after the bowl game before announcing anything? It will just confuse things around here. If you'll wait until after we get back from Hawaii, we can make an announcement and then have six months to do a search. Just promise you won't reveal this to anyone else."

Weaver was fine with that. To have let DiBiaggio know of his plans was instant relief, the first sense of real freedom he had known since retirement became an increasingly appealing thought.

A week later, DiBiaggio, Weaver, Perles, and half the MSU football galaxy, it seemed, had jammed into Long's Convention Center in Lansing for the MSU Football Bust. It was a happy enough evening. Plans for Hawaii were in place. Honolulu would be a nice consolation prize for a team that had gone 7-4, courtesy of a five-game, season-closing winning streak. Season-closing strong streaks were typical of the Spartans for years, a trend that was to completely reverse in the '90s and beyond.

DiBiaggio was about to dig into his chicken when Perles turned to him on the dais and said in a half-whisper:

"Doug's leaving. I'd like to be AD, too."

DiBiaggio's appetite began to wane. This wasn't what he wanted to hear. Not tonight. Not any evening, for that matter. It was precisely why he had asked Weaver to keep quiet.

The president was irritated and Perles knew it.

"George, you'll have to come over and talk with me," DiBiaggio said. "I have certain feelings about a person filling both roles. And we need a search, in any event."

The president himself wasn't sure if he was more stunned than mad. This reeked of a set-up. Even as a merry football celebration was taking shape on the banquet floor, DiBiaggio seemed to sense more than Perles that, for each man, it was the beginning of the end of a life at MSU they each had grown to know and love.

Four weeks later, MSU's official party was checking into the Sheraton on Waikiki Beach, adjacent to the pink and plush Royal Hawaiian Hotel, where an Aloha Bowl cocktail party was set for early evening.

Perles and his team already were in place. They eased into a late-morning team brunch as Perles read the papers and kibitzed with his three sons, along with Weaver and Kelley. Everything was the way Perles felt it should be at a bowl game: relaxed, laid back.

The coach flipped a page. News from the NFL: Dick Steinberg, New England's general manager, was moving to the New York Jets in the same capacity.

Sally Perles arrived in the dining room a few minutes later. She walked toward her husband's table and said, almost sheepishly: "George, can I see you for a minute?"

Perles knew something was up. Sally wasn't one to be cryptic.

"Dick Steinberg just called from the New York Jets," she said after they had stepped clear of the crowd. "He wants you to call him."

Steinberg's message implied nothing exceptional as far as Perles was concerned. A new GM would want information about players Perles had coached, maybe about assistant coaches he knew or had worked with.

He had different thoughts after calling Steinberg's secretary, only to be told Steinberg was in an important meeting. Perles knew enough about NFL front-office "meetings" to deduce Joe Walton was probably getting the axe.

Perles began to think Steinberg's call may have been an early feeler. Suddenly, there were two green-and-white teams occupying a coach's mind as he left with his team for an afternoon practice.

With the workout completed and a cocktail party next on the schedule, Perles headed back to his suite just in time to grab a phone call.

"Hi George," said the new GM for the New York Jets. "We're going to have a coaching change after the game this Sunday. Would you be interested in talking with me?"

Perles had an easy answer, given the current situation: Yes. He rushed to tell Weaver the Jets had called and that he was obliged to listen. The next move was Weaver's, who needed to tell DiBiaggio.

"George has to talk with you right away," Weaver said. "It's very important."

Perles didn't waste time or words once he shut the door leading into DiBiaggio's suite, joining the president on a balcony overlooking the Pacific.

"I've been offered a job by the Jets," the coach said, not sure how his boss would respond to yet another year-end bombshell.

DiBiaggio was irked, although not as much as he was fatigued. They had gone through this same soap opera two years earlier. At that time— January 1988—DiBiaggio was in Hungary on a business trip. He had stepped out of the shower when the phone rang informing him that his head football coach, fresh from a Rose Bowl victory, was preparing to join the Green Bay Packers.

"Tell him thanks for a good job," DiBiaggio said to the caller, MSU public-relations chief Terry Denbow, "and good luck on the next job."

It was now December 1989 and DiBiaggio was disgusted for several reasons. He knew the Jets' job was going to be used as leverage to get Perles the AD title, just as Perles had benefited from his earlier dalliance with Green Bay. The president was displaying classic CEO response to employees who dangle other employers and their courtships in front of a boss, particularly if it happens a second time: Get out of here and get on with your new job.

What had become, DiBiaggio wondered, of the man who once said MSU was the only head football-coaching job he ever wanted? What had George told Myles Tanenbaum, the Philadelphia Stars' owner, in 1982, when Perles was under contract to coach in the United States Football League ahead of his expensive hiring at Michigan State?

"Myles, if I have to walk to East Lansing, I'm going to take that job."

Five years after making that statement, Perles was flirting with the Packers and converting Green Bay's overture into a ten-year rollover con-tract at MSU, much to DiBiaggio's dismay. The president didn't get it. He understood how winning Rose Bowls could turn a head coach into a short-term deity, at least in the adoring eyes of MSU fans. What he didn't like was how trustees and executives were slobbering over Perles. What happened then was sure to happen now.

The president had it right, even if he wasn't being entirely fair to Perles or to his motives. Joel Ferguson, Bob Weiss, Larry Owen—the board's Democratic trustees—were keen on sports and of the opinion that Perles was indispensable and irreplaceable, at least at this point in time, and in light of MSU's ups and downs in the recent past.. Weaver had responded just as desperately in 1988 when he helped write a ten-year contract, spearheaded by then-vice-president Jack Breslin, with enough annuities and incentives to keep Perles in East Lansing and away from the NFL, presumably for a decade or longer.

This was going to be a repeat performance on the sands of Waikiki Beach. DiBiaggio knew it the moment Perles hit him with a follow-up question:

"Am I going to be the AD?"

Now, DiBiaggio was hot. What he wanted was for Perles to leave the suite, leave the hotel, and leave Michigan State for all he cared. This was a shakedown.

"George, I believe in the process," DiBiaggio said. "We have rules, affirmative action considerations. If there were minority candidates available, we would need to have conversations, all the more so in athletics."

Perles wanted to hear something, anything, which held promise. DiBiaggio made a single concession.

"George, if you really want to be athletic director—and I don't know why, because your salary will go down—I will violate one principle and we'll ignore a search, but on one condition: You'll have to give up coaching."

Perles' face darkened. He wanted a different arrangement.

"What about my assistants?"

DiBiaggio explained the assistant coaches would be paid for one year.

"What about my annuity?"

The coach was referring to a key sweetener in his ten-year contract negotiated after the Packers had called. It was an annuity that, after five more years as MSU's head football coach, would pay him the equivalent money he was turning down from Green Bay.

"We'll honor that and satisfy that," the president assured, explaining it would all be put into writing. "We'll have to talk about all of this later on."

Perles suspected there would be no "later on" as far as DiBiaggio was concerned. He left the president's suite feeling as if he had been sacked on fourth-and-goal. Weaver got the bleak update direct from Perles.

"This guy," the coach said, "doesn't want me around."

The situation was 180 degrees from the Friday mornings in the fall when DiBiaggio would take bagels and cream cheese to Perles' office so the two could discuss the game that would be played the following day. Those were the days when DiBiaggio seemed to love nothing more than visiting the State locker room after a big victory to congratulate the players and hug Perles.

By now, word had sailed across Waikiki that the New York Jets were firing Joe Walton and leaning toward Perles. News about Weaver's departure had already leaked days earlier, setting in motion a hiring process that would allow Weaver to leave by July 1.

MSU's pro-Perles political machinery was likewise moving at full-throttle with no regard for DiBiaggio's stance. The coach's camp would, ideally, engineer a dual role for Perles and avoid any interruption to the best stretch of football Michigan State had enjoyed since Biggie Munn and Daugherty had been in charge.

Weiss and Weaver met later that afternoon for a drink on the Sheraton patio.

"Do you think he can do both jobs?" Weiss asked.

Weaver was uninspired by the thought, but inclined to say yes. Weaver was leaving, after all. This was going to be Michigan State's and DiBiaggio's problem, not his.

The president would second that motion. He had reasons, plenty of them, for wanting to treat two very different jobs as two distinctly different entities at Michigan State.

On one hand, he thought the evidence was clear. Dual roles no longer worked on the major-college level. Basketball coach Jim Valvano had gotten into trouble with a two-title post at North Carolina State, landing his team on probation. Bo Schembechler was handed both jobs at Michigan and stayed just long enough to hire his coaching replacement, Gary Moeller, before bolting to become president of the Detroit Tigers.

You could not coach football at Michigan State University *and* run an athletic department, DiBiaggio contended, without having one, or both, suffer.

He had another motivation for wanting Perles held in check. DiBiaggio was a university president, keeper of a position the Knight Commission on Intercollegiate Athletics had determined must hold authority over institutional decisions regarding academic and administrative integrity. DiBiaggio knew the Knight Commission's creed personally. He had served on the panel, chosen by none other than Father Theodore Hesburgh, renowned past president of Notre Dame and a Knight Commission founding co-chairman.

DiBiaggio could cite from heart the Knight Commission preamble's second thesis:

"The responsibility and authority for the administration of the athletics department, including all basic policies, personnel and finances, are vested in the president."

That would be the university president, DiBiaggio reminded them. Boards of trustees, boards of regents, influential alumni, coaches' clubs, fan bases, sugar daddies—they were all subordinate to the university presidents in being accountable for significant academic and athletic issues.

Ferguson, Weiss, Owen and a good many Spartans fans disagreed. They could compliment DiBiaggio on his convictions and a president's noble philosophy. Michigan State, on the other hand, had George Perles at the helm of a critical university resource: the Spartans' football team.

They had watched for too long as Michigan strung together decades of success behind Schembechler and his boss, athletic director Don Canham. Michigan State had changed football coaches five times in ten years from 1972-82. In a nine-year stretch from 1971-80, the Spartans had five athletic directors.

Now, Perles' promoters contended, the best way to ensure that a recovering football program stayed on track was to keep its engineer in office. Two offices, if that were required.

The trustees' idea was to have Perles assume both jobs with an expiration date on his coaching tenure. Perles didn't object. He wasn't ready to quit coaching yet, not at age fifty-five with a solid team and momentum in his and MSU's favor.

In two, maybe three years—three, he told Weiss—he would be ready to hand over football and work exclusively as AD. Give him that arrangement, he confided, and he would stick with Michigan State and tell the Jets to look elsewhere.

What he most wanted in pushing for the AD's job, Perles had explained to intimates, was what DiBiaggio didn't seem to understand. This wasn't about money or power, per se. It was about avoiding Biggie-Duffy Part II. Perles liked working for Weaver. There were no surprises, no inordinate stresses and no petty jealousies. What a contrast to the Cold War-type culture that engulfed Munn and Daugherty's working relationship after Munn became AD and turned the Spartans' coaching job over to Daugherty in 1954.

If Weaver was gone, Perles figured the best AD to work for would be Perles. He had too much football yet to coach and too little faith in the brand of athletic director DiBiaggio would be inclined to hire to not fret about a new boss at Michigan State.

Just hours before the Christmas Day game against Hawaii, MSU's board and top executives were to meet at breakfast. Weiss ran into DiBiaggio in a hallway outside their private dining room.

"We don't want George leaving here for the Jets without the board having input," said Weiss, who was worried that February's recruiting class would be gutted if the head coach were to leave a month before national letters of intent were signed .

Weiss' view was shared by a pro-Perles bloc of fellow Democrats: Owen, Ferguson, and, as near as could be determined, Malcolm Dade. On the other side was a Republican flank headed by Dean Pridgeon. He had little regard for Perles in any context, let alone as a potential athletic director. Tom Reed appeared early on to be in the coach's corner but was being lobbied hard by Republican backers of DiBiaggio. Barbara Sawyer was the lone Democrat opposed to Perles taking a second job.

Kathy Wilbur was undecided.

Whatever their position, the trustees were about to ram head-on into one of the most divisive political issues in Michigan State's 135-year history. They would vote on who mattered most to Michigan State: the president or a popular college football coach. They would decide if a Knight Commission Report on Intercollegiate Athletics, constructed with input from MSU's own president, would carry as much weight as a football team's recruiting prospects.

They, in fact, would determine by way of eight votes the course Michigan State would follow during the next decade and beyond. Everything would be affected. Lines of succession in the president's office would likely be shaped. An athletic director's personal brand of stewardship over a massive department would be plotted. A football team and the imprint it bears because of the head coach—everything of visibility at MSU—was about to be influenced if Perles turned his latest NFL job bid into an either-or crusade for a dual role as Michigan State football coach and AD.

Perles, steadily, was bringing the issue to a crescendo. Steinberg was ensuring it with his daily calls. There would be a face-to-face conversation between the two as soon as Perles committed to a schedule.

MSU ripped Hawaii, 33-13, in a Christmas Day bowl game that saw Blake Ezor run for 179 yards and three touchdowns. DiBiaggio, interestingly, had a been a model of diplomacy when he smiled and told ABC-TV's Keith Jackson during a halftime interview that George Perles would get strong consideration to be MSU's next athletic director. DiBiaggio, of course, was speaking about one job. The last thing a shrewd president was going to do was paint himself in a corner or create a national issue out of an institutional spat—via Keith Jackson, anyway.

Steinberg wasn't letting up even as Perles tried to buy time. The coach was worn out and wanted a few extra days in Hawaii to relax before recruiting season's "dead" period ended and Perles would be back on the road.

Perles suggested to Steinberg that the two meet in Los Angeles. The coach could get off the plane between connecting flights at Los

Former president John DiBiaggio and his then-wife, Carolyn, enjoyed the fruits of a big-time football program until a dispute with head coach George Perles and the board of trustees soured him on MSU's high-profile athletic program.

Angeles International Airport and hook up with Steinberg, who was conveniently scheduled to be in Los Angeles at the same time.

Another bonus was that Weaver would be in Pasadena for the Rose Bowl and could meet with Perles afterward. This would ensure having an ally as a buffer between Perles and DiBiaggio at a tense time for both parties.

The GM and would-be Jets coach met for coffee the next morning at LAX, talking in detail about a Jets team that needed help in every facet of the game. Perles was only hoping Michigan State would end his anxiety before this romance got out of control and sent him and Sally packing for the East.

DiBiaggio had different thoughts. He was ready for a fight. This was a transparent power-grab, a political bushwhacking in the eyes of a president who had to draw the line and put a football coach in his place: on Spartan Stadium's sidelines, safely removed from the AD's office.

MSU's pro-Perles trustees were likewise sharpening their bayonets. Ferguson reminded all parties that there was no co-equality when it came to university authority. Something called the State Constitution had made that issue clear.

"The president reports to the board," Ferguson huffed as Perles versus DiBiaggio steadily turned into a statewide showdown. "And the board will not disqualify George Perles as a candidate for athletic director if he remains football coach."

DiBiaggio carried on with an air of confidence, appearing to be above a silly fray that would ultimately be settled in the president's favor.

"I made it clear that I felt the athletic director's position and the coaching position should be separate," DiBiaggio said, dismissively, during an interview with Lansing's WILX-TV, "and so that if he were to become athletic director he'd have to give up the coaching position."

DiBiaggio was as skilled at spin as Ferguson. The president said he doubted there was any agenda to Perles' discussions with the Jets. It was, DiBiaggio cheekily asserted, simply a matter of whether Perles wanted to coach in the NFL or in the college ranks.

If DiBiaggio's bravado was born of issues he believed to be ideologically pure, there was too little appreciation for what was politically practical. The board was probably one vote away from shooting him down. Still, the president was refusing to consider a Plan B, rejecting ideas of meeting with the board, ruling out any degree of compromise that might protect him from a defeat so damaging, so public, that DiBiaggio's reign at MSU would almost certainly be shortened and diminished.

Perles was enjoying a different experience. He was being fought over. Everyone who followed pro football intimately knew the Jets had eyes for one man: Michigan State's head football coach. CBS-TV's "NFL Today" reported on December 23, two days before the Aloha Bowl, that Perles was a favorite to replace Walton.

Steinberg had given Perles the same message, albeit in ways awkward and prolonged. He had called Perles at regular intervals, speaking with him about personnel issues in such a way as to imply Perles already was coach.

Not until the third weekend of January, more than two weeks after they had sipped coffee in Los Angeles and discussed the Jets, did Steinberg invite Perles to New York for talks that would plainly involve a contract.

Perles had been busy recruiting and was glad to be away from East Lansing. The town and campus were on fire. Owen, the board chairman, was answering tense questions and facing a lawsuit from the *Lansing State Journal* relative to possible private meetings at his home and at the Country Club of Lansing, where the board members had discussed Perles-related business in possible violation of the state's Open Meetings Act.

The pro-Perles bloc was about to hatch a strategy. It would be a bargaining chip based on the idea that the coach, if appointed AD, should be subject to a one-year review at which time his dual roles could either be sustained or cut short. It was, the Owens-Ferguson-Weiss camp reasoned, a failsafe method by which they might keep a coach and allow him at least the opportunity to succeed or fail at two jobs.

It was smart politics. However, it simply wouldn't appease the president. DiBiaggio and his allies—Pridgeon, Reed and Sawyer—in concert

Trustees Bob Weiss (left) and Joel Ferguson helped orchestrate George Perles' ascension to dual roles as AD and head football coach in the early '90s. Ferguson, particularly, wielded considerable, and sometimes controversial, clout in MSU athletics for years.

with most of MSU's faculty, kept the drum beating for their hoary cause: academics ahead of athletics. The president, they insisted, needed sufficient latitude to safeguard Michigan State's priorities.

Perles was nervous. He preferred staying in East Lansing, of course. He only wanted his bosses to appreciate the wisdom of allowing a Michigan State man to be *more* of a MSU man. It was what he feared—a new boss making his coaching life miserable—that primarily made him open to considering the job with the Jets.

By now the Perles-DiBiaggio standoff was being viewed statewide as a power struggle almost as sophisticated as a playground spat between two seventh-graders with black eyes and bloody noses. Perles had been strongly encouraged by his advisers to hang tough for a dual-role deal that MSU would ultimately offer. DiBiaggio had two masters he hoped to please: Father Hesburgh and the spirit in which he had placed DiBiaggio on his Knight Commission; and the parties who would reward his push for academic integrity with a five-year contract rather than the one-year deal now in place.

DiBiaggio and Perles had not spoken since Christmas. Jack Shingleton, MSU's retired placement director who had pinch-hit as athletic director during the middle 1970s, had been asked by Perles to act as mediator at a meeting where the two sides might finally settle their squabble and get on with MSU's affairs. Shingleton agreed and called the president's office.

"John, you need to talk with George," Shingleton said in a tone of voice that was more declaration than suggestion.

Shingleton and DiBiaggio believed Perles wanted a compromise. Perles had indicated as much to Shingleton. It was a first move toward resolution, which spurred Shingleton to arrange a meeting for a few nights later, a top-secret session at an East Lansing hideaway at which the feuding parties would appear.

On hand were DiBiaggio, Perles, Shingleton and trustee Tom Reed.

Perles quickly made it clear there would be no compromise. Whatever had been implied to Shingleton was no longer on the table. It was two jobs or the Jets.

DiBiaggio recoiled.

"Jack, this isn't what you told me," DiBiaggio said.

Shingleton, irritated: "It isn't what he told me, either."

The president got up from his chair and walked out. Now it was Shingleton who was steamed. Although he was on DiBiaggio's side with respect to Perles and carrying two jobs, what mattered to Shingleton was the University's stature. It was being assaulted. Ridicule would only mount now that Perles had reneged on a plan all sides could have lived with.

Perles was uneasy and feeling sheepish as DiBiaggio drove away. Shingleton wasn't letting him off the hook. He turned and said, in a school principal's voice: "George, where do you expect to be a year from now?"

Shingleton's implication was that Perles could win a battle but lose the war. A president so wedded to an issue of perceived integrity would never let it die no matter how a board might vote. George could have helped himself at the same time he got his school out of the soup if he had stuck to a compromise Shingleton had every reason to believe was coming.

January was slipping away and the trustees were still divided, 4-3, with Kathy Wilbur in the spotlight as an unpredictable swing vote. Perles flew to New York via Pittsburgh (accompanying assistant coaches Steve Furness and Dino Folino on a recruiting trip) for a Monday morning meeting with Steinberg he hoped would resolve a month-long exercise in melodrama.

The trustees needed their own resolution. They were either going to vote to retain Perles as football coach and give him the AD job, or hand DiBiaggio a personal victory and thereby trigger searches for a new football coach *and* athletic director.

Owen rounded up six trustees for an impromptu Sunday evening meeting in the Hannah Administration Building. The entire board would be on hand, save for Pridgeon and Reed, who decided to boycott a marathon session they concluded in advance would be an arm-twisting mission with Wilbur the target.

They had it right. By midnight, five hours after a roiling night of talking, cajoling and bargaining had wrapped up, the pro-Perles bloc had made headway. Wilbur was coming around. She, in fact, had been thinking the dual-title could work after a meeting with the coach a few weeks earlier. She liked the caveat that Perles would be subject to a one-year review.

Perles, who had been met at Pittsburgh International Airport by a wave of cameras and reporters privy to his double-purpose itinerary, was unaware of the eleventh-hour finagling taking place in East Lansing. Steinberg picked him up at his Manhattan hotel only a few hours after the trustees had called it a night. By early Monday morning, the coach was seated at a conference table with Steinberg and Jets president Don Gutman.

A contract needed to be hammered out even if Perles' heart was still tethered to East Lansing. Slowly, steadily, the coach understood as morning drifted toward mid-day that he had to face reality. No phone calls meant there was no progress in getting the necessary fifth vote. He had to begin thinking in terms of the NFL.

Perles delved into the numbers with Steinberg and Gutman, who were confident they could call a press conference for Tuesday. It was all very reminiscent, the coach thought, of a long day seven years earlier, in a hotel suite in Chicago, when he and Weaver had tied up details on a contract that would make Perles the highest-paid coach in the Big Ten—at a then-whopping $90,000 a year.

Now he was negotiating for millions over a handful of years. What a time-machine ride for a one-time Michigan State assistant who had drawn an annual salary of $11,000 in 1971, when he left Daugherty and MSU to accept an assistant's job with Steelers coach Chuck Noll.

Steinberg, Gutman, and the presumed new head coach for the New York Jets had settled on a contract by mid-afternoon. Gutman wanted a signature on a makeshift agreement printed on Jets stationery prior to formal language that would be composed before Tuesday's press conference.

Perles remembered the contract flap between MSU and the Philadelphia Stars seven years earlier—it ended in a $175,000 payment by MSU—and thought he should make one last call to Weaver, who, at that moment, was on a treadmill as part of getting a physical.

Perles next called home for Sally and got the answering machine. He tried Roger Wilkinson, MSU's vice president, who had worked to bring two sides together while at the same time unwittingly alienating himself from DiBiaggio. Wilkinson's sin was to see it as his obligation to make both Perles roles work.

Owen happened to be in Wilkinson's office when the phone rang.

"George," Owen said after Wilkinson handed him the phone, "we need one more vote. We've got Kathy Wilbur here and I think she's going to vote in your favor. Call me back in 45 minutes."

Perles was in a lovely jam with the Jets. Moments earlier he had pen in hand ready to sign a binding agreement with new employers who had been persistent and patient in chasing him. Now he wanted them to understand why they were being put on hold. Perles hadn't sweated so much since his Spartan playing days.

Forty-five minutes later, Perles phoned Owen who greeted him with the glee of a game-show host: "Pack your bags and come home. We got the vote."

Perles would have been just as giddy had he not been in so deep with the Jets. It seemed to the coach he had one option at a moment so unsettling: Have Owen talk with two executives who would be left to wonder if this episode was nothing more than a ploy to win Perles his coveted dual role at MSU.

Owen was ready. He told Steinberg and Gutman that Michigan State would not release Perles from his contract—unless he failed to get the necessary votes to make him athletic director.

Owen, of course, knew he had the votes. He also knew Perles could have gotten out of his MSU contract. As a legal or practical issue, Perles would have been free to leave. What mattered was that George had an excuse for staying at MSU and the Jets saw an obstruction to hiring him. MSU could proceed with making Perles coach/AD and get George and his supporters the deal they wanted all along.

Dealing with the University's constituencies and critics would be a separate challenge. Opposing camps—faculty, student groups and angry alumni—were about to slam Perles and his board supporters with heavy artillery, much of it rolled out for Tuesday night's 7 p.m. board meeting at the Kellogg Center's Lincoln Room.

It would be remembered even years later as a nasty town-hall session with all the rancor and divisiveness that marked student versus administration showdowns on campus during the Vietnam War. The war this time was between a coach and a president. It would draw an overflow crowd estimated at three hundred and fifty people, many wedged in against windowsills and pressed against walls. It was a roll-call vote unlike any other MSU trustees had confronted.

Of the fourteen people who spoke, all but one opposed Perles taking on two jobs. They included Dennis Martell, then a doctoral student and president of the Council of Graduate Students who had been a student liaison to the board of trustees for two and a half years.

"Look at the word trustee," Martell said, emphasizing *trustee*. "As students, as faculty, as staff, we put our trust into those people. We trust them to take our input and make a judgment on what's best for the University, not what's best for athletics."

There was an expectation that the vote would follow script. Reed had spoken during the pre-vote discussion to announce he would oppose Perles handling dual roles, which was no surprise. Wilbur, however, had been silent. Might she have backed away from her Sunday-Monday change of heart and sided with DiBiaggio?

The drama was as thick as the air in a hot and crowded conference room when voting began. Wilbur, seated to DiBiaggio's left, heard her name called.

"Yes," she said.

Gasps followed in tandem with applause from Perles' supporters. The coach—who had been watching the televised meeting in the basement of his defensive coordinator, Norm Parker—would be overseeing athletics as well as MSU's football team. A university president and his personal view of institutional principle had been defeated.

DiBiaggio's side saw no value in being gracious.

"I'm disappointed—enough that I have a pain in the gut," Pridgeon said, glumly, after the meeting had broken up.

Deeper debate was just beginning as three hundred and fifty people headed into a cold East Lansing night. Sentiment for a recall, aimed at five trustees who voted for Perles, was growing by the hour.

In a strident editorial, *The Detroit News* said: "Our front-page headline yesterday read 'Perles 5, DiBiaggio 3.' If space allowed, we would have added 'MSU 0'. The clock is still ticking, though. Citizens of Michigan should now express their outrage. Pro-Perles MSU Trustees Malcolm Dade and Larry Owen, who are up for election, should be forced to explain why academics should be subordinated to sports. Perhaps we won't have to wail till November. Recalls can start anytime."

The *Detroit Free Press* was less acidic in sharing a similar view:

"George Perles has many admirable attributes as a coach. He might or might not be a good candidate for athletic director. A good candidate for both? We thought that was a bad idea when the University of Michigan gave Bo Schembechler both jobs, and we think it would be bad policy at MSU. Above all, though, we think it's time friends of the universities, as opposed to friends of big-time football, started insisting that presidents have some voice in running one of the more highly visible parts of the university program. Athletics can be a real asset for a great university. Out of control, the sports program can also be a ruinous force."

Perles was doing little better with the national press, particularly New York pundits who charged him with taking the Jets on a one-way, self-promotional ride. The Perles-Jets charade, they said with barbed bluntness, was designed to festoon Perles with power made possible only by a romance with a NFL team.

Greg Logan of *Newsday*, a Long Island-based newspaper in the Jets' backyard, wrote: "Dick Steinberg isn't the first pro football executive to be played for a sucker by George Perles, but you can bet the Jets' general manager will be the last. The football fanatics at Michigan State gave Perles their endorsement as king-for-life when they offered him the athletic directorship. Fortunately for the Jets, Perles accepted."

As far as the Jets were concerned, Steinberg would leave the poison to other pens. He told the *New York Post*: "You're going to say he used us to get the athletic director's job, but we don't feel that's true. When he heard (Owen's) answer, he would have to be one hell of an actor to have the reaction he did. He turned pale, his eyes got glassy. He acted extremely shocked, and was almost speechless for several minutes. He didn't know where to go from there."

Neither, for that matter, did DiBiaggio. The president had been committed to a stance he believed was so lofty it could never be opposed by a university's trustees. He had been pristine, even pious, about academic integrity and its church-and-state separation. He saw the president as being the gatekeeper in such matters and could not fathom trustees, executives, coaches, or the general public, aligning in a contrary way.

He had drawn a bold and sacred line only to see five trustees obliterate it. What became clear in his written and spoken words in the ensuing days was that a public defeat had put the president into a deep funk.

"I want it known that I do not consider this action as a personal affront, but as one that could in the long run hurt the University more than the loss of any coach, any recruit, or any game," DiBiaggio said in a statement released after Perles was approved. "I am disappointed that perceived pressures of the moment were elevated over long-term benefits."

For a man who insisted he had suffered no "personal affront," DiBiaggio was doing a poor sales job. One significant administrative move appeared to be made out of pure spite.

Wilkinson was sacked as overseer of MSU athletics, his apparent punishment for not having been sufficiently supportive of the president's stance. David Scott, MSU's provost and a British Isles native who had gotten his doctorate in nuclear physics from Oxford, was now the person to whom Perles would report.

DiBiaggio was neither forgiving nor forgetting January's events. Three weeks after the trustees voted he delivered MSU's annual "State of the University" address. His tone was anything but conciliatory.

"No victory, no matter the level, no matter the court or playing field, is worth the winning if integrity and accountability are put at risk," DiBiaggio said, explaining that the transfer of authority over athletics to Scott's provost office would "put to rest any concerns loyal Spartans might have about perceived risks to academic primacy and to accountability."

Wilkinson had not appreciated the change in duties or the message it sent. He was ready to present DiBiaggio with a letter of resignation until board members talked him out of it. Not until later, during a private meeting between the two, was a relationship repaired.

DiBiaggio had only begun to fight, or, as some saw it, to pout. A letter sent to Perles on March 6 was obtained by the *Detroit Free Press* and published seven weeks later. It was a sensational statement by a spurned president who wanted it known he had no further interest or stake in Michigan State University athletics.

Sylvia Thompson, a longtime assistant to athletic directors dating back to Biggie Munn, had received the letter and cringed. She tried to persuade the president's office to squelch a petulant piece of correspondence that was bound to be made public.

"I must advise you that I feel that it is in the best interest of the

University that I distance myself from intercollegiate athletics and particularly from the football program," DiBiaggio wrote. "My participation will be very limited, focusing only on those activities that absolutely require my attendance."

DiBiaggio had responded to a February 28 letter from Perles in which the new athletic director had asked for a sit-down session with MSU's president.

"I am sorry that I have not had an opportunity to meet with you, but my schedule has been very busy these past several weeks," DiBiaggio said, with *faux* penitence, all before he cut to the chase: "I remain gravely disappointed by the board's decision, since it violated established University policies and severely undermined my authority to manage the University.

"Even more so, I think the integrity and the credibility of Michigan State University have been compromised, a situation that has been exacerbated by the manner in which the media has handled the entire matter."

Over and out, said the commander in chief. There had been a time, only months earlier, when DiBiaggio, Weaver and Perles had enjoyed the good life during drives to Cross Village on the Lake Michigan shoreline where Perles had a getaway. They were buddies, colleagues, leaders.

It was an arrangement some would have seen as destined to fail. Men and what they want from life, individually, make three-part harmony difficult to sustain.

CHAPTER 3

DOUBLE DUTY, DOUBLE TROUBLE

ALL A BIG TEN TEAM THOUGHT ABOUT IN 1990, well before a clumsy, contentious bowl-team clearinghouse known as the Bowl Championship Series evolved, was the Rose Bowl at Pasadena, California.

It was the best of all bowl games in every way that mattered.

Setting: The Rose Bowl itself was a beautiful, 100,000-seat stadium tucked within a deep canyon known as the Arroyo Seco. Watching a game from an upper-tier perch at the Rose Bowl afforded views of the San Gabriel Mountains on New Year's Day afternoons that typically were clear and sunny with temperatures in the 70s.

Prestige: The Rose Bowl was always prime-time, late-afternoon viewing in the Midwest and East. It was uncontested television entertainment for a broad college-football audience that gained a better appreciation for Big Ten football. The game also exposed West Coast teams to many American sports fans who were unfamiliar with them, mostly because of time-zone differences, and fewer televised games than today.

Environment: The Rose Bowl was a slice of Southern California at its best. You could enjoy all the trappings that Pasadena, Hollywood and Los Angeles offered, or zip down I-5 to Newport Beach or San Diego and savor even more of Nirvana at a time when the Midwest was freezing.

Twenty-two years after its last trek to Pasadena, Michigan State had slurped up all the Rose Bowl's sweetness during a 1987 trip to Pasadena and victory over Southern Cal on January 1, 1988. Now, in October of 1990, there was at least an outside chance Michigan State could make it two trips in four years, all because of a colossal, controversial victory over Michigan.

Beating Illinois at Champaign was the trick a week after MSU's stunning knockout of Michigan. Illinois was routinely tough and a miserable team to play on the road, especially after turnaround trickster Mike White had left Illinois and given way to John Mackovic.

Michigan State realized its trip to Champaign was the second half of a two-front war. Michigan, the primary target, had fallen a week earlier at Ann Arbor. Beating the Illini was going to be as tough, maybe more difficult, based upon the team's and the town's lingering bliss and head-in-the-clouds mindset following a 28-27 toppling of a rival ranked Number 1 in the land. What was needed most was adherence to the infamous "24-hour rule" established by George Perles: If we win, celebrate for 24 hours, if we lose, feel badly for 24 hours and then move on.

Balance was what Michigan State football featured in 1990. The Spartans' defense was tough in an old-fashioned, leather-helmet way. Their offense was sturdy behind quarterback Dan Enos and a couple of workhorse running backs with complementary styles.

Hyland Hickson was one of those second-chair recruits Michigan State had a way of finding and refining. He was out of Dillard High in Fort Lauderdale, Florida, where he smashed most of the records set by a running back who had left East Lansing a year earlier, Lorenzo White. State recruited Hickson even though everyone knew Hickson lacked White's speed, and would never be in the same class as a college or pro prospect..

Tico Duckett was a glitzy in-state recruit from Kalamazoo Loy Norrix High who had the profile any big-time college coach loved. He was an all-state-class running back and track man whose father was a coach. Super athlete from a super family, which explained why a duffel-bag full of recruiting letters had been arriving since his freshman year, when Iowa became the first college to send him a goodwill note.

"Where you going to school?" his dad, Ted Duckett, asked as Tico got on with his senior year.

Tico shrugged, not sure how to sort out the usual senior-recruit issues: UCLA was too far away. Florida and Nebraska might not offer. He

Tico Duckett was a big part of the Spartans' typically strong running game during the George Perles era.

had no idea what he was going to do.

"Why don't you pick out five schools within driving distance," Ted Duckett said, steering his son, who at that point wanted a nudge.

The candidates were Pitt (Tony Dorsett's legacy was alluring), Indiana, Michigan State, Michigan and Western Michigan. Western faded when Duckett found out his bowl-game and national television shots would come only if WMU was Mid-American Conference champion and made it to the Raisin Bowl.

Pitt was soon scratched off the list, as was Indiana, where big running back Anthony Thomas had hosted him during an overall pleasant visit. Michigan was next to get chopped.

"If you join us…" was a phrase Duckett remembered hearing during his weekend at Ann Arbor. It was a necessary way of phrasing recruiting pitches at U-M, where the best of the nation's high-school stable was always going to get a look, if not an immediate offer, from Michigan coaches who held out for the best.

His trip to East Lansing had been a different experience entirely. A hotshot runner/receiver was his designated host during a visit that had left him dazzled, as did the beauty of the campus, warm-hearted hospitality, and a social scene he tuned into. Everything was in place even before George Perles had his standard Sunday morning closeout discussion with all the visiting recruits.

"I've got Heisman written all over you," Perles said to Duckett in a voice an eighteen-year-old high school senior found to be positively paternal.

Two years later Duckett and Hickson were the 1-2 punch in a Michigan State offense Perles would have loved to turn into a template. Just as thrilled was running backs coach Bobby Williams, who liked how Duckett and Hickson tore at a defense in different ways.

Duckett was the slashing speedster who could get to the edge and outrun defenders. Hickson was powerful with excellent change of direction—and amazing vision. The two were rarely on the field together. Defenses had to cheat toward the outside for Duckett and contend with Hickson's power and swift changes in direction.

Their styles were no different from their personalities. Duckett was gentlemanly, a veritable Boy Scout. Hickson was noisy and, for all his popularity with teammates and coaches, a miserable cuss in the view of opposing players who would have loved stuffing his mouth with a football.

Hickson never quite forgave defenders who hit him along a sideline or touched him as he was skipping out of bounds. He would wag an index finger and chirp like an enraged magpie.

The referee inevitably would rush toward MSU's sideline and say to Perles: "Get him straightened out, Coach, or we're going to hit him with 15 yards."

Perles knew he had to appease the guys in stripes. He was just as keen that Hickson not lose his spirit when he grabbed his running back and pulled him close for a sideline conference.

"I want you to act like I'm ripping you," he would say to Hickson as players nearby grinned through their face masks. "Then you just keep doing what you're doing."

Michigan State's 1990 trip to Champaign could have gone down in MSU history much as MSU's 1987 game at Ohio State, when a 13-7 victory all but sewed up State's first Rose Bowl in two decades. It could have been a game as significant and as revealing in terms of MSU's heft and skill as the previous week's put-down of Michigan. It could have been a victory locked up late in the game at Memorial Stadium when MSU was leading, 13-12, and had Illinois sweating in its own end. The ball was snapped over Illinois quarterback Jason Verduzco's head, bounced off the artificial turf and straight into Verduzco's hands as the Spartans swarmed. What could have been a merry flight back to East Lansing instead went down as a 15-13 loss when Illini kicker Doug Higgins ripped a 48-yard field goal with 59 seconds left to win it.

Although standings and scenarios had to yet play out, what would become clear a month later is the Illinois loss had cost Perles and his bunch a second Rose Bowl. About all the Spartans could do was shake off Champaign and put together another of their trademark, season-ending five-game winning streaks that left State with a 7-3-1 record and Big Ten co-championship. Iowa won the Rose Bowl ticket thanks to its earlier 12-7 victory over State at East Lansing. MSU would be heading to El Paso to play in the John Hancock Bowl against Southern Cal and head coach Larry Smith.

MSU and Southern Cal were acquainted, of course. Overly so, thought some from each camp. Michigan State had beaten Southern Cal twice during the 1987 season: in the Labor Day opener at East Lansing, and then again four months later in a Rose Bowl where they could have greeted each other with, "Fancy meeting you here."

Perles had gotten wind that USC coach Smith yearned for a MSU-Southern Cal rematch. He thought the better team had lost once, if not twice, in the '87 season, and Perles suspected USC wanted a shot at evening the scorecard. Whether the I-want-you stuff was distorted or not, Perles saw a chance to use it like a cattle prod on his players. This was a team that loved the thought it could knock your block off in a tough-man contest.

Perles got busy when the Spartans gathered for practice at El Paso.

"You're co-Big Ten champions," he said, pumping some helium into his boys. "You could have gone to a lot of bowls. So you wanna know why you're here?

"Larry Smith hand-picked us. Larry Smith wants to play Michigan State. That's why we're here, guys. He wants to play you. He wants to beat you."

Smith and Perles weren't faking the bad blood. They got into a schoolyard spat before the game when Smith had said he wanted the Sun Bowl Stadium turf watered. It was a one-sided demand, expressed in a tone of voice that seemed haughty to Perles, who figured the playing field was an equal-opportunity surface.

"I don't care," Perles huffed. "You can water the parking lot, water the grass, I don't care. Water whatever you want."

Brotherly love was also in short supply at the prerequisite bowl banquet. Roosevelt Wagner—a Spartan defensive tackle who would have later repercussions for his coach—was acting as if he were the second coming of old Oklahoma linebacker and reputed tough-guy Brian Bosworth.

"I'm Big Rose, Number 50," he would say to Trojans players in a beach-bully voice. "I'm comin' after your ass."

It was all under-card entertainment. The main bout was ballyhooed to be terrific sports theater.

Southern Cal and quarterback Todd Marinovich—the no-McDonald's-hamburgers-for-you prodigy who had been physically and psychologically groomed as a quarterback since birth—was piloting a Trojans team loaded with linemen who looked like stunt doubles for Paul Bunyan. It was the biggest team State players remembered seeing on any field at any time.

USC led, 7-0, and was ready to make it 14-0 when Marinovich fumbled near MSU's goal line. Momentum turned and when Hickson scored on an 18-yard run, it was squared at the half, 7-7. Attitudes on the field were just as tight. Nasty stuff that had begun earlier in the week spiraled after kick-off. Spartan guard Eric Moten had gotten whacked by a Trojan defender and followed up with his own punch, which was good enough for the guys in stripes. Moten and his sparring partner were tossed from the game.

On the sideline, Perles exploded.

"You have no compassion," he yelled at the Big Sky Conference referee who had clearly over-reacted. "You must not have any kids of your own to treat players like that."

Perles never missed a chance to turn an event or an incident into motivation, no matter how much he had to amplify or hype. In Moten he had an instant halftime locker-room speech. The Spartans, he said, were going to dedicate the second half to their ejected left guard. They were to hit the Trojans with everything but night sticks. Perles' order: make the next thirty minutes the most physical half of football Michigan State had ever played.

If the Spartans fell short of fulfilling the order, it wasn't by much.

USC went ahead, 10-7, in the third quarter. Then Courtney Hawkins took an Enos pass, pulled a slick fake-and-pivot, and sprinted 21 yards for a touchdown that put MSU on top, 14-10.

Football pads popped like shotgun blasts. Dixon Edwards had set the tone even before halftime when he blew up a USC screen pass with a tackle so violent it had Perles pumping his fist.

After Michigan State took its second-half lead, Freddie Wilson, who had already intercepted a pass, put a head-snapping hit of such percussion on a USC receiver it might have resonated on the Mexican side of the Rio Grande.

Mike Iaquaniello, like Wilson, intercepted a Marinovich pass, and also nearly broke a Trojan in two on a hit-'em-high blast as the ball-carrier was sinking to the turf. John Langeloh's 52-yard field goal set up by Wilson's pick finished it for MSU. Final score: Michigan State 17, USC 16.

Perles and his staff had seen enough football games to do precise autopsies afterward. Never was there any mystery about the cause of one team's defeat: Turnovers, better opposing athletes and skills, a single instance of execution—coaches could always reach consensus on what had decided a particular game.

Michigan State had beaten the Trojans, they agreed, because Southern Cal had been pummeled to death. The Spartans had hit Smith's team with such unrelenting fury that USC—in the MSU staff's estimation—had all but waved a white flag after three quarters.

Why it so often seemed a Perles team had to get to the season's second half before it turned ornery may have been more than a scheduling issue. Before returning to East Lansing as head coach, Perles had worked in the NFL where teams have a four-game exhibition season. Beyond padding cash registers and helping cull rosters, pre-season competition serves to put pro teams at least closer to a point that will define their particular operating speed.

College football has no such structure. Teams scrimmage against themselves until the season opener at which time there is, within days or even hours, a zero-to-60 culture change. Perles teams may well have started gently and finished like Pamplona's bulls no matter how the schedule was sprinkled with tough versus beatable teams. It seemed to be a trait manifested in the head coach's football personality and preparation.

How that preparation might have been challenged by earlier events in 1990 was a question on most of MSU's football minds heading into what would be the last bowl game, indeed the last winning season, for Spartans football under George Perles.

His victory over DiBiaggio in January of 1990 had been Pyrrhic. Both men, both camps, had been damaged deeply—even mortally, in the president's political self-assessment—by the no-ground-ceded stances of two University icons who represented competing interests not easily reconciled.

There was festering antagonism between the two sides. There was obvious bitterness on John DiBiaggio's part after Perles won a 5-3 vote to assume the dual titles of coach and athletic director. So wide was the rift that no less than a United States ambassador tried to bridge the gap.

Peter Secchia, the Grand Rapids businessman and former Michigan Republican party chairman, had been talking with both men throughout a month-long imbroglio as he handled ambassador duties in Italy. Secchia lived in a sixteenth-century palace in Rome, named Villa Taverna, which Perles was only too happy to visit when he and Sally were on vacation three weeks after the vote.

Secchia explained his diplomatic mission in a conversation with *Detroit News* political reporter George Weeks:

"John DiBiaggio is a friend of mine and the best president the University could ever have," the ambassador said. "George was like a tennis ball between two large rackets: a hardworking president and a hardworking board that really care about the University. I understand both their situations, and I wanted a win-win situation for both of them."

DiBiaggio knew who had won—it wasn't the president. To a university's chief executive who understood politics every bit as much as an ambassador and GOP veteran, DiBiaggio saw Secchia's "win-win" assurances as Pollyanna proclamations more aimed towards placating constituents than soothing a battered president.

Perles had a different, more pleasant agenda as he and Sally flew home from Europe. He was already arranging structure and strategies for an athletic director's job he would officially assume after Doug Weaver headed for retirement at the end of June.

He would report to a new boss, provost David Scott, and preside over six assistant athletic directors: Bert Boyko, a longtime staffer and financial overseer; Gene Kenney, another veteran who was in charge of facilities; Charlie Wilson, the department's academic supervisor; Gus Ganakas, the one-time Spartans basketball coach who was now responsible for advertising and marketing; Kathy Lindahl, who was assigned non-revenue sports; and the returning Clarence Underwood, who had been at Michigan State previously as an assistant athletic director before joining the Big Ten as a deputy commissioner. Perles was bringing Underwood back to East Lansing as director of compliance and student affairs. This would put Underwood in a position to appropriately monitor athletes, rules, academic progress and the everyday challenges so often faced by kids who were theoretically students first, and athletes second.

Perles dug into both jobs, and one of the people who had strengthened his push to combine AD and football jobs gave him a kind of rough blessing: None other than Bo Schembechler, who had filled both positions for two years at Michigan before taking over as president of the Detroit Tigers.

In a conversation with the *Detroit Free Press*, Schembechler said in typically pointed words: "All the uproar (about Perles) ought to be put to rest. He's a highly qualified guy and if he wants to do it as badly as he does, let him. It isn't like he's taking over the presidency of General Motors."

Perles wanted people to understand several things he figured had been overwhelmed by the political heat:

He really wanted the AD job. That was the reason he took not a penny extra in compensation from his $123,000 salary as head coach. He believed he could be an effective athletic director. He was convinced of this for two reasons. First, because of his bond with the University. Second, because he believed that values make the ultimate difference—cases in point for him were people like iconic former president John Hannah, and athletic directors he admired in the persons of Biggie Munn and Doug Weaver, not to mention his old coach, Duffy Daugherty.

He had plenty of ideas, too. Perles understood money and what it could do with proper stewardship, and he had an idea that revenue and prudent spending could be expanded in fruitful ways. Facilities, coaches' salaries, team budgets, and creative marketing initiatives—Perles believed money would flow to good ideas and proper judgment.

He was going to work his trousers off. Perles knew that his days and nights, already full in the fashion of a major-college head coach, would be lengthening. He was now overseeing not one sport, but twenty-five. What Perles could not comprehend is how the focus before his appointment had always been on the dual-job debate. Why had his boss—and the media for that matter—not made a bigger issue out of his obvious inexperience as an administrator? He was a lifelong football coach. Yes, he had presided over the University's highest-profile sports program, but to move from a football office to CEO of Michigan State's multi-faceted athletic program was more than a quantum leap. Had he revealed his innermost fears, Perles would have confessed to some concerns.

What he also knew about himself is that his sponge-like brain absorbed and retained information. He could observe and process. He had a powerful memory. Soon Perles had a plan: He would visit Weaver's office each day for two hours and simply observe how the respected AD Weaver did his job. Perles could listen in on conversations, see how an expert negotiated contracts and business deals, and understand communication protocol with the conference, the NCAA, and with other ADs. He could get a feel for the ebb and flow of an athletic director's days—and nights.

Perles was confident this approach would work because first and foremost he and Weaver were friends. There would be nothing uncomfortable for an outgoing AD in having George hang around to soak up the nuances of life as a major-college athletic director.

Clarence Underwood had seen, in ways that stunned him, how Perles was already changing when they met in May to discuss Michigan State and Underwood's return to East Lansing, something that Underwood previously viewed as unlikely. He had been accustomed to hearing Perles speak during Big Ten meetings at Schaumburg, Illinois, and had viewed him as a brass-tacks football man concerned about football matters.

Perles had differed in that regard, Underwood thought, from a man like Schembechler, who seemed to view football as being one aspect of a complex outside world filled with overlapping issues. Schembechler saw the relationships there. Perles, while outspoken, tended to focus on football-specific topics: staffing, rules, bowl-game business, salaries.

Only if he were heading back to East Lansing as athletic director was Underwood entertaining thoughts of a return to Michigan State. He finally agreed to talk with Perles, who was intent on adding a sixth assistant athletic director who could supervise rules compliance and student-athlete issues.

Underwood spoke with the incoming AD for one hour and was shocked. A man he had viewed as pigskin personified was talking in substantive ways about all the right things: about having a "model compliance program"; about renovating facilities; about upgrading women's athletics and non-revenue sports; about fund-raising efforts that were not only ambitious but also realistic. Underwood had never anticipated that Michigan State's hardcore head football coach could have spoken so authoritatively and sincerely about so many dimensions of intercollegiate sports.

Underwood stepped from Perles' office and headed for the phone. He needed to call his wife:

"Noreese," he said, still blown away by his one-hour conversation, "this guy has sold me." Underwood accepted and would return to Michigan State.

As impressed as Underwood was, it was no more so than some of MSU's coaches who had initially feared the worst. Having a football man in charge of the department sounded to some of them like having Mobil

Oil in charge of United States energy policy.

Perles understood these anxieties and began heading them off even before Weaver moved out. He met with each coach—whether of a revenue or non-revenue sport—and told them more money was coming. He was adamant that funding would and could be found to give them the salaries they deserved, plus the scholarships, and the budget latitude they needed to run a competitive program.

He was about to embark on a plan for putting new scoreboards in Spartan Stadium and Munn Arena. It figured to be a costly investment until Perles spearheaded a drive to get six advertisers to pledge $125,000 each year for five years. In return for the exposure—the advertisers would also be part of scoreboard promotion at the Breslin Center—Michigan State got new scoreboards at no cost as part of a $3.5-million deal that brought new revenue to the athletics budget.

A new radio contract was in the works, as well, one that would turn $85,000 in annual revenue into a $400,000 deal and provide expanded statewide coverage.

Perles was showing another attribute not everyone had expected: imagination. When MSU headed off to the John Hancock Bowl in December of 1990, Perles had hatched an idea to buy two thousand seats for the game and give them away to troops at a nearby military base. It would accomplish three things: It would create a sellout, which would increase revenue for the Big Ten; it would be excellent public relations, particularly when TV cameras panned the crowd and mentioned how they were guests of Michigan State; and it would prevent MSU from getting stuck with a tab for returning unused tickets.

Perles was proving, also, during his first six months on the job to be good at delegating. There were daily staff meetings that brought together the assistant ADs, as well as those in charge of other areas, among them: Don Loding, MSU's ticket manager; and John Breslin, son of the late MSU vice president, Jack Breslin, and, like his dad, a former Spartan football player Perles had hired from the hotel industry to work in marketing.

With a staff he considered to be deep and versatile, thanks greatly to Underwood's arrival, he could parcel out responsibility and be assured an intricate department was functioning smoothly, at least on the surface.

Perles had another idea. It was bold and it was ambitious. He wanted to remodel the west side of Spartan Stadium and install big-ticket private boxes that had become the rage with professional sports teams and, increasingly, with major colleges.

He was going to enter into a partnership with Mike Ilitch's Little Caesars Pizza empire. There would be a sharing of the bounty from twenty-four luxury boxes over twenty-five to thirty years with MSU expecting an annual cut of $500,000. Ilitch's company would put up the cash to build the boxes, as well as $60,000 for a feasibility study.

It was all a little too adventuresome to suit Perles' boss, David Scott, the provost who was in his initial months overseeing athletics. Scott decided to table the stadium renovation, as well as another idea hatched by Ken Hoffman, MSU's sports information director, for a Michigan State satellite office in Detroit. The Detroit office would serve as a base for selling tickets and merchandise and for hosting media sessions that always forced Detroit stations and newspapers to travel to East Lansing. It was no wonder, Hoffman and Perles reasoned, that the University of Michigan seemed to fare so much better with Detroit media. Logistics were invariably part of the equation.

Scott, however, was of no mind to do anything daring. He was an Oxford man whose British Isles background made the world of American sports an alien experience.

"I know what balls are," he said once, speaking about baseball, "but what are strikes?"

Jackie Robinson, Joe DiMaggio—Scott had no idea who they were.

Perles and Scott otherwise enjoyed a civil, courteous relationship. Whether Scott's unfamiliarity with sports accounted for it or not, Perles began to act with increasing autonomy in his first year as AD when he felt it necessary or expedient. There was a certain irony to it, thought executives who had known him for almost a decade.

Perles was a man who found clichés useful for conveying bedrock virtues, values and policies. "Following chain of command" had always been one of George's pet dictums, but he made an exception of himself.

Often he viewed the implementation of an idea or a plan as a one-man initiative.

He was running into another problem. Women in the athletic department were finding in George Perles that male chauvinism was alive and well in 1990. It may have been subconscious, inadvertent, or benign in the realm of a man who cared genuinely about people. It mattered not to MSU's inner-department women whether Perles was incapable of looking at them as equals or whether he simply had a comfort level with men who had roots tracing back to his own football days.

What mattered was what the women experienced. What they saw developing was a blatant old-boys network extending from George to Kenney to Larry Bielat, an old Perles buddy and staffer who was now working in the athletic department. They saw that men were honored while women were, at best, tolerated, and, they believed, held in contempt.

Meetings were a window into the mindset of a man who made it easy for women to feel threatened or slighted.

"Come sit by me, Johnny boy," Perles would say with obvious appreciation for Breslin.

Part of the culture change had less to do with gender, perhaps, than with a difference in style from Weaver to Perles. Weaver was the man for whom Michigan State had named the Oilcan Award, and honor awarded annually to the football player whose humor kept his team loose.

Weaver had brought much of his native, rural Indiana ways to East Lansing and had maintained a Huck Finn kind of personality throughout his tenure as AD. He listened to Willie Nelson music in his office and remained so tied to his old football days that in the days before a game he became as nervous as a player or coach.

Perles loved having him stop by on Friday mornings during home-game weeks for bagels and coffee, even if not every coach was wild about Weaver's passion.

Aware of Nick Saban's dead-serious football demeanor when he was defensive coordinator under Perles, Sylvia Thompson, Weaver's assistant, would give Saban a reluctant heads-up that the AD was coming by to talk some defense.

"You can run and hide now," she would say, exasperated by Saban's impatience. "Doug's on the way over."

Saban: "I don't want him here."

Thompson had adored Weaver. He had this amazing capacity to be sensitive to people, their dignity, and their feelings. There were moments when Weaver needed to rip someone for personal irresponsibility or screw-ups and yet the person he targeted would invariably leave the AD's office smiling. In that respect, Weaver reminded her of Daugherty, for whom she had been secretary before transferring to the athletic director's office.

Perles was still spending weekends and vacation time at his summer home at Cross Village, on Lake Michigan's shoreline west of Mackinac City. As the weeks went by, he was making it clear he was no Weaver in his approach to women.

Thompson would drive north with boxes of mail that they would sort through at Perles' dining-room table. It was the best favor an assistant could have extended to her boss. Why, then, should she be made to feel as if she were nothing more than a servant? Whatever was at the root of it—any sincere feeling that Perles may have that females were inferior, his ineptness when it came to dealing with them, or his insensitivity to sexist words and actions—it was making life difficult for plenty of women who had to deal with the new boss.

Perles would have countered with defense witnesses, beginning with Mary Kay Smith, the longtime assistant to a half-dozen coaches. She was skilled at dealing with football's occasional caveman culture and simply handled it adroitly. She was so effective and so comfortable working with Perles she would rejoin him years later, after her retirement from MSU, when Perles became executive director of the Motor City Bowl.

How Perles was dealing with gender issues was not DiBiaggio's primary concern as Perles settled into his new duties. DiBiaggio was still bent on reclaiming authority he viewed as integral to a president's ability to govern MSU and to safeguard its academic character.

DiBiaggio was about to get help from November's elections. Malcolm Dade, who had voted in favor of Perles, was not running for another term on MSU's board of trustees. Larry Owen was a high-profile Democrat who had been a ramrod in getting Perles his dual jobs and who, because of his support, was one of the trustees who had been the target of failed recall efforts earlier in the year. He was beaten as two new Republican trustees—Dee Cook, a high-school classmate of DiBiaggio, and Jack Shingleton, the former interim AD who had supported DiBiaggio's stance—stood to shift the board's power dramatically and almost certainly in the president's favor.

Perles was about to lose another heavyweight political ally: James Blanchard, the two-term Michigan governor. Blanchard was a Perles friend whose limo could, on occasion, be seen parked in the Duffy Daugherty Building's parking lot as the governor and coach enjoyed a chat in Perles' office. Blanchard had been knocked off in the same November election by John Engler, a MSU alum who would be steering clear of Spartan football and focusing on his political agenda.

Perles was becoming marginalized by the day. If he failed to appreciate it fully, or react to it nervously, it was probably because his football team had caught fire in November 1990 before its trip to El Paso and the John Hancock Bowl.

Perles, Weaver and DiBiaggio once upon a time had been close enough friends to make weekend trips to Cross Village for fun and fellowship. Even after their political falling out, Perles could revert to towel-snapping moments with a president he had beaten and seemed to enjoy tweaking.

Their interaction, infrequent as it was, could be borderline juvenile. They would be in a small group discussing university business, and sabers would be drawn from their scabbards.

"Somebody ought to tell the athletic director," DiBiaggio would begin, cattily, "that (such and such) should be the policy here …"

Perles, hackles raised, would slide languidly into his response.

"Well," he would say, drawing out his words in molasses-slow tempo, "somebody ought to tell the president that (such and such) is already being done …"

Perles had begun to enjoy the rift. It was over, anyway, as far as he was concerned. Either by virtue of the board's vote last January or because the new board was going to take actions beyond his control, he could afford to yank the president's chain.

There was a day late in 1990 when he and Michael Kasavana, MSU's faculty representative to the NCAA, had arrived at DiBiaggio's office for a conference. They sat waiting for the president to finish one phone conversation when he was quickly interrupted by another. It was evident the caller was DiBiaggio's realtor.

"Uh, guys," the president said, wanting some privacy, "I've got to take this call."

Perles turned to Kasavana and said in a mischievous half-whisper: "Don't get up."

The two camped on office furniture as DiBiaggio talked real estate, his back turned to them. Perles found his own insolence amusing. Aching to do something, anything, that would stick another needle into the prez, he spotted a Christmas-season poinsettia plant sitting forlornly on a nearby lamp stand.

Perles grabbed it. He stepped toward the office window, delighted that Kasavana was grinning at this impromptu comedy act. Perles opened the window and pretended to heave the poinsettia into thin air as DiBiaggio, his back still turned, talked about mortgages and counter-offers.

By the end of 1990, DiBiaggio was getting everywhere in his political and academic struggles with a renegade AD. He was getting nowhere in subduing Perles himself.

The coach and athletic director remembered all too clearly DiBiaggio's March letter: The president would no longer be participating in team events or functions save for those a president absolutely was obliged to attend. It was a spiteful note, coaches and others thought, spurred by nothing more than bitterness toward the Perles vote.

The coach indulged in more fun two weeks before he and the Spartans would fly to El Paso. Perles' football team had finished as 1990 Big Ten co-champions and commemorative rings would soon be worn by coaches, players, key staffers, etc. John Hancock Bowl pins festooned men's lapels and women's jackets campus-wide.

"John," Perles said, cranking up for the kill, "what's your ring size?"

"I don't want a ring," DiBiaggio barked. "I don't want anything to do with that bowl."

Perles laughed off the protest and tried to put a John Hancock pin on DiBiaggio's suit coat. No go. Perles smiled devilishly and threw a pin on the president's desk.

On the way out the door, he turned, straight-faced, and said, "What about a ring for your wife?"

The president was not amused. He had lost in grand and humiliating fashion eleven months earlier on a matter of principle he could not yet believe had been subverted by a Big Ten university's board of trustees. George may have had his fun this year, the president had reason to believe. But with a new board and new determination on DiBiaggio's part to turn the tables, the pins would soon be sticking in an athletic director whose best days at Michigan State were about to slip into the past.

CHAPTER 4

PERILS OF PERLES

FROM HIS DAYS GROWING UP as a street-tough kid on Detroit's southwest side, to his family and to his career, George Perles was proud of a personal life story and those who had helped craft it. Nothing had elevated a football coach more than having been part of Chuck Noll's Pittsburgh Steelers dynasty during the 1970s.

Perles had four Super Bowl rings to show for it, not to mention countless friends and contacts from his days tutoring an august cast of Steelers defensive linemen including Joe Greene, L.C. Greenwood, Dwight White and Steve Furness. It was a sexy football background he could advertise to high-school recruits who perhaps had more interest in playing pro football someday than they otherwise might have had for attending Michigan State the next four years.

Perles made sure prep superstars bombarded with scads of major-college spiels were aware of his network. If a quality player failed to be drafted by a NFL team, Perles could point to ex-Spartans who had been signed as NFL free agents and who had careers of varying lengths, in part because Perles had made a phone call and offered an endorsement.

Never had Michigan State's head coach done a better job of sending players to the pros than following MSU's 1990 co-Big Ten championship season. Six Spartans were drafted: Percy Snow, Travis Davis, Harlon Barnett, Bob Kula, Jim Szymanski and Ventson Donelson, and more would sign as NFL free agents.

Veteran talent had helped Michigan State take a six-game winning streak into the 1991 season, just as those fourteen departing seniors cued a slew of new starters for '91, quarterback included, where a strong-armed sophomore named Jim Miller was set to replace Dan Enos.

At least the schedule stood as a plus for a truly green Spartan team. Three of MSU's first four games would be against Central Michigan, Rutgers and Indiana, schools MSU could expect to clobber with the mounds of muscle Perles had been amassing through his eight seasons in East Lansing.

Spartan players tended to like their head coach—in most cases, a great deal. He had an appealing personal touch bolstered by the manner in which he knew almost everything about a kid and his background. He proved that during one-on-one conversations that could run the gamut: discipline, sympathy or counsel on family issues, dorm life, academic realities, girls, etc. Whether the kid was from the inner city or fresh from a sugar-beet farm in Michigan's Thumb, Perles had a way of relating to players with his simple bromides and no-frills code of conduct.

Tico Duckett, who would be joining Hyland Hickson in a backfield that stood as one of MSU's strong suits heading into '91, had considered Perles the best teacher—after his own father—of life lessons he would ever know. He remembered how Perles handled a particular player with sure signs of a drug problem. Perles put the player on a weekly drug-testing routine and stopped a brewing crisis cold. The player two years later became an early-round NFL draft choice.

There was the day Perles had been given a report that chilled him: Someone had been taking items from players' lockers. He could handle kids flunking classes or getting into mischief on a Saturday night. Stealing from your teammates was about as low as a football player's moral code could sink.

Perles brought it up during a team meeting, using words his players recalled with a grin fifteen years later:

"I don't want any of you guys finding anything before someone loses it," he said, artfully avoiding the word "steal," or even the implication of dishonesty.

He had another clever saying players came to understand. It was comically contradictory until you saw how a head coach applied it:

"I treat everyone fairly," Perles would say, "but not equal."

In other words, kids demanded different approaches. Some responded to a coach's paternal side, particularly if they had never known an at-home father figure. Some of them needed a timely taste of penance running stairs at Spartan Stadium until their legs felt as if they were melting. Some kids had grown up in circumstances of poverty so unspeakable the coach could barely talk about it. When problems cropped up they were cut more slack than kids who came from good homes who knew that getting drunk Saturday night was out of bounds and not the kind of behavior their parents would abide.

Perles had been having his own battles the past eighteen months as his team got ready for MSU's 1991 season. Spartan players had been following along with everyone else the showdown with John DiBiaggio over George's two-job stint as MSU athletic director and football coach. Most viewed their coach's in-house fights as irrelevant, largely because Perles had been ordering them to think about their own business as opposed to his.

"You let me handle what's going on in the outside world," Perles would say to players who were uneasy about losing the only college head coach they had ever known. "Come in, practice hard, and act like I'm not going anywhere, because I'm not."

As far as his coaching job was concerned, Perles was correct. It was his tenure as athletic director that was about to be chopped short. New trustees were aboard—Jack Shingleton, Dee Cook and Melanie Reinhold, who had been appointed by Governor John Engler to replace Kathy Wilbur after she resigned to take a state job. It seemed clear there was a three-vote shift swinging the way of DiBiaggio and his push to undo one man's title to two high-powered jobs.

How they were going to do it was DiBiaggio's problem. Perles had made things sticky by faring well in his first year as AD. The athletic department was making money (not a common occurrence in the Big Ten in 1990-91) and moving progressively on projects Perles had, in many cases, conceived or directed. Likewise, MSU's football team had been to four consecutive bowl games, which made it tough to conk the coach for any sideline shortcomings.

DiBiaggio's strategy was to craft an amendment to the board's 1990 resolution making Perles coach and AD—subject to a one-year review. The new board could approve wording that held to Perles' review as AD, but would re-visit the concept of one man holding two jobs.

To use a legal corollary, the amendment would ignore precedent and re-submit DiBiaggio's case to a new set of judges. Perles' evaluation by provost David Scott would mean zilch if the greater issue in DiBiaggio's mind—keeping Perles from holding two jobs—became the board's primary action. The language was adopted at a June 7 board meeting by way of a 6-2 vote consistent with the board's new makeup. Textual machinery was now in place to trim George Perles' workload by one-half.

Scott would get rolling with an evaluation expected to take three months. One question Scott would answer on his evaluation had made DiBiaggio's intentions and expectations clear: "To what extent, if any, has this dual arrangement affected the credibility and integrity of the department of intercollegiate athletics?"

Perles had few options but to keep an eye on business at Jenison Fieldhouse, where athletic department offices remained based, and to get busy with the football season and State's September 13 home opener against Central Michigan.

It had been the coach's idea to schedule in-state schools like CMU. Playing the Chippewas—or their Mid-American Conference siblings at Eastern Michigan and Western Michigan—seemed to Perles to be smart, even unselfish, strategy. Michigan State played a tough enough schedule and owed no apologies for playing Herb Deromedi's crisply coached gang from Mount Pleasant. Playing a team seventy miles away would also be good for gate revenues that would help both schools.

Perles also liked the idea, from a sentimentalist's standpoint, that a lot of game-day money was staying in Michigan. This was good scheduling and good citizenship, he thought.

Not everyone on MSU's football team was as glad to see 1991 as

Perles had been following his long off-season as AD. Even if Michigan State were bringing a six-game winning streak into the CMU game, events behind the scenes and beneath the football program's surface were hinting at trouble.

Recruiting had been falling off. Players could see during visits they hosted the previous two winters that there was slippage in high-profile kids and in their potential to replace talent that was leaving East Lansing.

Assistant coaches had either moved on to other jobs or away from coaching. Morris Watts had left in 1991 to join the Tampa Bay Buccaneers. Steve Furness had departed for the NFL in 1990. Steve Beckholt was gone. New coaches like Bobby Williams were solid teachers, but staff adjustments meant transition time for players who liked continuity in their football routines.

Perles himself was a separate issue. The head coach had dropped a notch in intensity. Clearly, his AD duties had left him divided and too often distracted.

Players had remembered how Perles would berate them like a prison warden if they fumbled during practice. He was softer now, less incensed by screw-ups.

There had been times when ten minutes into practice the head coach's cell phone would ring. It was clearly an athletic-department matter in need of the AD's intervention. Players might not see him for a half-hour.

As the head coach's energy seemed to wane, so, too, did his staff's in the eyes of players who had been around long enough to compare. There were too many fights during practice, too much disorder, compared with teams that Perles had managed in previous years.

They might have been college kids, as the perception went, but twenty-one-year-olds knew enough about football to wonder if State might be headed for a tumble in 1991. All the wrong elements were in place: a new, though talented, quarterback in Jim Miller, new offensive line, too many new people on defense, and a coach fighting two-front wars on the gridiron and in Jenison Fieldhouse's increasingly commotion-filled offices.

Players were also unsettled by the game-week routine leading into MSU's opener against CMU. Michigan State was practicing as if the

Spartans were playing a Saturday scrimmage: two-a-day drills, heavy practices on Thursday. It made no sense even if the Spartans were expected to clean up on a MAC team that could hardly match MSU's muscle.

It didn't take long for the Spartans' hopes, plans and momentum to go up in smoke. Central Michigan waxed the Spartans, 20-3, in the opener as State fans groaned. Notre Dame partied a week later at South Bend with a 49-13 romp. It couldn't get worse—but it did. On week three, in East Lansing it was Rutgers 14, Michigan State 7. And still worse, the next game was a 31-0 disgrace at Indiana.

MSU had been outscored, 114-23, and was 0-4 and now faced the toughest part of the schedule. Miller, for all his talent, was having a rough start. A bad line in front of him and slow feet beneath him made a lethal combination for a sophomore trying to get a feel for the speed of major-college football.

Duckett was turning into a one-man offense for the Spartans as well as into hamburger. Example: He would carry forty-two times against Wisconsin on the way to 4,212 career yards, the most by any MSU running back other than Lorenzo White, who had finished with 4,887.

Duckett had been advised by friends to think about exchanging his senior season for a ticket to the NFL draft. He decided to stick in East Lansing, only to wonder a year later if his friends might have had the right idea.

At the NFL Combine in Indianapolis, Duckett was approached by New Orleans Saints coach Jim Mora, Sr.

"Son," Mora began, "why should I draft you?"

"Because I had almost five thousand yards at Michigan State," Duckett replied, proud to present a NFL coach with evidence of his skill and endurance.

"Why, son," Mora said, "that's like buying a used car to me."

Michigan State's 1991 season carried on, ruinously, when the Spartans dropped to 0-5 after losing at home to Michigan, 45-28. After their season-ending six-game winning streak in 1990, MSU was now one game from becoming a .500 team in their last dozen games. The Spartans instead beat Minnesota, 20-12, in a homecoming turnaround. But that result was no preview of things to come. Ohio State and Northwestern won the next two Saturdays to drop MSU to 1-7. State completed its disastrous 3-8 season after beating Wisconsin, 20-7, and then nipping Illinois at home, 27-24. Thus ended an autumn of ignominy that saddled Perles with his worst season as Spartan coach.

Life was little better on the political front.

DiBiaggio was sharpening his axe despite Scott's review, which suggested, to some people's surprise, that the head coach should consider bagging football to become Michigan State's fulltime AD.

Perles had received an evaluation grade of 77.6 percent on a university scale where 55-60 was generally regarded as favorable. He had scored 80-plus in four separate categories: leadership skills, commitment to MSU, professional achievements, and management of programs and resources.

In only two areas had he scored less than 60: commitment to diversity and pluralism (gender problems were showing up here), 59.2; and relations with academic governance, 50.7.

On the plus side were statements such as, "Among his recognized personal strengths are self-motivation and the ability to generate new ideas. Mr. Perles appears to most to have almost limitless energy and to be prepared to devote extraordinary amounts of time to work."

On the flip side was testimony in keeping with a football coach who had been a fighter since his days growing up along Vernor Highway in Detroit: "Mr. Perles, at some times and particularly when under pressure, reportedly has a confrontational style of dealing with people and their shortcomings. Some have described this as an approach in which people are immediately put on the defensive and questions are asked later …"

The review pleased Perles every bit as much as it infuriated DiBiaggio. Adding to DiBiaggio's ire was the fact that trustee Joel Ferguson had leaked the document prematurely to keep the president from "twisting things around," in Ferguson's words.

DiBiaggio had no intentions of twisting anything. He had plans, rather, for slicing. Perles was going to lose one, if not both of his jobs, in keeping with DiBiaggio's two-year stance and in step with a board of trustees disposed to do business the president's way.

Perles knew what was coming and began forming an exit strategy. In great part due to 1991's football disaster, he had decided it might be time to give up coaching and concentrate fulltime on an AD's job he had come to like.

He and the Spartans were on their way to West Lafayette, Indiana, on November 15, a week before the season would end, when Perles and attorney Donald Reisig released a statement that followed Ferguson's leak and DiBiaggio's outrage over it. In the president's irate view, "The entire process is jeopardized by the selective distribution of materials to media, incredibly even before three-fourths of the trustees had seen these documents."

The coach's statement made it clear that compromises he had earlier dismissed were now in play.

"Regretfully, it now appears my dual appointment has brought a degree of controversy that I never anticipated," Perles said in words Reisig helped craft. "The issues have distracted attention from other important issues facing this great university.

"This was never my intent. I want to be part of the solution to this issue and have it all behind us."

Later that day his new attitude became even clearer in words to Lansing television station WLAJ.

"I've said it for a long time that I'm always ready to sit down and compromise," he said, "because I want to get it over with and go on and do what's best for MSU."

In fact, Perles had been agreeable to a compromise Ferguson and Scott had discussed: He would stay on as head football coach for one more year and then move fulltime to the AD's office. It would help protect his assistants and give Perles a shot at having input on his successor.

DiBiaggio wanted none of it. Seven days later, DiBiaggio got the retribution he had been chasing for twenty-two months. He released a statement saying Perles would be occupying only one job—athletic director, if he preferred—for the duration of a three- and-a-half-year term that would begin January 1, 1992. It would end five years to the day Perles took over as AD from Weaver.

"I am informing our board of trustees, George Perles, and our athletic council, that I have accepted Provost David Scott's recommendation that we separate the positions of director of intercollegiate athletics and head football coach. I have considered such a dual appointment inappropriate from the start. The jobs are separate and distinct, and a mistake was made when they were joined over my objections."

DiBiaggio continued to fly the flag of academic integrity as he pressed his two-year case against one man functioning as AD and football coach. What the president avoided saying might have made a legitimate case with many of Perles defenders: that separate from "academic" concerns—the president could have spoken in the context of proper athletic department administration—no single man should be running a football program and athletic department on the scale of Michigan State University's two entities.

DiBiaggio, perhaps needlessly, had made the Perles episode a referendum on academic piety. The issue of Perles occupying two seats was as debatable from a straight intercollegiate athletics point of view as it had become for an academic-integrity camp that had conflated a college sports controversy. The cold war had never been about academics vs. athletics as much as it had been about a president versus a coach and a board.

"At the same time," DiBiaggio said in what could have been construed as a personal declaration of independence, "I have been disappointed in the responses of others who assign to intercollegiate athletics a priority that far exceeds the appropriate role of athletics in the university. From such people (Ferguson was in the crosshairs here), I have received opinions that focus solely on what allegedly would be best in terms of wins and losses."

His offer to Perles of the AD's job would protect Perles' annuity, which would kick in if Perles were still coaching on January 1, 1993. It was what DiBiaggio's offer did not promise that would startle Reisig and ultimately scare away Perles. The president's statement spelled out that if he agreed to drop coaching and become AD, Perles would "receive salary and benefits commensurate with those offered to athletic directors in the Big Ten Conference."

In other words, he could expect something in the range of the

$137,000 he was making in base coaching salary at Michigan State. There were two huge problems in the coach's view: Perles was pulling in $400,000 a year in overall compensation, thanks to his television show, endorsements, etc.

He could buy into a new, single-track life as Michigan State's athletic director, but not at a paycut approaching $1 million over three-plus years. Just as ominous was that "three-and-one-half year" timeline. His football contract was good for six-and-a-half more years. Agreeing to chop his earnings and shorten by nearly one-half his contract at Michigan State did not strike Perles as the shrewdest of business moves.

Within a day Perles had second thoughts. A new football coach would mean trouble for his staff of assistants and their families. Taking on the AD job would be personally fulfilling but financially crazy. There could be no such deal. He would stick as football coach for one more season and continue with his AD duties.

Or, rather, that was his opinion. Terry Denbow, MSU's vice president and spokesman on significant issues, was representing DiBiaggio when he said: "If his preference is to coach the MSU football team, the contract is already in place for that. But he couldn't be athletic director.

"The dual appointment has been canned. He will have to make a decision."

Perles would have two weeks to consider options. The board was to meet on December 6 and would be giving DiBiaggio his way on the Perles issue, at least. Still to be decided was DiBiaggio's double-barrel request— issued on the day he clipped Perles' wings—for authority to hire MSU's four athletic-department kingpins: athletic director, and head coaches for football, basketball and hockey.

Perles was losing leverage by the hour. Neither DiBiaggio nor the board was going to budge. He would not forfeit his football income or abandon his staff. On November 29, a week after DiBiaggio figuratively nailed his own 98 theses to the president's office door—along with Perles' hide. The coach faced facts as he met with reporters to tell them he was staying on as coach.

"I never had a choice and didn't make a choice," he said, describing the coach-or-AD decision as "take it or leave it."

"I'm just going to work hard and not say much and see what happens."

Perles was no more finished with business than DiBiaggio had been in January of 1990. He was going to "keep his options open"—code language for possible litigation against MSU. He had already applied for the now-vacant job as MSU athletic director, a search process Scott was overseeing. That window slammed shut in March when Perles was formally notified he was not among the final eight candidates.

He had dallied once more with the NFL. In January he and the Indianapolis Colts had discussions that bordered on the demeaning as Indy considered a new head coach. The Colts seemed only slightly more interested in Perles than he appeared smitten by them. Indy ended the unease by hiring its top choice, Buffalo Bills offensive coordinator Ted Marchibroda.

Three months later, Perles got more news that did not cheer him when MSU named Merrily Dean Baker as his successor—and Big Ten's first female AD. A job Perles once had, a job he could have yet been holding had he so opted, was now in the hands of a woman who would be his boss. The coach was not feeling terribly well as spring football wrapped up in April.

About the only good news from Perles' perspective was a May 19 announcement that rocked East Lansing: DiBiaggio was leaving. He had accepted a job as president at Tufts University in Medford, Massachusetts. Perles had spent the past twenty-nine months in various stages of warfare with a president who had affected his life as no other man had ever done. The coach was in no mood to overnight-mail olive branches to DiBiaggio.

"He got everything he wanted," Perles told the *Detroit News,* still spitting mad at the president's 1991 power play. "I'm just glad I'm here. I'm glad I'm not at Tufts."

No one, Perles included, seemed overly glad as Michigan State turned from the political battlefield to a comparatively genteel world known as Spartan football. Enthusiasm was at a premium heading into the 1992 season. Michigan State had put together in 1991 the worst year of football since Muddy Waters and the Spartans had finished 2-9 in 1982, paving the way for Perles.

Lots of fans had hoped Perles would stay in the AD's office. Listless football, mediocre recruiting, those weary wars with DiBiaggio—college football fans live for hope and for the excitement of new blood when times turn sour. In preparing for another season of Perles as head coach, MSU's camp seemed resigned to the same old tune.

The Spartans were, in fact, running out of gas. Michigan State's defense typified their slow decay. The Stunt 4-3 had been a marvelous innovation when Perles arrived in 1983 to vex offensive coordinators conference-wide with a shell-game front he had brought straight from the Pittsburgh Steelers.

That was then. Opposing teams had begun handling the Stunt 4-3 as easily as they blueprinted a game plan for any team's defensive wrinkles.

On offense, Perles seemed locked onto the same predictable sets and tendencies. Michigan State could shift into a three-receiver, one-back attack, but was still too often an I-formation team in love with play-action passes thrown by strong-armed junior Jim Miller. There was little chance the Spartans could explode on an opposing team, offensively or defensively.

The start of the 1992 season bore an eerie similarity to 1991. CMU, that friendly MAC school up the road, turned MSU's home-field season-opener into a 24-20 face-slap by the Chippewas. More gut-aches followed. Notre Dame won, 52-31, a week later at Spartan Stadium. A trip to Boston College the next Saturday turned into a 14-0 nightmare for Michigan State. With a 0-3 start following a 3-8 debacle in 1991, Perles was in as much trouble with fans as he had been a year earlier with DiBiaggio.

Michigan State football was deteriorating before the eyes of customers who were increasingly choosing to avoid a gridiron deathwatch in East Lansing. Spartan Stadium's crowd for Notre Dame had been an overflow turnout of 76,188. Four weeks later, homecoming at Michigan State, attendance was 65,516. Ohio State drew 70,037, but audiences for Wisconsin (45,219) and Purdue (36,803) were pitifully small for Big Ten games in East Lansing.

After a 35-10 waxing in Ann Arbor by a Michigan team that would go undefeated, State at least managed to win four of five games from mid-October through mid-November—the only loss was to Ohio State—and had a shot at a 6-5 record and a bowl ticket if the Spartans could win their season-finale at Illinois. To most fans, it was simple justice that the Illini won, 14-10. This Spartans team had beaten second-division Big Ten talent, exclusively, and was hardly worth shipping to a bowl game where State would likely be walloped.

Perles was left to contemplate the year's biggest victory, at least for a head coach who was getting awfully tired of the everyday grief: DiBiaggio's spring departure for Tufts. Gordon Guyer was MSU's interim president and a man appreciated by most of MSU's community, Perles included.

There had been a tradeoff. He had a new boss at Jenison Field House. Merrily Dean Baker was MSU's new athletic director, recommended by David Scott, the provost who had since turned executive oversight of athletics back to Roger Wilkinson.

Perles liked to think he had people skills. He tended to get along with just about anybody. An exception, he realized, was having a woman and outsider as his new supervisor holding a job he believed should be his.

The coach had gotten off to a bad start with Baker when he said, upon hearing of her hire: "I'll be watching her." Perles had also told his staff at a final meeting that he would forthwith be working from the Duffy Daugherty Football Building and would never again set foot in Jenison Fieldhouse.

Baker had heard all about George's vow. When she called Perles to arrange a first meeting after her arrival in May, she said to the coach: "George, I know you're busy, I'll come to your office."

It did not go well. Baker walked into an office where three tape-recorders were blinking. She had brought her teenage daughter, Jennifer, as part of the introduction to a football coach who was as immovable as one of his old Steelers linemen.

"Why doesn't that man like you?" Jennifer had asked her mother as they left the Daugherty Building.

"He liked me, honey," Baker answered, soothingly. "But he wanted this job."

He soon wanted her out. Baker had made the mistake of stepping into a new and entrenched culture at MSU forged heavily by interpersonal relationships. The blood could be thick, particularly between coaches. A new athletic director would be wise to at least give proper evaluation to people who had been in place before jettisoning them.

When he began work in East Lansing in 1983, Perles had brought with him Larry Bielat, a friend and coach who been Perles' teammate at Michigan State and later worked for him at Detroit St. Ambrose High and with the Philadelphia Stars. Bielat had moved to Jenison Fieldhouse as a facilities staffer in 1990.

Baker concluded after a couple of weeks on the job that Bielat was excess baggage and should be fired. He most certainly would not succeed Gene Kenney, the retiring assistant athletic director. Perles was enraged. Bielat was a good man functioning in a job Baker could not have had time to fully assess. Find him another job in the athletic department, Perles said, but do not fire a man like Larry Bielat.

The coach took his case to Guyer and the interim president moved Bielat into a job with the alumni association—which did little to appease Perles. As far as he was concerned, things had turned personal. An athletic director did not mess with a man and friend as valued as Larry Bielat; moreover, an AD did not create enmity with George Julius Perles.

Baker got a taste of paybacks at that November's MSU football banquet, another semi-melancholy affair signaling the end of a second consecutive losing football season for the Spartans.

George Perles stood at the lectern rising from a dais at Long's Convention Center and dutifully introduced all the dignitaries seated at MSU's head table. All, that is, except Michigan State's new athletic director, Merrily Dean Baker.

Across the audience a murmur rolled. This had been a football coach's public stiff-arm to his boss, a stunning insult. Guyer was there and had been introduced—he saw it and he heard about it for days afterward.

The thumbed nose to Baker reflected accurately the demeanor of a

George Perles had some triumphs and some turmoil at the lectern during his twelve-year MSU coaching career.

man who had withdrawn to an on-campus island. Perles and Michigan State were essentially stuck with each other in November 1992. The coach was fifty-eight years old with five years remaining on the ten-year contract Weaver had cobbled together in January 1988. But now Michigan State had to deal with the current reality. Five years earlier, the Spartan camp had grown giddy over a trip to the Big Ten's football Shangri-la at Pasadena after State's 1987 season. Objectivity anywhere in East Lansing during the ensuing days and weeks was about as common on campus as Maize and Blue merchandise. In that single-minded atmosphere Perles and Green Bay had talked about a deal that came close to making Perles an NFL head coach, all before MSU intervened with Weaver's one-of-a-kind contract enticement.

It was vintage Michigan State. The pattern had long since been chronicled; it would be repeated in years to come with respect to football coaches. Act impulsively or reflexively when selecting or retaining a coach. Be over-generous when restraint was needed; be tight-fisted when a bold and extravagant decision could lead to years of success.

Perles could be bought out for $2 million if Michigan State were convinced, as most fans were, that it was time to bring fresh energy to the Duffy Daugherty Football Building. Getting someone to write the check and make the change was another issue altogether.

The heavily Republican board was sick of strife and controversy and in no mood to meddle in affairs it had spent so much time and capital during 1991 investing in the president. Geyer was an interim president not inclined to fire a coach, particularly one who stood to get a $2 million parting gift.

These were issues that would have to await a new president and another football season. Michigan State could afford to wait and get a bead on each in the autumn of 1993.

Perles and his staff had a hunch '93 would be better. Eighteen returning starters suggested as much. One of those starters, Miller, was a senior quarterback on his way to the NFL. He could figure on help from a dazzling all-purpose receiver in Mill Coleman, standout offensive linemen Shane Hannah and Brian DeMarco, as well as first-rate defenders such as Rob Fredrickson, Myron Bell, Steve Wasylk and Juan Hammonds.

Smart-alecks might also have suggested Michigan State had done a better job of scheduling in 1993: MSU was no longer at risk from Central Michigan in its season-opener. The Chippewas had been replaced by Kansas, and MSU pummeled the Jayhawks, 31-14, at Spartan Stadium for Michigan State's first season-opening victory since 1989. Two weeks later, CMU, which had been shifted to the season's third game, finally tumbled, 48-34, as State got ready for another home game the following week against Michigan.

Miller had a big day and the defense looked as if it had found its old Perles crunch as Michigan State beat Gary Moeller's Wolverines, 17-7. State was 3-1, revived, off to its best start since 1979.

As MSU headed to Columbus for a get-together with the Buckeyes, the team and fans acted as if the Spartans were about to go 4-1 and send fans sprinting to their travel agents for Rose Bowl arrangements. The Spartans, though, had lost their touch in the previous two dismal seasons for finishing big games. They lacked confidence against a good team on the road that, unlike MSU, had the moxie to rally. Ohio State, which had been down, put together a late, lightning-fast, 70-yard drive to win, 28-21, steal-ing from Michigan State the kind of game coaches knew MSU would have won a few years earlier when talent and experience were in better supply.

It was evolving into a wild season, both inspiring and tormenting. Michigan State beat Iowa, 24-10, on homecoming only to lose the next week at Indiana, 10-0. The Spartans followed with tight victories over Northwestern (31-29) and Purdue (27-24) only to lose on a late field goal at Penn State, 38-37.

After all that, Michigan State was going to a bowl game. That much seemed certain as the Spartans packed for one of their crazier football trips, a journey to Tokyo to take on Wisconsin. It was all part of a deal spawned two years earlier when Perles was coaching at the Japan Bowl and representatives from Coca-Cola asked him if Michigan State would have any interest in playing a regular-season game there.

Perles was all for it as long as MSU kept its home-game schedules and got an opponent to give up one of its home dates. Wisconsin, which was just getting rolling under new coach Barry Alvarez, had been a bowl shutout during too many previous seasons. Alvarez thought a Tokyo trip would be just the exotic adventure Badgers players and fans needed.

Alvarez never imagined Wisconsin would be playing in Tokyo for another bonus trip: a plane ticket to Pasadena. The Badgers had ambushed the Big Ten and needed only to beat Michigan State to grab their first Rose Bowl spot in thirty years.

It was not a trip that thrilled Perles or his staff. The Spartans had just lost a crusher at Penn State and now had to fly to Japan. Wisconsin had been off the previous week and arrived as fresh as a team can pull into Tokyo after a twelve-hour flight.

Perles was weary and was also angry with himself for having gotten Michigan State into such a tangled arrangement. He was not terribly happy that Alvarez had said yes to the guys from Coke. This game was turning into a set-up, Perles concluded, and the Spartan coach regretted he had agreed to it.

Still, Perles decided to enjoy it as best he could. He was treated gra-ciously along with MSU's contingent that included Baker and MSU's new president, M. Peter McPherson, who had taken over in October. Perles decided he might as well have a scotch and kick back at the welcoming banquet he and Alvarez were obliged to attend, in company with both schools' executives. In attendance would be a room full of Japanese businessmen, wives at their sides dressed beautifully in kimonos.

The presidents, McPherson and Wisconsin's Katharine Culbert Lyall, spoke before Alvarez and Perles, with the Spartans' head coach going last. As the evening had gone on, Perles had grown increasingly irritated that Wisconsin's Rose Bowl bid had made this a Badgers party all but sponsored by MSU.

George's neck was flushed when he stepped to the microphone. He wanted to pop Wisconsin's balloon with a single mock-playful putdown.

"I just want you to know," he said, aiming his words at Alvarez, "I don't give a shit about this game."

In a culture where bad manners are taboo and courtesy to your host or guest is paramount, Perles had all but created an international incident with one crass sentence. Throughout the room there could be heard a shocked half-whisper: The Japanese were reciting, in disbelief, their own version of Perles' choice word.

Baker was stunned, incensed, and adamant about her next move. She stepped toward McPherson and said:

"Your move or mine, he's fired. Get him on the first plane out of here."

McPherson had been on the job two months. For a coach to say a naughty word at a banquet—even in Japan—was hardly a hanging offense. If the coach were fired, public reaction and national attention would be cataclysmic and MSU had practical considerations to ponder if it sacked Perles for bad language. Baker's indignation was warranted. A firing, in the president's estimation, was not.

Following a 41-20 Badgers victory, Wisconsin went to the Rose Bowl and Michigan State went home, left with only a low-profile holiday trip to Memphis for a Liberty Bowl date against Louisville.

Perles was out of Japan with his job but hardly out of the woods.

An 18-7 loss to the Cardinals left the Spartans at 6-6. The three straight losses were not helpful to the head coach's job health. Baker had lost her bid for dismissal at Tokyo, but now she had allies in McPherson, and board members such as Dee Cook, who believed Perles had any number of liabilities, including his prodigious weight that had caused fellow board member and Perles booster Bob Weiss to roll his eyes.

"You know what," Weiss said in an aside to Wilkinson, "if George were winning, he'd look like Santa Claus."

Whether he knew it or not—and he gave no indication he did—Perles was about to be fired after the Liberty Bowl. McPherson had made that much clear during a post-game conversation with Weiss and Ferguson at the Adam's Mark Hotel that lasted until 3 a.m. The head coach, as of that moment, was all but gone.

Ferguson and Weiss argued against it strenuously. Perles had just taken his team to a bowl game. You could not fire a man with three years left on his contract for losing a post-season game.

The board had five votes to axe Perles and begin the search for a new coach. Still, McPherson was hesitant. He liked Perles, personally, and wished George had taken the AD job when he had a chance. The new president would have enjoyed working with Perles whom he regarded as having strength and perspective that could have been helpful to a new president. As the new year arrived, one man's decision to take the coaching option had left both men in a jam.

McPherson and Ferguson—the trustee who delivered the key vote in making McPherson president—agreed to formalize Perles' marching orders for 1994. The president would make public that MSU and Perles must have an "outstanding season" in 1994 if the coach's office were to avoid a makeover in 1995.

Ferguson understood the language to mean Michigan State must qualify for a quality bowl game if Perles hoped to survive. It seemed a fair expectation for a coach who had not had a winning overall season in three years. Perles had a different interpretation. He thought the word "outstanding" to be just ambiguous enough to all but guarantee his dismissal.

Breaking in a new quarterback was bound to make matters stickier in 1994. Tony Banks, a junior-college hotshot from San Diego, had been brought in to replace Miller, who was off to the NFL. Rarely could it be expected that an offense would click at the outset of a season under a new quarterback. Perles' teams had enough trouble in September even with an experienced QB. From 1987 to 1993, MSU's September record was 5-15-1.

After an opening loss at Kansas (17-10) and another loss to Notre Dame (21-20) ahead of a 45-10 home victory against Miami (Ohio), the dismal seven-year September slate had slipped to 6-17-1.

Perles and his job status got a boost when the Spartans moved to 2-2 with a homecoming victory over their Tokyo travel companions, Wisconsin. Beating the Big Ten's Rose Bowl team ought to be a lift, Perles thought, heading into the following week's game at Michigan and the guts of a Big Ten schedule.

But MSU was bashed, 40-20, at Ann Arbor, and then beaten again on consecutive Saturdays by Ohio State and Iowa. Michigan State was 2-5 and McPherson made a phone call to Ferguson. McPherson was in favor of getting on quietly with a selection process that now seemed inevitable. Ferguson was initially opposed, but within days the board's most powerful trustee sided with McPherson.

"The truth is, under any definition, this is not an outstanding season," Ferguson told the *Detroit News*, "and winning the last four games won't make it an outstanding season."

Trouble of a bizarre nature was about to make George Perles' time at Michigan State even more flamboyant. In its November 1 editions, the *Detroit News* ran a story quoting former defensive tackle Roosevelt Wagner—the player who had taunted Southern Cal at the 1990 John Hancock Bowl—as having stalked Perles for two days in 1992 in an attempt to kidnap and shoot his former coach. Wagner believed Perles had cost him a career in the NFL.

Wagner had been delusional about his NFL prospects and had gotten involved with an agent who invested $130,000 in a vain attempt to become Wagner's agent. Wagner told the *News* stories about drug dealing, his bogus academic life at MSU, and wild spending sprees, including outfitting a new Jeep—paid for by the agent—with $3,000 gold wheels and a $5,000 electronics package.

When Wagner watched NFL teams bypass him on Draft Day in 1992 (scouts clearly considered him sub-standard), Wagner decided someone other than he had to be responsible. The head coach.

"I had this whole scenario made up in my mind," Wagner said in a tape-recorded interview with *Detroit News* reporter Fred Girard. "I was gonna kidnap him and take him and shoot him somewhere out there in all them woods in Mason. Wouldn't nobody ever found the body."

Perles obtained a restraining order against Wagner, who at the time was twenty-four years old and living with relatives in Ohio.

A football season continued. Four days after the Wagner publicity caused a statewide stir, MSU beat Northwestern to move to 4-5 with two games to play. It mattered not one iota what Michigan State would do against Purdue and Penn State in its last two games. Perles had been a goner since the three-game slide in October.

On November 7, a Monday, McPherson asked Perles to meet him that evening in the library at Cowles House. The session was not acrimonious. It didn't help that a reporter from *Sports Illustrated* was in town to look into the Perles/Wagner situation, possibly for a cover story.

"George, we agreed to a particular standard before this season began," the president said. "In fairness, it hasn't worked out. While you know I like you and enjoy your company, and we have a rapport, I just don't think we can continue."

The next morning—which coincidentally was Election Day in Michigan—Perles and his attorney, Monte Story, hammered out termination language with McPherson during a meeting at the Duffy Daugherty Football Building. The president had talked with Perles about making Saturday's game against Purdue a celebratory event—it would be "George's last home game." This occurred simultaneously with Ferguson being voted out as trustee (he would be re-elected two years later).

That day, when Perles walked out of his office and headed to practice, he was shaking his head.

"These guys are amazing," he said to no one particular. "They want to fire a guy and have him love it."

CHAPTER 5

NO PETALS FOR A PIONEER

OF ALL THE FOUR SEASONS THAT UNFURL so majestically across Michigan State University's five thousand acres, springtime in East Lansing has the greatest touch of Valhalla. Driving onto Michigan State's campus the morning of May 18, 1992, would have been a most pleasant experience. The visitor would breathe in the springtime aromas and see the aesthetic treasures a Midwest Land Grant College had been nurturing for nearly a hundred and fifty years.

Flowering trees explode in bursts of white, pink and lavender. Grass becomes lush and warm enough to cushion a blanket perfect for a picnic or for sunbathing. Into this postcard-pretty world drove Merrily Dean Baker for her first day as MSU's new athletic director.

She parked her car, strode up venerable Jenison Fieldhouse's concrete steps, then up another flight of stairs, past the portrait of Ralph Young, and past the trophy cases. She walked into the foyer leading to assistant Sylvia Thompson's small work area and, finally, to her spacious office.

Merrily Baker was the Big Ten Conference's first female athletic director. She was beginning to feel good about her new job at a university whose people were steadily displaying warmth and reassurance.

Baker had arrived in East Lansing two days earlier with her daughter, Jennifer, and her dog—and with the moving van on her heels. Saturday night, she had been to dinner and to the theater with MSU president John DiBiaggio and his wife, Nancy. Baker was going to like this place after all, she concluded, as she sat down to begin overseeing an intercollegiate sports program of considerable size and stature, with challenges to match.

Thompson buzzed her. The president was on the line, her first incoming call as MSU athletic director.

"Hi, John," Baker said, delighted that DiBiaggio was extending to her a welcome-to-the-job greeting.

"Merrily," the president began, in a serious tone that surprised Baker. "I've just finished talking with my mother and with my sister and now I'm calling you."

Baker felt a chill.

"John," she said, "I'm not sure I want to hear what you're about to say."

DiBiaggio had just accepted the presidency at Tufts University in Medford, Massachusetts. The man who had called her a month earlier, offering her the opportunity to become Michigan State's new AD, was leaving MSU and East Lansing. More than that, he was leaving the new athletic director to fend for herself at a university so notoriously political the president himself was fleeing. She had been hired because of a feud that had cost her predecessor, George Perles, his job as AD.

In Baker's mind, the wrong person was departing.

Had she suspected for a moment DiBiaggio's intentions to leave, she never would have come to East Lansing. Michigan State had a reputation, and not a good one, from the perspective of a woman whose most recent venue was as an NCAA assistant executive director. She was aware of the long and public wars between a president and the school's football coach, between a board of trustees and the president, between a coach and an athletic director and a board that ousted her predecessor from the position she now held.

David Scott had finally prevailed. MSU's provost had called her in February after the search committee requested Baker's resume. Would she be willing to meet with Michigan State's interview panel in Detroit?

Yes, she said. Baker at least knew a couple of administrator's in East Lansing who seemed like good people, and were considered very professional. Gwen Norrell was a former NCAA faculty representative from MSU and was held in high regard, as was the current faculty representa-

Merrily Dean Baker was appointed athletic director in 1992—and moved into her East Lansing home literally on the day president John DiBiaggio announced his resignation to become president at Tufts University.

tive with whom she was familiar, Michael Kasavana. Kathy Lindahl was an associate athletic director who oversaw non-revenue sports at MSU. Baker was aware that DiBiaggio had served on the Knight Commission panel and considered his experience there as another plus.

Baker's background made the gender distinction less of a barrier and more of a novelty as Michigan State considered candidates to replace Perles, who a couple of months earlier had finally lost out on his bid to hold dual jobs as AD and head football coach.

Six people would be interviewing for the position: Clarence Underwood, MSU associate athletic director; Debbie Yow, athletic director at St. Louis University; Gene Smith, athletic director at Eastern Michigan University; Max Urick, Iowa State athletic director; and Jim Livengood, athletic director at Washington State University.

Baker's qualifications were blue chip. She had been an associate athletic director at Princeton for twelve years and then spent six years as director of women's athletics at Minnesota before joining the NCAA in

1988. She had an undergraduate degree from East Stroudsburg University of Pennsylvania, a master's from Temple University, and sterling verbal skills that would be heard during subsequent interviews conducted at the Detroit Metropolitan Airport Marriott Hotel.

DiBiaggio was clearly ready to hire a woman, or a person of African-American descent—just about anyone, for that matter, who would assure MSU of new direction and adherence to academic values in the athletic department. He figured the football team would get on an even keel and not require heavy involvement from the AD. What he wanted to see reflected in the new AD was the competence and stature to address the greater university issues and concerns. Scott, who was presiding over the search process and who would make a final recommendation, was in agreement.

DiBiaggio would likely have focused on either of two candidates had he, and not Scott, been charged with the search. Gene Smith, at EMU, struck him as the right kind of person. He was black, progressive, and as far as DiBiaggio was concerned, had the right priorities. The president was happy that Smith would be interviewed.

DiBiaggio was also interested in an iconic Spartan football player from MSU's 1960s heyday whom DiBiaggio believed he could have brought to East Lansing: Gene Washington, who was with the 3M Worldwide Corporation in Minneapolis.

Washington was a native Texan who had come to MSU during the 1960s for the same reason other superstar Spartan players such as Bubba Smith of Beaumont, Texas, and George Webster of Anderson, South Carolina. Motivated by racism and segregation of schools and teams in the South, Smith, Webster and Washington had arrived in East Lansing and built the framework for MSU's1965 national championship team and its 1966 powerhouse. Washington had been denied admission to the University of Texas and the University of Houston. That brand of background was powerful and dramatic, indicative of the personal strength DiBiaggio would have loved at Jenison Fieldhouse in the person of Washington.

Scott's group began to sort itself out during interviews. Yow was not likely to be chosen, and soon withdrew as a candidate. Underwood, for whatever reason, was not making headway with Scott anymore than he had with DiBiaggio. The reluctance to strongly consider Underwood was baffling to many at Michigan State and frustrating in the extreme to Underwood, who had all the credentials necessary: MSU background, doctorate, African-American heritage at a time when diversity was being celebrated, intimate knowledge of MSU's sports landscape, and his own life story as a Southern-born male who had overcome entrenched societal racism.

Underwood stood as the coaches' preference and had more than two-dozen letters from MSU staffers supporting his candidacy. DiBiaggio had implied early in the process that Underwood would be a likely favorite, even if Scott were heading the search.

"I just want to ask you a couple of questions," DiBiaggio said during a meeting when Underwood was being interviewed. "What's your relationship with George Perles?"

Underwood disliked the question. It spoke of bias, if not bitterness, he thought. It had no relevance to a man's candidacy for MSU athletic director.

"I like him as a friend," Underwood said, aware that he was walking a tightrope. "But if I'm athletic director, friendship is one thing and job performance is entirely different."

As for Scott, he increasingly liked Baker. She had been so facile in handling every question the committee had thrown at her. She was clearly smart, tough, and, Scott was convinced, the kind of person who could put a house in order no matter how divided the president and MSU athletics might be.

Scott informed DiBiaggio of his choice. The president was concerned.

"Are you sure, David, that you can appoint a woman and the coaches will be responsive?" DiBiaggio asked. Privately, he believed there was no way it would happen at Michigan State.

"I'm going to support her," Scott said. "I don't anticipate any undue problems."

DiBiaggio: "Then I'm not going to second-guess your choice."

But DiBiaggio knew better than to think it would go smoothly. He met with Joel Ferguson for breakfast at Kellogg Center on the day Baker's appointment was to be announced, March 17.

"We don't need to celebrate women's volleyball," said Ferguson, who had been pushing for Underwood. Ferguson was adamant that any AD must have an institutional knowledge of Michigan State and familiarity with its sports culture. That had been his position for years.

"If you pick Clarence, you'll have a five-year contract," Ferguson said, realizing that the best way to push the president's button was to vow board support for DiBiaggio's own job security.

DiBiaggio, in fact, had been getting nowhere in his quest for a long-term contract at Michigan State. Although he had no idea he was two months away from taking another job, DiBiaggio had decided he must listen to offers from other colleges, twenty-six of which had inquired at one time or another about his availability.

Two weeks after Baker was announced as AD, it had become apparent to DiBiaggio that a rolling one-year deal was the only commitment he could wrest from Michigan State's negotiators. On an April night in 1992, DiBiaggio returned to Cowles House and told his wife:

"Enough."

He would interview with Tufts during the next few days, a spontaneous decision by both parties. Tufts had been less than excited about the finalists for its presidential vacancy. DiBiaggio simultaneously had decided he was finished wrangling with MSU for a long-term contract. In thirty days his appointment at Tufts would be a done deal—ironically consummated on the very May morning Merrily Dean Baker was moving into her home in East Lansing.

DiBiaggio was determined to keep confidential the decision to go to Tufts, except for conversations with his attorney. That, he rationalized, precluded him from saying anything to Baker later that day when they went to dinner and to the theater.

Eli Broad, the business magnate and MSU benefactor for whom a MSU school of business is named, had been tipped off about Tufts' courtship of DiBiaggio. It was an unethical intrusion, in DiBiaggio's mind.

Now the gears were turning in an eleventh-hour bid to keep

DiBiaggio at MSU. Governor John Engler was calling. Politicians, even a majority of MSU trustees, phoned feverishly. They all had the same question: "Are you going to Tufts?"

"I've made my commitment," he said.

Could this not yet be negotiated, they asked as Saturday night approached Sunday morning. DiBiaggio knew that a majority of the board had placed its faith in negotiators to get a multi-year deal done, though for naught.

"It's too late," DiBiaggio said. "I would never have used this (Tufts) offer as leverage. This (inability to get a long-term contract) simply should never have happened."

DiBiaggio went for a long, late-night walk across campus, blinking away tears.

His phone call to Baker would wait until Monday morning in deference to Tufts' wishes. The politicos who were aware of his move were, strangely, keeping quiet throughout Sunday. On Monday it would all blow sky-high, especially for Baker.

She would get assurances from various corners that things would be all right. Dee Cook, a DiBiaggio high-school classmate, came by quickly to tell Baker the board's majority would be behind her. It was the minority opposition on the board that worried Baker—Ferguson and Weiss had voted against her appointment. Winning them over would be difficult, if not impossible, but necessary if she were to make the kind of lasting progress she envisioned, particularly given Ferguson's clout.

Baker knew she needed to meet with Ferguson. By the time she called for an appointment, Ferguson, a key trustee, had decided she was late in paying homage. He did not appreciate a slight that Baker was unaware she had committed.

They met at the television station Ferguson owned, WLAJ, in a posh office marked by rich desk furnishings, a private bathroom, and by a sofa and love seat arranged perpendicularly around a coffee table. Ferguson had, prior to this meeting, been cordial. He motioned Baker to sit on the love seat as he stretched against the sofa.

He took off his shoes and raised his stocking feet to the top of the table, and all but in Baker's face. The tone had been set.

"What are you going to do now that your boss (DiBiaggio) has left town?" Ferguson asked.

"Well, I was told they (board members and key executives) would take care of me," Baker answered.

Ferguson, shaking his head: "They couldn't save DiBiaggio. How are they going to save you?"

The board's most powerful member then made it known why he had voted against her.

"Why hire someone whose forte is volleyball and gender equity," he asked, hardly bothered by the distortions, "when alumni and fans want to win at football?"

Baker had indeed decided Michigan State needed a push into the twentieth century, let alone the twenty-first. Women's intercollegiate athletics, not to mention non-revenue sports in general, suffered from steerage-class status at most schools, Michigan State included, if her early appraisals were correct.

She had also picked up quickly on another slice of Jenison Fieldhouse reality: The guys weren't keen on working for a woman. Bothered most were the men loyal to Perles: ticket manager Don Loding; sports information director Ken Hoffman, whose office was at Olds Hall; and Larry Bielat, an assistant facilities manager whom, Baker learned, was already derisively referring to her as "Olive Oyl."

Baker had been dealing with the "Men Only" sports culture for most of her life. She only hoped the early chill at Michigan State would thaw as had the opposition she initially faced at Princeton in 1970 when she asked the internationally renowned coach Pete Sparhawk if he would help with Princeton's women's rowing team.

Sparhawk, feet spread, thundered: "There will be women in this boathouse over my dead body."

It took two years, but Sparhawk came around. Princeton's women's team went on to win the national championship.

Ferguson was by no means the only person at MSU concerned about Baker and her agenda. She had manifested early a one-for-all, all-for-one philosophy about intercollegiate athletics. Even some of the egalitarian males on the search committee had wondered if MSU's high-profile sports might be pruned if Baker looked at football as simply a means to support MSU's overall athletic program.

"My father was the only one in our home who worked," she had said, allegorically. "But we all ate."

Baker wanted no misunderstandings about her holistic vision. She believed a university's football program must excel. As long as academic integrity was honored, an athletic department's policies must promote football and basketball—and hockey—to the greater benefit of the department and the university.

It was a pattern of expression Scott found irresistible. As for DiBiaggio, he was not terribly concerned how Scott and Baker and MSU's new president, whoever he or she was to be, might conduct business in the days ahead. He was off to Tufts. Baker was under new management at Michigan State.

"You owe me bigtime, John," Baker had said to him in her parting shot.

Underwood felt the same way. MSU's assistant athletic director had lost out on a job that he and many others at MSU believed should be his. He had been pleased by his interviews with Scott and with Roger Wilkinson, who was soon to return as executive overseer of athletics. He had every reason to believe he was on his way to appointment.

Underwood was sitting at home with his wife, Noreese, when news broke on that night's local television news. DiBiaggio had named Merrily Dean Baker as Michigan State's new athletic director. Nobody from MSU's executive circle had called to tell him of the hire or that Underwood had lost out.

Underwood had dealt with disappointment throughout his life, and would do so again. As Baker settled into her new role, Underwood figured he could work amicably with a new boss. He and Baker went to dinner at Hershey's in Baker's first days on the job and Underwood was calmed by Baker's amiability. There were no big promises, no unsettling agendas. This revelation at least settled Underwood's wife, Noreese, who had not been encouraged when Baker arrived. A reporter had asked Baker how she expected to get along with an assistant AD who had lost in his bid to win the job she now held, to which Baker responded:

"All Clarence needs is love," she said, "and I'll make sure he gets it."

But soon there was friction on several issues: Perles wanted to hire another graduate-assistant coach and misunderstandings ensued that left Perles and Baker both perturbed with Underwood, quite unfairly he thought. There was the ongoing issue of Larry Bielat, whom Baker had decreed was not qualified to pursue MSU's facilities director job. MSU's personnel heads had decided otherwise after looking at Bielat's resume, a point of view Underwood shared. Baker was displeased with Underwood's "disloyalty."

There had been chain-of-command squabbles about bowl-game considerations, as well as a falling-out over Underwood's absence from a staff meeting because of a Martin Luther King Jr. event at the Lansing Civic Center. No matter who was right or wrong, two people were becoming irreparably distanced.

Baker had no such problems with interim president Gordon Guyer. Then again, no one at MSU seemed to have conflicts with Guyer. When it came to the Michigan State president's office, nothing assured peace and harmony quite like the word "interim." It was a happy fact of life to which Edgar Harden might have testified after he served as transitional president during the late 1970s, between the Clifton Wharton-Cecil Mackey administrations.

Scenery, though, was about to change on the executive level. M. Peter McPherson, a San Francisco banker, lawyer, and Republican political appointee, was named MSU president in October 1993. He was a Michigan native from Lowell, a rural community in the state's west-central region, and had spent his undergraduate years at Michigan State. McPherson's attractions included the sort of business background that MSU power-brokers tended to like as in the transition from DiBiaggio—a dentist by trade and self-styled academic vicar—to McPherson.

McPherson did not know a great deal about sports. He had not been to a football game since his undergrad days. Baker could have construed this to be a plus. She had been dealing with locker-room testosterone from the board room, to Jenison, to the Duffy Daugherty Building, and could handle the thought of a man indifferent to athletics occupying the Administration Building's fourth-floor office.

McPherson concluded fairly quickly that Baker had problems at Michigan State in much the way oil and water don't mix. He had gotten re-acquainted with a culture heavy on football and its visible role in the Big Ten Conference. He knew MSU was intrinsically a male society. He knew that Baker, for all her laudable experience and credentials, was an outsider even more than M. Peter McPherson was in 1993.

M. Peter McPherson reigned as president from 1994 to 2005, taking a strong hand in athletics throughout his MSU career. He quickly lost confidence in AD Merrily Dean Baker, paving the way for Clarence Underwood.

Despite all of this, Baker had been making changes—and for the better, most had agreed. Men's wrestling was under new direction and had moved from the bottom of the Big Ten to the upper tier. Renovation of the Spartan Stadium press box and a lowering of the football Stadium's field— offshoots of plans Perles had earlier proposed—were accomplished. Jenison Fieldhouse was refurbished and fitted with a five thousand-seat competitive arena. The athletic department offices became fully computerized, ending the days of processing ticket applications by hand, along with other fan-unfriendly, archaic practices in the ticket office.

Another project was re-organizing the athletic department to match a model with which Baker had been familiar with at Minnesota. It called for the athletic director to be more involved in national affairs, fund-raising, and public-relations duties. It switched responsibility for day-to-day management of MSU's interior athletics to assistant ADs such as Underwood and Greg Ianni, who had been hired as director of facilities (the job Bielat had hoped to get). In that respect, Baker's plan was much like the vision held by one of her predecessors, Joe Kearney, who fifteen years earlier had wanted to bring in former Illinois AD Cecil Coleman as an athletic department manager, freeing Kearney to travel and press the flesh.

The delegation of duty was made more necessary by Baker's status as one of only three women athletic directors in the country (along with Debbie Yow at St. Louis University and Barbara Hedges at the University of Washington). She was in demand. Everywhere, that is, but in East Lansing, where the old guard continued to make life tough.

Ferguson got wind of her reorganization plans and leaked to the press an absurd distortion that Baker had relinquished control of football, basketball and hockey. Ferguson, her least favorite trustee, was a chronic irritant who was not about to let go. Life with Perles was not much better. Assistant coaches had been instructed to not so much as mention Baker's name inside the Duffy Daugherty Football Building.

Two exceptions to the anti-Baker sentiment were MSU's head basketball and hockey coaches, Jud Heathcote and Ron Mason. Each was respectful, each was supportive, Baker knew, no matter if there were occasional and inevitable disagreements. She wondered why the rest of MSU's men couldn't adapt with similar maturity.

Perles, of course, was in a galaxy unto himself. Baker had made her bid to fire the football coach after he used gutter language during a speech while on a November 1993 trip to Japan for a game against Wisconsin.

What she failed to realize was an innocent indiscretion of her own could be used against her.

It had to do with wardrobe color.

Michigan State had arrived at Memphis during the days just prior to Christmas for a Liberty Bowl date against Louisville. At an afternoon cocktail party on the afternoon leading into Christmas Eve, executives from both universities joined bowl organizers for drinks and Merry Christmas wishes.

Baker wore a seasonal red dress, the same color that women normally wear to a party that was, unofficially, a Christmas Eve gathering. Unknowingly, Michigan State's athletic director was wearing the team colors of MSU's bowl-game opposition, Louisville. Ferguson jumped on the *faux pas*. This was treasonous, he said, indicative of an athletic director's poor taste and even poorer judgment. Weiss, who had joined Ferguson in voting against Baker, agreed completely.

Perception was trumping reality, Baker and her defenders argued, as they wondered how indictments against Michigan State's AD could become any sillier.

By the summer of 1994, even McPherson clearly seemed to be separating himself from any form of executive relationship with his athletic director. He had been pressing, via memos, for a master plan on MSU's athletic vision. Baker needed to get some things straight with the president ahead of any such blueprint.

She wanted his thoughts on how much emphasis there should be on winning. How much on fund-raising? Baker repeated to Wilkinson that she needed to get the president's take on areas fundamentally tied to a chief executive's philosophies before creating the master plan.

But McPherson was preoccupied with other business. When the athletic director returned in late summer from a two-week vacation, she was greeted by a two-line note from McPherson. The president was steamed that no master plan had been presented.

Perles was at least on the way out in 1994, she realized, as another bad football season spelled his doom as coach, week by suffocating week. His dismissal would free an athletic director of an arch-enemy and, better yet, give her a shot at having input on Michigan State's new coach.

Ferguson, meanwhile, had decided to run for the U.S. Senate, a bid that would end in August's Democratic primary. He wanted everyone to know he was not stepping away from Baker and the frothy world of irrelevant athletics he decided she was overseeing in East Lansing.

"The only nickel she's raised is one she found in the parking lot," Ferguson said during a long diatribe that was, ostensibly, supposed to have been a political appearance.

In reality, Baker had figures to prove she had raised more money than Perles. What was Ferguson talking about? This was outright character assassination.

Others had come to the same conclusion as Baker. For the next week, driving around East Lansing or Okemos, Baker's car would stop at an intersection. She would be recognized.

"You hang in there, Merrily," she heard more than once. "This is a bunch of crap they're trying to dump on you."

When things turned personally nasty for his boss, Jud Heathcote had arranged a much-needed positive delivery. Baker arrived home one day to find a flowering bush on the doorstep.

"Hang in there," the note from Heathcote said. "This isn't your issue. It's someone else's issue."

Baker would feel better about events in November of 1994. Ferguson had been defeated in his bid for re-election to the board of trustees, an ecstasy-inducing piece of electoral news for the AD.

Michigan State was also beginning its search for a new football coach. Baker liked the idea of sitting and listening to men articulate their particular football ideology. She could look forward to being impressed, to being excited about Michigan State's new football face, just as McPherson was relishing these next days and weeks.

Baker sat in on a half-dozen interviews and found Penn State offensive coordinator Fran Ganter particularly impressive. Baker had known PSU's head coach Joe Paterno for years and could see that Ganter had studied hard at the knee of a master. The athletic director was convinced that Ganter represented precisely the balance MSU needed to strike in moving football from the locker room, exclusively, to the greater university stage.

But Baker began to realize as the process evolved that she had a small voice, dismissively small, in whatever football coach McPherson ultimately hired. She had pressed to add Tyrone Willingham to the interview list. He was a running backs coach with the Minnesota Vikings, had played quarterback for MSU in the 1970s, and was African-American at a time when diversity was a NCAA hiring issue. McPherson wasn't interested.

Baker had initially been pleased by McPherson's response to Ganter. He clearly had the same read as she about Penn State's top assistant. Later, though, as all the signs pointed toward Ganter moving to East

Lansing, the president seemed to be cooling on hiring him. Ferguson, she concluded, was at work in this regard. Ferguson wanted Nick Saban as MSU's head coach and would deftly lobby the president, even though McPherson was already growing wary of Ganter's increasing reluctance to leave State College, Pennsylvania.

Baker had been no more in favor of Ganter than she had been in opposition to Saban. It was a matter of style, the athletic director decided. She wanted no part of a head coach who breathed fire — "a shrieker and screamer," she said. Ganter had the right temperament for Michigan State and its football values. As the athletic director saw them, anyway.

It was now the first weekend in December. Michigan State was days from naming a coach who McPherson and Baker hoped would push aside the Perles era and bring a fresh football culture to East Lansing. McPherson wanted a Saturday morning summit meeting at Cowles House to review a final list and get some late-stage input on the person he would name.

Baker got a call from Underwood. Where are you, Underwood wanted to know.

No one had informed the athletic director of any Saturday meeting. Furious that she had been sidestepped by somebody, she drove to Cowles House, boiling. If I needed any more certain sign of where I stand in the old boys' network, she said to herself, this insult confirms everything about gender and my status at Michigan State.

After a tortuous week, Saban ended up as McPherson's choice. Special considerations and last-minute pressures combined to make the Cleveland Browns' defensive coordinator Michigan State's new football coach.

Roger Wilkinson called Baker two weeks later to extend an invitation.

"The president wants to meet us for dinner tonight," he said. "I think it's to congratulate us and celebrate getting Nick hired."

Baker was pleased. This was going to be an appropriate thank-you from the president for everyone's work in resolving a tough transition. For all their haggling, false starts and exhaustive discussion, they had named a coach who was already energizing Michigan State's football base.

She and Wilkinson arrived at Hershey's restaurant and waited forty-five minutes for the commander in chief to join them. They were two minutes into their conversation when McPherson turned to Baker and said:

"You know, I just have to tell you," the president said in a tone Baker found instantly alarming, "I don't have confidence in you."

Baker caught her breath.

"OK ... can you elucidate on that?"

"I really can't," the president answered. "It's just a gut feeling."

Baker was stunned, outraged. She looked at Wilkinson, realizing the vice president was just as shocked as she at McPherson's revelation.

Moments later she excused herself and drove home.

Wilkinson called her at 11 p.m.

"How are you?"

"Perplexed," Baker answered.

"I had no clue when he invited us," Wilkinson said, although Baker knew as much.

Baker left for a long Christmas break at her home in Ostero, Florida. There was time to think, to assess what was right, what was wrong, what had been done, what could change, what was futile.

She called Wilkinson after returning to Jenison and said: "I need to see you and the president this afternoon."

"Anything specific?"

"No, it will be very short."

She stepped into the president's office. It was best, Baker had decided, to keep things simple.

"It's very clear you want someone else in this seat," she said. "As long as I'm taken care of for what I've done here, you can get on with your preferences."

McPherson was relieved, but also concerned. Baker could make things messy for him and for MSU if she went ahead with a sex discrimination suit that a battery of lawyers had been pressing her for two years to initiate.

McPherson became solicitous in the ensuing days.

"How are you feeling?" he would ask. "Can you talk today?

Then, in words and tone that showed Baker how much the president was in touch with his lawyer roots, he would say, "Let's do this."

"Peter," Baker said, "unfortunately this is the most in-depth conversation we've had in the last two weeks. I just don't feel you're there to support me."

It would be a month before language and separation provisions were finalized. Baker would depart the AD's office at the end of March 1995. She would officially remain with Michigan State through June. Her financial settlement would be $260,000—about two years of salary.

McPherson was only three months removed from a safari that had bagged a new football coach for Michigan State. Now he had to reconvene some of his coaching selectors to track down a new athletic director.

Underwood was a leading candidate, as he supposedly had been in 1992. Gene Smith, the former Eastern Michigan AD who had moved on to Iowa State, was back in the mix. Another person of interest was Toledo athletic director Al Bohl.

McPherson wondered if it might be time for Michigan State to take a non-traditional approach to naming an AD. All the president had to do was consider personal experience. He had been brought to Michigan State from a banking job in California. McPherson might have been the first to applaud MSU's imagination in looking for candidates outside of academia who could perk up the gene pool. It was worth keeping an open mind as the AD applications piled up.

A person who fit the unconventional tag was Lansing sportscaster Tim Staudt. He was an East Lansing native and MSU graduate who had grown up with Michigan State. He had been Duffy Daugherty's neighbor and had covered Michigan State for Lansing-area television and radio stations for almost twenty-five years.

He had a high profile, locally, and knew the University's history and issues. Staudt had picked up on marketing principles from his father, Tom, who had been an executive with Chevrolet. He had energy and charisma to go with a sportscaster's requisite points of view. Staudt had even gotten a plug from *Detroit News* columnist Joe Falls. What Staudt lacked was a graduate degree, not to mention practical experience working within a university structure. McPherson was thinking outside the box, but Staudt, to him, was a candidate on the fringe.

The president had hired an outside search firm to cull national names and filter them to MSU's selectors. One of the people contacted was a former Wisconsin football player and color man on Badgers football broadcasts who had been serving on Wisconsin's athletic board the past four years, Dr. Merritt Norvell. He worked for IBM in personal-computer sales to colleges and universities. He had three degrees, including a doctorate, and had two sons who played football, one at Iowa, the other at Wisconsin. Norvell got a phone call in late December of 1994.

"We're looking for a guy who understands athletics and who has a corporate business background," said the consultant, Neil Stein, who gave no further information.

Norvell mailed off his resume and headed for Tampa, Florida, for the Hall of Fame Bowl, where Wisconsin was meeting Duke. A few weeks later he got another call from Stein.

"We like what we see," Stein said. "Can you come down to Chicago for an interview?"

On his way to the Madison, Wisconsin, airport a few days later, Norvell picked up on a talk-radio report out of East Lansing. Merrily Dean Baker was out as athletic director at Michigan State.

Norvell met Stein at O'Hare Airport's Northwest World Club and had barely finished shaking hands when Norvell said: "You're talking about Michigan State."

"You're not supposed to know that," Stein responded.

Stein's scouting report was strong. A get-acquainted session at Michigan State followed when Terry Denbow, a University vice president, met Norvell at Capitol City Airport and drove him to Kellogg Center, where he was checked in under a fictitious name. Norvell later took a stroll around campus that included a stop at a true MSU museum piece: Jenison Fieldhouse, which five years earlier had given way to the Breslin Student Events Center as home of Michigan State basketball.

Appalled by what he considered sheer neglect of a venerable building, he said to himself: "If I get this job, this (Jenison) is gonna change."

He was about to be grilled by a search committee laden with women, many of them African-American, who were serious about gender issues. It seemed to Norvell fairly obvious MSU was as well.

McPherson had been at work contacting people of prominence in Wisconsin who would know all about Norvell. Lee Dreyfus, the state's former Republican governor, put in a nice word to MSU's Republican president. Donna Shalala, the Secretary of Health and Human Services under President Bill Clinton, who also had previously been chancellor a Wisconsin, glowed when McPherson asked about Norvell.

"If you don't hire this guy," she said, "you're crazy."

CHAPTER 6

ENTER NICK SABAN

TWELVE YEARS AFTER HE HAD FIRST MARCHED into East Lansing in December 1982 as Michigan State's latest football messiah, George Perles was another pink-slipped head coach giving way to a school's need for new scenery. For the fifth time since Duffy Daugherty had moved out in 1973, twenty-two years earlier, MSU needed something transforming to take place at Spartan Stadium.

Perles unceremoniously ended his topsy-turvy reign with a 59-31 loss at Penn State, on November 12, 1994, four days after he had formally been fired by president Peter McPherson. A coaching search that had unofficially begun weeks earlier had now, as November unfurled, turned into an FBI-grade manhunt.

There were a handful of possibilities the Spartans' camp regarded as either popular or acceptable. Heading the list was Gary Blackney, Bowling Green State University's fifty-year-old head coach who had gone 36-8 in four seasons at a strong Mid-American Conference outpost. As much as his record, MSU fans liked the idea he had geographic intimacy with State's primary recruiting radius.

Had fans been polled in the days following Perles' exit, Blackney would have been hired by voice vote. But there were other men out there, a few of them as interesting to the season-ticket buyers as they were to Michigan State's coaching search committee, which was anchored by president Peter McPherson and a band of MSU staffers: Merrily Dean

Baker, Roger Wilkinson, Clarence Underwood, Michael Kasavana, Jay Morris and Terry Denbow.

One lock for an interview was Sherm Lewis. He had been shooting for the job since Denny Stolz departed in 1976. Lewis could have been brought on when Darryl Rogers fled to Arizona State in January of 1980. But whatever the problem—and college football's critics would begin by saying Lewis' key failing was that he was African-American—he hadn't impressed MSU's bosses as the guy who should be in charge.

Another ex-Spartan player—and an African-American—would get a formal interview. Jimmy Raye, like Lewis, was a Spartan star during the 1960s and had long wanted the Michigan State job. Like Lewis, he had tons of NFL coaching experience as an assistant. But Raye's supporters had the same feeling about Raye's chances as did so many who wanted Lewis. Whether it was perception, bias (MSU's leaders were furious at that notion), or the simple belief other personalities were better suited to the job, Raye was anything but a hot candidate.

Jim Tressel at Youngstown State was another possibility. Everyone knew he had been a consistent winner, that he was respected as a head coach, that he was steeped in Ohio and Midwest recruiting. What they weren't sure about was his status as head coach of an NCAA Division II school. Youngstown State was no Michigan State. East Lansing wasn't in a gambling mood as Perles departed.

McPherson would do the hiring, no question, thirteen months into his job as MSU president. It was no different from a new man in the White House insisting on picking his own attorney general or secretary of state. No matter how much scholarly input flowed from others, McPherson was going to pick a football coach who would, primarily, bring his idea of integrity to the sidelines and put an end to political squabbling and factionalism that had dominated Perles' latter years.

That he was a newcomer to the business of selecting college football coaches was understood by those who knew McPherson's background. That he was essentially clueless about sports wasn't necessarily appreciated. During a moment early in the process, McPherson had been advised he should have a conversation with Ara Parseghian, the great Notre

Dame coach who had faced off against MSU in 1966 when both unbeaten teams met in what was then billed as the Game of the Century. Parseghian had expertise only a Notre Dame legend could have amassed. He knew coaches and he knew universities and how they fit in college football's cosmos. McPherson had only one problem with calling Parseghian: Until someone filled him in, he had no idea who the man was.

Neither McPherson, nor those who formed MSU's search and selection committee, was isolated when it came to vetting candidates in the late autumn of 1994. They had help from old allies. Roy Kramer, the longtime football coach at Central Michigan University who had gone on to become commissioner of the Southeastern Conference, was brought on as a scout. So, too, was Joe Kearney, who had been MSU athletic director from 1976-80, before he joined Darryl Rogers in hotfooting it to ASU.

Kearney, like Kramer, had background as a conference commissioner (Western Athletic Conference) and knew the coaching landscape, particularly with respect to schools west of the Mississippi. One of the people Kearney was asked to contact, in an exploratory spirit, was a young defensive coordinator with the NFL Minnesota Vikings. Tony Dungy was the hottest young African-American head-coaching candidate in the land. He was also a native of Jackson, Michigan, who had been recruited by MSU in the mid-1970s. Only after State didn't buy into Dungy's urge to play baseball alongside football did he opt for the University of Minnesota.

Even though Kearney had a hunch what Dungy's response would be, he called him. Yes, Dungy wanted to become a head coach. No, he was not interested in Michigan State. College coaching wasn't his mission. Dungy was shooting for a job in the NFL, which he would soon land at Tampa Bay before moving to Indianapolis.

Another name, hot with Spartans fans, was gaining momentum by the hour. Nick Saban was defensive coordinator of the playoff-bound Cleveland Browns and had a glorious resume, in part because of his years as a young defensive coordinator under Perles. It was a stint that included State's 1987 team that went to the Rose Bowl.

Saban had credentials almost impossible to match, beginning with his knowledge of MSU and his familiarity with every inch of State's prime recruiting turf. He was a West Virginia native who had been an assistant at Ohio State, Navy and Syracuse, and who had played football at Kent State. He had coached for two NFL teams (the old Houston Oilers and the Browns), and had even spent a year as head coach at Toledo, where Saban was 9-2 before moving to Cleveland as Bill Belichick's defensive coordinator.

Moreover, he and his wife, Terry, had a thing for East Lansing. Saban kept up with news and events at Michigan State, football matters in particular. It was the school—and the community—he and Terry had most enjoyed during their years moving up the coaching ladder, gaining at each stop a splash more exposure to other coaches, systems, and insight into a sport Saban positively devoured.

What he hadn't received as Perles' days began to dwindle—Perles' fate, although not officially declared, was obvious to all—was any indication MSU was the least bit interested in him. In fact, Michigan State, or, rather, McPherson, had no intention of hiring a coach who had been any part of the Perles regime.

With respect to things that made him nervous about Perles, McPherson didn't distinguish between a head coach and the coach's staff. He did not care about specific times and events—issues that brought on an NCAA investigation, for example—and whether those episodes had the least relevance to a coach like Saban, who had departed East Lansing weeks after he had overseen a defense that took the Spartans to the 1988 Rose Bowl.

"I want a clean break," McPherson had been heard to say, privately, when Saban's name was mentioned.

Saban went on with his Browns business until a phone message from a *Detroit News* reporter arrived in his office on November 5. Would he, by chance, have any enthusiasm for the MSU job after Perles was gone? Although his profile as Browns defensive coordinator was growing by the week—steadily setting him up for an NFL head-coaching job—would there be any passion for returning to East Lansing and replacing his old boss?

Saban called the *News* reporter back, stealthily, on November 7. It was clear that anyone who doubted his interest in MSU's job was brain-dead. He wanted it, badly. But he had two serious concerns: How could he express his interest in a coaching position that hadn't yet officially opened? And how could he remain a live candidate in the Spartans' search without compromising his position as Browns defensive coordinator, especially at a time when Cleveland was headed for the NFL playoffs.

Saban, strangely, hadn't been mentioned as media scuttlebutt mounted ahead of Perles' inevitable firing. Some of the inattention was understandable because inside information had it that McPherson wanted a complete divorce from the Perles era. If it seemed irrational to blame an innocent long-departed assistant for more recent problems of a head coach, McPherson didn't care. If it meant bypassing a candidate who seemed destined to become a prime-time head coach at some level—college or pro—there were other safer and more fitting choices in McPherson's view. If it required slamming the door on a young defensive whiz who at age thirty-two had become Michigan State's defensive coordinator under Perles, it was of no consequence to the president.

In the November 9 edition of *The Detroit News*, Saban carefully crafted a diplomatic statement about the Michigan State situation. It was meant to convey to literate East Lansing observers that he definitely wanted the job and also that he owed appropriate consideration to Perles and to the Browns:

"I have a responsibility and an obligation to the Cleveland Browns and to the players to do a great job here, and at the same time I'm sensitive to what George has just gone through," Saban said, polishing his words. "I hope Michigan State has a fine finish to its season, and right now I wouldn't care to comment one way or another on any job opening."

Saban's smoke signals were understood by the Browns and Belichick. It is a reality within football coaching's galaxy that timing with respect to job openings is almost always bad. Coaches get fired at the precise time candidates with hot names are either preparing for a bowl game or for the NFL playoffs. Belichick was secure, loyal to his staffers, and intent on helping get Saban a good head-coaching job he by now deserved. Likewise, Browns owner Art Modell wasn't about to shackle Saban. He was intent only that MSU not drag Saban's name into a public search and then reject him for the job. In Modell's view, that wouldn't be fair to his defensive coordinator, or to a Browns team that had its own responsibilities and prestige at stake.

McPherson wasn't a student of NFL protocol anymore than he was familiar with football's bigger names. "Who's this Belichick guy I've got to call?" he asked, irritated that MSU couldn't get busy hiring Saban if, in fact, Saban was the man State wanted.

There lay the question McPherson had to answer. He was neither wild about Saban nor eager to abandon his no-Perles-ties edict. It was a mind-set that opened the door for another candidacy as interview schedules were arranged a couple of weeks before Thanksgiving.

Terry Denbow, MSU's chief media spokesperson, had been at Penn State before his move to East Lansing. He knew of a longtime assistant there, Fran Ganter, who was Joe Paterno's offensive coordinator—not the worst calling card in a year when the Nittany Lions had just broken MSU's 1978 Big Ten record for points-scored-per-game.

Denbow, who was acquainted with Ganter's wife, Karen Bruno Ganter, phoned her as Michigan State weighed the sensitivities of inter-viewing a conference opponent's assistant coach. It was an otherwise unorthodox move that seemed reasonable for the simple fact Ganter had been with the deity himself, Paterno, as a player or coach for twenty-seven years. Denbow knew the kind of person McPherson had in mind. Ganter's background, he decided, might be a match for his boss and MSU. McPherson was intrigued.

"We have a football coaching opening here at Michigan State," Denbow said after Karen Ganter answered the phone. "Would Fran be interested?"

Ganter's answer, delivered a day later, was firm: Yes. Ganter became one more name added to the committee's lengthening list of candidates.

Most of the selection team's interviews were to be conducted at the Marriott Hotel at Detroit's Metro Airport—a convenient site for incoming candidates, especially because it offered cover for the coaches, as well as for the MSU contingent, which didn't want job applicants showing up under East Lansing's spotlights.

The interviews were so secretive that they needed precise choreography. A van would be parked behind Jenison Fieldhouse. The search committee would dart from an out-of-the-way door or vehicle and duck into the van. And then the gang would make a run for Detroit, hoping they and the candidate could skip undetected into a suite and get on with the grilling.

Up first was Blackney. If it is bad luck to be first on any list of interviews, Blackney's responses became double trouble. He had, by all accounts, the worst session of anyone MSU considered. Blackney struck the interviewers as too self-assured, too brash. His candidacy was dead within an hour.

"I'll bring all my coaches," he said when asked about assistants he might hire. "They're all transferable."

Underwood at one point asked Blackney: "How many of your assistants are black."

"None."

Dead silence. Blackney later had a staffer call and explain, as best he could, why there were no African-American assistant coaches at Bowling Green and why there would be black staffers at Michigan State. It was a clumsy attempt at a diplomatic mission that helped MSU decide they didn't want to raid BGSU's coaching offices.

Blackney's greater problem was that he had been getting so much press as MSU's leading nominee. He seemed, in the committee's estimation, to be too full of himself. As days unfurled and Blackney saw the handwriting, he withdrew his name from consideration—a face-saving gesture.

Raye's interview, also at the Marriott, was much better. Raye, a running backs coach for the Kansas City Chiefs, was a personal favorite of Underwood, who had insisted to Denbow and others: "If you bring Jimmy Raye here, he's going to win."

Raye's problem was that he seemed so lacking in contemporary knowledge of Michigan State football. He also made a couple of unfortunate statements.

"Who would you hire as assistant coaches?" asked Wilkinson, repeating a favorite question.

"You already have some of the greatest coaches in the world on George's staff," Raye answered, sharply.

McPherson trembled when he got wind of Raye's plans to re-deploy the Perles gang. Another minus with McPherson was Raye's low-key, almost morose, speaking style. Underwood seemed to acknowledge that energy levels were low when he said to someone afterward about Raye: "He's one serious guy. Boy, is he serious."

The president had a different read. He told Underwood afterward he didn't believe Raye would be tough enough as a head coach.

Underwood shot back: "Jimmy Raye is the kind of guy who'd kick you all over campus and not apologize for it!"

No go. McPherson had other ideas about MSU's new football coach. There was a specific image he had in mind. A football commander-in-chief would be appointed, someone with stature and experience and a record clean enough to earn him a clerical collar.

It wouldn't be Raye or Blackney, or as it turned out, Sherm Lewis, who had flown from Green Bay for what became—much to Underwood's indignation—a kind of courtesy interview in Grand Rapids. It seemed with each of Sherm's ongoing candidacies that his standing as a serious candidate diminished. What had never been satisfactorily explained is why he couldn't get hired, either as a college head coach, or as a head coach in the NFL. The mystery wasn't so baffling to men like Underwood, who concluded Sherm Lewis' ethnicity had clobbered him earlier in his career, when he might have had a chance to break out as a young, vibrant coach with both college and NFL experience. NCAA football remained an industry that talked about minority presence. It rarely fulfilled it.

McPherson had one other name in mind. It would be a longshot, yes, maybe even a crazy notion. But if it somehow were to work out—and McPherson was intent on doing whatever it took to bring him to East Lansing—the MSU president wanted his football team to be in the exalted hands of a coaching colossus: Nebraska's Tom Osborne.

McPherson had established casual rapport with Osborne through the years. They had met at national events, functions more political and academic than purely athletic, befitting Osborne's bigger-than-football status and his future job as a member of the U.S. House of Representative.

Tom Osborne was the embodiment of what McPherson had determined was The Perfect Coach for Michigan State. In Osborne he would have a Mount Rushmore presence who could marry academic and institutional integrity with crowd-pleasing football.

What would that be worth to a university—and to a president's governing stature? McPherson figured market prices for coaches could be tossed out the John Hannah Administration Building window if Osborne might somehow be tempted to consider Michigan State.

McPherson was aware of something else about Osborne: He wasn't perfectly happy in Lincoln, Nebraska—the coach had been slighted two years earlier, an affront that still chafed Osborne.

It had to do with a matter MSU especially could relate to: a head football coach who wanted also to be athletic director. In the case of Osborne and Nebraska, there was precedent.

Bob Devaney had worked as athletic director at Nebraska during his latter years as Cornhuskers head coach. Osborne, who had spent two decades building on the football grandeur Devaney had introduced at Lincoln, believed he was entitled to the same executive privilege after Devaney retired in 1992.

Nebraska instead hired Bill Byrne as athletic director, making it clear Osborne was in charge of football, exclusively. He could forget about handling AD duties that had grown exponentially since Devaney assumed both roles in 1967.

During a lull in the interview schedule at the Metro Airport Marriott, Baker offered a startling comment, exciting McPherson with a new possibility.

"I hear Tom Osborne may be looking," Baker said.

Jaws dropped. The committee might as well have heard that there had been a Vince Lombardi sighting.

Tepid to the people MSU had so far considered, still looking for his version of a MSU football messiah, McPherson decided to do with Osborne what he tended to do with accomplished people from all avenues of life: He would give him a call. If the temperature were warm enough, he would explain to Osborne that Michigan State was prepared to go where no university anywhere in America had yet gone for a major-college coach.

He would offer Tom Osborne a financial package worth one million dollars per year.

Osborne, to McPherson's delight, was interested. It had nothing to do with the money. He had turned down bigger pay elsewhere, with Houston in the NFL. For that matter, he had thought at one time about taking the Colorado job, even when it couldn't match Nebraska's compensation.

What hooked him was timing. Osborne had been getting his share of flak at Nebraska. For all the Cornhuskers' success, there was squawking about his bowl record (the Cornhuskers had lost six straight), which was an irritant separate from his rebuke on the AD role following Devaney's departure. He was also interested in Michigan State. Osborne had an understanding of the place, its roots, its personality and its past, courtesy of Devaney, who had coached under Biggie Munn and Duffy Daugherty and who had entertained Osborne for years with stories of football at East Lansing.

It was a couple of days before Thanksgiving, 1994. Nebraska's regular season was about to end with a 13-0 record and a victory later that week against old rival, Oklahoma. There would be a trip to Miami for a second straight Orange Bowl date against Florida State (it would become Osborne's seventh consecutive bowl defeat).

Osborne told McPherson he needed to talk with his staff and with his wife, Nancy. Give him a day to get back.

The coach, fifty-seven years old and a long way from retirement, stepped into a meeting room where most of his assistants (Charlie McBride, Frank Solich, Milt Tenopir, Turner Gill, George Darlington, Kevin Steele and others) were huddled.

He told them of McPherson's call and the invitation to transfer Nebraska's entire coaching staff to East Lansing. Life in the Big 12 would be traded for dramatic new scenery in the Big Ten. Nebraska versus Oklahoma would be out. Michigan versus Michigan State would be the staff's new rivalry.

"What do you think?" Osborne asked.

His assistants didn't know what to think. On one hand, they couldn't believe Osborne was serious. Nebraska was two games from a national championship. Virtually every year at Lincoln meant another shot at grabbing one of those national titles 'Huskers fans had been expecting Osborne to deliver.

Besides, Osborne had listened to job offers before and had always opted for the place he knew best and probably loved most, no matter how perturbed he had been over the Devaney-Byrne succession.

McBride, who was Nebraska's defensive coordinator and a man who spent his summers in Michigan, thought Osborne might bolt. McBride would have adapted. He had thought seriously at one point about joining Michigan State's staff when Perles and he talked about a possible job.

Dispositions changed a day later. It didn't make sense, Osborne concluded, to leave what he had spent twenty-two years nurturing at Nebraska for a new conference and new school that didn't have the status Michigan State held when Devaney had been there.

Tom Osborne knew his assistants weren't keen on relocating. Their families were comfortable in Lincoln. They had homes, friends. Why would he and they leave all this to take over at struggling Michigan State? Why, particularly, when Nebraska was on its way to a national championship, if not this season, then very possibly in 1995 because of everyone who was coming back?

The coach knew he was a single word from rocking the college football world. He realized also that fans who viewed him as a coaching profession's definition of bedrock would wonder if, by going to East Lansing, he had gone off his rocker.

Osborne called his staff into his office. He phoned McPherson, making sure the speaker was on. A coach wanted staffers he had considered relocating to hear the conversation themselves.

Osborne told the president he needed to stay at Lincoln. He had appreciated the offer, had thought seriously about Michigan State and its potential to be a good fit for all parties. But it would be impossible to leave

Nebraska then, with a national championship in Osborne's grasp and a staff so entrenched.

McPherson was deflated, mostly because Osborne had seriously considered his offer. McPherson could imagine the reception such an announcement would receive. He had been so close to bringing an icon to East Lansing, a man who would embrace McPherson's concept of how academics and athletics should function, and in precisely that order. Those priorities were critical to McPherson.

But Osborne was now out of the picture, so McPherson and his committee went back to work. They had interviewed good people, but none that left the new president overwhelmed. There was the difference: Committee members had thought Saban was by far the best of all presenters during a week of interviews. The president, though, stayed cool on the candidacy of a man who was neither an established head coach nor free of stain McPherson believed had to have been absorbed during his years under Perles.

Saban, in fact, had softened McPherson on the first point. He had written a heartfelt pre-interview letter to the president explaining why he wanted to become MSU's head coach. He talked of growing up in West Virginia, of rising at daybreak to serve as an altar boy, of riding a bus his dad drove, loaded with Pop Warner football players whom his father, Nick, also coached. McPherson was impressed. The letter was sincere and self-revealing.

Committee members were more enthused and for different reasons. They saw during Saban's Marriott dinner interview that he had an agenda, a vision for Michigan State football. He was more prepared than were any of the candidates. He was more ready to seize and respond to any question the group fired at him.

Had he seen any of Michigan State's games during recent seasons? What did he think could have been done differently by a head coach?

Saban, in fact, had seen plenty of Michigan State football. He explained, with diplomacy the group appreciated, that he thought George Perles could have perhaps made a few more halftime adjustments.

Wilkinson followed up with his pet question about staffers. Saban scored more points when he rattled off a comprehensive list of coaches from which he would handle interviews and hiring.

He talked about academics, integrity and discipline. He forayed into areas of inspiration and motivation, which he believed to be at the heart of a good head coach's capabilities and responsibilities. He gave a rundown on specific areas he had overseen during his stint at Toledo: academic support, strength and conditioning. He covered every topic the committee had outlined. And he never slipped up. Saban was so absorbed by the session that he never touched his silverware or the uneaten club sandwich.

It was too much for Baker. "Oh here," she said, moving toward Saban's untouched plate, "let me wrap that up for you."

Saban flew back to Cleveland knowing he had nailed the interview. He had been wanting to bombard the committee with everything his twenty-plus years in coaching had taught him was correct and successful about coaching football. He wanted the people at Michigan State to know that this was but a taste of what they would be getting if Nick Saban were named MSU's new head coach.

Saban might have been a consensus pick by the committee at that point, but McPherson still wanted to talk with Ganter. The president was as enthused about having discovered Ganter's candidacy as he was about the idea of hiring someone so affected by Joe Paterno.

Ganter would not be appearing at the Marriott. He would be interviewing in East Lansing, and would bring his wife, Karen. McPherson wanted Ganter to get a first-hand look at a campus and at a job McPherson believed Ganter would take, as long as everyone else at MSU was as prepared as McPherson to buy into Penn State's offensive coordinator.

The interview took place at Cowles House, the longtime residence of MSU presidents. Very quickly Ganter was on his way to turning off the other committee members. He was nice enough, a real gentleman. But there was about him a hint of standoffishness that some saw as a red flag. Ganter's interview answers were a separate problem.

"This is the way Joe Paterno does it …"

"I don't know … I'll have to check with Joe."

"This is what we do at Penn State."

The last thing most committee members wanted was a head coach trying to establish Penn State West in East Lansing. Another rebuilding job at Michigan State begged for a fresh blueprint custom-drawn for the Spartans in 1994. No one seemed particularly enthused about the forty-five-year-old Ganter's potential except for the one person whose vote counted: McPherson.

The president was acting as if he had his man, a coach who would hammer the boss' personal stamp on a football program that could now look forward to the kind of leadership and stature Penn State had gotten from Paterno.

It was why he had pursued Osborne with such fervor. McPherson understood he needed a football man to run a Big Ten football team. Football, though, unquestionably would run second to academic leadership in McPherson's system of institutional values.

In Ganter he saw what mattered to a new president disgusted by MSU's recent grid history. Ganter would be a guaranteed Boy Scout on NCAA compliance. Ganter had been groomed by a coach and by a school that were American football institutions. Ganter was stable and solid, not likely to surprise in a negative way.

Adding fuel to Ganter's candidacy was a simple fact, apparent to other committee members, that Peter wasn't the only McPherson high on Fran and Karen Ganter. Joanne McPherson was in accord with her husband. In the McPhersons' joint view, there was no way Michigan State—or the president—could lose by appointing the Ganter pair from Penn State to put George Perles and his era in the past.

McPherson had now moved from courtship to closing the deal. He thought Ganter should get acquainted with his new campus. That it was now approaching midnight was positively peachy as far as McPherson was concerned. Clarence Underwood could drive Ganter to the Duffy Daugherty Football Building on a wee-hours mission perfect for keeping a visitor under wraps. No one wanted any media or snooping observers blabbing that MSU's top choice for football coach was in town or on campus.

The dead-of-the-night orientation proved to be less than secure. No sooner had Underwood unlocked the Daugherty Building's door than he saw Gary Van Dam, the recruiting coordinator who was still on board, hanging around in the office, as recruiting coordinators tended to do even after the season ended.

Ganter looked around. If he were enthused or excited about setting up shop here, he had a peculiar way of showing it. He asked elementary, even irrelevant, questions about the facilities. At one point he shocked Underwood with a single query: "Whom should I hire?"

Apparently Ganter wanted to find out which of Perles' assistants Underwood favored. The question made Underwood uneasy. A head coach had to decide those things, not an associate athletic director.

Underwood went home an hour later convinced MSU was about to make another Muddy Waters-style mistake with its football program. What he would not do is offer McPherson any endorsement when the two met the following morning.

"How'd it go?" McPherson asked.

"I was disappointed," Underwood said, darkly. "Frankly, he asked a lot of stupid questions. I don't think Ganter is prepared at this time to become a head football coach at Michigan State."

"Why not?" McPherson asked in a tone more irked than surprised. "You told me yesterday you thought he was a good candidate."

Underwood said he agreed Ganter's credentials and personal pedigree were a match for Michigan State. But the Penn State-flavored interview and Ganter's uneasy ways during their midnight-express stroll through the Duffy Daugherty Football Building offices had left him with a bad feeling about Ganter's potential.

McPherson ended the conversation, upset and annoyed. Ganter clearly hadn't impressed the committee, most of whom thought Ganter had too little passion for the job in East Lansing. Without zeal and fire for taking on Michigan State's mess—the kind of passion that Saban, for example, had shown—an incoming head football coach would be dead before his first spring practice.

Regardless, McPherson pressed ahead with plans to bring Ganter aboard. The coach's attorney, former Penn State football player Bob

Mitinger, was working on contract elements as the Ganters did a bit of morning house-browsing around East Lansing. They, the McPhersons, and Denbow later had lunch at Cowles House before the Ganters departed. At that moment, McPherson would have been surprised to know that Fran Ganter would not return to Michigan State for almost a year—and that visit would be in his existing job as offensive coordinator for the Penn State Nittany Lions.

Joel Ferguson was now lobbying hard against Ganter, and not having Ferguson behind McPherson's decision, the president knew, would be asking for trouble down the road. That the committee didn't seem enthused was less a political problem than a window into how MSU's football community would likely respond—or, in Ganter's case, not respond.

McPherson, who for days believed he had his man, now had to admit, at least privately, he too was worried and nervous about Ganter's attachment to Penn State. It was unusual to find a coach who had been at one school his entire career. Why weren't other schools chasing him? Why hadn't a career assistant made any movement toward a head-coaching job?

McPherson was being careful. Ganter could reasonably assume he was in line for the job, but McPherson, who was also a lawyer, had not formally offered Ganter a position at Michigan State.

What had begun as a cordial courtship quickly devolved into a fencing match. Ganter and his wife left East Lansing feeling as uneasy about Michigan State as MSU had become toward a career Penn State assistant.

When Ganter talked with Paterno after he got back to State College, his rapidly chilling feet got even colder. Michigan State would be a tough job for anyone. Ganter, who was considered by most at Penn State as The Man Most Likely To Succeed Paterno, didn't need a messy experience at a place so foreign to him.

The deal had dissolved because of concerns by both parties.

Ganter phoned McPherson the next day, requesting that his name be removed from consideration. The president was both relieved and deflated by Ganter's fade. MSU's hardcore football camp, on the other hand, was relieved *and* elated.

Now the door seemed open for Saban. His candidacy had been cheered from the start by fans who remembered Saban as the tough defensive coordinator from State's '88 Rose Bowl team, and who now knew him as a high-profile defensive strategist for Belichick's Browns. East Lansing movers and shakers like Jim Epolito, Gregory Eaton, Gil Haley—important allies with influence—had pushed for Saban from the get-go. Newspaper columnists, radio talking heads—everyone seemed to be on a figurative convention floor holding up "Saban For Coach" signs.

When Nick Saban coached football at MSU, there was never a question as to who was in charge.

There was only one hang-up. Ganter had been replaced by new front-runner Osborne—a candidacy so unlikely, so dramatic, so unfathomable, that it would shake college football to its footings if the deal were pulled off.

Saban couldn't figure out what was going on. His interview had been excellent. He appeared to be the leading candidate and still he hadn't heard anything substantive from MSU. On December 10—two weeks after the Osborne flirtation and a few days before MSU would finally decide on its head coach—the Browns stopped Dallas tight end Jay Novacek at the Cleveland one-yard line as time ran out in a huge nationally televised showdown between the Browns and that season's eventual Super Bowl winners.

Cleveland, which was about to nail down an 11-5 regular season, won the game, 19-14, and Saban thought to himself as Novacek dropped just shy of the goal line: "This is gonna be helpful. A lot of people saw this game."

In a couple of days, Saban would get wind that Ganter's candidacy had heated up. His spirits sank. He had gone from believing he would be MSU's guy to concluding that he was now out of the running.

Saban called McPherson on Wednesday, December 13, requesting that his name be stripped from MSU's candidates list if he wasn't McPherson's choice. Saban understood that a drawn-out, failed run at the State job would bruise his standing and simultaneously make the Browns look bad. It was a point Art Modell had made to McPherson when the owner of the Browns warned State not to mar Saban's name or insult the Browns should Saban lose out to Penn State's offensive coordinator.

Saban had also explained to McPherson, for one final time, that he wasn't a Perles protégé. If the new president was so paranoid of anything Perles that he was about to exclude Saban for the simple fact Saban a decade earlier had been on Perles' staff, then Saban needed to get things straight with the prez.

McPherson told Saban not to withdraw. It was already apparent to McPherson that Ganter wasn't coming to East Lansing. The top-secret bid for Osborne had gone nowhere.

"Then I'd like to know tomorrow (Thursday) by noon if I'm going to be your choice or not," Saban said.

McPherson phoned Saban at the Browns' offices the next morning. His tone and words indicated Saban was back on top. That evening, McPherson called Saban again to begin the rough outlines for an agreement. The deal was done. Money would be no hang-up. Saban was going to become Michigan State's new head football coach once contract language was straightened out Friday.

Late Friday night, McPherson and Saban could both talk privately about a new era of football headed for East Lansing. Nick Saban was going to be introduced at a news conference the next day at Kellogg Center, the first public moments for two men whose relationship during the next five years would know its extremes.

CHAPTER 7

ALL SABAN, ALL FOOTBALL

NICK SABAN'S PRICE FOR WINNING ONE FOOTBALL-COACHING JOB in December of 1994 was to assume responsibility for two. Michigan State's new head coach had been named successor to his old boss, George Perles, as the last step in an awkward, ever-shifting dance that had seen Michigan State finally land Saban, perhaps in spite of itself.

Saban's dilemma was that he already had a job as NFL defensive coordinator for the playoff-bound Cleveland Browns. It was tough enough at any point of any season to be a right-hand assistant to ever-revved Browns coach Bill Belichick. Now it would get stickier as Saban, six weeks past his forty-third birthday, began trying to squeeze in head-coaching tasks at MSU from a car phone as he made the two-way commute from his home in Medina, Ohio, to Browns headquarters in Berea.

Typical of the craziness was a call to his former strength and conditioning coach at the University of Toledo, where Saban had been head coach in 1990. It was 1 a.m. when Ken Mannie's phone rang. "Do you want to be strength and conditioning coach at Michigan State?" Saban asked as he headed for home and a few hours of sleep before another day of straddling tasks began.

Saban quickly added staff: Bobby Williams, who had been an assistant at Eastern Michigan when Saban was at Toledo, was retained from Perles' staff; Charlie Baggett, an assistant on Perles' staff when Saban was there in the '80s, and who had gone on to the NFL, was coming back; Gary

Tranquill, Saban's head coach at Navy, was joining as offensive coordinator; Dean Pees, Jim Bollman, Greg Colby, Glenn Pires, Mark Dantonio and Pat Shurmur, who had played on Perles' teams when Saban was at MSU earlier—all were coming aboard, in most cases well ahead of their boss, who was on playoff duty with the Browns.

Saban's early-stage plan was to put his assistants on the recruiting road during the week as he took care of Browns business. On Friday evenings, he could fly into East Lansing where his wife Terry was already in place as a recruiting hostess. He would stay through Saturday before rejoining Belichick's staff before Sunday's game. It worked for the Browns. It would have to work for Michigan State until Cleveland either lost a playoff game or made it through the Super Bowl.

Saban had been following the Michigan State football story for half of his twenty years as a college and NFL coach. East Lansing was his top-of-the-heap stop, as close to home as a hard-driven, semi-nomadic football man had known during stints at Navy, West Virginia, Syracuse, Ohio State, Kent State, Houston of the NFL, and Toledo, which preceded his move to the Browns. No place had made Nick or Terry Saban feel quite as anchored as those five seasons he had spent at Michigan State from 1983-87.

Saban had kept up with the football news in East Lansing. He checked the scores each week, picked up scuttlebutt from other coaches or friends who might still live in MSU's backyard: Jim Epolito, an insurance executive and former Spartan linebacker and teammate of Kirk Gibson; Gregory Eaton, a prominent Lansing businessman and MSU booster; and basketball coach Tom Izzo.

He knew of the political fire that had charred Perles in his skirmish with John DiBiaggio. He was aware of the alarming decline of a football program that had been at its apex when he left for Houston, just after the 1988 Rose Bowl.

Rather than being impediments, these were reasons why Saban wanted the job all the more. You could win at Michigan State. Anyone who recruited as zealously as he, any coach as passionate about making football players better than they imagined they could be, had at Michigan State all the resources and community capital a Big Ten school required to win football games.

He did double duty until Cleveland lost in the playoffs. With his staff of assistant coaches in place, he stitched together a passable recruiting season in only a few weeks, and got busy assessing what he had inherited from a 1994 Spartans team that had finished 5-6. The more he got acquainted with State's returning players, the more he understood why Michigan State had posted merely one winning regular-season record since 1990.

What had happened to that old Spartan work ethic he had known during the 1980s? He shook his head at a talented offensive tackle, Flozell Adams, who weighed a blubbery 367 pounds. This was the brand of self-discipline that had to change, pronto, if MSU were to make anything out of Saban's first season as head coach.

Overall personnel was a separate issue altogether. Big Ten-caliber players at MSU were down from what he had known just seven and eight years earlier. Academics had thinned the ranks to some degree; disciplinary issues had sent a few more home. Only on offense was there much strength, primarily in skill players: Tony Banks, a second-year junior-college quarterback; significant Perles recruits in receivers Muhsin Muhammad, Derrick Mason and Nigea Carter; and Scott Greene, a fullback who had more heart than raw skill.

Players realized in about two-fifths of a second that the Duffy Daugherty Football Building's new boss might, forty years earlier, have been a great choice to run Alcatraz. He had an explosive sense of energy and dynamism about him, like a quick and efficient fighter jet.

"This is how it's gonna be," he said at a first team meeting where spellbound players sat silently as the new coach laid out his plan and requirements. "You don't like it, you don't commit to it, you're gone."

Saban had already made clear to his assistants that MSU football would stick to a clear, inviolate set of principles:

He would imbue players and coaches with an extraordinary sense of team. Physical conditioning was about to grow in intensity and surpass any existing thresholds. Recruiting was going to change in scope and in focus: Michigan State intended to blanket a three-hundred-mile radius—every promising locale within a five-hour drive of East Lansing, making sure the states of Michigan and Ohio were pounded particularly hard. Any players taken from a state such as Florida would be regarded as a bonus.

Off-season conditioning was a first taste of life with Saban for players who were about to embrace a cultural overhaul, like it or not. Players reported at 6 a.m. and worked as strenuously as if they were going through August two-a-day drills. Levity was scarce. Serious football was the rule.

Saban's ally in turning MSU football into an NCAA version of Marine Corps boot camp was Ken Mannie, whom players could see was as fanatical about his strength-training job as Saban was about coaching. Players accepted as part of football reality that there would be times during extreme conditioning when a player would throw up after running drills. Saban was about to take things further.

"You people are gonna be throwing up while you're lifting weights," Saban had said. "I guarantee you."

In fact, some did. It was a seismic shift from those latter years under Perles when players referred to MSU's weight room as "the hamburger stand." There were days under Perles when players did more television watching than weight-lifting. Perles had always been loud and clear about his players adding muscle, but conditioning had grown softer in step with other facets of State's football personality during that coach's waning years.

Executives, academic heads, and athletic-department staffers saw the same profile of Saban as Tough New Coach. They all came to see Saban in his initial months and thereafter as football personified. He believed in football as science, as craft, as inspiration to young men to become successful student-athletes. He believed passionately that his sport had the power to transform them academically and athletically. Saban saw football as a drive-train spanning spirit, mind and soul—as something akin to a profession of faith. Precisely because he believed the game of football and the human psyche induced bodies to produce at amazingly high plateaus, Saban—a student of motivation philosophy and techniques—

expected his team at Michigan State to excel.

If Michigan State's inter-departmental personnel wanted to argue with any of that, go ahead, make his day. The coach could be compelling, if not downright intimidating, during debates about academic standards, about athletes and lifestyle issues, on whatever point he believed MSU's people and resources could do to make Spartan football players and a football team better.

Saban could get physically impassioned at these meetings with administrators and athletic-department people. He might slam a fist on a table, more out of conviction than anger. Another sure sign Saban had entered The Realm came when his knee gyrated like a paint can shaker. The more the knee bounced, the more consumed Saban was by an issue or point of view.

Still, players, at least privately, were like everyone else from MSU's football galaxy in the late summer of 1995: No one knew whether the won-loss column would change dramatically when MSU's overall talent was at about the same level as it had been under Perles in 1994, if not a bit lower.

On the first day of full team practices in August, players on the sidelines watched a simple sequence foreshadow MSU's strong suit in 1995: big-play potential. Tony Banks took the snap, dropped back, and fired a pass at Muhsin Muhammad, who was running an eighteen-yard come-back route. Muhammad grabbed the ball, spun, turned the cornerback into jelly, and sprinted forty yards for a touchdown.

Muhammad was big and powerful and not a bad recruiting story. When he came out of Lansing Waverly High, he was a running back and linebacker with raw skills and nice upside. Michigan State went for him with no set position in mind. In time, Perles had decided Muhammad should be moved to receiver. He was fast, tough, and no matter that he lacked finesse skills, MSU was thin at wide-out.

It was an idea the head coach liked a lot more than position coach Charlie Baggett.

"He'll never make it as a receiver," said Baggett, who saw in Muhammad zero ability to catch passes.

There was a game at Minnesota in 1992, Muhammad's red-shirt freshman season, that left Baggett grimacing years later. Muhammad ran downfield chasing a long pass from Jim Miller. He misjudged the pass, stumbled and fell, and looked so inept everyone at the Metrodome was either embarrassed or humored.

He sat out 1993 on a gun-possession charge MSU officials regarded as out of character and a stupid, dangerous slip-up by an otherwise solid kid. It was not until his senior year that he turned himself around in all respects. He was the quintessential big, fast receiver who would light up NFL scouts and, when blended with Mason and Carter in 1995, give Banks a shot at becoming an upper-tier college quarterback in his second and final season as State's starter. Muhammad would show his skills for more than a decade in the NFL.

Muhsin Muhammed was another fairly low-profile high school athlete who would go on to star in the NFL. Coach George Perles had a knack for uncovering and developing talent, as did Nick Saban, his successor.

Defense was going to be a different story, a tougher one to accept for a coach like Saban, who was all defense all the time. Many of the Spartans' defenders were small and had mediocre tackling skills. Saban wanted big defensive backs who could match up with opposing receivers, knocking away passes and pummeling pass catchers. He wanted big linebackers and up-front Goliaths who could get their hands on a pass before it crossed the line of scrimmage. He instead had smaller defensive backs on the level of Ray Hill and Sorie Kanu, linebackers (Reggie Garnett, Ike Reese and Carl Reaves), all of whom he liked as players but who were somewhat undersized, as well as defensive linemen (Yakini Allen, Robert McBride, Jabbar Threats and Chris Smith) who were capable enough, but not game-changers by any means.

Saban wished his defense were as tough as that of MSU's season-opener opponent: Nebraska, ironically enough. A new head coach breaking in with a wobbly team needed a first game against the Cornhuskers the way Custer needed Little Big Horn. Final score: Nebraska 50, Michigan State 10. The crowd let out a gasp and cheerful applause when the Spartans began the game in shotgun formation, a move that demonstrated that a new era had dawned at Michigan State.

Saban was deflated. He may have been away from college football for four years, but standing on Spartan Stadium's sidelines the second Saturday of September 1994, MSU's new coach concluded he had a terrible football team. Even as super-talented, deep and fast as Nebraska appeared to be, Saban was stunned by Michigan State's competitive effort, or lack thereof, and berated the team in the post-game press conference for quitting midway through the second half. Saban continued with scathing public criticism, something Perles never would have done—it was indeed no longer the Perles era at Michigan State.

Nebraska coach Tom Osborne, who nine months earlier had mulled—for twenty-four hours, anyway—taking the job Saban now had, said as they met on the field afterward: "You know, Nick, you've got a better team than you think."

He thought about Osborne's words after Michigan State beat Louisville a week later, 30-7, on the road. He understood even more what that wise Cornhuskers coach had meant when MSU upset Michigan, 28-25, on a cold November evening at Spartan Stadium. And, later that season, Saban thought again about what Osborne had said, after Nebraska had won the national championship.

The U-M game was an MSU classic. The Spartans took a final lead on a late, pulse-pounding drive featuring big fourth-down passes to Scott Greene and to Muhammad. Those plays set up a pass over the secondary and into Nigea Carter's cradling hands as he crossed the goal line in the waning moments.

That gave MSU a 5-4 record, and they upped it to 6-4 a week later at Indiana (31-13), setting up a season-ender against Penn State. One question remained: Which bowl game for MSU?

Penn State helped answer that question when the Nittany Lions rallied with seconds left on a fourth-down pass to a lunging Bobby Engram to win, 24-20. Michigan State had come within a couple of ticks of the clock of a major win. Among the what-ifs and coulda-beens: one completed pass to Engram after an injury had knocked play-stuffing linebacker Ike Reese out of the game; one passed-up chance by Tony Banks to run for a touchdown when State was poised to finish off a victory. Just one play away from finishing 7-4 and winning for Saban a bushel of votes as Big Ten Coach of the Year.

MSU was at least back in the bowl-game rhythm with a trip to the Independence Bowl at Shreveport, Louisiana. That pitted MSU against LSU, a school that, years later, would have far more bearing on Saban's and MSU's football lives. As for the game, the more talented, much faster Tigers captured that, 45-26.

Getting to the Independence Bowl pleased Saban for one big reason beyond MSU's winning regular-season record: University president Peter McPherson had seriously considered giving up the chance for Saban's team to play the game. It was to be part of the school's self-imposed sanctions in the wake of a year-long internal investigation that was accompanying another NCAA probe, each announced in the waning days of George Perles' administration.

It was a probe tied to former Spartan defensive tackle, Roosevelt Wagner, who had told *The Detroit News* in October 1994 a bizarre tale of stalking Perles for two days in an effort to shoot the coach, whom Wagner blamed for his failure to get drafted by a NFL team in 1992.

Wagner's story included such nuggets as $100,000-plus in cash from an agent and a new Jeep with gold accessories. His account meshed with stories of academic fraud told by ex-players, including defensive lineman Aaron Jackson, whose father said grade-tampering had been keeping his son eligible for five years.

The charges were dynamite for a university that had a history of scrapes with the NCAA. Most notable was the January 1976 three-year probation sentence that crippled MSU with the loss of a significant number of scholarships and knocked them out of bowl games and off television. The fallout included a series of firings in what became a Black Sunday bombshell in East Lansing.

MSU decided its best defense in the late autumn of 1994 would be an internal offensive. McPherson hired the Overland Park, Kansas, firm of Bond, Schoneck and King—experts at NCAA cases—to counsel MSU during an A-to-Z internal investigation that would cost the school nearly a million dollars. The hope was it would lead to lesser penalties if the University handed over all the facts, acted contritely, and punished itself appropriately.

There was plenty to probe.

The testimony presented by athletes and other people involved was particularly gruesome on the academic side. It cited grade changes and petitions for academic credit; improper inducement made to instructors and tutors, at Michigan State and at Lansing Community College, where some athletes had taken courses; bogus medical reports as excuses for missing classes; backdated University grade-change forms; and fraudulently written papers. It ultimately led to department reassignments and to the firing of Greg Croxton, a former Spartan lineman in the mid-1970s, and now an academic adviser to the football team.

THERE WERE OTHER MISDEEDS on the recruiting and boosters front, all of them leading back to a phrase the NCAA used as a catch-all for universities it regarded as being slipshod in following the rules: "lack of institutional control."

There were problems with a south Florida recruiting contact, Dan Calloway, a deputy sheriff and director of a youth recreation association, who became a close ally of Baggett. Calloway was found by investigators to have covered the cost of meals for recruiting contacts. His absence of any formal ties to Michigan State cleared MSU there. (Calloway had long worked to get area athletes scholarships, regardless of whichever university, including ex-Michigan football superstar Anthony Carter, and U-M basketball player Richard Rellford). McPherson, in fact, had personally met with Calloway in Florida, and was comfortable with Calloway's role and what was clearly a detached relationship to MSU.

Michigan State released its own findings in April 1996, and decided to self-impose a long list of sanctions:

- Two years of probation.
- Forfeiture of all five games MSU won during the 1994 season.
- MSU reduced by one the number of assistants who could recruit off-campus from 1996-97.
- MSU cut incoming football scholarships for 1996-97 from 25 to 23.
- The school scaled back total football scholarships for 1996 from 85 to 79.
- It cut the number of visits by recruited football players for 1995-96 from 56 to 48.

As State prepared in the autumn of 1995 to offer the NCAA its long list of self-inflicted penalties, McPherson suggested, at the law firm's urging, that MSU forfeit its opportunity to play in a 1995 bowl game. Saban fought the president hard on that point. These were infractions that had occurred in earlier years, under someone else's watch, Saban reasoned. Michigan State was hitting itself hard enough. There was no justice, he argued, in keeping a team from a bowl trip it desperately wanted and would certainly deserve, all because of bad acts from earlier years.

McPherson pushed Saban to reconsider as MSU prepared to play Indiana at Bloomington on November 11. The Spartans were 5-4, and there were bowl representatives on hand who knew of McPherson's stance.

"Do you want to give up the bowl?" McPherson asked Saban one more time.

"No way."

"Well," McPherson said, "if you lose this game tomorrow we won't have to worry."

Saban: "We're not gonna lose this game."

MSU won, 31-13, and so did Saban. The bowl-game flap was his and McPherson's only disagreement concerning an internal investigation the coach believed MSU's president had otherwise handled deftly.

By September 1996, the NCAA had its own verdict. It went along with MSU's self-imposed penalties, and added a few of its own:

- NCAA probation would be extended from the two-year stretch MSU had recommended to a four-year sentence.
- Michigan State was ordered to disassociate itself from two other "representatives." One was a steel-company owner who had employed a football player at a slightly higher pay scale ($7 versus the minimum wage of $5.50). Another had helped a visiting recruit and his family with transportation from Detroit's Metro Airport by providing use of a rental car.

The NCAA, however, hadn't yet pounded the gavel. Though Michigan State's probation was going to be extended from two years to four years, in contrast to the devastating three-year sentence handed down against MSU football in 1976, the Spartans would this time be allowed to play in bowl games and appear on television.

The NCAA also lopped seven scholarships for a total of 18 from MSU's 1997-98 roster. Added to earlier washouts that had mounted because of academics, discipline, transfers, etc., Saban and MSU were heading for trouble on the roster front. College teams could get by with 85 scholarship players, but not many fewer than that.

The infractions were considered, on balance, to be "secondary" violations that helped avoid a sentence as devastating as the three-year, no-bowls, no-TV crusher handed down twenty years earlier. It would have its intended effects nonetheless, particularly with respect to squad numbers on Saban's team. By 1998, Michigan State's number would be at 71, or twenty percent fewer troops than MSU was facing against teams with full rosters.

It was simply one more thing to deal with for a coach intent on retooling a football program. Saban was trying to straighten out a program that, during the decades, had most often messed up because of its own misadministration.

Still, for all the turmoil and unease Saban inherited in a job that had turned so many predecessors into casualties, he was settling in as head coach. He was growing more comfortable with MSU's place in Big Ten football and with its potential just a year after McPherson acceded to hire him.

Recruiting was about to pick up. Saban's first class had been respectable, considering he was still coaching for the Cleveland Browns until mid-January. A year later he could get busy round-the-clock with an aspect of coaching he genuinely liked.

Saban was tailor-made to recruit. He could get by with little sleep, he was organized and efficient with his time, he had solid relationships with high-school coaches, many of whom worked in the football-rich region of Ohio.

He was excellent in one-on-one meetings with recruits and with parents. For all the heat and fury he generated on a football field or in a team meeting, Saban was likeable in get-togethers at high schools, at homes, or during the recruits' weekend visits to East Lansing. He was serious, yet courteous. He was not without a sense of humor, but it was of a subdued sort and he seldom displayed it. What he specialized in was speaking clearly, directly, comprehensively, about football and about the value of a football experience at Michigan State University.

He was most impressive when visiting a recruit's home for dinner. He and whatever assistant coach he had joined would sit in the living room, or at the dinner table, with a high-school senior and his parents, grandparent, or siblings. Whatever the particular family structure might be, Saban was able to relate. He had been raised simply in West Virginia's coal-mining hills and could adapt to a lower-income or impoverished circumstance far removed from the at-home experience most incoming college freshmen knew.

He enjoyed talking technical football with parents who knew a bit about the game. He relished getting into conversations about defensive schemes and tactical football subjects that recruits invariably found as impressive as they marveled at the depth of this man's football knowledge.

Herb Haygood, a prime-time running back out of Sarasota (Florida) High School, had placed Michigan State as well as Ohio State on his list of visits. He had arrived in East Lansing for a mid-December weekend tour, and was delighted by East Lansing's weather, which at the time was unseasonably mild.

"Is it like this all the time?" Haywood asked Saban.

"Yes," replied the coach, with a sly grin that let Haywood in on the joke.

Haygood visited Ohio State a few weeks later during a weekend blizzard. Even if his geographical knowledge told him East Lansing was farther north, Haygood decided—as he battled the snow and wind of Columbus—to sign with Michigan State. It was a decision affirmed when Buckeyes coach John Cooper told him later that weekend: "If you don't sign with Ohio State, you'll never be anything."

Recruits invariably commented on Saban's intelligence, how prepared he was, how nothing could catch him off-guard. Those qualities melded nicely with what they liked about MSU's campus. Beauty, intimacy, attractive young women, East Lansing's night-time charms accessible by way of a stroll across Grand River Avenue—the setting could dazzle a high-school senior. It even drew admiring comments of an opponent player on the lofty scale of Michigan receiver Desmond Howard. Howard had shaken hands with Tico Duckett after one Michigan State-Michigan game in Ann Arbor and gave him the evening's itinerary from the view of a future Heisman Trophy winner. Duckett, a workhorse on George Perles' teams during the early 1990s, had forged friendships with MSU's rivals down the road and invited Howard to spend the evening in East Lansing.

"I'll be up," Howard assured him, and a few hours later, he and a few teammates were partying with Duckett and his gang in East Lansing.

"You guys might be winning down there," Duckett said when he cornered Howard for some rival ribbing. "But what do you do after a game? You come up here."

Adjusting to Michigan State's administrative layers was proving, on some days, to be less exhilarating for Saban. Early on he found his boss, MSU president Peter McPherson, to be approachable and was comfortable with him. He very much liked MSU provost Lou Anna Simon, as well as Barbara Ward, even if they had occasional disagreements about admitting a particular high-school senior whose grades did not impress Simon. He had the same good feelings toward vice president Roger Wilkinson, who had been given back his old duties as executive overseer of athletics.

The relationships were so good, across the board, Saban felt as if he never had to fight a worthy battle standing alone. Another plus was his friendship with Tom Izzo, who was breaking into his own new job as State's head basketball coach. Saban and Izzo were close enough in age—when hired, Saban was forty-three and Izzo thirty-nine. They were they were both all-around jocks who had been MSU assistants during the 1980s and were so steeped in each other's games that they became complements to each other in recruiting and in tackling Michigan State's particular coaching challenges.

Saban was proving to be of help in recruiting Izzo's Number 1 program prospect, Mateen Cleaves of Flint Northwestern. Izzo, in fact, would escort basketball recruits to football practice as part of his showcase tour. He also worked with Saban to bring to MSU two brothers from Flint: Antonio and Robaire Smith, who were to become for Izzo and Saban among the most extraordinary people they had ever coached.

Izzo's feel for football was explained, to a great extent, by his best-friend status with Steve Mariucci, the head coach at the University of California who had been in the NFL at Green Bay, and who eventually landed with the San Francisco 49ers and Detroit Lions.

Izzo and Saban had a friendship few major-college football and basketball coaches had ever enjoyed. They played golf together and hung out socially. They were much alike in their substance and even in style—if you sidestepped public-relations charm and instead focused on their intensity, recruiting zeal, and drive to get the maximum out of whatever talent they had assembled.

Saban's relationship with MSU's athletic director was a different story. Saban and Merritt Norvell quickly got under each other's skin. Saban would blame himself years later for having been too sensitive to an AD who had a CEO style and ego, which, for the most part, was benign. It was a veneer that should have been recognized as such, Saban later concluded, even if others were having the same problem with Norvell's inadvertent haughtiness.

Clarence Underwood, the assistant athletic director who had lost out in his second bid to become AD, was developing a deep hostility toward Norvell and a manner of governance Underwood found to be "imperious." It went back to that initial introductory press conference—the "my coaches" phraseology that had made administrators like assistant AD Clarence Underwood and coaches like Saban and Izzo all cringe.

MSU's 1995 trip to Louisville, Saban's second game as coach, was a particularly low moment. It was raining hard in Kentucky on a Saturday afternoon in September when Norvell and his wife, Cynthia—a favorite even among Norvell's critics—headed for the press box at Cardinal Stadium. Not as fortunate were other members of MSU's party: Underwood and his wife, Noreese; Wilkinson; trustee Joel Ferguson; as well as Terry Saban and the Saban's son, Nicholas, who was only five years old. They sat in the rain, covered in black plastic trash bags as a deluge ruined an otherwise splendid day for Michigan State.

Norvell's defense was that he had asked Terry Saban the previous Thursday if she cared to join him and Cynthia in the press box. Terry Saban had replied that she would be sticking to custom and sitting with the coaching staff's wives, although she had reason to believe at the time that such seating was also in the press box.

Saturday proved to be a different experience. When Norvell saw Terry Saban after the game, he had one word for her appearance: drowned, a description her husband unfortunately shared.

After MSU's party boarded the charter flight for East Lansing, Saban left his seat in the first row of coach and strode toward Norvell, his blood boiling.

"Why in the hell did my wife and son sit in the rain?" he thundered. "My kid's gonna have pneumonia!"

Norvell decided the team charter was a poor place for a conversation or a fight and tabled the discussion for a later and more private time. They met Monday, in Saban's office, where the coach's knee was moving at about the pace of a hummingbird's wings as the AD arrived.

"The first thing you need to understand," Norvell said, his voice rising, "is you don't scream at me like that ever again."

It was nearly 48 hours after Saturday's game, and Saban had barely ceased steaming.

"I don't get any respect from you," the coach said, hotly, explaining that the athletic director should have seen that the head coach's wife was taken care of.

"I asked her Thursday if she wanted to sit with me and she said no," Norvell replied. "I'm not responsible for your wife."

Now, Saban was apoplectic. He pelted Norvell with words that were more like hailstones.

"You wouldn't holler at the president like that," Norvell admonished.

"I don't regard you as my boss," Saban answered.

The tone was as toxic as the damage was permanent. Several days later, Saban's assistant, Linda Selby, called Norvell's office, a routine act for someone who made all of Saban's calls.

"Nick," Norvell said when Saban came on the line, "let me teach you some things about protocol. Don't ever have your secretary call me again."

Saban pounced.

"Merritt, you don't have to worry about me ever calling you again," said Saban, who indeed never again phoned Norvell.

Saban was in the process of excluding from his life a man who, though technically his boss, was becoming marginalized by a coach and by a president who, at least in the autumn of 1995, was more disposed to listen to Saban.

Michigan State's football players had learned, as well, that one voice counted when it came to anything having even a tangential relationship to football: Saban's. When the Spartans convened for a team meeting there was a hush when the door opened and the head coach walked in, head down, carrying coffee in a Styrofoam cup he placed upon the lectern from which he spoke.

Instantly, the coach would be into a game-plan address, some matter relating to Saturday's opponent—whatever the coach's subject, it would be serious and relevant to the moment and how it factored into Michigan State's football consciousness.

Players would unfailingly be in their chairs by the time Saban appeared, which was in their self-interest. When the coach called a meeting for 3 p.m., it was going to begin at 3 p.m. and not a second later. Woe to the player who dared, even once, to show up late.

If a cell phone went off, players understood they might as well pick it up and smash it against the wall as atonement for a sin the coach found indefensible. Nick Saban could make you wish you had never seen a cell phone, so withering were his verbal bombardments.

Assistant coaches sometimes had it no better than the players.. An assistant who had incorrectly diagrammed coverage or an offensive set during a position meeting could be brushed aside like a bad blocker.

"No," Saban would say, heading to the overhead projector, irked that heresy had crept into Saturday's preparation. "You've got to have the guy *here!*"

A win the previous Saturday meant nothing when it came to Saban's disposition at the start of a new week, and with it the preparation required for a new opponent. Mondays were infamous for the verbal pummeling players could expect during full team meetings when Saban would analyze film from the previous Saturday's game.

Players dreaded it. Mistakes were noted and the perpetrators were going to get a public skin-scorching from the head coach.

Practice sessions were a separate experience, and experience was the word. There was no wasting of a second and no inefficiency tolerated. Nobody could ever "take a play off" or even catch a half-breath on a blazing August afternoon during two-a-day drills.

Saban's credo was that a team during practice was either going to get better or get worse. If he believed the squad was leaning toward the latter, he would blow his whistle and order the team to begin practice all over again. Everything would revert to square one, right down to repeating stretching exercises.

It might add an hour or more to the day's schedule—delaying dinner and that night's study routine—but Saban would not abide a wasted practice. The re-do, which could occur just as easily during winter conditioning sessions, always seemed to work. Players would get so mad they would tear into drills with the intensity and fire Saban demanded.

Practices, the players learned painfully, were designed to be mini-games. Saban wanted Michigan State's mental and physical approach to be identical from one practice session to another, from one week of game preparation to Saturday's final act. If a player injured a quadriceps muscle during practice and had to pull out of formation, he hobbled to the sideline. No one was permitted to lie on the field unless the injury was truly serious. Saban had seen too many players who had been helped to the sideline actually be healthy enough to return two plays later. His team was going to be tough, impervious to fakery, resistant to the kind of bang-ups endemic to football.

Saban tried his best to keep his players corralled, on and off the field. He understood percentages. By the time you factored in walk-ons, he was in charge of more than a hundred players. There were going to be problems no coach, or parent, could control. All you could do was create a reasonably restrictive culture and mindset. You could instill in players a sense of discipline that would affect them on the field as well as away from practices and team meals and study sessions.

Bye weeks presented a unique set of problems. The troops had a weekend pass on the one Saturday each autumn that a team was given a schedule break. Practices were not as focused, game-week rhythms were a mess, players were looser, ominously so when it came to Friday and Saturday.

Saban minimized laxity by calling meetings and practice for 10 a.m. He made sure the players were occupied until at least 3 p.m. That left them little time to get into mischief and it ensured they were worn out enough to throttle down Saturday night's combustion.

Relationships between the head coach and players were fairly standard: He ran the football team; they played for him. If you wanted to have a serious conversation about football or about your role on the football team as it related to your greater mission as a student at Michigan State University, then Saban was your man. If you wanted to drop by the office and have a warm and folksy conversation about life, or home, or your parents, or girlfriend, or about anything sentimental or schmaltzy, you might as well call Dial-A-Friend.

Walking down a hall when Saban was walking toward you was a standard-issue experience in the impersonal. The coach more than likely would not say a word, would not acknowledge you even with a nod, and generally left the impression he never saw you. Most players decided not to take it personally. Nick Saban was so consumed by football, so fixated on thoughts about preparation and what was next on his schedule, the name of a player he had just passed in the hallway probably never registered.

It was pure Saban. Get accustomed to it, players would tell themselves.

His staff could be just as cantankerous as the head coach, Gary Tranquill in particular. Tranquill and Saban had coached together at West Virginia, Navy (Tranquill was head coach there) and later with the Browns, where Tranquill had been quarterbacks coach for, most notably, Bernie Kosar and Vinnie Testaverde.

Tranquill was a brilliant offensive football coach the players nicknamed "Yoda" because of his trademark ears. He was regarded by players—particularly by quarterbacks—as a master assistant who could not be disputed with or second-guessed. Begin to stammer an excuse after throwing a pass to the wrong spot, and Tranquill cut you off in a nanosecond. He was above reproach, unlike other assistant coaches who had their human moments.

A scripted set of plays would be in place for a particular practice. The plays changed throughout a week and season, and were of such complexity that an assistant could be excused for occasionally mixing up a right-side or left-side protection's choreography. Tranquill never erred, never deployed any player other than the place he was required to be. It gave him immense credibility when he would blow his stack, throwing down his coaching cap, jumping up and down, and letting loose with verbal thunder that—with his Yoda-like looks—could leave defensive players across the field cracking up.

His quarterbacks missed the humor. These meltdowns were almost as bad as Saban's.

"If you can't handle this from me," he would roar as a quarterback's head sank, "how are you gonna handle things when you've got seventy thousand or a hundred thousand screaming people at Iowa or Michigan or Notre Dame?"

Saban and his staff were turning around a Spartan football team by way of altering its very makeup. Michigan State had undergone the most dramatic change in personality a Big Ten team could have experienced after one year of Nick Saban's influence. Work habits, discipline, attention to detail—changes made all the more pronounced by players and their fear of screwing up—had turned Michigan State into the kind of team that made opponents uncomfortable.

Saban's style struck observers as a coaching demeanor similar to that of Michigan's longtime deity, Bo Schembechler, who put the fear of God into players with a relentless, fire-breathing, you-will-win approach to football that forced players to perform with optimum intensity and purpose.

Schembechler had built and run a football program with supreme efficiency and was an equally compelling recruiter. Saban was steadily becoming Michigan State's counterpart, with one exception: He was having a more difficult time winning over some of the locals. It was mostly due to a personal style fans found rigid, icy or uncompromising in a coach who believed his responsibility was not to engage in public relations but to prepare a football team for battle.

Saban was revealing himself to be a different kind of head coach from anything Michigan State had ever experienced, with the possible exception of taciturn Denny Stolz, Duffy Daugherty's successor. Stolz coached only three years (1973-75) before losing his job in the aftermath of MSU's 1976 NCAA probation sentence.

In the somewhat intimate setting of mid-Michigan's version of twin cities, Lansing and East Lansing, Michigan State's community had come to view their head coaches as friends, neighbors and ambassadors. Daugherty had personified the role of football coach as endearing celebrity. Duffy had been a joke-telling, crowd-pleasing Irish charmer who had followed another icon, Biggie Munn, and in the process built upon Munn's work that gave Michigan State a commanding coast-to-coast football profile.

Daugherty was viewed with a sense of ownership by folks in Lansing and East Lansing. Perles had tapped into this heritage when he arrived almost ten years to the day after Daugherty resigned. Much like

Daugherty, Perles loved the social setting football provided. He enjoyed the friendships, particularly the closeness with teammates, and how the sport and its battleground forged enduring qualities in men. He also valued the relationships football engendered with men who were accomplished in other area, men such as Frank Kelley, Michigan's venerable attorney general.

With Saban it was going to be different. He understood the value of playing in alumni golf outings, and for standing behind a microphone as Michigan State football's primary presence. He was committed to the charity efforts in which he and Terry were involved.

What he would not become was a latter-day Perles, Daugherty, or even a Jud Heathcote, the droll basketball coach from 1976-94 who could reduce a crowd to giggling rubble with his dry one-liners. Saban would hit up Heathcote for jokes but they could hardly be transferred because Heathcote's humor demanded spot-on timing and intonation. It had to have about it a touch of the acerbic, and Heathcote was unparalleled at putting all the elements together while Saban had to be Saban. He enjoyed a good laugh and a good quip, but comedy was a no-show on his agenda. Saban was going to talk football—with energy and intellect running at full throttle—whether he was addressing his team or the Downtown Coaches Club.

By the late winter of 1996, fifteen months after he had been hired, Michigan State football was, A to Z, a Nick Saban production. He had just wrapped up his first full recruiting class at Michigan State, a group that included a nationally ranked Florida running back, Sedrick Irvin, as well as a crackerjack kicker, also from Florida, Paul Edinger.

Day by day, Nick Saban was placing his imprint on MSU football and on the University. He was bringing in his brand of players and shaping the ones already on hand into Saban-grade warriors. University officials were beginning to adjust to him, as well. Let it never be said that a man who had been nominated to attend the U.S. Naval Academy by West Virginia Senator Robert Byrd was deficient in his appreciation for academics or for time-honored values. Saban believed in the classroom. He believed in students who could still be students and at the same time the best football players their skills and minds and hearts would allow.

It was clear to those who had been around for a generation or two that there had never been anybody quite like Nick Saban at the helm of a team, any team, in MSU's hundred-year sports history. He had been around for only a single football season and followers were already wondering what was in store for MSU football.

CHAPTER 8

MATTER$ OF PRINCIPLE$

NICK SABAN HAD MET MORE FOOTBALL PEOPLE by age forty-five than some coaches meet in a lifetime. He knew them from his college stops at Kent State, Syracuse, West Virginia, Ohio State, Navy, Toledo and Michigan State. He knew them from the NFL, where he had coached for Jerry Glanville at Houston before joining Bill Belichick in Cleveland, where Ernie Accorsi had been the Browns' general manager before becoming GM for the New York Giants.

Saban had even been interviewed for a previous NFL head coaching job, with the expansion team at Carolina, when he was Browns defensive coordinator. He watched his good friend from Kent State days, Dom Capers, get the nod instead. But he knew there would be a day when he and the right NFL head coaching job would probably click.

The Giants were looking for a football coach—again—in 1996 after Dan Reeves was fired following a 6-10 season. Accorsi had offered his boss, George Young, a name of particular interest: Nick Saban, head coach at Michigan State, which was on its way to the Sun Bowl to play Stanford following MSU's 6-5 season.

Young called Saban a few days after Christmas and asked him to think about the Giants and a return to the NFL.

Saban was in a mood to listen. He no longer had any relationship with MSU athletic director Merritt Norvell, and he was beginning to chafe at the way in which MSU president M. Peter McPherson viewed sports in general, and the football coach's contract, specifically.

"I can talk after the Sun Bowl," said Saban, who left with his team for El Paso, Texas, just as word was leaking in New York of the Giants' interest. The leak created the kind of public buzz that leaves an employer uneasy, especially after the coach and his team get socked in their next game, 38-0, which was the case as Tyrone Willingham's Stanford Cardinal slaughtered the Spartans in one of the worst losses a Saban-coached team had ever endured.

Saban flew to New York to meet with the Giants' brass: Young and Accorsi, as well as the ownership team of Wellington and John Mara and Robert Tisch. This came during the thick of recruiting season and Saban was uncomfortable with all the attention (the courtship had been made public) and how it was going to affect players and their commitments to Michigan State, and its impact on recruiting.

"George, we've got recruits coming in Friday," Saban told Young as the drama—and New York's indecision—played out in mid-January. "I'm making a statement tonight either way."

Saban talked and haggled with McPherson throughout that day. He wanted a raise and a fortified contract more in line with the Big Ten's top tier of head football coaches. McPherson was opposed to any boosts in pay but saw no practical options. Minnesota had just hired Glen Mason from Kansas at an annual salary of $625,000, the benchmark used by Jimmy Sexton, the agent representing Saban, as well as Mason.

During a conference call with vice president Roger Wilkinson, McPherson, still miffed by the Sun Bowl collapse, asked, indignantly: "Why do I have to pay $625,000 for a .500 coach who just got his brains beat out against Stanford?"

Nonetheless, by Thursday evening, the coach and McPherson had agreed in principle: Saban would stay at Michigan State. The announcement would be formalized later that evening by way of a press release.

The Giants weren't dissuaded. Young called Saban.

"Give me another day," he said. "You're gonna get this job."

"George, I can't do that," Saban replied. "I've already told the president this was it."

MSU's announcement about Saban broke just ahead of Thursday night's 11 p.m. news. Michigan State's football faithful, weary of coaching changes and worried about Saban's departure at a point when things were at least moving forward, went to bed satisfied MSU's head coach was sticking in East Lansing to wrap up what stood to be a big recruiting class.

At 7:30 the next morning, Saban's office phone rang. John Mara was calling. The Giants were offering their head coaching job to Nick Saban.

"John, I made my statement last night," Saban said, appreciatively. "I'm standing by it."

Saban was being polite. He knew that he likely would have turned down the Giants even if he hadn't come to an agreement the day before with McPherson. He was two years into a job he was absorbed by, the Norvell and McPherson irritations aside. He and Terry and their two children were settled. Leaving the calmer life in East Lansing for an NFL job in New York was going to be less than thrilling—at this juncture, anyway.

Saban felt better about the Giants' overture than did his boss, McPherson, who had a typical CEO's attitude toward employees who entertain offers from other employers: Do it once. An employee in good stead with his company can establish his market value and earn an adjustment that makes both parties happy. Repeated dalliances, however, are likely to lead to good-riddance farewells from bosses who want loyalty to be part of the relationship, no matter how legitimate the employee's points may be.

Saban had also seen a crack develop in his growing bond with MSU fans. The Giants' courtship made them nervous. For too many years Michigan State had dealt with abandonment issues: Darryl Rogers leaving for Arizona State in 1980; George Perles coming within an eyelash of going to Green Bay days after MSU won the 1988 Rose Bowl; Perles again nearly leaving for the New York Jets.

Michigan State fans were tired of wedding themselves to coaches they wanted to believe were Spartans for the long haul and who so often seemed to view MSU as an interlude. They were unsettled about Saban after his flirtation with the Giants. Only the knowledge Saban was staying and could put the lid on a good recruiting season, and their distaste for another coaching search, offset fans' doubts about how long a coach who seemed so much like a NFL coach would remain in East Lansing.

McPherson had offered to renegotiate Saban's contract even before the Giants called. Saban was pushing for something in the $600,000 to $700,000 range—up from his $450,000 package. McPherson liked the idea of building deferred compensation into Saban's re-done contract. His compensation would increase $50,000 to $500,000 and his radio-television return would be worth another $100,000, which brought him to $600,000.

McPherson's idea of giving his coach more cash and clout was to offer Saban a one-million dollar loan from a University-managed portfolio. Saban would pay six percent interest and allow the marketplace to work either in his behalf (forecasts were more than promising), or against him in the event the economy suddenly tanked. The University was making fifteen to nineteen percent on such portfolios. Saban saw the wisdom of gambling $60,000 against prospects of making three times as much as he would with McPherson's offer.

The 1996-97 market, highlighted by exploding tech stocks, worked nicely in Saban's favor. It worked too well to suit McPherson, given his knowledge of how money affected university politics. Saban was about to rake in cash that would take his combined income closer to the $750,000-$800,000 range—too much, McPherson thought, to avoid trouble with certain board members.

"You've really done well on the stock portfolio," McPherson told his coach in July of 1997. "We're going to withhold the hundred-thousand-dollar raise on your radio-TV until next year."

Saban was incensed. McPherson was essentially back-loading a structured pay-raise Saban had gambled on and won fair and square. McPherson made good a year later, paying the hundred-thousand-dollar radio-TV add-on—it was a catch-up payment that brought MSU even with Saban—but the coach was bitter. It seemed peculiar to Saban that a former banker and businessman steeped in financial principle would play a shell game with money the coach believed he legitimately earned the previous year.

Saban's grumbling gave way to bigger issues, such as Michigan

State's oncoming 1997 season. His team was thin and was getting thinner. Scholarships had been chopped the previous winter as a result of penalities the school incurred at the end of the Perles era, but the schedule figured to help. MSU's first six games would be against Western Michigan, Memphis, Notre Dame, Minnesota, Indiana and Northwestern

State's quarterback, Todd Schultz, had game experience from 1996 and could manage an offense, aided by a pro-caliber running back in Sedrick Irvin and a solid receiver and return man in Gari Scott.

Schultz had been a Perles recruit out of suburban Chicago who struck some teammates as cockier than his ability warranted. Others thought he ran a good huddle and had the moxie to lead a team.

In his ability to make sure everyone knew what they were doing when a play was called, they viewed him as a helmeted version of Gary Tranquill, Saban's offensive coordinator. "Be sure to do this," Schultz would say, grabbing a teammate and repeating instructions, or, "watch out for the blitz." But he had an intellectual streak that made teammates listen.

Irvin was a more talented player than Schultz, whose running skills were matched by a personality players tended to appreciate. He was nicknamed "Swervin' Irvin" for his tendency to run east and west in a bid to juke tacklers, which often happened.

"Just give me a block, just give me a block and I'm gone," he would say before breaking off a 10- or 20-yard run, after which he would trot back to the huddle giving high-fives to his offensive linemen.

The Spartans romped in their first five games, winning by a combined score of 185-54, including a 23-7 road whipping of Notre Dame. Michigan State was 5-0, ranked eleventh in the country, and on its way to Evanston to play a very beatable Northwestern team just before a game that had two potential unbeatens meeting in East Lansing: Michigan and Michigan State.

MSU players were peeking ahead and Saban knew it. He breathed fire throughout the week and kept heat on his team all the way to Ryan Field. At halftime, with Northwestern on top, 16-7, Saban was on a rampage.

"You are not playing at a competitive level," he roared, in one of the milder phrases he uttered during a locker-room verbal strafing that left no one untouched.

Late in the fourth quarter, needing a field goal to win as Northwestern guarded a 19-17 lead, Schultz and the Spartans' offense put together a drawing-board drive. Mixing Irvin's runs with Schultz's controlled passes, MSU pushed to Northwestern's 11-yard line, leaving Chris Gardner the field goal distance any kicker would have wanted to ice a game: center of the field, 28 yards.

Chris Gardner lined up for a chip-shot kick that, if successful, would leave MSU unbeaten and begin an incendiary week of Michigan-Michigan State heat in East Lansing. But Gardner's kick barely cleared the butts of his bent-over linemen and was stuffed by Northwestern defender Anwann Jones. That sent MSU's unbeaten record and grand plans for Michigan spinning like that football now twisting on Dyke Stadium's turf.

Saban gestured to Gardner, raising his hand upward, as Gardner came off the field: Put some air under it, the coach was saying, trying to tread the line between blaming and instructing.

Michigan took care of the Spartans a week later in East Lansing, 23-7, and Ohio State followed by ripping State, 37-13, also at Spartan Stadium. A team giddy after opening 5-0 was now 5-3 and headed for a place considered by most teams to be the toughest place to play in the Big Ten: Purdue, where fans were vicious and loud, and where a sophomore quarterback, Drew Brees, was a miserable cuss to defend along with Joe Tiller's high-octane spread offense.

Saban liked the challenge of going against a hotshot quarterback. He was a defensive coordinator before he became a head coach and he coached defensive backs before he became a coordinator. As a head coach he was known to personally take control of the secondary and a defensive team's choreography to prepare for a gunslinger QB—that was precisely what Saban did in prepping MSU to play Purdue.

Michigan State gave Brees all the trouble a defense could manage against a deadly passer who almost always had three or four options on any set play. The Spartans were leading, 21-10, after Schultz hit Octavis Long on a 65-yard TD pass with 10:08 to play.

Eight minutes later a football game collapsed on Michigan State. A blocked field goal was brought back 62 yards for a touchdown that, when the two-point conversion failed, cut State's lead to 21-16. There were two minutes to play. MSU had only to chew some clock or get a first down. If necessary, State could afford to punt the ball downfield and let Brees go to work with too little time for even him to stage a miracle. That, of course, was after State had secured the onside kick that was sure to follow.

The onside kick bounced 10 yards and was a free ball. It settled into the hands of the Boilermakers as Purdue set up at its own 45 with a shot at taking the lead.

Saban was going nuts on the sideline.

"If we lose this game," he snorted over his headphones back to the assistant coaches' box, "I'm going to kill myself."

Purdue took the lead, 22-21, on a three-yard run with 40 seconds showing. Ross-Ade Stadium's crowd had turned manic, although Michigan State still had a shot. Schultz hit on a couple of big pass plays that, coupled with a Purdue offside penalty and a Marc Renaud 1-yard run to the middle of the field, gave State, incredibly, a shot at kicking a 43-yard field goal to win it with 0:07 on the clock.

Saban thought about the Northwestern game. He glanced at freshman kicker Paul Edinger, an important recruit from Lakeland, Florida, who had a fabulous leg and just as much poise. Saban wanted to give him a shot at salvaging a game MSU probably had more business winning than it had losing. Edinger, though, was five months out of high school. Instead, Saban sent out his senior, Chris Gardner.

Gardner not only missed the uprights, he also almost missed the football. Years later, Saban would call the Purdue loss his most heart-sickening defeat as a head coach, rivaled only by a last-minute cave-in by Saban-led LSU at Arkansas on Thanksgiving weekend, 2002, when the Razorbacks hit on two big pass plays against a prevent-defense to win a game LSU had apparently iced.

MSU took its 7-4 record to the Aloha Bowl to meet a fast, physical Washington team. The Huskies slammed the Spartans, 51-23, an unsatisfying climax for a team that had lost its shot at a prime-time bowl because of two galling one-point losses at Northwestern and Purdue.

Nonetheless, Saban was making headway with a team and with a

program. He was recruiting
effectively, even with reduced
numbers that put pressure on a
coaching staff to land a contributor with every recruit they
signed. He was getting his share
of playmakers and making
progress in toughening up a
team. Players were even improving academically, which would
go a long way toward pleasing
his bosses.

The Spartans' community
still seemed unsure about Saban
after three years in East Lansing.
Fans wanted to love him as a
coach, but found it tough to
stoke their ardor after 6-6 and 7-
5 seasons. They wanted to like
him, personally. It was just that
they wondered if they could ever
warm up to a coach so driven, so
serious, so volcanic on the side-

*Tailback Sedrick Irvin ran 25 yards
untouched on second down to beat
Indiana in State's first-ever overtime
game in 1998. His three-year career
began with a four-touchdown effort
against Purdue that turned heads
throughout college football.*

lines, so unwilling or unable to be warm or gregarious in public, despite
the fact that he was handsome, polite, and spoke in compelling style
before groups.

Legions of acquaintances would come by the Saban house, just off
Walnut Hills Country Club, for an evening of celebration after a Saturday
victory. Losses invariably thinned the crowd to a hardcore group: his
mother and uncle from West Virginia; Denny Fryzel, a great friend from
Ohio State coaching days; basketball coach Tom Izzo; and Jim Epolito, an
insurance executive and Spartan linebacker from the 1970s.

Saban's wife, Terry, might cook chili as part of a full-flavored spread,
or the group might send out for pizzas. A downstairs television carried

whatever college game was on that night as Nick settled in on a stool against the bar. The coach would smoke a couple of Salems, drink a couple of Budweisers—about the only time a man who wasn't much of a drinker did so. In an instant, he would plunge into MSU game analysis that was a blur of high-tech Xs and Os.

Ex-players such as Epolito knew college football—or so they thought until Saban dived into a hyper-complex re-creation of certain game moments. He would diagram plays and talk about "edge players" doing this or that, and then perhaps refer to a conversation he might have had with his old boss, Bill Belichick, earlier in the week about a particular set or scheme.

Diagrams would fly across a cocktail napkin. "We were going to use this," he would say, "but we used this instead …" Saban had not a Plan A or Plan B for any particular moment in a game. He had Plans A to Z.

Izzo would be standing nearby, holding a can of Diet Coke, absorbed not so much by the specifics of what Saban was saying as much as by the mental schematics of a coach that could leave another very good coach in awe.

After the blackboard session had cooled, Saban would drift into more philosophical discussions of football, often centered around his MSU players. He loved how individuality of personality and character could not substitute for, but could, at sublime competitive moments, overwhelm physical skills. It was why he was such a student of history, military history in particular, from which he took lessons that, to him, perfectly paralleled in so many ways decisions and responses that played out on the sidelines, at practices, or in the coaching offices.

He would delve into ethics and justice. He knew compassion was absolutely necessary for a coach to have, no matter how tough or hard-boiled he was obliged to be, at least if that coach were human and, more important, had respect for other people, beginning with his players.

What was fair, he would ask himself and others gathered in his home? What was just? He would discuss a particular player or disciplinary problem, perhaps a player who had been in a scrape at a party. Saban would probe his inner-self for answers as part of a broader discussion with his post-game group of intimates. He had similar discussions with MSU administrators, many times over academic issues with respect to admission.

Saban believed genuinely he was not only a football coach when he argued for opportunity on behalf of an academically marginal recruit. Sometimes, he lamented, the inflexibility of rules denied opportunity. It made him crazy if people thought his point of view was driven by a self-serving football motivation. He had grown up in the hills of West Virginia. He understood poor America. He had seen how thin the line could be between productive versus constrained lives.

"We should leave a guy in school," he would say during such discussions with someone such as Lou Anna Simon, MSU's provost and future president, with whom Saban had a strong relationship, "until he shows he cannot succeed at school."

The downstairs post-game colloquy might last until 3 a.m. Saban, who never seemed to need much sleep, was inevitably the last to pack it in. Six hours later he would be at St. Thomas Aquinas Church for 9 a.m. mass, a personal Sunday ritual.

NO SEASON AT MICHIGAN STATE UNDER NICK SABAN would be as weird as 1998. It was a counterpart to the George Perles-coached 1986 team that lost four three-point games to finish 6-5 and miss a bowl berth a year before the Spartans won the Big Ten title and the Rose Bowl.

Quarterback was one issue heading into 1998. Schultz had graduated, which made left-handed junior Bill Burke the obvious starter. Burke had filled in at times for Schultz the previous two seasons and thus had game experience, although everyone at Michigan State was waiting to see a freshman named Ryan Van Dyke. This headline recruit had come on the scene a year earlier out of Marshall, Michigan, and fans wondered if he would eventually blow away Burke with his greater size and more powerful arm.

Burke had been part of Saban's eleventh-hour recruiting push during his first weeks as MSU coach. Burke was from Howland High in Warren, Ohio, and was not a top-tier recruit. Maryland had brought him in for a visit, but was keeping him on ice. Minnesota wanted him to visit. The coach at nearby Youngstown State (a man named Jim Tressel, who was a few years away from taking the Ohio State job) had already offered Burke a full ride.

One of Saban's quickly hired staff members, Jim Bollman, had spotted Burke's talent and asked him to send a highlights tape to Saban's offensive coordinator, Gary Tranquill, who thought Michigan State should offer. Burke signed with MSU.

Saban and his staff were going to be thin again in 1998 with only 71 players on scholarship, 20 percent beneath the NCAA limit, but the Spartans had been adding playmakers on both sides of the ball.

Plaxico Burress had a shot at being very good. He was a 6-foot-6 receiver out of Virginia Beach, Virginia, who might have been the best high-school safety Saban had ever seen. His problem was grades, which cost him a year of prep-school exile before he made it to East Lansing.

Saban had brought in a junior-college transfer possessing sensational speed: Julian Peterson, of Hillcrest Heights, Maryland. Peterson would help at an edge defensive position provided he could make a rapid transition to major-college football.

Saban had another NFL-caliber player at defensive end. Dimitrius Underwood was a senior with the brand of size, strength and speed to make a coach feel very sure about one of his defensive-end pillars.

Throw in Sedrick Irvin and Gari Scott on offense, Robaire Smith, Courtney Ledyard, Lemar Marshall and Robert Newkirk on defense, and Michigan State had impressive front-line talent—the challenge was whether Saban's team could stay intact, physically and psychologically.

Bad things began to happen in the season-opener, a 23-16 loss to Colorado State in East Lansing. MSU got annihilated, 48-14, a week later at Oregon, but almost shockingly came home to destroy Notre Dame, 45-23, as Peterson returned an interception for a touchdown and MSU exploded on both sides of the ball. It was a prelude to one of MSU's earliest-ever games against Michigan, September 26, at Ann Arbor. Michigan State was only briefly in the game against Michigan, losing, 29-17, to slip to 1-3 a month into its rapidly nose-diving 1998 season.

The next two weekends, MSU beat Central Michigan and Indiana at home. Indiana had been an overtime escape, State's first-ever OT game, ahead of a trip to Minnesota. MSU broke down in every conceivable way, including an embarrassing effort on a Gophers on-side kick. The day ended on a missed 32-yard field-goal attempt by Paul Edinger, which was remarkable if for no other reason than Edinger was developing into the kind of kicker his team wanted on the field for a game-winning kick. Minnesota escaped, 19-18, in a game State led most of the way.

Both the team and the quarterback situation were in flux. Saban had been going with Burke as his week-to-week number one quarterback. Six days after the crusher at Minnesota, Saban called in Burke, a customary five-minute chat the head coach had with his quarterbacks each week to see where their psyches were.

"We're gonna make some changes," Saban said in typically terse fashion. "Some other people are gonna get a chance to play."

That meant Van Dyke. Neither quarterback stood out that week in MSU's 29-5 victory over Northwestern, but Burke thought he had played well enough to get the start a week later at Number 1-ranked Ohio State.

On the morning of the Buckeyes game, Tranquill said matter-of-factly to Burke regarding his quarterback rotation: "We're going to alternate series again."

Burke, who had been fired up to play against his home-state team, was crushed. His funk, however, lasted one series. He made some big passes early and never came out as Michigan State started quickly and finished with a big second half to win, 28-24. A game-ending interception in the end zone by Renaldo Hill left Ohio State fans stunned in disbelief.

A week later, MSU was back on the teeter-totter. The Spartans put together another dandy defensive scheme against Drew Brees and Purdue, only to turn it over to the Boilermakers late in the game. That left just enough time for Brees to throw a TD pass for a 25-24 victory that drove a dagger through the Spartans and their season.

All in all, a peculiar year, right down to on-the-field, off-the-field eccentricities uncommon for a Saban team. Dimitrius Underwood had been one of the problems. He had an ankle sprain that seemed to every-one to be taking an inordinately long time to heal. Suspicious minds won-dered if Underwood's NFL plans might have something to do with his season-long recovery.

Players were convinced Irvin was heading to the NFL, as well, after his junior year. You could always see it in players who were convinced—sometimes naively—they had long and lucrative pro careers ahead of them: The final season tended to be a gear lower than the tempo they played at the previous year.

Whispers about Saban and his future—even assistant coaches were suggesting he might not be in East Lansing for the long haul—had become part of a season players wanted to forget even before Penn State closed things out with a 51-28 romp.

In November 1998, after MSU lost to Penn State in the last game of the year, its 6-6 record immediately knocked the Spartans out of the bowl pic-ture, which did nothing to enhance the relationship between Saban and McPherson.

Still, Saban's name remained a sizzler when it came to NFL job open-ings. Now it was the Indianapolis Colts who were talking with him when they shopped for a new coach in January of 1998 to replace Lindy Infante.

Saban and McPherson's annual discussions over contract and money were making life increasingly prickly for two men who were never going to get along terribly well.

"Am I talking with the same young man who said he wanted to be the coach here forever?" McPherson asked Saban during one of their discus-sions after a NFL team had called. "I must be talking with a different young man."

Saban was left to fume about an employer's perception that he believed was patently unfair. The coach's feelings were sparked by his football experience. He knew what was right and wrong about a football team and in his view there had been infinitely more wrong with Michigan State when he arrived in 1994 than his bosses, or most fans, recognized. Bad discipline, bad academics, too many years of tepid recruiting, NCAA violations that had led to probation and to a reduction in scholarships—a far more serious crisis for a team and a coach than was generally appreci-ated—had made MSU a long-term project. Saban doubted anyone knew the hoops through which he and his staff had jumped to squeeze out six- or seven-win seasons for the past four years.

Michigan State's 0-3 bowl record under Saban? Ha, the coach wanted to say. This was a team that was lucky to have played in three bowls. And what happens to a team that has marginally qualified for a bowl is gener-ally predictable: That team is likely to get smoked as part of mismatches MSU had found itself in against LSU, Stanford and Washington.

Still, Saban at least liked his and Michigan State's chances in 1999. It was going to be his fifth season as head coach and enough good things had been put in place to give State its best shot at winning since Saban came aboard.

Players realized it as soon as they showed up for August practices. Roster numbers were better. Suddenly, there was none of the position jug-gling that had marked earlier Saban teams where a player who probably had more natural skills for offense had to be moved to defense to plug an otherwise-gaping hole. Saban's 1998 team had an unsettling number of walk-on players who had earned scholarships. The '99 MSU team clearly had more thoroughbreds in their stable, and now they had experience.

The Spartans had four tight ends, just one example of how State's per-sonnel picture had changed. There was front-line strength on both sides of the ball and some genuine depth at most positions.

Michigan State had also grabbed the nation's top recruit, a line-backer and option quarterback from Kalamazoo Loy Norrix High named T.J. Duckett, who figured to settle in at linebacker for the Spartans. He was one of those potential all-world players who had enough talent to help as a freshman. It was the right forecast, but it turned out that Duckett's pro-jected position was all wrong.

Morris Watts had returned to East Lansing following a stint at LSU under Gerry DiNardo. He and the staff understood Michigan State had a potential problem with its running game. The Spartans had a fine tailback in transfer Lloyd Clemons, and a solid fullback in Dawan Moss. But they were having problems in short-yardage situations, particularly near the goal line. They needed somebody to blow up a stacked line and at least bulldoze his way for a yard or two.

They began giving the ball to Duckett in experimental plays at practice. The coaches liked what they saw. Even though he was spending the bulk of his time on defense, more and more Saban and Co. saw that in Duckett they had their own version of that hard-running plow horse gobbling up yards in the NFL, Jerome Bettis. Within weeks, Duckett's days at linebacker were history. He was a fulltime running back and MSU had the equivalent of a Panzer tank blowing holes in opposing defensive fronts.

Other elements in MSU's game-day structure began to come together. Amp Campbell, the cornerback who had been lost the previous year to a fractured vertebrae during the disaster against Oregon that threatened to end his career, was back. He was to distinguish himself not only as a marvelous comeback story but as a player who—for reasons no one could pin down—enjoyed one of the closest relationships with Saban any player or coach at MSU had ever observed.

It seemed to be a simple matter of chemistry. Saban found in Campbell a thick-skinned athlete who never withered during a coach's verbal strafing, but who only got better. He saw in Campbell, too, a marvelous story of inspiration—an athlete who had come close to permanent paralysis somehow work his way back to again become a productive player.

Campbell would end up scoring a turnaround touchdown by returning a fumble 85 yards in Michigan State's critical season-opening win against, ironically, Oregon. It was a tone-setter for a football season that would become one of Michigan State's best efforts in 35 years.

MSU's defense was back to old Saban form. State's linebackers—Peterson, T.J. Turner and Josh Thornhill—were a vintage Big Ten linebacker troika, while the up-front crushers (Hubert Thompson, Robaire Smith, Jace Sayler and Josh Shaw) were sturdy and mean. Campbell's cohorts in the secondary (Aric Morris, Richard Newsome and Renaldo Hill) were agile and good tacklers.

Edinger was a terrific place-kicker on his way to a long career in the NFL. Burke was back at quarterback, Plaxico Burress and Gari Scott were at the wide-out spots, and the Spartans had all those tight ends (Chris

Baker, Ivory McCoy, Kyle Rance and Brad Rainko) to go with a dynamite offensive front: Greg Robinson-Randall, Shaun Mason, Casey Jensen, Dave Sucura and a junior-college Samoan transfer who was becoming MSU's biggest surprise and contributor: Tupe Peko.

The Spartans even looked better from a sartorial standpoint in 1999. They had gone to a midnight-green jersey for a richer, more exalted appearance. And they were playing in just such a fashion.

MSU won the critical Oregon opener, 27-20, on a Thursday night, September 2 at Spartan Stadium. The Spartans ran off five victories in the next five weeks: Eastern Michigan, Notre Dame, Illinois, Iowa and Michigan. The Wolverines had two standout quarterbacks in Tom Brady and Drew Henson, but lost, 34-31, at East Lansing.

The Spartans were unbeaten and ranked fifth in the country heading into the one place,

Quarterback Bill Burke threw four touchdown passes to lead MSU past Florida in the 2000 Citrus Bowl, and give MSU its first and only 10-win season since 1966.

against the team that gave them the most heartburn: Purdue, site of State's infamous 1997 collapse.

Brees was a senior and as miserable on opponents as ever with his deep reservoir of receivers, most personified by Vinnie Sutherland. Saban had been through this routine before and figured MSU could keep Brees from going crazy. It was the other stuff that bothered Saban—the psychological odds against keeping a long winning streak alive at a notoriously wretched place to play. That was what weighed most heavily on the minds of a coaching staff.

Michigan State hopped to a 7-0 lead on a nifty drive off the opening kickoff. Then Brees got rolling. Purdue went ahead, 42-28, but Saban had seen these kinds of games before. State was moving the ball and Saban felt Michigan State was going to win. It might be 48-44 or some such silly score, but the coach knew comebacks, and this comeback was following a script displayed only by better football teams.

Of course, this was also West Lafayette, Indiana, and a predictable Purdue-grade disaster loomed. The floodgates cracked open when Burke threw an end-zone interception early in the fourth quarter. On the Boilermakers' next possession, Robaire Smith was flagged for a late hit, turning a punt situation into a drive-sustaining penalty that treated the Boilermakers to a huge touchdown—and Smith to a verbal sideline scalding from Saban.

Purdue's final winning score of 52-28 hardly reflected where the scoreboard and the momentum had been before Burke's end-zone pick. Almost unnoticed in the frantic scoring was that Purdue wide receiver Chris Daniels set a Big Ten record with 21 receptions and 301 receiving yards.

Coming off the Purdue debacle, State now could look forward to a trip to Wisconsin against a Badgers team that had size and muscle and depth, a combination the Spartans were ill-suited to face. State was not the physical bunch they had been during the last standout season Saban had known at MSU, 1987, when the Spartans had gone to Pasadena.

Wisconsin destroyed MSU, 40-10. The game was a mismatch in any context, set in motion by all that had happened at Purdue, and by too many missing players (MSU started merely four fully healthy defenders). It was a reminder of what various national pundits had been suggesting and MSU's staff privately knew: The Spartans were still a notch shy, physically, of becoming a legitimate Top 10 team. They were probably Top 20. But the difference in ten spots on the national scale was the number and size of bodies, and State was a year or two from matching up there.

Northwestern was plowed under, 34-0, a week later ahead of a season-ending, thrilling 35-28 knockout of Penn State, punctuated by a T.J. Duckett touchdown run that came with five Nittany Lions hanging onto him. The win left the Spartans 9-2 and headed for the Citrus Bowl in

Orlando, Florida, against a team that wasn't terribly fired up to be there: Steve Spurrier's Florida Gators.

Saban and McPherson were getting ready to talk money as the '99 season ended. It had been a triumph for a man in his fifth year as head coach in East Lansing, and Saban was looking forward to getting the financial side of his job cleaned up. It was a matter of justice, he thought. At the generally accepted five-year milestone fans and coaches expect to see a program ripen, Saban had delivered, just as Perles had delivered a Rose Bowl

T.J. Duckett (8), like Charles Rogers, came to MSU as the nation's top high school prospect. His nearly one-man show against Penn State in 1999—as a backup—set the tone for a brilliant career, which also included a controversial, last-second catch in the end zone against Michigan in 2001.

in his fifth season. Fans were now in Saban's corner. So, to an extent, was MSU's president, who had just finished up a fat contract extension for his basketball coach, Izzo, and who was now of a mind to make his more nettlesome football coach happy, at least to the extent possible.

McPherson's communiqué to Saban was just fine as far as the president was concerned: Michigan State would re-negotiate his contract following the Citrus Bowl. Saban, though, was in no mood to wait. He was still sore about the deferred stock-market compensation and, while he never begrudged Izzo his money, Saban knew enough about top-tier Big Ten schools to understand the football coach needed to be paid at least as well as the basketball coach, if not considerably more.

Saban sensed that McPherson did not necessarily share that view. It irked him that his boss was only grudgingly agreeing to discuss a fair and deserved contract re-structuring after five difficult years of rebuilding a deeply fractured football program.

McPherson had not been misunderstood. The president had reservations about MSU's 48-year-old coach, no matter what NFL teams or other colleges thought, Michigan included, which had seen Saban achieve in recruiting and in game situations the kind of presence U-M had known was possible if the right man were in East Lansing.

McPherson was a non-believer for various reasons:

The president had been bothered by State's second-half failures (Purdue during the Brees years; Northwestern in '97, Minnesota in '98, etc.), no matter that McPherson had not attended a single football game between his years as an undergraduate at MSU until he signed on as president. If he had, he would have seen more than one late-game collapse.

McPherson was troubled, as well, by Michigan State's bowl-game tumbles under Saban, particularly MSU's 38-0 disintegration against Stanford at the 1997 Sun Bowl (MSU had also lost, 45-26, to LSU at the '96 Independence Bowl, and 51-23 at the '97 Aloha Bowl). In the president's view, these were not defeats against better teams taking advantage of a MSU squad that had eked its way into a bowl game at an early stage of a football program's reconstruction. To McPherson, this was a clear message the coach had a weak strain.

Then, too, there was the matter of Izzo versus Saban. McPherson had been inclined to pay Izzo top dollar. The fifth-year head basketball coach had already won two Big Ten championships and been to a Final Four. Izzo had shown McPherson that basketball at MSU was in the hands of a master and commander. Accordingly, Izzo was pulling down $700,000 a year. That the football coach was, at least temporarily, trailing in a key category of recognition seemed fair enough to MSU's president, especially since the 1999-2000 Spartans basketball team was favored to go to another Final Four at the exact time Saban wanted to discuss his contract.

Saban had simply not convinced his boss he was in the same constellation as Izzo. They had been at the job for identical periods of time. Izzo had an amazing start on building his basketball program's trophy case. Saban had no Big Ten championships, no bowl victories, and no lack of ability for irritating a president who saw nothing wrong in comparing basketball and football programs, or in pitting—in a contractual context, anyway—one of his coaches against another.

Another sore spot for McPherson was Saban's taskmaster style and how it could make life difficult for players, not to mention assistant coaches. Never mind that players and assistants who had been under Bo Schembechler at Michigan had much the same experience. The specter of a fire-breathing head coach on the Red Cedar River's banks was not the portrait of civility McPherson thought should be part of Michigan State's athletic culture.

McPherson had an additional aversion to talking money with Saban: The coach preferred that his agent, Jimmy Sexton, handle negotiations. McPherson wanted no part of Sexton, whom Saban had met in 1993, when Saban was in Cleveland and Sexton was representing a free-agent defensive tackle bound for the Hall of Fame: Reggie White.

Sexton had become the agent for Sedrick Irvin and ultimately signed on to handle Saban's negotiations—and to keep an eye open for jobs that might prove more rewarding than Michigan State.

Sexton was getting busy. Carl Torbush was in trouble at North Carolina and Sexton knew Saban would be on the Tarheels' interview list if MSU's coach were interested.

Mack Brown had enjoyed some success at North Carolina. But other coaches had struggled. Saban could hardly imagine leaving East Lansing for Chapel Hill, an issue that never materialized after Torbush was retained.

Sexton called later in the week with another feeler.

"You wouldn't be interested in LSU, would you?" he asked.

"No," Saban answered, dismissively. "I don't know anyone there."

Saban went on with his business. It was Thanksgiving week. His players had exam schedules and Saban had practice sessions and a trip to Orlando to think about.

He got a call later that day from Gil Brandt, a venerable Dallas Cowboys scout from the Tom Landry era who was as plugged in as any man in the country to coaches and coaching vacancies. Brandt had been enjoined by LSU to help find a head coach. Gerry DiNardo was the latest casualty at Baton Rouge and LSU was determined this time to get it right, at any cost, and assume its former role as a Southeast Conference gridiron warrior.

Brandt gave Saban a long list of reasons he should think seriously about LSU. Great support from the top; a fertile recruiting backyard that had been mismanaged by too many predecessors; resources and a fan base waiting to be exploited; potential that exceeded anything he could attain anywhere.

Saban understood Brandt's perspective. He had been to Baton Rouge to work out players during his NFL years, and could never understand why LSU had lost its luster. The talent in Louisiana was extraordinary, and LSU was by far the biggest school in its state.

Saban phoned Sexton.

"I don't know about this," he said, "but Gil called me. He had good things to say."

LSU had been working Saban's perimeter, hoping to get enough people to express enough encouragement that Michigan State's coach would at least listen. Brandt knew—as did all football people—that Saban was as good as any young coach in the game. He had the substance, the experience, and just the right balance of youth and savvy, to make things happen.

Phone conversations occupied most of Saban's next 48 hours as LSU turned up the heat. An official offer came Sunday night from athletic director Joe Dean. LSU was about to hand Saban a five-year, $6-million package to leave East Lansing for Baton Rouge and a new life, in a different kind of football culture.

"You guys need to call Michigan State and get permission," Saban said, uneasy that one formality had yet to occur.

The next morning, LSU chancellor Mark Emmert called McPherson and received permission to formally pursue Nick Saban as its new head football coach. Terry Saban was already on a flight to Baton Rouge. She had been invited down to scout out the campus, to see LSU's facilities and new athletic academic center, to check on academic support, and to get a feel for the community. She had to determine whether she, her husband and two children, could ever think about relocating there.

Terry particularly liked the chancellor and his wife and how sincere they were about wanting the Sabans in Baton Rouge. Score one for LSU over Michigan State.

Terry phoned her husband late Monday afternoon.

"It's a diamond in the rough," she said. "The potential is all there."

By Monday, word was out and media attention was relentless. Saban was holed up in his office before escaping to his home in East Lansing, where his mother-in-law was taking care of children Nicholas and Kristin while Terry was in Baton Rouge.

During the interim, he had met with his team at the Duffy Daugherty Football Building to explain Monday's chatter.

"LSU and I have been talking," he told the players. "It's something I have to look at as part of my responsibility to my family. I'll let you know tomorrow where things stand."

At 4 p.m., McPherson called athletic director Clarence Underwood and told him to drive to Saban's home to find out what the situation was, what MSU needed to do to get matters settled.

Joel Ferguson accompanied Underwood. If anyone was going to get to the bottom of this, Ferguson determined, it was going to be the member of the board of trustees who had the power to single-handedly influence athletics at Michigan State University.

Neither side appeared comfortable when the three men sat down. Saban was fidgeting and talking evasively. Ferguson and Underwood, for all their earnest questions about Saban and about LSU, for all their queries about what he needed and what he wanted, seemed less than intent on keeping him in East Lansing.

"Nick, where's Terry?" Ferguson asked.

Saban was noncommittal.

"Isn't she down in Baton Rouge?"

"Yes."

"Have you taken the job at LSU?"

"No."

Saban disappeared for a moment and Underwood turned to Ferguson and said: "He's leaving. Let's get out of here."

Then the phone rang. It became obvious that it was Terry calling . Saban was doing his best to keep that to himself.

"Nick, before you do anything," Underwood asked, "will you give us another chance to talk?"

"Yes."

Missing from the session was another MSU staffer who would have had significant things to say: Tom Izzo, Saban's colleague and close friend. He was with the MSU basketball team at Chapel Hill for a game against North Carolina. Izzo would wonder for years afterward what might have happened with Saban had MSU's basketball schedule not interfered.

Terry arrived at Capitol City Airport, via private jet arranged for by LSU, and hustled home to begin a long, sleepless night of conversation with her husband.

Saban was confused, angry, melancholy, torn. East Lansing was home. For the first time in their married lives, he and Terry had enjoyed living in one place, working at one job, all wrapped within a beautiful town and campus.

Sleep was out of the question. They went over every aspect of their lives and how a new job would affect everything: The kids, Saban's thoughts on coaching college football or in the NFL—everything was going to be impacted by a move to LSU.

It was the atmosphere on campus and in East Lansing he wondered about. Nothing seemed as if it were clicking with McPherson, and not only with the president, following a 9-2 season that had represented such triumph after so many years of frustration. Saban felt that people complained about his personality, or about a bowl game, or about how few jokes he told compared with Jud Heathcote—there was always something, or so he imagined.

It was approaching dawn when the phone rang. Nick and Terry Saban had, at that hour, decided to stay at Michigan State University. There would be no immediate raise; nothing had been offered the previous night by Underwood and Ferguson. But money wasn't the reason a couple was considering LSU. It was about one word: appreciation. LSU was showing loads more of if than Nick Saban's current employer had managed. But they would at least stay in East Lansing for now and hope things got better after the Citrus Bowl.

Saban answered the phone. It was the president.

Saban right off the bat didn't like McPherson's tone. There was a "you're not going to do this to us" air to it that was, in an instant, making the coach realize why he had listened to LSU in the first place. It was also apparent to Saban that McPherson thought he was headed for Baton Rouge.

"Why is it okay for you to talk to me this way?" Saban asked.

He hung up, told Terry that was it, dressed and headed for the Duffy Daugherty Football Building. Linda Selby, Saban's office assistant, had already been on the phone early Tuesday morning telling players to assemble for a 7 a.m. meeting.

Saban met with his seniors inside the head coach's office. By the time they began shuffling into the corridor, silent and stunned, the underclassmen immediately realized Saban was gone. It was as certain as the tears streaming down the face of Amp Campbell, a player whose relationship with Saban came to embody all that was good, all that was inexplicable, about the most complex football-coaching tenure ever at Michigan State.

CHAPTER 9

OPTICAL ILLUSION

PETER MCPHERSON COULD VIEW NICK SABAN'S DEPARTURE from Michigan State with utter ambivalence. On one hand, he was glad to be rid of a football coach who had been unfailingly complicated for a university president who had better things to do. On the flip side, McPherson was now obliged to endure another sticky search for a coach who could provide for MSU a solid football program, image and presence consistent with McPherson's ideals and the fan base's desires. Not an easy assignment, especially when one considered MSU's tortuous football history.

McPherson's first choice was the same man he had tried to hire in November 1994: Tom Osborne, the retired Nebraska Cornhuskers icon who had wrapped up his football career in Lincoln two years earlier. Osborne had been to college football during his twenty-four years as head coach what Dallas Cowboys coach Tom Landry had been to the NFL: a stolid general who won games by the bushel and who brought unblemished glory to his team and to his job.

Osborne had retired from Nebraska after the Cornhuskers' 1997 national championship season with a 255-49-3 record that included a stunning 60-3 mark in his last five seasons at Lincoln. McPherson looked at Osborne and saw the perfect college coach. He was a Mt. Rushmore figure in the eyes of football fans and an impeccable educator from the standpoint of a university president. Osborne had a doctorate in educational psychology. He turned out academic All-Americans and football

All-Americans with equal frequency. He was a solid Republican from the American plains.

McPherson wanted Osborne and his cachet every bit as much as he had when he sought to bring him aboard five years earlier with an unprecedented one million-dollar-per-year contract MSU had creatively arranged. That bid, which had seemed so deliciously close to becoming reality, died when Osborne and his staff decided leaving Lincoln was too radical of a move for a head coach and his staff. There were families to consider, as well as a Cornhuskers team packed with promise.

This time, McPherson sensed he could pull off a coup that would knock college football's seismograph silly. The two men talked for three days. Osborne, retired and living in Lincoln, was staying busy enough. But he was a football coach. He had been more in favor of coming to East Lansing in 1994 than his staff, which had younger families to consider. Getting a shot at Michigan State, at the Big Ten, was just the jolt a sixty-two-year-old coach who loved college football could relish.

Phone lines burned between East Lansing to Lincoln: McPherson talking, selling, reassuring a man who knew enough about Michigan State to have been drawn to East Lansing even as he reigned over the Cornhuskers' empire. Osborne listened, counseled and countered as they constructed a contract that would make both parties eminently happy.

It was an elaborate series of ultra-secret negotiations, unusual in that rarely in college sports did a coach and a college president talk for extended periods, almost as if McPherson were acting as a foreign diplomat pressing for a treaty. At last they had a deal: multi-years for multi-millions. Tom Osborne was about to shake a university, and a college football galaxy that thought it had seen everything with respect to Michigan State and its endless knack for making more news off the football field than on it.

Osborne had only to nail down endorsements from a few intimates, including his doctor. He had physical concerns typical for a man his age and wanted his physician to give the go-ahead. His doctor, however, was opposed to Osborne returning to fulltime coaching and recommended the coach enjoy civilian life and stay away from the sidelines; this opinion was bound to carry serious weight with Osborne's wife, Nancy.

Osborne phoned McPherson. For the second time in five years he had to say no to Michigan State and to a university president who had made a lavish offer Osborne hated to refuse.

McPHERSON HAD AN OPPORTUNITY, he realized after Saban had left for LSU, to make the kind of personally satisfying hire he was prevented from making in 1994 when Fran Ganter faded and Osborne spurned an eleventh-hour offer. McPherson knew, as well, that he had assumed the high ground after Saban's departure, which to MSU's fan base appeared to be nothing more than a craven lust for money on the part of a greedy head coach. Their website indictments made it clear: $aban, as they took to writing his name, was all about ca$h.

McPherson had grown no closer to Saban following a remarkable series of conversations two days after the coach left East Lansing for Baton Rouge. Saban, who had already been introduced to the state of Louisiana and to an LSU nation praying Saban was its football messiah, could not believe what had happened inside of forty-eight hours. He had left his home, had left a football job he loved, and had set into motion the relocation of his wife and two young children to a culture far removed from the Midwest, where he had always felt such comfort. No longer would he and Terry and the kids be spending those lovely summer days at Walloon Lake in Northern Michigan. His friend and colleague, Tom Izzo, was no longer nearby. Neither was Jim Epolito, or Gregory Eaton, friends he had come to count on at all times, at any time, especially when things had turned tough with the president or with some other facet of a job that was ceaselessly difficult.

In the aftermath of his hiring and introductory press conference at LSU, Saban phoned to confide to trustee Joel Ferguson that he wanted to come home—that he wasn't so far into this crazy LSU experience that he could not reconsider. Ferguson, startled, called McPherson with the information. Clarence Underwood, who since April had been MSU's interim athletic director, was next to hear Saban say he wanted to undo this whole crazy week.

"I may have made a mistake coming down here," Saban said to

Underwood, dread in his voice.

Saban understood it was next to impossible to reconsider. This was a national story that would become a national embarrassment—for a respected football coach and for two giant universities—if he were to get cold feet now. But he needed to know, for sure, if notions about coming home were less outlandish than they seemed.

Underwood thought it was possible.

"You've got to fly to (Detroit) Metro Airport and hold a press conference right there," Underwood said, "and explain to the people of the state of Michigan why you left."

Underwood, who knew from personal experience how emotions can overwhelm a man taking a new job away from his family, calmed Saban and said he would call McPherson immediately.

The president, although intrigued by Saban's change of heart, decided any idea of bringing back a coach at this stage would be bad for all parties. Saban resigned himself to the same logic and got busy recruiting for Louisiana State University.

McPherson, who had made the call on Saban five years earlier, was going to run this 1999 selection process as well. McPherson would handle this himself, no matter that Underwood was athletic director and Ferguson was wielding his customary power as MSU's most knowledgeable and deft board member in matters relating to football or high-profile athletics.

A short list of candidates had been thrown together that included two well-known head coaches: Glen Mason at Minnesota, and Tyrone Willingham, the one-time Spartan quarterback who had prospered at Stanford. Either would have been welcome in East Lansing. The handsome Mason had done a splendid job turning around Kansas before arriving to straighten out Minnesota. He was forty-nine years old and knew the Midwest from his days as head coach at Kent State and Ball State, not to mention his current job with the Gophers. He had also had been on Ohio State's staff under Woody Hayes and Earle Bruce, which inspired the conventional wisdom that Mason would be bound for Ohio State as soon as John Cooper departed.

Notre Dame was another much-discussed destination for a Catholic head coach who fit the Fighting Irish's profile. McPherson and the selection committee thought East Lansing might provide Mason with resources—including money—and recruiting advantages such as a fine on-campus stadium he would be hard-pressed to match in Minneapolis. Mason tended to agree, which is why he authorized his agent to talk with MSU's selection committee.

Willingham was a different story. He had been a Spartan walk-on football and baseball star out of North Carolina at the same time another North Carolina quarterback named Charlie Baggett had found his way to East Lansing in the early 1970s. As a player, Willingham was a dead-serious, radiantly poised performer who had the makeup for coaching. He was a graduate assistant on MSU's staff under Darryl Rogers before hiring on as a three-year member of Muddy Waters' staff. There were stints at Rice, Stanford and North Carolina State, followed by three years as an NFL assistant to Minnesota Vikings coach Dennis Green, before Stanford decided Willingham should be its head coach in 1995.

It was Willingham's Stanford team that had pounded Michigan State, 38-0, in the 1996 Sun Bowl, a game McPherson remembered all too well for what it said, in his estimation, about the quality of coaching on the two sidelines.

Mason was first up. Michigan State's search and selection party consisted of McPherson, Underwood, provost Lou Anna Simon, vice presidents Fred Poston and Terry Denbow, faculty representative Michael Kasavana and assistant athletic director Greg Ianni. On December 1, the group hopped on a charter flight bound for Minneapolis and face-to-face interviews with Mason. That was two days after Saban's formal departure. Now they would interview a coach who had all the ingredients to give MSU as seamless a transition as possible from Saban to a new regime.

They found Mason seemingly less than enthused about moving to East Lansing.

"What's your non-conference scheduling philosophy?" he asked the group.

McPherson responded that Notre Dame would continue to be on the docket every year, at least if Michigan State had anything to say about it.

Mason nodded and McPherson countered: "What can you tell us about Ohio State and your future considerations there?"

The coach shook his head.

"Oh, no," he said. "That job isn't as good as it used to be."

McPherson was inclined nonetheless to think of Mason as Michigan State's next coach. Contract talks would begin between the two parties—Michigan State and Mason's representatives—and extend into the approaching weekend.

Willingham had likewise been on MSU's must-see list as the safari to name Saban's successor convened. He had at least been open to talking with Michigan State, although he was free to wonder why he had not been seriously pursued when Saban was hired at the same time Willingham was being tabbed by Stanford.

The MSU recruiting team was planning its trip to Palo Alto, California, to interview Willingham when word came from Stanford: Willingham had just signed an extended contract to remain Cardinal football coach.

McPherson was experiencing déjà vu—it was 1994 all over again. Osborne, his first choice, had said no. Mason's candidacy was lukewarm. Willingham was staying put at Stanford.

Bobby Williams, meanwhile, was back at the Duffy Daugherty Football Building minding the store. As Saban's assistant head coach and running backs lieutenant, Williams had been given charge over Michigan State's orphaned football players after Saban departed. Williams himself wanted a shot at becoming head coach, although McPherson seemed reluctant to take his candidacy seriously. There was a general perception that Williams, a nice man who had never even been a coordinator, needed more seasoning.

It looked, in fact, as if he were about to get it. Williams had been interviewing at Eastern Michigan University, where he had once been an assistant, and was the front-runner to become the Eagles' head coach.

He had returned from Ypsilanti earlier in the week to take a call from Underwood: "We'd like for you to be interim coach, and to coach us in the bowl game."

Williams had no problem with that as long as it would fly with EMU. He was going to get the job there and everyone knew it.

By late that week, two days after Mason's candidacy unraveled, attitudes were beginning to change in East Lansing. Spartan players were at the heart of an impromptu push to make Williams head coach.

Dozens of them arrived en masse at Cowles House, home of the MSU president, knocking at McPherson's door in an organized effort to get Williams hired. They wanted security in the wake of Saban's sudden and unsettling departure. They wanted continuity, familiarity, and no surprises from a new coach who, at that point, could have been anyone in the country.

They wanted Bobby Williams as the Spartans' new head football coach. They were backing up their plea with a polite threat: If Williams weren't hired, players would take a dim view toward playing in the Citrus Bowl game. It was a statement McPherson did not take entirely seriously, but one he could not totally dismiss.

McPherson was more moved by the players' feelings toward Williams. The president had not been a fan of Saban's stern ways with players and could warm to the idea of a favored assistant coach taking over as a kind of popular, compassionate leader. That would be an antidote to any toxins still in the system after the Saban regime.

Williams' post-Saban week was turning into a blur. He was shuttling between Ypsilanti, where he was about to be hired as head coach, to East Lansing, which now wanted him to function as interim coach. He had to get things ready for MSU's first Citrus Bowl practice, as well as for the first weekend of visits by recruits. At the same time, Eastern Michigan was playing in a basketball tournament at Breslin Center, which was to correspond with Williams' formal offer of the EMU job.

Williams decided to get aggressive. He told Underwood and Fred Poston, the new vice president for finance and development, that he wished to be interviewed for the MSU head coaching position. They arranged a formal session Saturday morning, four days after Saban had left for Baton Rouge.

McPherson was warming to Williams' candidacy. In principle, he liked the idea of hiring from within and avoiding all the entanglements that came with hiring someone outside Michigan State. It was a cleaner transition, not having to pull an existing coach from his team for an upcoming bowl game, as LSU had done with Saban. It would enable an important recruiting season to continue with minimal interruption—a huge consideration in the eyes of people such as Ferguson.

There was something else to like about Williams in the president's view: He was African-American. Michigan State needed to put its money—and its coaching appointments—where its considerable mouth was on the issue of diversity.

Despite Williams' candidacy, there remained the clear sense Mason would do well in East Lansing. There was no guesswork to him, no apparent risk. He knew the Midwest and had established himself as a Big Ten head coach. He was young and polished. He had no taint.

The question with Mason was: Did he really want to come to East Lansing? And if he did, why were contract talks moving in such frustrating fashion as the parties headed into Saturday evening? Mason and his agent, Neal Cornrich, were asking for $1.2 million a year—about a half-million dollars more per season than Saban had been pulling down. Even if Mason's heart was in a new job at East Lansing—and nothing suggested that was the case—the agent's demands were making clear Mason would move for money and for no other motivation. Underwood and Poston, who were handling the contract from MSU's end, both were sour on negotiations that increasingly looked like a hold-up. Objectively, most would consider the MSU position a better college football job than Minnesota—especially when the Spartans were coming off a big season.

By late Saturday night, Michigan State was ready to offer the job—either to Mason, or to Williams, depending upon how the evening's business transpired. The group included McPherson, Underwood, Ferguson and Poston, as well as trustee Bob Weiss, whom McPherson had called when it appeared Michigan State was getting close to a deal, perhaps with Mason.

"What the hell are you doing?" Weiss asked the interviewing team. He figured East Lansing would be nothing but a layover for Mason ahead of his move to Ohio State. "You'll be doing the same thing in two years—looking for a new coach."

Ferguson didn't disagree with Weiss, whose ongoing theme was that Michigan State needed continuity in its coaching offices. Ferguson's greater concern was recruiting. Coming off a splendid 9-2 season and headed for the Citrus Bowl, MSU needed to capitalize on the December, January and February crusade in order to get blue-chip athletes committed to East Lansing.

Ferguson was also in favor of an African-American head coach—the majority of MSU's players were black. At some point logic was going to win out, he thought, and there was no reason why it shouldn't prevail now with the appointment of Williams.

It was after midnight when Ferguson and McPherson stepped away from the conference room and into the Jenison Fieldhouse hallway. Moments later they came through the door with McPherson announcing that Bobby Williams was going to be offered the job as Michigan State's new head football coach.

Underwood phoned Williams, who was at home, wondering what negotiations were going on at Jenison. He had no reason to believe he was being hired.

"Come on back to campus," Underwood said. "We'd like to meet with you."

When Williams got to Jenison he saw that a mixed group had assembled, including Tom Izzo and his wife, Lupe, who had been on hand for that night's basketball game.

There were strings attached to the appointment: McPherson had insisted that the assistant coaches stay if Williams were to be retained. There was no hang-up there. The assistant coaches had houses and families and, in most cases, kids in school. They weren't terribly interested in uprooting for a new life in Baton Rouge, Louisiana.

Williams would get a four-year contract at $435,000 per year, about five times the money he had been making as associate head coach. One thing the president knew: Williams would not be asking for an immediate salary adjustment. Nor, the president might have said to himself, teeth clenched, would Williams likely be leveraging NFL offers, at least in the near term.

McPherson immediately arranged with Williams and Morris Watts, State's offensive coordinator, to have the entire MSU football coaching staff ready for a power-house meeting at 7 a.m. Sunday at the Duffy Daugherty Football Building. It was put-up or shut-up time for assistant coaches who had been unified in their call to make Williams the head coach.

"This is gonna be a team hire," McPherson said to Williams. "The assistant coaches all wanted you—I want them to sign on, too. If I'm hiring you, then I want them to tell me they're staying to make this work."

McPherson had resolved that nobody was leaving MSU's staff to join Saban at LSU. That would be a form of piracy, in his estimation, that would de-stabilize Williams' staff and, at MSU's expense, enhance Saban's.

It was a legitimate concern, especially since Saban was in town to finish business before heading back to Louisiana. He had preferred to take as many as three or four assistants from his MSU group; he wanted at least half of his new staff to be steeped in the state of Louisiana and Southeastern Conference landscape.

A private jet was waiting at Capitol City Airport in the event any of his assistants were coming with him. But at 8 a.m. the next morning, when the plane took off, it was carrying only Saban and his mixed emotions. He would have preferred having a handful of MSU assistants whom he knew and who likewise knew his style and system. But to make immediate gains in recruiting and to become immersed fully in a new job in a new conference, hiring a staff familiar with that landscape had its benefits.

Williams was introduced formally as head coach during a Sunday afternoon press conference at the Clara Bell Smith Student Athlete Academic Center. MSU's camp, as surprised by events as Williams had been, was waiting with a collective embrace. Saban's departure had antagonized fans in much the same fashion as Darryl Rogers' departure for Arizona State—along with then-athletic director Joe Kearney—had infuriated fans and the University in January 1980, triggering complaints about carpet bagging that were being voiced again over Saban's exit.

For all the years he had worked at MSU—nine since joining Perles' staff and remaining with Saban—Williams was not very well-known. He had been a hotshot high-school running back from St. Louis when he signed with Purdue, moving from running back to defensive back after he injured a knee his sophomore year just days after he and the Boilermakers had pulled off a big comeback victory against Michigan State in September 1978.

The 1978 Spartans were a high-flying offensive team that held the Big Ten record for scoring until it was eclipsed by Penn State in 1994. MSU was led in 1978 by All-American wide receiver Kirk Gibson, and by quarterback Eddie Smith, who broke his hand during the Purdue game, which enabled the Boilermakers to turn a 14-0 Spartans lead into a 21-14 triumph for Purdue. MSU finished with seven consecutive victories and a 7-3-1 record that made the Spartans Big Ten co-champions. They missed out on a Rose Bowl trip because of a three-year NCAA probation sentence that was in its final year.

After Williams' playing days, he went on to become a graduate assistant at Purdue under Leon Burtnett, then was an assistant at Ball State before moving to Eastern Michigan for five seasons. He had spent three months on Glen Mason's Kansas staff when George Perles (MSU assistant Charlie Baggett had told Perles about Williams) called in 1990 with an offer. It was an easy choice for Williams—if irksome to Mason—given that Williams' wife, Sheila, was from Detroit, and Bobby had spent five seasons in Ypsilanti.

Now he was Michigan State's head coach after a most improbable seven-day sequence of events. Dressed in jacket and tie, and wearing glasses, Williams was soft-spoken, yet impressive at his December 4 unveiling; it was seventeen years to the day since Perles was named MSU head coach. Williams smiled often and easily—MSU knew it was in for a change there—as he stood flanked by his attractive wife, and by his son and daughter. His comments were reassuring, even healing, for a Spartans football community that had an almost masochistic relationship with pain.

He talked about turning Spartan Stadium into a fearful place—"The Woodshed," he called it—where opponents would play at their own risk.

Above all, he made the most of his staff's decision to stay at Michigan State. When Williams spoke about "an airplane that was ready to take off this morning for LSU," he was evoking imagery more dramatic than significant, but tailored to MSU fans who loved anything that suggested rejection of Saban and commitment to Michigan State.

A prevailing view among fans as they studied up on Williams was that Michigan State could be in better shape now than the Spartans had been under Saban. MSU had built a football program under Saban's watch, no question. If recruiting could be sustained—and people such as Ferguson were more than betting on Williams there—MSU was showing signs of becoming a self-perpetuating, rollover program on a par with what Izzo had going at Breslin Center.

As Williams settled into Saban's old office, he knew that he would not be regarded as a passive head coach. He was going to place his imprint on a football program to which he had already given nine years of his life. He had seen what had gone right and what had been patently wrong, from 1990-99. He was going to

Thomas Wright helped the MSU defense make a statement against Florida's Steve Spurrier-coached Fun 'n Gun offense.

change the culture, although no one—on December 4—quite understood how much MSU's football environment was about to shift from Saban's administration.

Williams fundamentally wanted a different setting for his players. He was going to ease up on the drill-sergeant stuff and treat his players more like young men. Williams believed in carrots over sticks and figured his players would respond to such after so many years of borderline oppression under Saban.

He was also going to establish that he and his staff were totally in charge of MSU football. Nick was gone. Bobby was coach. There needed to be an instant delineation just as Saban had insisted upon a scrubbed-clean start when he took over from George Perles.

Players loved it.

Practices were more relaxed, as were meetings. No longer did players' blood chill when they saw the head coach entering a meeting room. A cell phone might go off without a firing squad being instantly assembled. Players who were guilty of mistakes when film was broken down were no longer subject to being verbally skinned.

As the next order of business, the Spartans could look forward to their New Year's Day Citrus Bowl game. The felt good about their upcoming trip to Orlando, Florida, to take on Steve Spurrier's Gators. Williams would see to it, as well, that this bowl trip was appreciated as an opportunity for Michigan State to showcase its talent, and also as a reward for its success in 1999.

Workout schedules in Orlando during the week between Christmas and New Year's Day were pure Williams. Some practices and meetings were adjusted to give the players a chance to enjoy themselves. Players were reveling in telling everyone that Michigan State football was now enjoyable. The wicked warlock had fled for Louisiana—a benevolent ruler was now in power.

At a hoary Florida-Michigan State affair—The Great Squeeze-Off, where Spartans and Gators had an orange-squeezing contest—jabbering and trash talk began to escalate, much as it had nine years earlier when MSU and Southern Cal met at the Sun Bowl's team banquet and the year before that, 1989, when MSU and Hawaii got into it.

On game day, January 1, 2000, various Michigan State players behaved more like students on spring break as the two teams warmed up on the Citrus Bowl Stadium's turf. Florida wasn't keen on playing a bowl game in its own backyard and was already in a foul mood. They were not about to be dissed by a bunch of green-and-white renegades from the north.

Here and there a Michigan State player had taped a homemade, inflammatory taunt to his arm; such conduct a month ago would have drawn Saban's wrath. Some players were wearing their socks at different lengths; some weren't wearing any at all.

Hubert "Boo Boo" Thompson, a Spartan defensive end and genuine piece of work from Hillside, Illinois, had decided he was playing in the Citrus Bowl sans socks. During pre-game warm-ups, officials picked up on his wardrobe rebellion and notified Williams and his staff that if Thompson did not adhere to NCAA regulations on dress, he would not be allowed on the field at game time.

Thompson was in a go-jump-in-the-lake mode when Williams and other coaches approached him in MSU's dressing room before kickoff. The officials are serious, they said. Put your socks on, Boo Boo. You won't be allowed to play.

"Ain't puttin' my socks on, Coach," Thompson said, shaking his head. "Nope, ain't gonna do it."

"C'mon, Boo Boo," Williams said. "Put your socks on. Please, just put 'em on."

Thompson was resolute.

"Nope," he repeated. "Ain't gonna do it."

Assistant coaches headed for their places in the press box resigned to the fact Boo Boo Thompson—a key starter on defense—was going to sit out the Citrus Bowl because of a conscientious objection to wearing socks.

Only later, at kickoff, did they realize assistant coach Brad Lawing had finally prevailed. Thompson relented. He would wear his socks, although they were going to be worn at a personally determined length, in keeping with other players who were taking liberties new to MSU.

When a scuffle broke out during the second half, Thompson, who during one scrum had been lacerated by an overly zealous Florida player, grabbed the Gator and did a full-body suplex—essentially pile-drove the Gator into the turf. Thompson's body was covered with tattoos and teammates likened his wild-eyed disposition to the tattooed character played by Robert DeNiro in *Cape Fear*.

Michigan State went on to capture one of its greatest bowl victories. It was decided when Paul Edinger did something that had not been done in a MSU bowl game since Dave Kaiser managed it in the 1956 Rose Bowl. Nor, for that matter, was MSU ever known through the years for dramatic, waning-moments, game-winning field goals. It simply was not part of MSU's football heritage. This time it was going to be different for the simple reason Edinger was so different.

"Money," his teammates called him. You could bet your IRA account on Edinger. Away from the field he was quiet and serious. On the field he simply did not miss a kick. The more tense a game got, the better he got, a trait that he would take into the NFL. With the score tied, 34-34, the Spartans pushed downfield on a crisp last-gasp, possession drive with Bill Burke blending in passes to complement the Lloyd Clemons-led running game.

With just a few ticks left on the clock, State got to Florida's 22-yard line to set up an Edinger 39-yard field goal try. Burke was the holder and

Paul Edinger puts his foot into the game-winning field goal against Florida in the 2000 Citrus Bowl.

would not so much as make eye contact with Edinger, a player who was perpetually locked in. Burke got a nice snap, put the ball down, and stared ahead as it ripped on a line, dead-center through the uprights. Edinger knew in an instant the kick was perfect. He was running for MSU's locker room as the ball was still sailing, getting such a head start that Burke and his teammates had to chase Edinger down to celebrate—MSU had beaten Spurrier and Florida, 37-34.

Williams had a dramatic win in his first game as the Spartans' head coach, thanks to a field goal he never saw. The coach had known along with everyone else that Edinger's kick was good from the second it left his foot. But even before it split the uprights, Williams was getting a bath from players who dumped a Gatorade bucket on his head, knocking off his glasses and making a happy mess of a head coach who didn't mind that he never saw Edinger's kick sail high above the crossbar.

It was a victory that made academic all the pre-game banter, the wrist bands, the trash talk, the socks worn at whatever length a player preferred. It had been an acutely public debut for a head coach who had inherited a team a few weeks earlier and could now feel validated by a big bowl-day victory that left his team with a 10-2 record and momentum that was going to be important on all fronts, especially recruiting.

SINCE THE DAY HE WAS MADE COACH, Williams had been working on an extraordinary senior from Saginaw High School: wide receiver Charles Rogers, a majestic 6-foot-4, 200-pound speedster who was a state sprint champion and far and away the state of Michigan's top recruit. Like Duckett before him, he may have been the nation's top recruit.

Williams and assistant coach Reggie Mitchell had identified the people close to Rogers, beginning with his mother and with a grandfather who had helped raise him. They had a relationship with his high school coaches and had gotten to know his father, who lived in Pontiac and who was now in his son's recruiting picture. They knew Charles had a child. They kept in regular touch with everyone who could help Rogers feel comfortable about a new head coach and an opportunity to become a box-office college receiver prior to his certain move to the NFL.

Fans who slurped up recruiting info were turning giddy about Michigan State's 2000 class. Rogers looked as if he might be on his way to MSU, and a nationally ranked quarterback had already committed—Jeff Smoker, from Manheim, Pennsylvania. Smoker had become impressed with Saban during a speaking engagement in his hometown. Penn State already had commitments from two other quarterbacks and spurned Smoker, who was sought by Michigan, Kentucky and North Carolina. Penn State fans were unhappy their school failed to recruit Smoker.

Current team members were feeling as good about football life at Michigan State as coach Williams, who was enjoying the fact a different kind of approach could still produce winning football.

Players could not fathom how opposite Saban and Williams were in their personal and professional ways. The new coach had an open-door policy that was just that—an office in which players were welcome to stop in and talk about anything. A player might notice cigars piled in a humidor behind the head coach's chair, leading to an impromptu, non-football discussion on another topic. Girls, studies, movies—you could find yourself talking about anything with Bobby Williams.

"Hey, Mr. Harker, sit down, what's going on?" Williams would say to a player like Paul Harker, the big offensive lineman from Ohio. "How's school going, how's your mom and dad? We're excited about this year. What are your thoughts and feelings? Let's go out for spring ball, stay focused, and get on with a big year."

Harker remembered meeting with Saban following his freshman year, in 1998, when injuries had forced him—a young lineman four months out of high school—into State's starting lineup. Saban met one-on-one with all the players who were coming back to gauge their status and plan for what they needed to think about heading into a new year.

"I'm a little disappointed with how you performed last season," Saban said. "I thought you had a chance to do more things."

Harker would have been crushed if he weren't more tempted to laugh. He was supposed to have been redshirted as a freshman. He ended up starting. He knew he had played half-decently, or he never would have been in the lineup.

Harker also knew Saban's psychology. If you did not instill in a player the intense desire—the absolute need—to get better from season to season, the player was unlikely to reach his potential. Even if you understood Saban's motivation, Harker and others concluded, playing for Williams was more enjoyable.

It would remain true as long as Michigan State continued winning. The Spartans were managing that nicely at the start of their 2000 season. They beat Marshall, Missouri and Notre Dame to go 3-0. Smoker got his chance when Ryan VanDyke suffered a hand injury in the opener against Marshall. However, the fast start concealed a reality about Michigan State's offense: Going with a true freshman at quarterback, no matter how talented he might be, would ultimately leave your offense vulnerable. All three wins were close—and the Notre Dame win almost downright miraculous as State hit on a fourth-and-10 pass to Herb Haygood in the waning moments.

Smoker had fine skills, but he was less than a year removed from a high-school football field. State's offensive coordinator, Morris Watts, was forced to keep MSU's game plan almost rudimentary until Smoker became seasoned enough to read defenses, make progressive choices on receivers, etc. He could not do it as a freshman, nor could MSU expect T.J. Duckett to make Michigan State an effective, single-dimensional running team. Charles Rogers, the hotshot receiver who had signed with MSU, was academically ineligible to play as a freshman. MSU—and Smoker—would have to wait a year for Sir Charles.

Four straight losses followed the 3-0 start, including three in a row when State's offense showed its impotence: 21-16 at Iowa, 17-10 on homecoming against Wisconsin, and 14-0 at Michigan. All were games State could have, and probably should have, won. Michigan State was following its 10-2 breakthrough year under Saban with a 5-6 thud in Williams' first year as head coach.

Worse from the assistant coaching staff's perspective, Michigan State was suffering from a bad case of anything goes off the field. It seemed players were involved in every misdemeanor in the book. Meetings, practices, classroom matters and general conduct had all begun to slip.

Wide receiver Charles Rogers joined State as the nation's most highly touted prep prospect. He mostly lived up to expectations during his three years in East Lansing, before injuries and a four-game suspension for substance abuse cast him as a disappointing first-round draft pick of the Detroit Lions.

Bobby Williams was a consummate nice guy who had a tough time cracking the whip. The way he had treated players at the Citrus Bowl had legitimized, in his mind anyway, that football players could be allowed their freedom and their fun and could still be counted on to perform on the field and off.

"If this happens again," he would tell his players at a team meeting, detailing the specific consequences for any repeat acts.

But it would happen again and rarely did punishment follow.

Assistant coaches were caught between wanting to knuckle down on players and being regarded as disloyal or oppositional to the head coach. Players began taking advantage of the split. If it came to a showdown between assistant and player, Bobby Williams was likely to work something out in favor of the athlete.

It was a matter of time, staffers thought, before the inmates would be running the Duffy Daugherty Football Building's resident asylum. That is, if they already weren't.

The quality of play on the field figured to improve in 2001. Smoker was now a sophomore with a bruising year of on-the-job training behind him. Rogers was getting ready to line up at wide-out, where he would be giving Big Ten defensive backs seizures with his size and speed.

The season started niftily as the Spartans beat Central Michigan and Notre Dame. State should have avoided a 27-26 loss at Northwestern in the 2001 season's third week. Williams blamed himself after Northwestern connected on a big pass that set up the winning field goal late in the game when MSU had only ten men on the field. It was a cross-up between defensive back Lorenzo Guess and linebacker Mike Labinjo, who had just gotten hurt on the kickoff and whose absence signaled to Guess that MSU was out of its nickel package. Northwestern made a hurry-up snap and hit a long pass against ten defenders.

After the frustrating loss to the Wildcats, Michigan State got better. The Spartans surprisingly rallied after halftime to wallop Wisconsin, 42-28, at Madison, coming back after a gruesome injury to cornerback Tyrell Dortch, a converted tailback They returned home for an epic against Michigan. In a thrilling climax to a tense battle, Smoker threw an end-zone pass to Duckett with one second on a game clock for a 26-24 victory. Michigan fans would forever point to this game as the worst case of home-cooked clock manipulation in NCAA football history.

The fun lasted all of one week. MSU lost three straight: 37-28 to Indiana, at East Lansing, no less; 24-14 at Purdue; and 42-37 to Penn State at Spartan Stadium. The three losses were all caused by sloppy mistakes and poor execution, particularly against the Hoosiers and Boilermakers.

State closed out the regular season with a game with Missouri that had been moved to December 1 from September 15 because of the 9/11 terrorist attacks. The Spartans destroyed Missouri, 55-7, in the makeup game.

MSU was 7-5 and headed for the Silicon Valley Bowl against Fresno State and the country's hottest quarterback, David Carr. Getting back to a bowl game was nice, but like 2000, when State believed it should have won seven or eight games, the Spartans understood they should have been playing somewhere on New Year's Day.

Smoker was almost as good as Carr in a game that saw two quarterbacks combine for a phenomenal 907 passing yards. Carr, who was on his way to the NFL Houston Texans, got 531 of them that afternoon in San Jose, California, with 35 of 58 passing with two interceptions. Smoker, who hit Rogers for an MSU-record 270 yards on ten catches, finished with 376.

Rogers had 184 of his yards on three passes: touchdowns of 72 and 69 yards, and another 43-yarder that set up MSU's winning TD. It meant he and NFL-bound junior running back T.J. Duckett (184 yards on 27 carries) combined for 454 of MSU's 586 total yards.

Duckett was less than four months from becoming a first-round pick by the Atlanta Falcons. Rogers, who had forfeited his freshman year because of NCAA Proposal 48 restrictions, was clearly headed for first-round terrain in another year when he would become draft-eligible.

It was the price you sometimes paid for signing talent so exceptional—and Rogers, in particular, was from another realm. Coaches thought of him as Andre Rison with size. He had sprint-class speed in the 4.3 to 4.4 range, which was about the rate at which Rison burned down a football field.

He had hands every bit as good as Rison, or Mark Ingram, another Flint receiver who had teamed with Rison before he marched off to the NFL. It was his 6-4 altitude, his exquisite ability to leap and to stretch, that made Rogers unstoppable.

Coaches would see Rogers during practice perform some kind of unprecedented pass-catching acrobatics and say to themselves: "He didn't do that," just as they had whispered in disbelief over Rison's gravity-defying antics almost fifteen years earlier.

Then they would review practice film and shake their heads: "He *did* do that."

Rogers was proving to be Rison's lesser in another area, however: durability. He would feel a twinge in his hamstring, or get dinged on a tackle, and suddenly it was game day and Rogers might have practiced once that week. The coaching staff rarely said anything—you weren't about to let opponents know Rogers was nicked—when he so often turned around on Saturday to provide ESPN's *SportsCenter* with a show's worth of highlights.

It was something the NFL would probably want to consider in another year when scouts would see in Rogers a franchise-caliber receiver who could break up games the way he had smashed up the Silicon Valley Bowl.

Bobby Williams and the Spartans were hardly concerned about Rogers and his 2003 draft status. They were far too enthused about the coming season. Rogers would be a junior. Smoker would be a junior and in his third year as starting quarterback.

Williams, likewise, was feeling better, more established, as he began season number three as Spartan head coach.

It was going to be a big year, 2002. There were several "ifs." If key people stayed healthy, if the team remained emotionally intact, and if bad luck decided to befall another team. If those things went the right way, Williams and his players figured the upcoming season could be wildly spectacular.

The Spartans were football players, not prophets. But they were right about 2002 becoming a spectacle. They simply could not have imagined the bizarre way the coming autumn would unfold.

CHAPTER 10

SIGHS AND SIGNS

LIFESTYLES HAD BECOME AS LOOSE AND AS WILD AS THE RUMORS wafting
through the Duffy Daugherty Football Building as Michigan State's 2002
football season arrived. A renowned party school had been burnishing its
reputation—deserved or not—in the life and times of its Big Ten college
football team.

Too many players were majoring in fun. And their teammates knew
what was going on. Even if they were shy on details, they were aware
that some of the prime-time Spartans were enjoying their nights well
into the morning.

One of those players was a surprise, given his background and the
position he played. Something definitely was up with Jeff Smoker, MSU's
junior quarterback, a genuine straight-arrow from a model Pennsylvania
family. Players guessed, or already knew, there were substance-abuse
problems, probably in the plural.

A teammate's girlfriend had seen MSU's quarterback at a fraternity
party, collapsed in the corner and dead drunk. They knew, as well, that he
was hanging around with an element not known for exemplary citizenship.

Coaches began to wonder what had happened to a quarterback who,
even as a freshman, had been diligent and clear-headed. Smoker as a
freshman or sophomore would watch film, take down notes, and delve
into questions the coaching staff had asked, and by afternoon's practice
have processed everything. Now he seemed lost, confused and inatten-

tive. His responses were puzzling. The staff wanted to believe these behaviors were symptoms of pressure. It probably hadn't helped that Smoker and sublime wide-receiver Charles Rogers had their likenesses stretched across murals on the exterior of Spartan Stadium as a 2002 football promotion.

Jeff Smoker became an instant star at MSU when his 68-yard, fourth-down touchdown pass to Herb Haygood beat Notre Dame in 2000. Smoker's subsequent personal problems were key to coach Bobby Williams losing his job at MSU in 2003, but Smoker bounced back his senior year under a new coach, John L. Smith.

If there were some kind of off-the-field influence—and with Smoker that seemed doubtful—the coaching staff figured it was nothing more than marijuana. It was commonly known that some players were smoking grass. But this was also a major university in 2002. Pot remained the illicit activity of choice for lots of college kids.

If there were deep-seated behavioral or disciplinary problems threatening MSU football in 2002, Bobby Williams was sufficiently unaware—and personally not disposed—to meet them head-on. Heading into Williams' third season as head coach, "Don't worry, be happy," seemed to be the team motto. MSU's football culture had taken on a Club Med personality. And this was a team that even the coach claimed could challenge for a national championship.

Matters grew steadily worse as fall practices convened in August. Players were by now certain that Jeff Smoker had a drug problem. Those who had been hearing stories about Smoker's night-into-morning stints of cocaine-snorting believed that behavior explained his on-the-field antics.

Jeff Smoker had always been razor-sharp in the huddle during his sophomore season, and even as a freshman. Now, he might hunch over to take the snap and then babble as he caught himself calling the wrong play: "Oh, wait, wait, wait, wait, wait … this is it."

As Smoker and the team struggled to prepare, Michigan State caught a soft first half of the season from the schedule-maker. Eastern Michigan and Rice were coming to East Lansing as part of a lineup that opened with five consecutive home games.

The Spartans dutifully destroyed EMU, 56-7, then rallied to dispatch Rice, 27-10. But the 2-0 start created false optimism in those not attuned to life within the Duffy Daugherty Football Building. What had been laxness was turning into defeatism.

It is a mindset not exclusive to football, but best represented by football's comprehensive makeup, which tends to stipulate that coaches as well as players thrive on intensity and passion under-girded by discipline.

Game-day performance is wrought from grueling practice elements of violence, painful conditioning, practice fatigue, dry meetings, and extreme punctuality. Unless a heightened brand of militaristic zeal, order and *esprit de corps* governs a team, it will almost surely begin to disintegrate.

The Spartans were one week from seeing their cracks turn into canyons. California struck the first blow. The Bears tromped through MSU, 46-22, at Spartan Stadium. A week later, Notre Dame arrived to squeak by State, 21-17, on a ridiculous 60-yard pass from Pat Dillingham to Arnaz Battle with 1:15 to play, a game-winner set in motion when Spartan cornerback Broderick Nelson fell down on the play. The score negated a brilliant, back-of-the-end zone grab by Charles Rogers moments earlier to apparently give MSU a win.

Michigan State was suddenly in a slide that would see the Spartans win only once in seven games—39-24 over Northwestern. The nosedive spanned one bleak loss after another: 44-16 at Iowa, 28-7 to Minnesota on homecoming in East Lansing, all ahead of a 49-3 annihilation by

Michigan at Ann Arbor.

In two short months, high hopes had dissolved into a mess. The carnage was complete: Discipline. Morale. Offense. Defense. Attitudes. Relationships.

Williams and his offensive coordinator, Morris Watts, got into a public spat following the Minnesota game. Williams had told the media, " I need to get more involved," in MSU's woeful offense.

Watts was unaware of what had been said until he got a heads-up that Saturday night from John Lewandowski, MSU's assistant athletic director for media relations. Lewandowski clued him on remarks that were bound to incite a coach who had been having his headaches, primarily because of Smoker's problems. MSU remained unaware officially of Smoker's traumas. Further complicating matters was Williams' insistence on a rigid ground attack that put the clamps on Watts' play-calling and passing preferences.

Watts was still furious when he got to Williams' office the next morning. He was going to resign on the spot.

"I've coached forty-one years and I don't want to be part of something where I'm going to be second-guessed," he told Williams. "I've been loyal to every guy I've worked for. But I will not coach for a second-guesser. If you don't have confidence in me, maybe I shouldn't be part of this thing."

Williams calmed Watts and the two agreed to get on with business. Watts had recognized Williams' remarks for what they were. Things had begun to fall apart and the head coach was becoming as desperate as he was exhausted by the stress. Watts was not insensitive to the pressures on Williams, but he needed answers for himself as well as to get to the bottom of the puzzling behavior of MSU's quarterback.

Smoker had been unraveling by the week. Only because he had never been a particularly good practice player were his junior-year mess-ups somewhat less alarming to a staff that had always seen Smoker put things together on Saturday. The difference now was that bad practices were running seamlessly into bad football games.

He would miss receivers in practice and on Saturday. A quarterback who did not have the strongest arm but who had been unfailingly accu-

rate in his first two seasons was now missing everyone. Rogers was losing at least a touchdown per game because of under-thrown passes.

MSU players had decided to stop the charade and press the issue.
Williams heard directly that Smoker's teammates knew something was
up and that their information was solid: It was cocaine. It would also have
not surprised them to know alcohol was a separate challenge for a man
four months past his twenty-first birthday.

Smoker had reached rock-bottom after the Minnesota game, a rancid
contest that had led to the Williams-Watts skirmish. He came into
Williams' office at the start of the week, plopped down in front of his head
coach, and said in a voice that signaled surrender:

"I need help."

"Hey," Williams said. "That's what I've been trying to get you to ask
for is some help."

In fact, Smoker's obvious drug problem was the worst-kept secret on
campus among players, as well as coaches. Various students and outsiders had also become privy to his night-time habits. Williams had
intended even before the third week of October to pull Smoker from the
starting lineup and take whatever steps were necessary with MSU officials to get an increasingly visible problem addressed.

Those plans changed at the last second. It was back to status quo.
Until something public happened, this was going to be Smoker's call.
Which, soon enough, it became.

He finally crashed on October 20, 2002. Smoker, a college junior living
an out-of-control nightmare, turned to coaches, to parents, and to MSU
executives and invited them into his darkening interior life.

Williams called Smoker's parents as a first step. Ron Mason, who was
only a hundred days into his new job as athletic director succeeding the
retired Clarence Underwood, was phoned, as was MSU president Peter
McPherson. Each was told that MSU football—and one of its highest-profile players—faced an enormous crisis.

Getting the appropriate medical help for Smoker was an immediate
goal. He was clearly going to need time to heal at a substance-abuse clinic, most likely Maplegrove, the West Bloomfield, Michigan, center affiliat-

Bobby Williams took over as interim coach for the 2000 Citrus Bowl, and rode the glory of an upset win over the Gators to become successor to Nick Saban as head coach. There would be fewer and fewer celebrations as his career unceremoniously ended with dismissal in mid-2003.

ed with Henry Ford Hospital.

McPherson, Mason, Williams and MSU officials met to decide on action that would ensure Smoker's privacy—a legal imperative, given the tough laws protecting students, NCAA athletes and their personal lives. They also had to deal with an enormously public event in the realm of college football.

The decision was to suspend Smoker indefinitely and to religiously suppress details of his condition. Williams would make junior Damon Dowdell MSU's new starting quarterback.

Williams told players before Wednesday's practice that Smoker was entering a rehab clinic to deal with substance-abuse problems. He would likely not be coming back to the team that season. Dowdell was MSU's new starting quarterback. Make sure both young men have your support, the coach said. We need to get on with the football season and make it successful.

As October melted away, chances of anything "successful" happening for Williams and the Spartans were all but delusional. Michigan State was outscored, 92-27, in its next two games against Wisconsin and Michigan.

As badly as things had turned in Williams' third season since replacing Nick Saban, few in East Lansing would have guessed that he was in his final days as head coach. MSU had never replaced a coach during the regular season and its normal practice would be to wait until a miserable autumn of football had dragged to a halt before Williams was fired, which by the day was becoming more probability than possibility.

Mason had one expectation with respect to football as he shifted in July of 2002 from Munn Arena to a new office at Jenison Fieldhouse: He was anticipating a bowl game and the likelihood MSU would re-do Bobby Williams' contract after his third year as head coach. Mason might have been a career hockey man, but he knew football and had a feel for coaches. When the season started, he had sensed things would be fine as Williams, Smoker and Rogers settled in with a schedule that looked so promising for Michigan State.

But for new athletic director Mason, red flags began waving by mid-season, not so much because of MSU's sudden string of losses, but more due to the problems cropping up away from Spartan Stadium. Smoker's crisis was frightening, of course, but almost encouraging for an athletic director who saw how model parents and proper intervention by MSU's medical staff had combined to give a young man a shot at recovery.

By October, Mason had begun preparing for the possibility Michigan State would be changing football coaches. Williams and the Spartans had a long way to go and anything was possible, even after Smoker left the team. But Mason had been told long ago by Joe Kearney, MSU's athletic director during the late 1970s who had hired Mason in 1979, that a university AD always needed to maintain a short list of candidates in the event he needed suddenly to hire a coach.

The Spartans' team was coming unglued so rapidly, in ways public and private, that Mason would have conceded what fans were steadily concluding: Williams was all but a goner. MSU's build-up to the November 2 game at Michigan was more like a death-row vigil. Michigan State had no chance, and everyone from Ann Arbor to Beaumont Tower knew it.

After the Wolverines barely worked up a sweat in winning by 46 points, Williams shuffled from MSU's dressing room after the game to an interview area where media had gathered and cameras had been stationed. It was going to be a miserable session. Michigan State had managed three points. The Spartans had offered zero resistance. MSU football had deteriorated into a kind of malaise on an autumn afternoon in front of 111,542 fans who might have been excused for covering their eyes.

"Do you think you still have control of this team?" asked Mickey York, from Fox Sports Net Detroit.

Williams seemed exhausted, disgusted, and out of answers and energy when he shook his head. In a low, hopeless voice he said: "I don't know."

It was the death knell for a forty-four-year-old head coach who had, in three words, forfeited any shot at finishing a job that fundamentally called for a man to remain in charge. Without control, Williams had no authority, no basis for leadership, and without those essential requirements for governing a football team, Williams—from MSU's executive perspective—no longer had a job.

Mason, McPherson, Lewandowski and Denbow met the next morning at Cowles House to discuss the unavoidable. The only debate was whether Williams would finish out the season or be replaced with three games remaining.

The group went back and forth, McPherson paying close attention— he knew that he needed Ferguson's support on any matter of significance, especially on this issue over the coming days. Ferguson was the premier power broker on MSU's board of trustees, and his backing was important. Mason, as well, hoped to have Ferguson's backing as Michigan State prepared for the likelihood that Williams' firing would be branded as racially motivated.

The decision was to fire Williams, effective at the end of the season. Legal language had to be worked out, but the formal announcement would be made Monday or Tuesday.

Williams, McPherson and Mason met through the morning on

Monday as Michigan State's execs made it clear they wanted Williams to finish the season. Williams, though, by Monday was having reservations about going quietly. Sunday's shock had worn off. There would need to be statements made.

McPherson feared Michigan State was headed for an ugly street fight fueled by racial interpretations that could make the old George Perles-John DiBiaggio feud look like nursery school by comparison. By Monday afternoon, the decision had been made: Williams was to be fired, effective immediately.

Mason was in his office at Jenison when he called Williams at about 5 p.m. and told him they needed to talk. It was not uncommon for the AD and head coach to huddle from time to time, often in Williams' office, where Mason was now heading, as uncomfortable as he had been at any moment in his twenty-three years at Michigan State.

But rather than meeting in Mason's office, they would assemble in a small counseling room at Clara Bell Smith Center.

John Lewandowski told Williams, "Bobby, Ron wants to see you at the Center."

"What's he gonna do," Williams replied, "fire me?"

When Williams walked into the room, there would be no chit-chat.

"Hey Bob, I've got bad news," Mason said. "We can't do this any longer."

Williams felt as if he had been clothes-lined by one of his defensive linemen. It hardly mattered that there had been endless talk for the past month suggesting Williams was a goner. The shock was staggering, so much so that Williams found himself instinctively in control mode. There were no outbursts, there was no outrage. Williams was composed as the athletic director outlined plans for finalizing contract obligations and making a formal announcement the next day.

Morris Watts had been around coaching long enough to know Williams was out. He was less sure why Mason wanted to meet with him.

"Morris, I've just fired Bobby," Mason said as he stepped into the meeting room. "I've talked it over with the president and I want you to be interim coach, with no guarantees of anything for you and the staff."

Watts was in no mood, or position, to argue. Nor, for that matter, did he have any problem taking control of a team that in another circumstance he would have enjoyed coaching.

He first needed to talk with Williams. Watts understood that criticism and job insecurity were things a head coach had to live with every week of every season he spent in football. Williams was today's lesson in reality. But a head coach was owed absolute loyalty from his assistants. Watts had stuck to his guns there for four decades and needed Williams to understand it now that Mason had filed his request.

When he met Williams in a meeting room a few minutes later it was as if the ousted head coach's face had frozen. Knowing you were leaving at the end of the season was one thing. Being evicted at the end of a Monday practice was crushing.

"Bobby, I've been asked to be interim head coach," Watts said. "They've asked me, and I'm thinking about it. I'll probably do it. Somebody's gonna have to do it."

Williams turned without saying a word and walked out of the room. Another man had his job and there wouldn't be any fellowship. He was gone from Michigan State football, avoiding even a farewell address to players who were showing a range of responses to the firing of Bobby Williams.

Watts got a first taste of the lingering bitterness when he met with each player Tuesday morning in his first appearance as interim head

Offensive coordinator Morris Watts served under George Perles, Nick Saban and Bobby Williams, eventually becoming interim head coach when Williams was fired in 2002 after an embarrassing loss to Michigan.

coach. It was an attempt to heal and to reassure players that whatever was right about Michigan State football, whatever was worth retaining from a difficult season, was going to be left in place and made better over the final three weeks.

One player stunned Watts when he said: "Coach, I don't think I'm gonna play Saturday."

"Well, are you hurt?"

"No," the player said. "I just don't know how to handle this."

Watts was hours into a new job that had already turned sticky.

"Do you want to be a first-round draft pick?" he asked the player, who nodded.

"Do you think they want to draft a guy who can't handle things when they've fallen apart?"

Watts enlisted the help of African-American faculty members and executives in talking with various players, realizing a joint effort by educators and coaches, black and white, was the only way around a catastrophic team split. If it happened, it would be reminiscent of Michigan State's January 1975, walkout by black basketball players minutes before MSU hosted Indiana in the Big Ten opener. The walkout became a delayed fuse that blew up on Gus Ganakas and cost him his job as head coach fourteen months later. Watts had no illusions about becoming a head coach. He also wanted no part of presiding over a rift as nasty as this stood to be if things turned crazy.

Charles Rogers had been one of the players considering boycotting Saturday's game. He had been lobbied by, among others, Thomas Wright, the defensive back and co-captain from Lake Wales, Florida, who had met with several other players Monday night at Williams' house, where they had decided to go through with the boycott.

Not every player was so disposed. Dowdell, the new starting quarterback, was against any walkouts. Rogers, after getting counsel he trusted, likewise decided to play against Indiana. Players settled in by mid-week and practices were smooth.

Watts' first game as interim coach was even better: Michigan State romped over the Hoosiers, 56-21, as Rogers had a huge day: two touchdowns, 102 yards on only five catches. Watts at least wanted the satisfaction of finishing the season with some sizzle and leaving the team with good feelings about the way they had closed after a miserable autumn filled with turmoil. Smoker had gone through his personal crisis. A head coach had been axed eight weeks into the season. A little fun in the final twenty days of football was the least a staff and a hundred football players deserved.

Watts had enjoyed getting his offense back against Indiana. He shelved the grind-it-out stuff Williams had been insisting upon and aired out the football, which had pleased Dowdell as much as it did Rogers. Some players had suspected, incorrectly, that Watts was pulling his punches until he became head coach.

Purdue was next, the only home game Watts would work as head coach. He was still dealing with a bruised co-captain in Wright and had toyed with the notion of keeping him off the field against the Boilermakers. On a fourth-and-8, make-it-or-break-it moment with 3:18 on the clock, Purdue quarterback Kyle Orton (Brandon Kirsch had gone out with an injury on the previous play) lofted a 40-yard pass over Cedric Henry's head and into the hands of John Sandeford for a touchdown that beat MSU, 45-42.

Michigan State was now, certifiably, a dead football team. Practices before the season-ender at Penn State were so bad they might as well have been canceled. The Spartans were slaughtered at Happy Valley, 61-7, in a game that, over a three-hour span, was as ugly as an entire 2002 season that would go down as the most tumultuous ever experienced by a Michigan State football team.

ATHLETIC DIRECTOR RON MASON had already been tearing into the job of picking a new coach. He had been asking for advice ahead of the most important task an athletic director confronts—an assignment he was tackling less than five months into his new job.

Mason called an old confidant from Lake Superior State, Bud Cooper, the athletic director for whom he had once worked. He called Andy Geiger at Ohio State, who had just hired Jim Tressel following John

Cooper's retirement. Although he was being given latitude to find a new coach, he knew he needed help, which led to the hiring of a college coaching head-hunter, Jed Hughes, who had worked with Geiger.

He drew up a strategy that was sanctioned by his bosses, McPherson and Poston:

(1) Mason wanted no deadline on naming a new coach. He was afraid that a deadline could lead to impulsiveness when it came time to choose.

(2) He needed to be the person doing the interviewing. This time around there was going to be no search and selection committee grilling candidates. Mason had the green light and relished it. If he knew anything from his years in athletics, he knew who could coach.

Mason was sensitive to notions that autonomy would be perceived as arrogance. He handled that by asking for a broad-based advisory committee of almost three-dozen people who were asked to list all the components and qualities they wanted in a new football coach. He included ex-athletes, alumni, boosters, business people, students and faculty. Mason was pleased to learn that MSU's constituencies wanted exactly what he had decided football at Michigan State needed, beginning with longevity.

MSU had watched Nick Saban leave for LSU in the closing weeks of a hugely successful season. Twenty-three years earlier, Darryl Rogers had split for Arizona State a year after finishing in a tie for the Big Ten championship. In each case their successors—Muddy Waters and Williams—had lasted only three seasons. Michigan State was tired of interim coaches, of interlopers and carpetbaggers and all the other short-timers who had either left or been forced from a job that demanded people who were committed to the football mission in East Lansing.

Mason and Hughes were putting together essential data that would provide a virtual computer printout of people with coaching DNA that was a match for MSU in December of 2002. Mason wanted not only a coach who would stick at Michigan State for the long term, but also a man who, preferably, had sufficient head-coaching experience—an antidote to problems Mason and Michigan State believed were a product of Williams and his inexperience.

Mason's printout listed six names:

- Marvin Lewis, defensive coordinator for the Washington Redskins
- Norv Turner, former Dallas Cowboys head coach and now assistant head coach and offensive coordinator for the Miami Dolphins
- Les Miles, a one-time University of Michigan player and assistant coach who was head coach at Oklahoma State
- Doug Williams, head coach at Grambling
- Jimmy Raye, the former Michigan State quarterback and career NFL assistant who was now assistant head coach for the New York Jets
- John L. Smith, head coach at Louisville.

Lewis was Mason's first choice for various reasons, all compelling: He had a rich football pedigree, charisma that would win over fans, great cachet with recruits because of his football background, and African-American ethnicity that would be appreciated by a football team featuring a black majority, which had been particularly wounded by Williams' departure.

He was also a hot name in the NFL, where it was assumed he would quickly return, even if he were named head coach at Michigan State. That possibility was going to make it difficult for Michigan State and Mason when an expressed goal was to hire a man who would be in East Lansing for at least five years.

As for Smith, Mason had already made a casual visit to see him in Louisville, before formal discussions and an official request for permission to interview him, simply to get a feel for whether Smith and MSU would have mutual interest. A ninety-minute conversation at Smith's home, during which their wives walked around Louisville, made it clear the answer was yes.

Next up was a lengthy interview with Lewis, at Lewis' home in the Washington, D.C., suburbs. Mason had a good feeling about Lewis even before they sat down to talk for nearly four hours. The interview was so smooth Mason was saying to himself early in their conversation: "This guy has all the qualities."

Lewis, however, had the answer to a question they both had to confront:

"My decision is whether I want to go to college or to the NFL," he acknowledged, repeating to Mason a choice only Lewis could make.

It was possible that a coach so torn might opt for Michigan State now, and the NFL later. Mason had seen enough coaches put MSU through the anxiety grinder to want any repeats there.

"Ron, if I commit to you, I'll commit for five years," Lewis said. "And if I do come to MSU, you can put a buyout clause in that contract that will shut up everyone."

Lewis needed to visit State's campus, to get a taste for East Lansing, and to get a sense for whether college coaching could replace his greater professional passion: to become an NFL head coach.

He and his wife, Peggy, flew to Lansing and checked into the East Lansing Marriott at University Place Hotel. Then Mason and Greg Ianni, the associate athletic director, took the couple on a campus tour. They saw Spartan Stadium and stopped by the Duffy Daugherty Football Building.

Lewis quickly concluded: "We need to upgrade Duffy."

He had done his homework about MSU. Lewis knew details about the University, its size, scope, history and relationship with the Big Ten. He was crackling-bright and compelling.

Mason would have been pleased to announce that Marvin Lewis would be Michigan State's next head football coach. Peter McPherson would have been just as delighted following a breakfast at Cowles House the next morning, where fifteen to twenty MSU dignitaries had gathered to meet a man who was going to become coach—if he wanted to.

The Lewises flew back to Washington late that morning. Lewis and MSU each needed time to think, a process that was going to mean extra time for Lewis as he and NFL teams looking for head coaches increasingly became linked. The more Mason thought about it, the more he realized Lewis had his heart set on the NFL. There was no point in amplifying Michigan State's sales pitch. One month later, Lewis got his wish when he was named head coach of the Cincinnati Bengals.

So, Mason was back to his list. And back on the plane.

Having talked with Smith and Lewis, Mason then visited each of the remaining four candidates on, or near, his home turf. Miles, Williams, Turner and Raye all had their strengths, and each had varying degrees of passion to coach at Michigan State.

Smith had been winning on two fronts: He had head-coaching experience and he was asking all the right questions, the same ones Mason
knew he would have been asking before taking a job at another school in
another state. Mason had done it himself when he and Kearney talked
twenty-four years earlier, when Kearney selected him over Jerry York of
Miami (Ohio).

Mason liked another reality about Smith and his resume: Smith had
turned around three different programs: at Louisville, at Utah State and at
Idaho. Still, he wondered why Smith—who had a good program going at
age fifty-four—would want to leave Louisville for a brand new conference and region.

"Ron, we can't get to the BCS here," Smith said, facing an essential
reality about a school from Conference USA, even if it were in the process
of becoming a Big East member. The BCS and its four-game college bowl
showcase were going to be the province of elite conferences: Pac-10,
Southeast Conference, Big 12 and the Big Ten. Outsiders simply could not
match all those BCS computer points generated by the big boys.

Smith understood that wanting a BCS ticket and getting one could be
two different galaxies of dream and reality. Mason had clued him in:
Michigan State football was in some disarray. Jeff Smoker's loss to substance abuse was by no means an isolated case. Academics had slipped,
badly. Attrition was a threat until Michigan State got discipline reinstated
and scholarship numbers in line. How many washouts might yet occur,
Mason could not say, but there was work to do for an athletic director and
definitely for a new head football coach.

Smith realized there would be some reconstruction, more, probably
than anyone was banking on in December 2002. It was the nature of college football. Everyone wants to believe their school can get to the prom-
ised land—in a hurry.

Diana Smith had a sense East Lansing was probably right for them. It
had to do with a wife's perspective on her husband. She had known better than anyone what Smith had done at Idaho (53-21 record), at Utah
State (16-18, but two six-win seasons after inheriting a dismal program),

and now at Louisville (41-21).

"One of the things you do best in your life is rebuild," she said. "Don't close your eyes to something that could be good for everybody."

Smith was in a mood to agree. Michigan State had a place on college football's big stage. It had all that glitzy history from the Biggie Munn-Duffy Daugherty decades, not to mention a team that had gone 10-2 only three years earlier. The paychecks were going to be fatter (Smith was making $800,000 annually at Louisville on a contract that ran through 2008).

This was the right job if Michigan State thought he was the right man.

Mason was abiding by CIA-grade secrecy as he and Jed Hughes arranged interviews and kept media speculation to a minimum. Lewis and his candidacy were public. Les Miles was known to be on Mason's list, as was Doug Williams. Norv Turner had been mentioned. Smith had escaped scrutiny, mostly because word from national coaching circles was that he had a prohibitive buyout arrangement at Louisville. But there was no such compensation due Louisville if Smith were to take a better job. It allowed Mason to get busy settling on a coach who, among all the six he was considering, ranked the closest to matching up with his categorical wish list for MSU.

Mason had been thinking deeply about commitment—about a future coach's loyalty to MSU and about a university's obligation to a good head football coach. He had been planning on offering the right man a long and lucrative contract. Mason had seen Saban leave East Lansing three years earlier because of penny-wise, pound-foolish dollar squabbles that set in motion a messy, and unnecessary, departure that had left MSU football years behind where it should have been in December of 2002.

Money would be no object this time. A six-year contract in the ten-million-dollar range was there for Smith if he pushed for it. Michigan State would choke off any financial inducement to leave East Lansing by making him the highest-paid head coach in the Big Ten. It was time for Michigan State to quit fooling around, to shut up and put up, and pay John L. Smith, a certifiable football fix-it wizard, what he was bound to make in a few years, anyway, considering the way markets were headed for a coach who was destined to succeed.

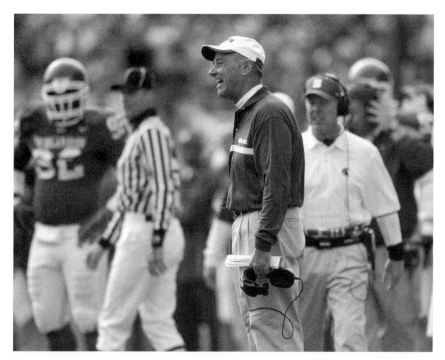

Football coach John L. Smith started surprisingly well at MSU in 2003 with QB Jeff Smoker at the helm, but seasons of 5-6 and 5-7 clearly added pressure heading into 2006.

Mason was hiring Smith with a sense of certitude that came naturally to a man who was as self-assured an athletic director as he had been behind a hockey bench for more than thirty years. Mason had followed a failsafe blueprint in selecting a failsafe head coach. Michigan State was about to triumph because of the appointment of John L. Smith, a proven winner, a seasoned and solid football man, as head coach and leader of a soon-to-be-revived program that would get progressively stronger throughout the decade.

Negotiations remained stealthy, so much so that Louisville officials were not formally approached until December 17. Smith had a bowl game to coach—the GMAC Bowl on December 18 at Mobile, Alabama. Michigan State had decided it wanted no part in grabbing a head coach ahead of his final game, or even officially contacting him, as had been the case when Saban left for LSU. Even if that meant recruiting would get a late start, Mason concluded it was not worth the disruption or the ill will that would be created with Louisville.

Smith's candidacy remained top secret a week before Christmas. Only in the early evening of December 18, two hours before Louisville and Marshall were to take the field at Ladd Peebles Stadium in Mobile, Alabama, was John L. Smith's name linked in any credible way to the job vacancy at Michigan State. It came by way of ex-Spartan star and former World Series hero Kirk Gibson, who was working with Eli Zaret and Gary Danielson as one-third of *The Locker Room* radio program on WXYT-AM in Detroit.

Gibson had been tipped off. John L. Smith and Michigan State were now a public romance as media and Internet sites got hold of a breaking story just as the Cardinals were going through their pre-game routine. Mason's secret, known only to three or four people was now about to turn a nationally televised bowl game into a debacle that would make a spectacle of John L. Smith's shift from Louisville to East Lansing.

Mason was watching the game on TV at his home in East Lansing, becoming more angry and embarrassed by the moment. Louisville players could be seen on the sideline talking into their cell phones, yammering about a head coach who was about to become their former head coach as news broke coast to coast that Smith was bound for East Lansing.

About as many people in Louisville had been aware of Smith's romance with Michigan State as knew about it in East Lansing. Mason had waited until the day of Louisville's bowl game to formally ask athletic director Tom Jurich for permission to talk with the Cardinals' head coach. Informal conversations could, in most circumstances, occur between a school and a coach as long as they adhered to the spirit and letter of "informal."

Hammering out a contract was going to require dispensation from Smith's long-term arrangement with Louisville as well as formal permission for the two parties to negotiate.

"I'd like to come down the day after the bowl, or whenever you get home, and officially talk with John L.," Mason told Jurich, who said there would be no problem.

Problems, instead, were cropping up in East Lansing. They included an unhappy Joel Ferguson, who had been screened along with other trustees from direct involvement in a hiring process that was all Mason's.

"I hope he doesn't accept the job," Ferguson said as news broke Smith was bound for Michigan State.

Ferguson had been irked by Williams' firing, and was in no mood to see an Idaho-born, fifty-four-year-old cowboy coach strut into East Lansing as the new Spartans football sheriff. That, however, was what Ferguson and Michigan State were about to get.

Still stinging over the previous night's fiasco, when a football game turned into a sideline gossip fest, Mason flew via charter to Louisville the next day to pick up Smith and nail down contract details. Louisville's 38-15 loss to Marshall in Smith's last game was almost a sidelight to Smith's introduction as MSU's new coach. The formal coronation took place that Thursday evening, one week before Christmas, at a press conference in the Clara Bell Smith Center.

No one quite knew, late that cold night in East Lansing, what to make of someone so different from the previous strain of head football coach at Michigan State. Smith was unlike any of his predecessors. He was animated in the manner of a televangelist, but with a kind of Great Plains voice. There was nothing low-key about his demeanor, as there had been with Williams, with Saban, or even with Perles, who offset football-field fire with a kind of good-humored, easy breeziness. Go all the way back to the crinkle-eyed Irishman himself, Duffy Daugherty, and it was clear Smith was cut from a different bolt of coaching cloth.

"I promise you this," he said in carnival-barker fashion, "you're gonna see a good product. You're gonna see a good product on the field, you're gonna see a good product in the classroom, and you're gonna see a good product downtown in the community."

Smith had done his homework and understood the clean-up was going to extend beyond MSU's won-loss record. Diplomatic challenges were just as dicey, beginning with Ferguson, the powerhouse trustee whose affinity for Michigan State sports meant he and the football coach would be intersecting.

As he knew and had prepared for, Smith was asked at the media gathering how he expected to get along with a high-profile trustee who opposed his hiring.

"Where is he?" Smith barked in *faux*-angry fashion. "He and I are gonna fight."

There were a few chuckles.

Smith turned serious.

"People are not going to agree," the new football coach said, "on all the decisions people make."

Smith was keeping two of Williams' assistants, Reggie Mitchell and Jeff Stoutland, but new staffers were otherwise being hired and jumping into an eleventh-hour recruiting rush that, by the first week of February, 2003, had landed nineteen kids, some of whom were going to eventually help: Jehuu Caulcrick, Pete Clifford, DeAndra Cobb, Greg Cooper, Mike Gyetvai, Terry Love, Kaleb Thornhill and Joe Toth.

Once his salvaged recruiting season ended, Smith could get down to the business of his existing team. It was not a pretty picture.

There were big academic problems. As of spring, 2003, there were thirty-three kids in academic peril and destined for summer school. It was worse than ironic that the falloff in academic performance came just as a six-million-dollar treasure known as the Clara Bell Smith Student Athlete Academic Center was operating at full steam.

Deeper analysis came to show that the Smith Center was an oasis for kids whose academic skills were already reasonably well-developed. High-risk students were another issue. They tended to be from poor urban areas where schools, and at-home structure, can be more than challenging. They needed more hands-on help and attention than they were getting as dozens began to slip and regress in the classroom.

Demetrius Marlowe, who was director of MSU's student-athlete support services, was accountable, and soon was replaced by Jim Pignitaro, a former MSU athletics academic counselor who had left in 2000 for the head academics job with Eastern Michigan University's athletic department. He was brought in to clean up immediately a situation that could have gutted Smith's first-season team.

Smith was awakening to a more dangerous situation that had become part of too many players' lifestyles.

"Here's the deal, gentlemen," the new coach said at his first major team meeting. "We have a few cut-and-dried rules, and the first is, no drugs. Period. End of story."

When the first drug-test results were forwarded, Smith was appalled. There were positives galore.

Clearly, some of the existing players were about to become former players. Evidence of marijuana—and worse—was heavy. This was by no means a case of isolated substance abuse, the kind that had caused Jeff Smoker to leave the team at mid-season and be admitted to a recovery program.

Although Michigan State had a standard practice of testing players each week during the season, a number of players under Williams had been figuring ways to beat the inspection. They would know a test was coming after practice. Too often, they were excusing themselves from practice before completion for one inventive reason or another. It was a football culture run amok.

Smith in any event was going to plug in his system, with whatever players survived the off-season winnowing, and give it a go. He had respectable front-line talent, if not much depth. What no one knew was whether Smith would have the quarterback he needed to run his spread offense with its sets of four-plus receivers.

The triggerman he needed was Smoker. Whether a player who had come so close to destroying his career, if not his life, could make it all the way back was a 50-50 proposition, at best. Smoker, though, was doing everything within his might to recover fully from addiction, and resume his life as a student and one of the country's better college quarterbacks.

As a first step, he apologized to his teammates during a meeting at the Duffy Daugherty Building. Working his way up from the equivalent of walk-on status was another mission being accomplished. Getting up for 5 a.m. running and workouts was not a difficult hurdle for a young man who months earlier had been losing nights not to sleep but to addiction.

Smoker was looking like his old, healed, self during spring practice.

He got no breaks on the depth chart. Damon Dowdell was listed as starter and was ahead of Smoker who, technically, was in position to win back his old job if he played with skill and command as the new season progressed.

From the beginning of fall drills it was evident to coaches and to teammates he was back. Smith restored him as Michigan State's starting quarterback prior to the season-opener against Western Michigan. The Spartans won, 26-21, beginning a seven-week uprising that saw MSU go 6-1. The only loss came in the closing seconds to Louisiana Tech, 20-19. Smoker, Smith and the Spartans were the Big Ten's big surprise.

It was surprising only when contrasted to the poor performance of the 2002 team. The 2002 Spartans had finished 4-8 and gotten Williams fired in the process. Now, Smoker was back and so was an offense that was tank-tough up front (Paul Harker, Sean Poole, Joe Tate, Chris Morris, Steve Stewart) and had enough skill in the backfield (Jaren Hayes) to complement a skilled squad of receivers: Kyle Brown, Agim Shabaj, Aaron Alexander and tight end Jason Randall.

There was muscle on defense, as well: Greg Taplin, Matthias Askew, Kyle Rasmussen, Clifford Dukes, Ronald Stanley, Seth Mitchell and Mike Labinjo, although the secondary was young and on the light side: Darren Barnett, Greg Cooper, Jason Harmon and converted receiver Roderick Maples.

The Spartans were acting as if Smith's BCS Bowl thoughts had been clairvoyant. Reality set in the next two weeks with losses to Michigan, 27-20, and to Ohio State, 33-23, ahead of another customary dismantling by the Big Ten's resident bar-room bouncers, Wisconsin, which destroyed the Spartans, 56-21. But State rallied with a regular season-closing mop-up of Penn State, 41-10, at Spartan Stadium.

Smith had lost three conference games in three weeks, but still finished in a tie for fourth place, which was enough to make him Big Ten Coach of the Year.

MSU had taken advantage of a cooperative schedule (seven home games, no Purdue, no Northwestern) to paint over a deeper structural problem: The team was thin, especially on defense, and was no match for brawny Big Ten teams, as had been evident against Michigan, Ohio State and Wisconsin. State's bowl-game draw was going to provide more of the same: Nebraska, which was meeting the Spartans in the Alamo Bowl at San Antonio, Texas.

Nebraska pounded MSU's defense early and took a 17-3 lead at the half. It ended up as the final score in a game where Michigan State's biggest loss had nothing to do with a scoreboard. It was a knee injury to freshman quarterback Drew Stanton, who was scheduled in a few months to replace the NFL-bound Smoker as MSU's starting QB.

Smith was about to take his first fusillade of industrial-strength flak from Spartans fans who had not been keen on Stanton's role as a punt-team performer. Smith had been aware of the risk, but thought it was a good gamble. Michigan State had too few bodies, and the multi-skilled Stanton wanted to play on special teams if it got him into a game.

Stanton was a solid tackler with great hands, a talented football player, and Smith had decided when the season began that he had too few of those to worry about his understudying quarterback getting hurt. Earlier in the season, Stanton's muff of an onside kick against Louisiana Tech had perhaps cost MSU a win, but a week later his recovery in a similar situation against Notre Dame had resulted in victory.

Attrition was, in fact, the story of Michigan State football as Smith's regime unfolded. Washouts due to bad grades, bad habits, or transfers, had sent scholarship numbers into a nosedive. Just as Nick Saban had only 71 scholarship players—14 below the NCAA 85-man limit—in 1998 when the Spartans finished 6-5, Smith was losing ground that could not be made up when single-class recruiting was limited to 25 players.

JOHN L. SMITH'S 2004 TEAM would have it only slightly better: seventy-seven scholarship players, a figure that would drop to seventy-three in 2005. Previously under Saban, attrition and NCAA probation had left State with an under-numbered rebuilding program. Saban had slogged through his first four seasons in East Lansing from 1995-98, giving way to a 10-2 breakout when scholarships edged past the eighty mark in 1999.

Smith, however, was dealing not with NCAA probation, but with players lost, mostly because of slovenly behavior. Off-the-field conduct had deteriorated quickly under Williams. MSU was going to remain dramatically down in the number of able Big Ten-caliber bodies available—and, significantly, in the number of fourth- and fifth-year seniors—until Smith strung together enough consecutive recruiting classes of viable kids to make a team complete.

One sure way to decide if a team heading into the season had a chance was to count scholarships. A team stuck in the seventies, the lower seventies especially, could expect second-half breakdowns and blowout losses against physical teams. Injuries and fatigue commonplace in an NCAA Division I football season made the eighty-five-man limit a bare minimum for any successful program.

Players tended to like Smith at the outset in a way that was very different from the manner in which they had enjoyed Williams when he took over in December 1999. Smith was light-hearted, he could joke, and he would smile. He brought an element of fun to the football field, even as he tightened MSU's ship overall.

Players had never encountered a coach who could make them believe football—even when it was drudgery—was fun, and that playing well made it all the more gratifying. Players had concluded halfway through the 2003 season that as bad as things had been at the same point a year earlier, they were now every bit as good under Smith.

Winning football could be another issue. Smoker was gone and Stanton was coming back steadily, if slowly, from his bowl-game knee injury. By the fourth game of the season, against Indiana, Stanton was starting quarterback ahead of Dowdell and Stephen Reaves.

The 2004 Spartans had massacred Minnesota, 51-17, on homecoming at MSU to move State to 4-3 with a trip to Ann Arbor against Michigan next on the slate.

Smith's first season-and-a-half at MSU had been solid, if not necessarily dramatic. He and his program needed one of those Sunday front-page-headline victories. They needed a landmark game to bring into the national spotlight a coach who—for all his climbs up Mount Kiliminjaro and his sprints with the bulls at Pamplona—kept a modest profile.

What better place to make a real statement that State was back than in Ann Arbor?

With 8:43 to play, DeAndra Cobb took a misdirection handoff from Dowdell and tore past stunned safety Earnest Shazor on a 64-yard romp to put the Spartans ahead, 27-10. Dowdell was in the game after Stanton, who was having a colossal day, got his shoulder mauled on yet another keeper that was part of an 80-yard, twelve-carry afternoon for State's two-way dynamo.

Then Michigan got busy against a MSU team, proving how low scholarship numbers and frayed personnel had left MSU vulnerable to a team and to a program that was MSU's direct opposite in depth and endurance.

Braylon Edwards, a tremendous game-breaking talent, took apart a much shorter Spartan cornerback, Jaren Hayes, who also happened to be a running back converted to defensive back as Michigan State had sought to patch one of its ample holes on defense.

Edwards scored slam-bang touchdowns on passes of 36 and 21 yards. In five minutes, 44 seconds, it was a blinding seventeen-point rally with Edwards' TD grabs from Chad Henne, an onside kick the Spartans couldn't recover, and a 24-yard field goal by Garrett Rivas. With the score 27-27 and 2:59 to play, 111,000 hearts were beating like conga drums.

After a couple of overtime field goals it was 30-30, then 37-30 after Jason Teague put MSU back on top with a three-yard run. Michigan quarterback Chad Henne hit Jason Avant on a five-yard TD to tie it again, after which Henne hit—who else—Edwards with a 24-yard laser to make it 44-37. After State missed on its chance to tie, that was the ballgame.

Long before this November 1, 2004, football game between Michigan and Michigan State had become a rivalry classic, MSU fans had become fatigued to a point of anguish by Michigan's ability to stick it to the Spartans in college athletics' biggest sport, and most public annual benchmark of superiority.

Spartans fans were sick of losing and disgusted by U-M's dominance. They were more sick than angry, more angry than frustrated, when the Wolverines showed such brilliance, not to mention the kind of luck that had seen an onside kick go U-M's way, as well as Edwards strip a perfectly defended pass from Hayes. Branch Rickey, however, had it right: Luck was the residue of design. Michigan, quite clearly, had designed a self-perpetuating college football program. It bred excellence that would continually draw the best recruits, put Michigan in the best bowl games and, in this first weekend of November, invite ESPN-high-light finishes over its ego-bruised rival. Michigan State wanted for itself the kind of success to which Michigan was accustomed. The 2004 game had made clear—again—how different were the fortunes at two neigh-boring Big Ten universities.

The Spartans lost the next week, as well, this time to Ohio State, 32-19. MSU's only victory in its last five games was a surprising 49-14 walloping of unbeaten, fourth-ranked Wisconsin. Losses at Penn State (37-13) and Hawaii (41-38) finished a 5-7, no-bowls season for Smith and the Spartans.

Michigan State was in for a longer reconstruction period than most fans had forecast when Smith was hired. On the surface, State was in decent shape with a veteran quarterback and deft skill players. Defense, though, was going to be an issue again in 2005 as the earlier attrition left a Big Ten team far too light and thin on defense.

Recruiting was going reasonably well—national rankings of State's classes were fairly uninspiring, although Smith's had signed a second-year class with respectable promise after making it to a bowl game in his first year. Still, the personnel were limited in numbers and in strength, particularly on defense.

IN THE EARLY AUTUMN OF 2005, there was little to find wrong with the MSU football team, apart from its wobbly kicking game. The Spartans rocketed to a 4-0 start, thanks, notably, to an overtime victory at Notre Dame when Jason Teague sprinted down the right sideline for MSU's winning touch-down after taking a last-second pitch from Stanton. That had been a huge boost in self-esteem and national prestige.

MSU's season, however, was about to be defined by a series of mid-season mishaps and revelations.

The deterioration began a week later, at Spartan Stadium, against the old villain, Michigan, which had enough of its usual moxie to polish off

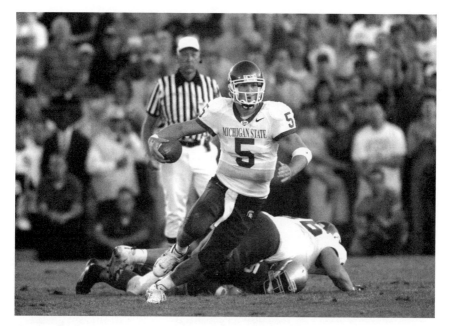

Quarterback Drew Stanton carries the ball in 2005 against Notre Dame, one play before his flip to Jason Teague would result in a game-winning, overtime, touchdown.

the Spartans, 34-31, in overtime. A bad year for the Wolverines (7-4 regular-season record) might have been catastrophic had MSU's wheezing kicking game been even average.

John Goss and his shaky ways had come to define MSU's kicking hang-ups in 2005. What must be remembered is that kicking is a psychological exercise even more than it is physical, and never is it a complete surprise when a player becomes rubbery-legged. Booting a football between narrow goal-post uprights, with 100,000 or so folks looking on, sometimes with millions more watching on television, with a team's and a university's fortunes hanging in the balance, is pressure disproportionate to the act, particularly for a twenty-year-old. Still, that is what kickers do, and by the time they have ascended to a starting role in college or in the NFL, their performance capabilities have generally been established.

Generally, that is. Makeup still has everything to do with the job. Paul Edinger had been a perfect match of mind and kicking skill during his days at MSU in the late 1990s. Dave Rayner had been solid during the Bobby Williams and early John L. Smith era. Goss, however, had won the job in 2005 primarily because he was not seriously challenged. It was not an ideal outcome for him, or for his team. His confidence waned as he slogged through the early season.

Against the Wolverines, Goss missed a 23-yard field goal in the fourth quarter that could have won the game, and a 37-yarder in overtime that would have put pressure on Michigan. Garrett Rivas, Michigan's more dependable kicker, had helped offset Goss' misses by cobbling a 27-yarder with 48 seconds left in regulation that would have won the game for Michigan. Rivas missed, in every bit as ugly a fashion as Goss had stumbled, but got a second chance from 35 yards during overtime, and this time Rivas connected.

As Michigan won the football game, Smith lost his patience. In between general indictments of a team that had invited U-M to win a game MSU had every opportunity to grab, the Spartans' head coach got to the point about two very manageable, and two very missed, field goals.

"The kicking stunk," growled Smith, who was still in a lousy mood at his press briefing two days later.

"We're going to open it up and see if we can bring in some guys from campus to find a kicker," Smith said. "Why not? We have some young kids here, and it may even be a freshman."

Smith's words, which struck the coach and others as simple candor, bothered plenty of MSU fans who thought a young man was being personally blamed for a lost football game.

Smith was not sympathetic. Quite apart from the missed kicks, he wanted from Goss a different disposition, which the head coach believed was basic comportment for any player or any kicker. If it sounded as if he were beating up on one player, so be it.

"Psychologically, I could care less," Smith said. "You either become more mentally tough, or somebody else will kick, and that's how I approach it."

The Spartans were now headed for Columbus, Ohio, and for what figured to be more trouble, no matter who kicked. Michigan State instead played excellent football through two quarters. State's vertical-horizontal offensive schemes made a mess of OSU's defense just as MSU and Stanton had managed against other teams in earlier games. MSU took a 17-3 lead against the Buckeyes, hushing up another rabid bunch of 101,000-plus at Ohio Stadium, and was set to make it 20-3 as the Spartans drove deep in the first half's closing seconds.

Stanton needed only to spike the ball on fourth down to kill the clock with a few seconds remaining, which would have allowed a chip-shot field goal by a kicker who, as MSU knew all too well, was not necessarily a sure thing.

Neither Smith nor his assistants felt as if anything was amiss as MSU made its decisions in those closing seconds. There had been clear headset communication among coaches on the sideline and in the press box. Stanton was going to take a snap, spike the ball, and stop the clock with a few seconds showing. A slam-dunk field goal – no matter who was kicking it—would follow.

Suddenly, Josh Harrica, a graduate assistant coach, yelled "go" to the field goal team. There was a Chinese fire drill of bodies passing one another as the clock began to run. Stanton ran off the field as Goss scrambled to get a rapid-fire snap and boot the ball before time ran out.

The kick was blocked, scooped up by Ohio State's Ashton Youboty, and with all of Ohio Stadium roaring like a squadron of B-2 bombers, Youboty sped 72 yards for a touchdown that turned what should have been a 20-3 lead for the Spartans into a 17-10 momentum pirouette for the Buckeyes.

In one monumentally ugly moment, State's chaos had turned around a season.

Smith was greeted by ABC-TV as he trotted off the field. Through the years, lots of coaches had said lots of things during these generally insipid briefings. John L. Smith was about to re-invent the heading-for-the-locker-room halftime interview.

"The kids are playing their hearts out and the coaches are screwing it up," he wailed, sounding as if someone had just set his house on fire.

But it was not a single game that had just turned to ash in the span of one badly timed sideline bungle. An entire season had just gotten black-flagged. The Spartans were all but finished. A soft Spartans defense, characterized by inadequate size, numbers and skills, was going to be as evident in the waning weeks as bad kicks and bad coaching calls had been on display earlier. State beat only one team, Indiana, in its final seven games.

The Spartans finished 5-6 in the third year of John L. Smith's coaching regime. If nothing else, it was going to ensure that $85 club-seat tickets were going to be available in abundance in 2006, as they had been in 2005, the season Spartan Stadium unveiled its new luxury suites and posh club-ticket locations.

No one had to tell a head coach halfway through his contract that the next season or two in East Lansing needed to be better. Smith realized as much each time he strolled through the Duffy Daugherty Building and pondered those portraits on the wall. They were former coaches. Over the past thirty-five years, their average length of time as MSU head football coach had been five seasons.

CHAPTER 11

CHEW 'EM UP,
SPIT 'EM OUT

MERRITT NORVELL BEGAN TO UNDERSTAND soon enough what his old Wisconsin football teammate, Pat Richter, had meant when the University of Wisconsin athletic director spoke to him as a friend early in 1995.

"You've got to be careful," Richter said to a man who was on the short list to become athletic director at Michigan State University. "That's probably one of the most political places I've ever seen."

Michigan State had come quite naturally by its reputation for extraordinary in-house conflict. The malevolence had occurred during decades of warfare between rivals who endlessly vied to exert influence in a high-profile Big Ten athletic department.

Biggie Munn and Duffy Daugherty had been bitter enemies throughout the 1950s and 1960s in ways that were not always private. It was a squabble simply explained. Munn, a former head football coach—and certified Michigan State legend—resented the incoming coaching celebrity, Daugherty, after Munn moved to AD in 1954. Daugherty, for his part, would not, or could not, ease a relationship that turned increasingly acrid.

The man who succeeded Munn as athletic director, Burt Smith, had three highly politicized years as AD before he ran out of reprieves in 1975. Vice president Jack Breslin angrily banished Smith to a cement-block office in the bowels of Munn Arena.

Joe Kearney, one of MSU's most qualified athletic directors ever, had become so nervous about MSU president Cecil Mackey's agenda that he fled in 1980 for Arizona State, vacating the AD office and taking head football coach Darryl Rogers with him.

George Perles and president John DiBiaggio engaged in one of the most public and poisonous spats in MSU history during a two-year show-down, pitting the president's power against an MSU sports giant who wanted to assume dual jobs: head coach and AD.

Many of the skirmishes in which various trustees were entangled in MSU's political thicket were quite possibly of their own creation. Acrimony in MSU athletics became as familiar as the Red Cedar River on State's campus. With far too much frequency, intrigue and ill will flowed and bubbled across Michigan State's sports terrain as a kind of natural feature.

Merrily Dean Baker's hiring and ultimate departure had been the lat-est moment of marquee melodrama at Michigan State. She was gone, as much by her choice as by MSU's, which had initiated a split when presi-dent Peter McPherson told her, and not in a subtle way, that she no longer had his confidence.

In deciding to become MSU's new athletic director in May 1995, Merritt Norvell believed he could defy history, as well as the presence of personalities about whom he had already been warned. McPherson was first on the list. Although the president might have a different characteri-zation of his style, Norvell had heard through the grapevine that the pres-ident was a micro-manager. Even if he were not particularly meddlesome, the new AD understood that McPherson had a clear sense for how he wanted Michigan State athletics to operate.

Comportment, compliance, accountability—McPherson wanted MSU to undergo an athletic-department makeover. He had seen enough outrageous behavior in his first year as president to know Michigan State athletics were too often a tail wagging the dog. Thus, the incoming AD at Michigan State, like it or not, was going to become McPherson's partner in shaping a president-driven mission for MSU athletics.

Norvell was fifty-four years old as he arrived at East Lansing in July

1995. He still had the bearing of a football player, which he had been at Wisconsin alongside Richter in the early 1960s. He had a strong and articulate speaking voice that suggested strength on a CEO scale. His wife, Cynthia, was attractive and outgoing. McPherson understood Norvell was not without political capital or shy on community good will as Norvell and his wife arrived in East Lansing. These strengths were bound to bolster an athletic director who was itching to make changes and please a boss and constituency that wanted a different and dynamic athletic department for Michigan State.

There were assorted issues and crises already percolating as Norvell moved into his Jenison Fieldhouse office. Of immediate concern was the NCAA's ongoing investigation of Michigan State's football program, which had begun the previous year and was coming to a close.

The investigation had spurred McPherson to push for more oversight in compliance, which was about to come in the person of an attorney, John Hardt, who had been at Syracuse and was now an associate athletic director, in step with four others who were part of a new and more corporate structure at Jenison.

The others were Mark Hollis, an MSU graduate and assistant AD at the University of Pittsburgh, whom Norvell was about to hire from Pitt as head of marketing; Peggy Brown, another MSU graduate—and granddaughter of the legendary ten-letter winner Lyman Frimodig—who was overseeing the athletic department's business operations; Greg Ianni, also an MSU alum who was retaining his supervision over facilities, but who was now Norvell's liaison with Spartans football; and Kathy Lindahl, a lawyer who had been supervising non-revenue sports, but was now watching over hockey and women's basketball.

Norvell understood another reality: The athletic department was a Superfund site. Toxins bubbled from the offices and corridors, remnants of ugliness that had been brewing for too many years between the George Perles and Merrily Dean Baker camps, and from others before them.

Ianni had been told about it in chilling words passed on by longtime baseball coach Tom Smith, when Ianni was considering leaving Ohio University (where he was assistant AD) for a job at East Lansing.

"Greg, I'm not sure you want to come here," Smith said. "There's turmoil everywhere. People don't get along."

Ianni was undaunted, saying to Smith: "This is a great place. I've always dreamed about coming back here."

As quickly as Baker hired him in 1993, Ianni learned that Smith, if anything, had understated the reality. He could not fathom the depth of hostility between Jenison Fieldhouse and the Duffy Daugherty Football Building. He came to think of the area between the two facilities as "The DMZ"—harkening back to Vietnam War days when the "demilitarized zone" was part of the public lexicon.

Doors would close when Ianni arrived at the football building. A person from Jenison was simply not welcome there, although Ianni had noticed that Perles was professional and remained above the fray, as Baker had managed in her own relationships. But now there was a replay of the same old script with the evolving rift between Saban and Norvell.

"I've become a 240-pound punching bag," Ianni complained to Norvell after one particularly unpleasant visit to the Duffy Daugherty Building. "When I'm there at 8:30 a.m., all I do is get beat up."

Ianni's first years on staff came to be the harshest, most difficult professional times the forty-year-old had ever experienced. It was a side of human nature he had never seen, nor would have imagined existing on Michigan State's seemingly friendly, fresh-air landscape.

Norvell referred to the problems as "vertical silos" that staffers had erected as a means for self-preservation because of tensions and factionalism that for too long had been rampant within a department. Those silos needed to be imploded, demolition work Norvell was aching to do.

He wanted to take action elsewhere, as well, beginning with adjustments in non-revenue coaches' salaries, which he considered appalling as he looked at the list of people who were being paid salaries only in the twenty-thousand-dollar range.

There was nearly ten million dollars in the athletic department's reserve fund and Norvell was going to tap into it pronto to dish out raises. The whole structure of salaries and revenues was messed up, he thought. The athletic department was giving 50 percent of concession money to the general student scholarship fund. It made him just as indignant that the athletic department was required to buy game-day parking from the University.

Norvell called one of his predecessors, Doug Weaver, wondering how a business framework like this had been allowed to exist.

"Where in the hell does it say I've got to give the University 50 percent of all the concessions?" he asked Weaver.

Weaver laughed.

"Hell, you ought to consider yourself lucky you've got 50 percent. They wanted all of it from me."

There were other concerns Norvell wanted settled in the new AD's favor and conflicts that needed to be resolved.

Lou Anna Simon, the University's provost, had been aggrieved by "special case" kids—admissions exceptions during the Perles era—that she believed had a corrosive effect on MSU's academic integrity and the athletic department's well-being.

Coaches, as well as Norvell, were nervous. It appeared Simon was going to win in her bid to be more restrictive when it came to admitting athletes with fringe academic credentials.

Although Simon's concerns were shared in plenty of offices across campus, an admissions privilege had suffered its share of abuse during previous years, and had been part of a frayed football culture that ultimately brought on NCAA investigators. Regardless, the athletic department eventually prevailed.

Adjusting to a new Big Ten school was another challenge for Norvell, although he seemed to appreciate it less than his staffers. They were aware that he was often calling Richter at Wisconsin, or Richter's associate, Vince Sweeney, to consult on problems.

He was caught a time or two referring to Michigan State as "Wisconsin." It may not have helped that he was sometimes seen jogging in red-and-white togs reflective of his years with the Badgers.

Likewise, Tuesday morning staff meetings in Jenison's conference room were no benefit to the boss as far as his associates were concerned. The sessions would begin at 8:30 or 9 and last up to two hours. Specific issues that associates thought could have been handled rapidly and tidily could drag on in prolonged, long-winded ways that led to fatigue or deteriorated into downright silliness as staffers tried to break the tedium.

Norvell was famous for distributing an annual *War and Peace*-sized NCAA Convention report at the end of a week for his staffers to peruse. At the next Tuesday staff meeting, he might decide to read aloud lengthy portions of the report as his staffers twiddled thumbs and rolled eyes. The AD's soliloquy became self-parody.

A man not known for levity—Clarence Underwood—became so giggly during one of Norvell's readings that he had to leave the room, teary-eyed, when men who had decided for a moment to become kids again turned one particular session into seventh-grade, school-room comedy.

The playfulness was not so much a case of not liking Norvell, or doubting his decency. Staffers considered him a fine and bright man, and they liked his wife immensely. They only wished he had shown more humility, that he would have known when to lighten up and when to be serious.

He drew off his marketing background and wanted associates to recognize that he had cutting-edge skills there. If he went on a road trip and saw something at another university or facility that he thought was relevant to MSU, he wanted to incorporate it at once. It might have been creative graphics on the video board at Wisconsin, or a corporate tie-in at Ohio State. Norvell was attempting to instill in his troops the most *avant-garde* marketing techniques.

Along the way, Norvell had become tight with Tom Goss, his counterpart at Michigan, who helped fill Norvell's head with thoughts that the AD wanted implemented instantly in East Lansing.

"We've got to get the Internet going," Norvell would announce, although it was an exorbitantly priced website system at Michigan that became one of the reasons Goss was fired a few years later.

Norvell did succeed in bringing first-class video capabilities to MSU's sports facilities. He also wisely chose a far less expensive and more efficient Internet system than the one Goss had implemented at Ann Arbor.

Underwood throughout remained the good soldier. An associate ath-

Dr. Merritt Norvell (right) served as athletic director from 1995-99. He's shown here before MSU took on LSU in the 1995 Independence Bowl in Shreveport, Louisiana. Ironically, it was LSU that spirited away Nick Saban just four years later.

letic director who had learned throughout life to walk the fine lines between acceptance, endurance and perseverance, he was doing his best to get along with a boss whose job he knew he should be performing.

Underwood was forced to assume another role as Norvell tried, not always successfully, to realign and unite an athletic department that had split into many camps. He became the athletic department's de facto staff psychologist. Underwood through the years had seen and absorbed about everything an athletic department could dole out in frustration and injustice. Staffers who found their ideas rejected, who found that no good deed in any athletic department went unpunished, who had done precisely what they were asked to do only to learn political realities had turned their work into a project that became a liability, had only to go to Underwood to get perspective and consolation.

They often needed it. Mark Hollis and Greg Ianni each aspired to be athletic director at Michigan State, and each took his job seriously in the way expected of men who might as well have been called apprentice ADs. Hollis was creative and bold, traits that did not particularly endear him to McPherson.

Hollis had arranged a plan whereby the television show featuring MSU's football coach would be transferred from an over-the-air outlet to cable, saving the University $400,000 annually. When McPherson found out the show would be hosted by Tim Staudt, he deemed it one more manifestation of Hollis making unilateral decisions outside the chain-of-command. The disgruntled president fired Hollis, only to call him back thirty minutes later and rehire him.

Norvell's response to the flap was all-too-typical of many such instances when the AD was unable to protect them from above: "I don't know anything about it." It was the same out-of-the-loop excuse offered by Norvell when MSU trustees complained about murals that had been painted on the south side of Spartan Stadium. Norvell had been as aware as Ianni and Hollis of the artwork and failed to apprise various trustees whose noses were sure to get out of joint. It was one more lesson in political survival at Michigan State: An athletic director and his associates had to think about chain-of-command and about the political stakeholders on all fronts.

Ianni and Hollis began in time to bypass Norvell and deal more directly with Roger Wilkinson, the retiring vice president for finance and administration, or with his successors: Mark Murray, who later joined Governor John Engler's office before becoming president at Grand Valley State University, and after Murray, Fred Poston. Murray was cut from the same go-for-it cloth as Hollis—and, for that matter, as Wilkinson and Poston. He pushed for revenue streams. He was not opposed to ruffling feathers. He had likewise found a fan in Norvell.

Nick Saban, however, was proving to be a different story at a different venue, the Duffy Daugherty Football Building. The head coach was having nothing to do with the man who was, ostensibly, his boss: Norvell.

In his first year as head coach and Norvell's first months as AD, Saban and Norvell were becoming a modern-day version of Munn-Daugherty. Their relationship, to the extent one existed, was increasingly contentious. That might have been anticipated because their strong personalities seemed made for collision.

People who worked with Saban at Michigan State believed he could be summarized in one word: football. While he accepted intellectually that football at MSU had to know its humble place within a university's mission, his single-minded focus on his sport made him no less combustible when he didn't get his way. Saban wanted to build a nationally prominent football program and he wanted to build it now. Being thwarted by restrictions or whims or philosophical barriers—or by an AD whom he believed to be heavy-handed—sent him into orbit. Saban considered himself just as keen on academics and chain-of-command issues as any Michigan State professor, department chair, or athletic director.

Norvell was doing better with basketball coach Tom Izzo, perhaps because Izzo had a gift for diplomacy. Not that holding his tongue was easy for Izzo. It drove the basketball coach nuts when Norvell would sit on the Spartans' bench during pre-game warm-ups as if he were just another coach or player. Other moments could be even tougher, as when Izzo stood in the locker room after a game, listening to his boss talk for thirty minutes about that night's contest, about program-building philosophies, about a lot of stuff Izzo believed he could have done without at that particular moment.

Relationships between Michigan State's two primary head coaches and the athletic director were as different as the coaches themselves. Saban had long ago bailed out on Norvell and was drifting more and more into direct contact with McPherson, which became a prelude to him getting his fill of McPherson, as well.

Izzo could deal with issues more diplomatically. It probably helped that money was not the irksome issue it was with Saban. This basketball coach was less inclined to use salary benchmarks as an indicator of justice, of achievement, of appreciation. Saban had a different perspective. He was good with money, and paid attention to what it could do. It signified to him what a Saturday victory told him about his football team—that successful performance had been acknowledged and rewarded.

Izzo was a different animal. He tended to let his wife, Lupe, worry about financial things, probably because accounting issues would have kept Izzo from writing one more recruiting letter today or breaking down film from last winter's Michigan State-Wisconsin game. Save for his family, Izzo considered time away from basketball to be time misspent.

Norvell was in Izzo's office one day when he happened to find, wedged in a crevice between Izzo's desk and the wall, a $3,000 check. It had been lodged there for six months, never for a moment missed by the head coach.

Not that money was irrelevant to a man who wanted to be paid in proportion to his achievements. MSU basketball was becoming an elite Big Ten program in Izzo's third season, 1997-98, when the Spartans won a Big Ten championship and cracked their first NCAA tournament in three years. Izzo's team had ripped through first-round games against Eastern Michigan and Princeton, and was now on its way to Greensboro to play North Carolina in the NCAA regional.

MSU basketball was soaring. A head coach's salary needed to reflect it.

On the team charter headed for Greensboro, Norvell said to Izzo: "When we get back, we'll fix your contract."

McPherson had gotten wind of the conversation, and had decided any matters relating to Izzo's contract would be, at the very least, overseen by the president.

Norvell was at the NCAA Final Four at San Antonio when he got a call from Izzo, who was anticipating nothing uncomfortable as he filled in his boss.

"Peter called me at 6:30 this morning," Izzo said. "He offered me $625,000."

There was a pause. It was long enough for Izzo to realize Norvell knew nothing about any salary adjustments by McPherson.

Norvell was boiling. The president had done a contractual end-around without so much as including the AD in discussions. It wrecked an athletic director's credibility with his coaches, maintained Norvell, who complained to Roger Wilkinson, the MSU vice president in charge of finance. Wilkinson knew nothing about McPherson and Izzo's talks.

"I'll take this up with Peter," Wilkinson said, which led to a phone call from McPherson to Norvell.

"Mr. President, I need to see you," Norvell said, explaining that negotiating Izzo's raise over the AD's head "was disrespectful to me and doesn't make me look good in front of my coaches."

McPherson was not sympathetic. Money matters on this level were a president's concern, most definitely, he said. These issues needed to be handled at the executive level.

Norvell returned home that night. He had been at Michigan State three years. He had, after the Izzo end-around, taken his third strike. He turned to his wife, Cynthia, and said:

"It's time for me to leave."

It was a feeling that had been building for months. Too many essential working relationships were on the rocks. He had watched Underwood grow increasingly distant. He was clearly no longer in the president's good graces. His associates were going their own way. He was tired of pushing for ambitious projects that were getting nowhere with McPherson. He had championed new locker rooms in Spartan Stadium, moving the baseball field to a new location on Farm Lane, and getting on with the much-discussed west-side expansion of Spartan Stadium.

Norvell was having breakfast with a friend, Gordon White, a vice president for human resources at General Motors, when he mentioned in the spring of 1999 that he and MSU seemed on the verge of divorce.

"I need to do what you do," Norvell said to White. "It's not working here. I'm not getting along with the president, and he's not getting along with me."

White said: "Why don't you work for us?"

Days later, Norvell received a call from a top-ten executive search firm, DHR International, Inc.

"We know a lot about you," the representative said. "And we need to get into sports and coaching."

By mid-April, Norvell was headed to DHR as president of its newest division, delving into the world of placement for coaches and sports personnel. And Michigan State was preparing for yet another athletic director, the fourth in seven years at a university that once upon a time looked at the AD's office as a place of long tenure, where men such as Biggie Munn would settle in for the duration of their highly accomplished careers.

Clarence Underwood was sitting in his associate athletic director's office at Jenison on a Sunday morning in April 1999, when he got a call from McPherson, explaining that Norvell was resigning.

"What do you think I should do about the position?" the president asked.

Underwood answered in a tone of voice that suggested they both were aware of the obvious.

"If you don't have anybody internally," he said, "then you need to go outside. You can do what you've always done: leave the position open until you find your person."

Silence filled the phone line, after which McPherson asked: "Would you be interested in serving on an interim basis?"

Underwood sighed.

"I would under two circumstances," he said. "I need to have authority to move forward, and I need to be able to make decisions."

"Just listen to people," McPherson replied.

"No," Underwood said, firmly. "We've suffered from inaction for too long."

"No, just listen to people," the president insisted, pausing for a moment before his sign-off statement: "Talk it over with your wife."

Noreese Underwood had been through this routine enough to say to her husband: "If you can't make decisions, stay where you are."

McPherson phoned Underwood again the next day. McPherson was sticking with his theme from Sunday's conversation: "Just listen to people."

Underwood told him for a final time that if he were moving into the AD's office, even on an interim basis, he was taking the athletic department forward. He was not going to be party to the nonsensical habit of leaving athletics idling in neutral as a new AD was hunted.

McPherson said neither yes nor no. He told Underwood that if he were to become interim AD, he could not become a candidate for the permanent job.

"I want to have someone in there for ten years," the president said.

"I don't plan on being here for more than five," Underwood responded. "So I will not be a candidate in any event."

Underwood got to work. He was organizing the department's staff, moving ahead with a strategic plan for athletics that McPherson had been hounding Norvell to complete, and getting input from staffers on how MSU's sports mission could be made better.

Soon afterward, Underwood read a *Lansing State Journal* story by Jack

Ebling, saying that McPherson had offered the permanent AD job to former Nebraska football coach Tom Osborne.

Underwood was furious. Osborne was sixty-two years old. He was into his second year of retirement. Underwood was sixty-five years old. If the supposed "ten-year" job was good enough for Osborne, it was going to be good enough for Underwood.

Underwood promptly crafted a hand-written letter of application for the position and personally delivered it to the assistant for vice president Fred Poston, Underwood's boss.

The next day, Larry Lage of the *Lansing State Journal* called Underwood and asked: "Are you going to throw your hat in for the AD's job?"

"Yes, I am," Underwood replied. "I will become a candidate."

The news was reported in a *State Journal* column by Lage the next day. McPherson was in a rage when he put down the newspaper. He headed for Poston's office, furious, as he phoned Underwood.

The president was slamming his fist on a desk, accusing Underwood of having lied to him about the non-candidate pledge, and suggesting that Underwood was following the wishes of someone who wanted him in the job—a veiled reference to trustee Joel Ferguson.

"Let me be clear," Underwood said. "You first told me you wanted an AD for ten years. I abided by your wishes. But then when I saw you had talked with Tom Osborne, I changed my mind."

McPherson became even angrier. Underwood, he said, had flat-out deceived him.

"I did not lie," Underwood shot back. "You're the one who changed the criterion. I can serve as long as Tom Osborne."

Poston intervened. He had Underwood's letter of application in hand, he said. Had he read his mail that morning, he would have forwarded word to the president ahead of him learning about Underwood's candidacy by way of a newspaper article.

McPherson was not appeased.

Underwood, by this time, had decided enough was enough.

"I can make this simple for everyone," he said. "I can resign right now."

The president calmed down.

"No, you're doing a good job," he said. "I want you to continue as AD."

When it was implied, once again, that Ferguson was the inspiration behind this sudden push for the job, long term, Underwood heated up.

"The only person who controls Underwood," he said, boiling at the insinuation, "is Underwood and God."

Athletic director Clarence Underwood served in that capacity from 1999-2002. He was considered for the top job in the Michigan State athletic department several times before succeeding Merritt Norvell.

Underwood settled into his job in tandem with an athletic department that was growing more tranquil by the week. It was hardly a coincidence. Underwood represented the opposite of everything that had frustrated staffers about Baker and Norvell.

He knew the University fore and aft. He was secure because of his experience and achievements. He was inclined to listen and to infuse Jenison Fieldhouse's offices with a sense of commonality—that Michigan State's staffers were all hewn from the same rock and all in this together.

Associates appreciated his intellect and integrity, which was not to be confused with passivity. Underwood had a flash point sure to be triggered by any number of indiscretions. He had seen a boss or two from the distant past look at compliance issues—NCAA rules—as something quaint or irrelevant. An ultimate insult was personal disrespect toward him, which had been the all-too frequent experience for an African-American man born in 1933 to sharecropper parents in Marion, Alabama. Clarence Underwood Jr. was the fifth of thirteen children who, during his first twenty-two years of life, would become a scholarship athlete, serious student, future paratrooper in the United States Army, and after his Army discharge in 1955, a married student at Michigan State.

Underwood planned after high school on attending the famous black college, Tuskegee Institute, where he had a partial athletic scholarship because of his football and baseball prowess. Even with the scholarship it was going to be a rough road, financially, which inspired Underwood to join the Army and take advantage of GI Bill benefits afterward.

His thoughts about college began to change on New Year's Day, 1954, when Michigan State met UCLA in the Rose Bowl. Underwood was stunned to see so many black players performing alongside white Spartan teammates. A man steeped in rigid Deep South segregation was moved by what he was seeing a few months before Brown v. Board of Education was to end *de jurae* racial segregation in schools, and ten years before the Civil Rights Act was to end sanctioned racism in America.

Underwood looked further into Michigan State and decided to enroll in 1955, accompanied on a long train ride north by his wife, Noreese, and their seventeen-month-old daughter.

A life was about to be altered, enriched, affected in countless ways. Underwood during the next fifty years would know East Lansing as his primary home, and know Michigan State, at alternate times, as professional fulfillment or abiding frustration. He was about to feel the ambivalence that comes when opportunity inclusive of respect is cloaked in bias, or in condescension. There would be days both inspiring and disillusioning as a student, educator and athletic department administrator.

His experience in Depression-era Alabama had made him sensitive to how others would feel in a given circumstance. Underwood could empathize with black athletes who had come from poverty and who, unlike himself, too many times were the product of stressful one-parent homes. He understood, as only one can who has been on the receiving end of searing racism, how it can erode self-esteem, how it compromises educational systems that are in no way equal in their ability to produce college-ready students. He knew personally how it wounds to the soul a man or a woman who wants only to be considered on a par with all other people.

Thus, when he assumed the job as interim athletic director at

Michigan State in April 1999, he could empathize with the bruised or the discouraged. Nothing was more needed in MSU's athletic department in the spring of 1999 than healing. There had been a decade of strife, squabbling and division that was within an AD's power to repair.

Listening was Underwood's first obligation. Too many associates for too long had felt marginalized or insignificant. Creativity had been made subordinate to flow-sheet hierarchy. There was no oxygen in Jenison Fieldhouse. It was the key reason why a quarterly "picnic" for athletic staffers was arranged during a particular day's lunch hour. It was a small gesture that broke the department's rigidly routinized mode.

None of the shifts in policy or human relations would matter if Underwood had a credibility gap with his staffers or had been lacking in essential respect from associates. He had that respect, however, because of his personal makeup and his familiarity with so many with whom he was now working. He was one of them. There were no trap doors. No guessing games. No anxieties.

He simply had to deal with the occasional phone call that went with the territory.

Nick Saban, heading into his fifth season as MSU head football coach in 1999, was never far from the phone when his grievance *du jour* surfaced.

Sylvia Thompson was now the assistant to her ninth athletic director since she became secretary to Biggie Munn thirty years earlier. She had grown as fatigued as her bosses when Saban called.

"Oh, Nick," Thompson one day sighed in here-we-go-again tones.

"You are a PITA," she said, pronouncing the word as *pit-tuh.* "Do you know what that is?"

"No," Saban answered, irritated by Thompson's guessing game.

"Well," she said, "it stands for pain in the ass."

Saban was widely regarded as the man in MSU athletics most likely to make you consider a career in something comparatively relaxed, such as air-traffic controlling.

Underwood's predecessor, Norvell, was sitting one afternoon in the office of his boss, Roger Wilkinson, having an earnest discussion when the phone rang. A voice on the end of the line was angry, which meant it almost certainly was Saban.

Wilkinson listened to the complaint, closed his eyes in semi-torment, and put down the phone.

"I don't know how much more of this I can take," said Wilkinson, who otherwise had a good relationship with Saban.

Underwood's status as interim athletic director was about to change in December of 1999. McPherson realized Jenison Fieldhouse had calmed in the eight months since he asked Underwood to mind the store. Poston, who was dealing most directly with Underwood, regularly provided good reports about Underwood for the president. From the board of trustees' viewpoint (which meant Joel Ferguson's), Underwood needed to have the word "interim" removed from his job title.

McPherson agreed. The board approved Underwood's appointment as unconditional MSU athletic director on December 10, 1999. He would remain on the job at least through 2000 before his retirement. His tenure was later extended by eighteen months to run through June 30, 2002.

Having a timeline established was helpful to Underwood in allowing him to operate with minimal restraints, practically and politically. He still had bosses to whom he must be accountable—Poston, his direct supervisor, as well as McPherson, to say nothing of the trustees. Still, he could operate with relative freedom and, perhaps for the first time since Doug Weaver's heyday, a Michigan State athletic director was enjoying himself.

He could stop by Spartan Stadium following a Friday night practice before a home game, as he did before Bobby Williams' first regular-season game as coach, the 2000 season-opener when the Spartans were about to take on a Marshall team, nicknamed the Thundering Herd, which had the nation's longest winning streak—eighteen games.

Underwood delivered a speech that was not exactly a stem-winder. Rather, he made a team of football players chuckle and feel good about an AD who could speak to them in such an amusing, even endearing, fashion.

"Let me tell you something," Underwood began. "I know what a Spartan is. There's a statue of a Spartan at the entranceway to this athletic complex. A Spartan is a strong man, with a sword and a shield.

"What's a Thundering Herd?" Underwood asked, indignant that a team so named would have the audacity to march into East Lansing and take on mighty Michigan State. "I don't even know what a Thundering Herd is. I couldn't even find it in a dictionary. How's a Thundering Herd going to beat a Spartan?"

ONCE THE SNAKE PIT that had been Jenison's athletic offices turned civil, Underwood could get busy with an agenda he had planned to push from the day McPherson made him interim AD. His plans included:

- Giving coaches longer-term budget projections with which to work. The inability to budget beyond the upcoming year had been hand-cuffing coaches who needed to think farther down the road about costs and revenues.
- A half-dozen women's sports were lagging behind the NCAA limit on scholarships, so Underwood moved to give them parity with opponent schools that already were awarding full-limit scholarships.
- Inaugurating a west-side Spartan Stadium expansion, complete with skyboxes and club seats. This was imperative if Michigan State was going to produce revenue necessary from a sport that had long been the basis for an athletic department's support: football.
- Renovation of Jenison Fieldhouse's athletic facilities and locker rooms in an eight-million-dollar upgrade.
- Respect for student-athletes. It was a somewhat startling, even dubious, concern in the eyes of some, particularly outside Michigan State's campus. Underwood, though, had seen too many examples where college athletes were treated and perceived by administrators, staffers, and even coaches as commodities and not as young people worthy of respect and enrichment. He was not mincing words or thoughts: College students, regardless of back-ground or status at Michigan State, were to be seen as the University's future ambassadors.

THE FACT THAT UNDERWOOD had an established retirement date, June 30, 2002, meant there need be no hurry-up searches for a successor. Internal candidates had time to form strategies; outside applicants could be circumspect in checking out the Michigan State job without endangering their existing position.

Two internal candidates were sure to want the job: associate athletic directors Mark Hollis and Greg Ianni, who had been applicants before. Beyond those two, a successor was anyone's guess.

Ron Mason, now twenty years into his job as MSU hockey coach, was a possibility. He had been asked about the job ten years earlier, when Weaver left and George Perles was taking temperatures across campus.

"Are you interested?" Perles asked Mason.

"No, not at this time," Mason said. "I've got too much going on here."

"Well, if you're not," Perles said, "I'm going to look into it."

A decade later, Mason and his basketball counterpart, Tom Izzo, were having breakfast at Kellogg Center with a national headhunter MSU was employing in the AD search, Jed Hughes.

Hughes wanted a briefing from Mason and Izzo on precisely the qualities and requirements coaches needed in a new boss. They talked at length, speaking with zeal about each coach's personal AD wish list.

Mason was driving back to Munn Arena following breakfast when the thought struck:

"The guy we were talking about is me."

McPherson was aware that Mason might be interested and asked him to think it over. Poston made a follow-up call.

Ron Mason was warming to thoughts of a job change. He realized it could be his last opportunity to do something other than coach hockey, even if it made perfect sense to anyone else in the world that the most successful college coach in NCAA hockey history might want to stick with his day job for a few more seasons.

His daughter, Cindy, had a different perspective.

"Dad," she said, "you keep banging your head against the wall trying to win."

Mason had to agree. He could think back to previous winters, when he had beaten Michigan in a big CCHA playoff game at Joe Louis Arena in Detroit, and by the time he had gotten to the bus he was already thinking about the next game.

"Maybe," he said to himself, "it's time to get out of the rat race."

Having won a NCAA championship in 1986, Mason decided, was of no relevance to his decision since he wanted a second championship anyway. He decided to talk it over with confidants: Rick Comley, hockey coach at Northern Michigan; Steve Cady, vice president at Miami (Ohio), who had been Mason's assistant at Bowling Green; and with his old colleagues and bosses, Weaver and Perles, whose sense for whether Mason could do the job was imperative if he were to go for it.

On the negative side were true minuses: no more practices with his players. He loved those kids and he loved the games.

Then, there were the pluses: no more parents calling about their son's playing time, no pro teams meddling with underclassmen. He had grown tired of spending half his year recruiting program-dependent kids such as Ron Scott, Joe Murphy, Craig Simpson and Rod Brind'Amour, only to see them head for the NHL just as they were about to take MSU to the NCAA Frozen Four.

His apprehensions about the job, as well as his attractions, were significant:

- Mason was not a big meetings person, and meetings were going to become a way of life as AD. His remedy, he decided, would be to keep them short and to the point.
- He knew he had a good and experienced staff of associates and coaches.
- Facilities were in relatively great shape. The Clara Bell Smith Academic Center had been a marvelous addition. Breslin Center was a national model, as well. Upgrades to Spartan Stadium and to Duffy Daugherty Football Building could be worked on.
- The budget was in good shape, in great part due to Underwood's stewardship.

Mason, in fact, had asked Underwood a single question: "What am I going to spend most of my time on?"

"Budgets," Underwood answered.

Mason had some experience there. During summers he ran the

AD Ron Mason, shown here behind the bench, remains the winningest college hockey coach of all time. His twenty seasons at the MSU hockey helm included a national title in 1986. He became State's athletic director in 2002, replacing Clarence Underwood.

world's largest hockey school. He had a reasonable handle on finances and rink budgets, on overhead and revenues as they applied to a sport and to broad numbers of participants.

Poston was running a shuttle from MSU's Administration Building to Mason's office as Michigan State's executive wing pushed discussions. People were becoming suspicious as a vice president's visits mounted.

Finally Poston, who was reporting back to McPherson after his scouting trips, was given the green light to talk contract with Mason. The offer to Mason came during a formal discussion in Mason's office. Other conversations had already occurred with McPherson, with provost Lou Anna Simon, and with Dave Porteous of the MSU Board of Trustees. It was now official that Ron Mason would become MSU's next athletic director.

It was mid-season in hockey, and Mason suddenly realized he was two people: MSU's hockey coach and incoming athletic director. Fortunately, Underwood was staying on the job until July 1, which left

Mason to finish up his farewell season at Munn Arena, and even take an exquisitely peaceful three-week break during May at his off-season home on Florida's Singer Island.

Summer vacations at Singer had always been Mason's favorite way to decompress. There he could divorce himself from ice rinks and red tape and the usual hassles that were standard operating realities for any college coach. Totally detaching himself from a coach's stresses was another matter altogether. There were always aspects of a head coach's job you had to live with every day of every year: the present season or the season to come; eligibility; and dealing with realities tied to talented kids and their early exits for the professional ranks.

Mason was feeling particularly good about his May 2002 getaway. He had been coaching at Michigan State for twenty-three years, an entire generation. He was beginning to realize a surprising sense of fulfillment that ratcheted up his enthusiasm for the new job. One benefit after working so long in East Lansing was that he knew where the bodies were buried. He was coming into his Jenison Fieldhouse office as no stranger to Michigan State athletics.

Personnel decisions were tempting nonetheless. He was leaning toward an alteration or two, and wondered what his old friend and predecessor, Doug Weaver, thought about it.

"I wouldn't change anything for a year," Weaver said. "You need to find out what your team's like."

Mason later would say Weaver had it right. There was too much of everything to sort through during his early months as AD to have disrupted staffs in Jenison or anywhere else—such as the Duffy Daugherty Football Building.

Mason was one of several people at MSU who was unsure about Bobby Williams. What bothered him, even when he was hockey coach and a full year before he was recruited as AD, was the mediocre season in 2000 that followed a 10-2 year and Citrus Bowl victory. Why the falloff in a team that had sustained no more than the usual senior departures? Williams and the Spartans had done a bit better in 2001, beating Fresno State in the Silicon Valley Bowl.

Mason was planning on another bowl game in 2002 and as solid of a year as any AD could expect at MSU heading into a new season. Getting rid of Bobby Williams may have been on the to-do list for various fans who were never going to be happy with MSU's football coach. It was not on Mason's agenda in September of 2002.

Other projects, he knew, were likely to roll forward under his watch. Spartan Stadium's west-side expansion was heavy there. It had been discussed for years and had almost gotten a go-ahead during George Perles' brief stint as AD, when Perles wanted to farm out construction costs to Ilitch Holdings in Detroit, and rent the west-side luxury boxes and club seats from a corporate sponsor.

That plan had fizzled as Perles' tenure as AD had ended. Then Underwood had realized when he arrived in April of 1999 that MSU needed to make a move on Spartan Stadium. Football revenues could no longer remain static if the black-ink fiscal years of the '90s were to continue. There had to be dramatic new, high-margin cash streams available.

The best way to secure them was to spend $62 million on a stem-to-stern facelift of the stadium's west side that would give Michigan State layered levels of luxury-suite and VIP seating. It would be a 200,000-square-foot expansion and conversion of the old press-box area into three thousand additional seats—posh, big-ticket football hideaways geared to bringing MSU's bottom line seven-figure returns. It was Mason's responsibility to get ground broken and a tremendous new west-side edifice built.

It opened in time for the 2005 season. The stadium's west side was now a towering, brilliant reddish-brick fortress encapsulating luxury boxes, club seats, and a stunning press box—everything but sold-out seats.

Spurring sales was now the mission. Luxury suites had been reasonably successful in 2005. Club seats languished. A mediocre football team coupled with the sour economy in the state of Michigan had made the high-roller seats a difficult buy for people and business that, a few years earlier, might have been names on a waiting list.

It was 2006 and the MSU athletic department considered how it would approach a pivotal year. Mason was left to ponder several vexing questions with his staffers. They had to find the way to bring it all together, how to combine the recent initiatives with the established strengths. Into the mix went the Spartan Stadium's expansion, John L. Smith's football team, Tom Izzo's remarkable basketball program, and the other people and teams at MSU. Mason's challenge was nothing less than leading his people and marshaling his resources—combining talents, energies, passions and personalities—to build a better, more enduring society known as Michigan State athletics.

CHAPTER 12

TRANSITION RENDITION

SLAMMING HIS FIST onto a courtside table at Kemper Arena in March of 1986 had been Jud Heathcote's way of expressing everything a courtroom judge communicates with a crash of his gavel. Anger, injustice, a demand for order from disorder—Heathcote was feeling every impulse from his emotional repertoire (homicide, included) as he pounded the scorer's table, knowing a 15-second clock-stoppage had just jeopardized MSU's bid to beat top-seed Kansas in the 1986 NCAA regional semi-final.

MSU had, at the time, been on its merry way to the 1986 Final Four at Dallas. Kansas was Number 2 in the nation and top seed in the Midwest Regional and the Jayhawks looked worthy of their rank in taking a nine-point halftime lead. But the Spartans promptly unsheathed their three-guard scoring saber of Scott Skiles, Darryl Johnson and Vernon Carr, and with Barry Fordham knocking down a string of short jumpers, State led by six points with 2:20 to play.

It might as well have been with 2:35 to play. The added 15 seconds on the dead clock was just enough of a reprieve for Kansas to tie the game in regulation and then win in overtime. Two days later, Kansas and head coach Larry Brown beat North Carolina State in the regional final on their way to winning the national championship. Small consolation, but most college scouts would have picked MSU to beat N.C. State, as well, because of State's speed.

Heathcote could no more forget the Kemper Clock Crisis than

Michigan State basketball fans could put it in their pained past. The coach knew how skilled and how lucky you had to be to get to a Final Four. He had been a head coach for fifteen years and had been to exactly one: 1979, when Magic Johnson and Gregory Kelser had helped deliver a national title to East Lansing.

Now, three years after Kansas and Kemper, Heathcote could see with greater clarity how precious MSU's chance had been in 1986. MSU had not even made the NCAA tournament the past three seasons. Those three years were as dark as any time in the head coach's career: 11-17 overall, 6-12 in the Big Ten in 1986-87; 10-18 overall, 5-13 in the Big Ten in 1987-88; 18-15 on the season, 6-12 in the conference in 1988-89, with not much consolation coming from a five-game run and fourth-place finish in the National Invitation Tournament.

The Spartans' problems were easily explained. They had too few elite basketball players. The post-Magic years when Scott Skiles or Sam Vincent could single-handedly make State dangerous had given way to a kind of hardcourt haze when the Spartans were defined by lesser stars like Darrell Johnson and Carlton Valentine.

It was one of the reasons why Heathcote had wanted so badly to bring Tom Izzo back to East Lansing. Izzo had been lost to Tulsa in a kind of arranged marriage during the spring of 1986. Izzo needed a fulltime assistant's job that MSU was powerless to offer because of NCAA rules on staff size. The hang-up was resolved when J.D. Barnett, Tulsa's head coach and a man Heathcote knew would be good for Izzo, hired a paycheck-hungry, thirty-one-year-old assistant who someday figured to be back on Michigan State's payroll.

Two months later, Izzo was back in East Lansing, filling an unexpected hole on Heathcote's staff. The head coach sorely needed Izzo's help corralling talent—in-state, particularly—that might turn around a sorrowful stretch of Spartan basketball.

Izzo arrived back in East Lansing on a Saturday night in June of 1986. He had barely changed clothes before he was hitting the recruiting trail, beginning with a trip to Detroit. MSU wanted an update on 6-foot-11 high school senior-to-be Eric Wilson, who was working out at Detroit St.

Cecilia's gym, where much of Detroit's prep talent convened in the summer time. Heathcote arrived the next day to join Izzo for a look.

The head coach instead noticed another player.

"Man, I like that kid over there," he said, turning to Izzo. "Go get his phone number."

The player's name was Steve Smith, a skinny senior-to-be from Pershing High. Michigan State—if it wanted—could have exclusive Big Ten rights to a Detroit prep talent who had been missed on most blue-chip lists primarily because he had not been to the usual parade of summer camps.

Heathcote and Izzo were about to raise Smith's profile. They would make twenty visits to Smith's home over the ensuing months. Throughout, they were in a chase with Don Sicko, head coach at the University of Detroit, which had made Smith its Number 1 recruiting target.

At one of the St. Cecilia showcase games, Heathcote bumped into his old friend and one-time assistant, Don Monson, who was now head coach at the University of Oregon.

"What the hell are you doing here?" Heathcote said.

"Got a home visit," Monson said. "One of my assistants says this kid Smith is really a good prospect. Doesn't look like anybody in the Big Ten is recruiting him."

"Don't spend too much time here," Heathcote said. "He's one of our top recruits."

"You're kidding."

"And," Heathcote added, dryly, "he's number one on Missouri's list."

By November's early signing date, Smith was headed for East Lansing. Heathcote found himself the same week at the Detroit Athletic Club, joining two other head coaches—U of D's Sicko, and Bill Frieder of Michigan—speaking to a lunch-time group of businessmen and water polo players known as the Beavers.

"What about Smith?" someone from the audience asked after Heathcote had unloaded his arsenal of wry zingers and began to take questions.

"Bill's the expert on all the recruits," Heathcote said. "I'll defer to Bill on that one."

Guard Steve Smith came to MSU as a skinny but talented player from Detroit Pershing, and left as one of the greatest Spartans in history, not to mention one of the nicest. During a long NBA career, Smith found plenty of time to help with fund-raising, including construction of the Clara Bell Smith Academic Center, named for his late mother.

Frieder by now knew all about Smith. Regrettably, he had come to know him too late.

"Jud just got one of the best players in the state of Michigan," said Frieder, who, diplomacy aside, knew of Smith's skills and was mad at his assistants for having let a Detroit prep perform so anonymously for so long.

Not everyone was choosing East Lansing over Ann Arbor. Most of the hotshots belonged to U-M.

Glen Rice was one of them. A spectacular shooter out of Flint Northwestern, Rice was a prototypical in-state dazzler whom Frieder had made Michigan property. It had not helped that MSU assistant Mike Deane, while still with MSU, had gotten wind of Rice's bad grades and told Heathcote to forget it. A bad GPA didn't seem to bother Michigan. MSU got busy late in the game, but Rice by then belonged to Frieder.

Recruiting had always been problematic with Heathcote, the renowned basketball teacher and old-pro bench coach who was no charmer, no flim-flam man, no slickster when it came to signing players. Staking out high-school games to get a look at a particular player or to let him know Michigan State had arrived was a task he preferred his assistants to handle. Frieder, on the other hand, was the consummate gym rat, writing letters to prospects while they were still in junior high school.

Heathcote's discomfort with recruiting was but one manifestation of the head coach's personality compartments. He functioned best when he was in control. Being in control did not preclude him from being gracious or friendly. Nor did it keep him from being funny, or social, or helpful, or regarded as a good guy by nearly any bloc of constituents inside or outside Michigan State University. It was a simple matter of comfort level.

Recruiting, though, was an exercise carried out on a different plane. A coach necessarily *came down* to a player when he recruited him because in the basketball talent market, highly talented players were in short supply and there were many coaches competing for the limited supply. Heathcote, though, was no door-to-door salesman. He was a come-to-my-door type who liked being on secure, familiar turf. Trying to entice a high-school kid to accept a full-ride scholarship at your university was an opposite-end experience.

The head coach believed MSU's intermittent talent flow was largely a matter of Michigan State's basketball stage. Jenison Fieldhouse, empty, had the look and warmth of a C-130 cargo-plane hangar. Filled on a game night, it had skin-tingling energy and intimacy. Recruits, however, tended to see it in hangar mode as part of their campus tour. It was no selling point for a head coach who was not about to compensate with his personal spiel.

Sometimes it was a matter of him being too honest for his—and MSU's—good.

There was one interesting recruit who, during an MSU home visit, shifted to the subject of summer jobs. He was aware of athletes who had pulled down nice money working at tool-and-die plants.

"Oh, I don't think you want to do that," Jud said. "There was a football player at one of those places who lost his thumb in a press."

Izzo asked afterward if his boss might want to refine his presentation just a tad if summer jobs came up again.

"Jud," Izzo pleaded, half-laughing, half-anguished, "just tell him you can get him fifteen or twenty dollars an hour."

Neither had MSU's pursuit of Lorenzo Orr been a shining exercise in diplomacy.

Orr, a 6-foot-7 front-court sentry from Detroit Pershing High, was sitting in the family living room as his mother, Heathcote and Izzo talked about academic choices if Lorenzo opted for East Lansing. Orr's mother suggested that her son might want to major in computer science.

Heathcote shook his head.

"Computer science is one of the toughest curriculums at our place," the coach said, almost paternally. "He's not going into that."

Izzo smiled, wanly. Orr ended up signing with Southern Cal.

What allowed Izzo with his different recruiting style to remain so wedded to Heathcote was an ultimate appreciation for the coach and the ideals he represented.

Heathcote played the game right. He played clean with recruits, no matter that he wasn't the most adroit recruiter. It was why his opponent coaches—Gene Keady at Purdue, in particular, was a great Heathcote friend—liked him, respected him, enjoyed him, and appreciated his presence in a profession where carnival barkers were too often shaking down the customer.

MSU's staff nonetheless had relationship hassles, some of them in Detroit, where at least one Public School League coach had decided Heathcote was racist. That charge was made within earshot of Spartan assistant Stan Joplin and sent Joplin into a fury. He could acknowledge that Heathcote had his faults, same as anyone. Racial bias wasn't on the list.

"Our friendship is over," Joplin told the coach. "If you're gonna talk about Jud Heathcote and Michigan State, you're talking about me."

The loyalty shown Heathcote by his assistants was amazing for a coach who could be an ongoing pain in the tail. Assistants knew there would be plenty of times during an oncoming season when they would be "fired" for whatever Heathcote wished to make them accountable for at a given moment: a missed recruit, a missed free-throw, a bad in-bounds pass. Heathcote's assistants were going to pay the price. Everyone got "fired," Izzo more than anyone.

Sitting on MSU's bench, five minutes into a game, the opposing team would go on a 10-2 run and Heathcote would moan, "We're gonna lose this game."

"Jud," Izzo would say, "we're not gonna lose this game."

"I said we're gonna lose this game!"

"Goddammit, Jud," Izzo would snap, by now a pro at the script, "we're not gonna lose this game."

"Shut up. You're fired."

"Well, fire me after the game."

For their own part, players with frail basketball psyches would learn that Heathcote was not exactly Dr. Phil at crisis time.

A young player, perhaps on the road with a crowd shrieking and all sorts of paraphernalia being waved in his face by fans sitting behind the basket, would lock up on the first free throw and instantly hear his coach shrieking from courtside:

"DON'T SHOOT IT SHORT!"

Izzo would cringe.

"Jud, don't say that," Izzo would exhort in a kind of exasperated plea. "The kid's as nervous as a whore in church."

Heathcote, deadpan, would slip into his whack-the-assistant mode: "Shut up."

Even had Heathcote been serious during their mock-angry spats, Izzo's recruiting touch would have kept him afloat. He had a sense for how to approach a prep star, for how to nurture a relationship. So often with a recruit, Izzo understood, less was more.

LATE IN THE SUMMER OF 1986, days after Izzo had returned from his Tulsa exile, a junior-to-be at Warren De La Salle named Mike Peplowski received a phone call at the family home in Detroit.

Peplowski was already approaching his eventual altitude of 6-foot-10 and was being deluged with the standard duffel-bag full of letters from college coaches each day.

"Mike, I just want you to know that I just got an assistant coach's job here at Michigan State, and you're a priority recruit for me," Izzo explained during his first-ever conversation with De La Salle's hot ticket. "I've heard you're a guy who might want to do things a little differently. So how would you like me to handle things from here?"

Peplowski was barely sixteen. But he liked what he was hearing. Izzo's words meshed nicely with Peplowski's early-stage anxiety. Two years of oncoming recruiting pitches and pressures had already become overwhelming.

"You know, you're the first coach who has ever said that to me," Peplowski explained. "If you could send all the correspondence to my high school, it would be great. I'm not really going to get very involved in choosing a school until next year."

Izzo was content.

"OK," he said. "Good talking with you."

Izzo hung up. The two never spoke until the following autumn, late in 1987, as Michigan State's football team closed in on its first Rose Bowl trip in twenty-two years.

Peplowski called Izzo and asked: "Do you mind if some friends and I come up for an unofficial visit and go to a football game?"

Unofficial visits are loose get-acquainted sessions, always on the parents' dime. By this time, Peplowski's unofficial visits had become weekly rituals. Purdue ... Indiana ... Michigan. This sought-after player was going to stay close to home, not necessarily in-state, but within a five-hour drive of Detroit.

He was very much a product of his parents: his dad, Gerry, a magistrate, and his mother, Diane, a registered nurse. He was a National Honor Society student who was going to do something big with his life, basketball or not.

It explained why his unofficial trip to Ann Arbor had gone so badly.

In the locker room after an early-season game, Bill Frieder ushered in Gerry and Mike Peplowski and began with what he believed was a reassuring sales pitch.

U-M's head coach detailed how Mike's freshman year would be a carefully arranged adjustment to the rigors of U-M academics. Easier entry-level courses were to be scheduled, guaranteeing a soft landing for an incoming freshman.

"Coach, that may be how you run your program," Gerry Peplowski said, irked at Frieder's condescension, no matter how inadvertent it had been. "But that's not going to happen to my son."

It had been the same story at Indiana. Bob Knight's aura was real. So, too, was the passion with which a father discussed his son's future.

Knight had argued during the Peplowskis' unofficial visit that it mattered not so much where a young man earned his degree, but that he obtained his degree.

"So you're going to try and tell me," a heated Gerry Peplowski said, "that if my son earned a law degree at Harvard, or got an engineering degree from M.I.T., that a degree from Indiana would carry the same weight with a company's recruiters as the other two schools?"

"That's exactly what I'm telling you."

"Coach," Gerry Peplowski answered, "you've never been more wrong on anything in your life."

By the time Peplowski arrived on MSU's campus for his unofficial visit, Rose Bowl voltage was lighting the sky over East Lansing, adding to the electric energy everywhere on campus.

Michigan State was about to win a prized recruit because of a young man's uniquely personal responses to a Big Ten campus. Whether it was meeting coaches, or players, or professors, or deans or other students, Peplowski had found his match.

His unofficial visit had coincided with that of Mark Montgomery, a polished point-guard from Southgate Aquinas who was another hot Izzo recruit. They were two Detroit Catholic League stars that knew each other. They had seen enough to tell Izzo on their football-weekend trip that they were going with Michigan State.

Snagging a 6-foot-7 small forward from Grand Rapids South Christian named Matt Steigenga would require a longer courtship. Steigenga was the kind of all-everything athlete and veritable Boy Scout any big-time college wanted as Steigenga's senior year approached.

Michigan State was working hard on the kind of in-state recruit who too often signed on at Ann Arbor. Izzo had been involved since Steigenga's arrival as a sophomore at South Christian, a three-year high school. Everything had been going well in the interim for Heathcote's staff. Steigenga was considering Michigan State, as well as Arizona and

North Carolina. His first choice was Michigan. He had decided U-M's academics were more in line with his tastes and aptitude and expected to lock in with the Wolverines during his official visit in October 1987.

Things didn't go as expected. Steigenga anticipated a friendly welcome from U-M's resident stars: Glen Rice, Rumeal Robinson, Loy Vaught, etc. What he felt instead were cold shoulders. U-M coach Bill Frieder had been his usual energized self in handling Steigenga's sales pitch, but Steigenga was uneasy. Nothing was clicking.

He was thinking now it would be better to play at the place an hour from home, Michigan State.

Steigenga had a better sense East Lansing was a fit when he took his official visit the following week. It had been the policy for Steigenga, a terrific high-school golfer, to play golf (covering his own greens fees) with the coaching staff at the colleges he was visiting. At MSU, that meant a Friday afternoon round at Forest Akers West, since Steigenga was obliged to be at South Christian's state high-school golf regional the next morning before a return trip for that Saturday's Michigan-Michigan State game.

He, Izzo and Heathcote headed to the course on a crisp autumn afternoon when one of the best all-around athletes in the state would essentially host his own recruiting trip. Steigenga understood what golfers long have known about their game. During the course of a four-hour round people are revealed comprehensively. It was an open door into their minds, their wit, their integrity, their values, how they respond to pressure, failure, and anxiety.

He had played golf at North Carolina with the coach most actively recruiting him there, assistant Roy Williams, just as he had played in Arizona with Lute Olson and assistant coach Kevin O'Neill. Now it was MSU's turn.

On one hole Steigenga committed a sin others who played golf with Heathcote had always known was golf's most serious offense against the Spartans' head coach. Steigenga had stepped to the back of the tee box to watch at the ball's flight as it left Heathcote's club.

Heathcote, who on a golf course seemed to have six eyes in the back of his head, detected Steigenga lurking.

"Would you get the hell out of the way?" groused Heathcote, who wouldn't have cared if he were recruiting Michael Jordan. No one could stand within his peripheral vision during a backswing.

Steigenga loved it. Any coach who could be this straightforward and gruff during a recruiting pitch was going to be the real deal. He was now leaning toward MSU. Another factor was North Carolina's recruiting priorities. It had become clear North Carolina was chasing the country's two top recruits, Billy Owen and Alonzo Mourning. They had already had Rick Fox. Steigenga was interested in playing time and concluded it would be scarce early at Chapel Hill.

Everything changed when Owen shocked half the Eastern seaboard by going with Syracuse. North Carolina was now scurrying to sign Steigenga. Dean Smith, the Tar Heels' head coach, flew into Grand Rapids for a second visit. Suddenly, Steigenga was confused. Michigan State was nervous.

A few days later, the haze lifted. Steigenga was less than an hour's drive down I-96 from home. He could expect to play in a hurry at Michigan State. He was signing with the Spartans. Steigenga was joining Peplowski and Montgomery to forge the single highest-profile recruiting class Heathcote had signed since the 1977 bonanza that brought in Magic Johnson and Jay Vincent.

THERE WERE ONLY A COUPLE OF PROBLEMS as fall and winter, 1987, gave way to spring 1988. State had just put the wraps on a sickly 10-18 season and eighth-place Big Ten finish.

Equally unsettling had been February's news bulletin: Peplowski had wrecked his knee during the Detroit Catholic League semifinals at Calihan Hall. He and his Warren De La Salle team were tangling with Southgate Aquinas—Mark Montgomery's school—when, in the third quarter, Peplowski was going for a rebound amid a half-dozen twisting bodies. His massive body rotated sharply. Peplowski felt his knee pop.

He had torn his ACL, and just about everything else in the immediate vicinity of his right knee. Medical science was less sophisticated in 1988, even at the University of Michigan sports medical center, where

Peplowski had opted to be treated. His knee was restructured with a screw and six staples. He was on crutches for six months. His freshman year became a wipe-out—a redshirt season for a young man who had the size and skill to transform MSU's low-post game.

Another recruit, destined to be one of MSU basketball's landmark talents, was living a life of lesser celebrity as he got ready for his senior year. It was the summer of 1989 and Izzo was making his way through the customary maze of high-school camps and All-Star games on a sweat-filled safari in search of players who could bring Spartan basketball some much-needed protein. The past two seasons had produced lean results on the hardcourt and if the future was to brighten, State needed talent to piggyback with its two previous recruiting classes that had brought in Smith, Peplowski and other promising players.

Izzo stopped by the basketball camp at Rensselaer, Indiana, a rich hunting ground for college recruiters who, at these talents fests, either firmed up relationships they had already established with recruits, or sought new ones. Izzo was about to become campaign manager for a kid out of Detroit Bishop Borgess High named Shawn Respert.

Respert was a borderline Big Ten talent who was plainly south of the border heading into his senior year. The University of Detroit was interested in him and probably would get him, considering that higher-profile schools had other priorities.

Respert, though, was warming up in Indiana's July heat and humidity. In one, beautifully timed breakthrough game, he scored 40 points and eviscerated the Ft. Wayne prep hotshot who allegedly was guarding him.

Izzo got on the phone to Heathcote.

"We might want to take another look at this kid out of Borgess."

MSU's coaching staff had been at odds over Respert. Heathcote's assistants regarded Respert as more of a forward than a guard. They, in turn, liked a guard from Ohio named Eric Snow, brother of a fabulous MSU linebacker named Percy Snow. The head coach wasn't so sure.

Heathcote caught a later workout at Bishop Borgess and chatted briefly with Respert, invited him for a visit, and, by October—having come around to agree with his assistants—won a commitment.

Shawn Respert, driving past Michigan's Robert Traylor, redshirted his freshman year, 1990-91, with a bad knee. Observers at practice felt that even with the injury he was State's most talented player at the time.

Respert felt liberated. He no longer had to audition, no longer had to try to persuade a major-college coach that he could make it as a Division I shooting guard. With a scholarship locked up, Respert flourished as a senior and, suddenly, all of Detroit, all of the state of Michigan, knew the Spartans had a potential steal. That was Heathcote's feeling, as well, as he drove to Calihan Hall on the University of Detroit campus to catch the Detroit Catholic League championship game between Borgess and Southgate Aquinas.

Borgess was up by almost 30 points at the half and Respert had already hit 30 points. Heading back from the locker room, Respert caught sight of Heathcote sitting in the bleachers.

"Man," he thought, "I've got to put on a show."

A few minutes into the third quarter, Respert was gliding toward the basket on a fast-break when he stepped on a defender's foot. His left knee's ACL shredded. Respert's freshman year at Michigan State, if not his college basketball career, was now a question mark.

Respert healed as quickly as could have been hoped through the spring and summer of 1989. His rehabilitation program was on a faster path than the recovery plan for Peplowski, who had torn up his knee a year earlier during the Catholic School League playoffs at Calihan Hall, also against Aquinas.

Heathcote believed a red-shirt year was, for most players, a blessing.

He preferred it for a host of reasons, one in particular. A player could adjust to school and to the realities of big-time college basketball. High school stars invariably had a tough time appreciating how different from high school was the major-college game. As Heathcote loved to say, they not only wanted to start, they wanted to *star*, which was generally behind college basketball's annual parade of transfer requests from players unhappy with playing time.

Heathcote had a plan for making the most of Respert's red-shirt season. He was about to teach a Number 2 guard how to shoot the basketball. For decades Heathcote's ability to deconstruct and reconstruct a player's mechanically flawed jump shot had been a Heathcote coaching trademark.

Respert's problem was apparent to anyone who understood the fundamentals of sound shooting form. His left hand was overly involved. Rather than providing a base for Respert's shot, it had become part of the release mechanism.

Heathcote's remedy began with a roll of duct tape. He peeled off long strips of adhesive and began wrapping Respert's left hand inside mummy-like strands that encircled Respert's waist. Heathcote wanted Respert's left hand incapacitated. The coach understood that a guard with extraordinary shooting potential would be playing at half-gear if that ugly two-handed release weren't revamped.

Heathcote's plan was to have Respert shoot repeated shots from, initially, a five-foot radius extending from the basket, moving progressively to eight feet, ten feet, and beyond. Respert began to feel the ball's rotation as it left his hand. The release was becoming as smooth as his follow-through. By January, with his knee strengthening steadily, Respert could feature a newly capable, comfortable jump-shot.

Michigan State was getting better heading into the '89-90 season, dramatically so, because of the influx of new bodies and skills. Smith, Ken Redfield, Parish Hickman, and a hot-shooting guard who had become a game-buster in his final two years at MSU, Kirk Manns, joined with Steigenga, Montgomery, Peplowski and Dwayne Stephens. Heathcote now had his best and deepest talent since the near-miss in '86.

Michigan State started 6-0, moved to 14-2, then won eleven consecutive Big Ten games as Smith scored 36 against Michigan and followed with 39 at Minnesota. That set up a season finale and Big Ten championship showdown against the Boilermakers at Breslin Center, the gleaming new arena which that season had consigned Jenison Fieldhouse to mothballs for men's basketball. Heathcote's team had already locked up a share of the Big Ten championship with a regular-season game to go, but needed to whip the Boilermakers and Heathcote's buddy, Gene Keady, to win the title outright.

East Lansing was ready to rock. Basketball at Michigan State had shaken off its late '80s malaise and, in three-and-a-half months, had become the high-voltage campus sport it was when, first Magic Johnson, and later Skiles, were pushing MSU through NCAA tournament brackets with surprising ease. Smith had exploded to become one of the best players in the country, and was unstoppable by the regular season's end. The rest of the cast was filling roles and blessing Heathcote with an expanding bench.

The Spartans and Boilermakers met on Sunday, March 11, 1990, five hours before the 1990 NCAA tournament pairings were to be announced. Game officials were as keyed as the players when both teams stepped onto Breslin's court and into an atmosphere hot and electric.

Steve Welmer, one of the referees, pulled Peplowski and Boilermakers center Steve Scheffler together before tipoff.

"OK, guys, here's the deal," Welmer said. "I'm gonna let you play. I'm gonna warn you if things go over the line. And if you keep fouling, I'll call it. Otherwise, you're free to play."

The latitude made a Big Ten basketball classic even more extraordinary in the minds of opponents who liked and respected each other, and who would never forget the quality of basketball played that afternoon at Breslin.

Welmer kept his promise. Peplowski and Scheffler battled each other hard and clean throughout. They leaned against one another and backed each other low in ways that had not been allowed in earlier games. At moments when things more resembled sumo wrestling than basketball, Welmer was in their ear.

"Uh-uh, that's too much, Pep," Welmer would say. Or, "Watch it, Steve."

If they fouled each other, the fouls were clean and hard. Welmer and his partners blew whistles judiciously. Unless, of course, Purdue's coaching staff had been polled afterward.

Michigan State was down, 70-67, with 50 seconds to play when Kirk Manns hit a six-foot jumper from the left baseline to cut Purdue's lead to a point. A timeout gave both teams a chance to pow-wow, as if Keady's strategy was any mystery. The ball was going to Scheffler.

Purdue in-bounded and quickly shoved the ball to, of course, Scheffler. An instant later, there was Dwayne Stephens lumbering down the court like a water buffalo, driving all the way for a crashing slam-dunk that put MSU on top, 71-70, with 20 seconds to play. Steve Smith's free throw after a Boilermakers offensive foul finished it, 72-70.

Stephens had stolen the ball from Scheffler and had, in one slap—Purdue insisted it should have been a foul—grabbed the Big Ten title for MSU.

Keady never forgot the moment, the play, or the perceived shafting, anymore than he could forget to jab Heathcote or one of his Spartan tribesmen in the years ahead. In the summer of 1991, Keady was coaching and Peplowski was playing on the United States Pan-American team. Keady, whose edgy humor helped explain his friendship with Heathcote, kept needling the big guy from East Lansing.

"Stephens fouled him, didn't he?" Keady would say, playfully.

"Hey, Coach," Peplowski would answer, dishing it right back, "did they call a foul?"

Keady: "That doesn't mean he didn't foul him."

Peplowski: "Well, it kind of does. C'mon, Coach, you know in a game like that you have to tear off a guy's arm and have blood shooting across the floor before they're gonna call a foul."

Peplowski, pleased by how this mutual yanking of two chains was going, paused and said, with a grin: "Great game, though, huh?"

Keady, who even at placid times looked as if he were sucking on lemons, crinkled his face and sneered, not even close to seriously, "Yeah, for

Center Mike Peplowski hits his patented hook shot against Iowa. His career, from 1989-93, spanned a key part of the renaissance of MSU basketball that became more consistent when the Breslin Student Events Center opened for the 1989-90 season.

you," as Peplowski broke up.

Michigan State was back in the NCAA tournament in big fashion: ranked fourth in the country and a Number 1 seed at the regional at Knoxville, Tennessee. Murray State was the first-round competition and seemed unfazed being a sixteenth seed facing off against a regional's top seed, which became clear all too soon. Murray State's hotshot, Popeye Jones, scored 37 points and pushed State into overtime before the Spartans escaped, 75-71. It was a game that had nearly gone down as NCAA tournament history. Through the 2006 tourney, no sixteenth seed has ever knocked off a top seed.

MSU next slid past UC Santa Barbara, 62-58, sending the Spartans packing for the Southeast Regional at the Superdome in New Orleans. The opposition was Georgia Tech, the region's Number 4 seed and a tourna-ment-tempered bunch coached by Bobby Cremins.

It was viewed most simply as a battle between two All-American guards: Smith, who had been like a locomotive engineer in driving State through the regular season and, now, deep into the tournament; and Tech's Kenny Anderson, another lofty NBA-bound guard who was steer-ing the Yellowjackets.

Michigan State wobbled in the early going and was down, 39-35, at halftime before straightening out in the final 20 minutes.

The Spartans were still leading by four points when Heathcote admonished his team, "Don't let 'em drive in."

Seconds later, Georgia Tech's Kenny Anderson promptly ran down the lane and past Montgomery for a lay-up that cut State's lead to 75-73.

"Mark, what were you doing?"

"I had four fouls," Montgomery said.

Heathcote replied that a fifth foul was less risk than handing Tech an easy bucket in a four-point game with six seconds showing.

The Spartans were still up by two with five seconds to play and were going to ice it as Smith, the invincible one, settled in for a one-and-one free-throw sequence that would put MSU into the regional finals against Minnesota.

Smith missed. Tech rebounded, pushed the ball up-court and into Anderson's hands, who let fly at the three-point line as the horn sounded.

It fell through the twine, drop-dead perfect, and sent the Superdome crowd into a chill. Heathcote was off the bench, waving his arms at the officials, pleading for them to realize that Anderson had been on the line: no three-point basket.

The officials agreed. Michigan State and Georgia Tech were headed for overtime.

It was only after the game had ended, after Tech had managed to win in overtime by a point, 81-80, that CBS-TV's Jim Nance broke the news: Anderson's shot not only was not a three-pointer, it was not a basket. Not in regulation. Audio replays proved the horn had sounded before the ball left his hands.

Four years after the Kemper Arena clock fiasco had ripped apart a team that might well have been on its way to the Final Four, more national-stage injustice had just socked the Spartans with a monumental defeat.

One analysis for a game so important being decided with such imperfection is that it was a less technologically precise world in 1990. Officials did not automatically consult scoring-table monitors and video replays to determine what had actually happened during a particular moment if it were subject to dispute.

Post-game analysis had introduced one likely cause for the confusion. In the vast Superdome, the basketball court was situated in one end of the facility, a good distance from the game horn. When acoustic realities were considered in a building so immense, sound could require a split-second extra to be absorbed. Whether it was long enough to have permitted Anderson the nanosecond of time needed to get off a shot that had clearly been released after the horn blared was open to debate. But the horn's audio signal was, tellingly, scarcely an issue until CBS aired its replay.

Heathcote and his players were in misery, again, four years after the Kemper nightmare. Adding to his ire over one more potential Final Four ticket that had been ripped in two, the NCAA had interpreted critical media remarks about the Superdome's time dispute as being an indictment by Heathcote.

He was about to be fined $10,000 for unsportsmanlike statements.

"Check the source," Heathcote told NCAA staffers when they phoned with the news. "If you want to fine me, go ahead. But this is the second time this has happened to us, and if I'm fined I just might sue the NCAA. These mistakes are course-changing and they cost universities thousands of dollars."

Heathcote never heard another word.

SMITH'S UPCOMING SENIOR YEAR, 1990-91, stood to be a good one, a make-up for the gut-ache game against Georgia Tech that sabotaged State's 1990 season. MSU was on everybody's cream-of-the-crop list. The Spartans had the right people back, the younger players were a year older, and those who knew how long injustice can stay in a team's mind figured MSU would make the Georgia Tech shafting a rallying point straight into March.

The Spartans instead lost a half-dozen squeakers to finish 18-10 in the regular season and 11-7 in the Big Ten. They got by Wisconsin-Green Bay, 60-58, when Smith hit a stunning, last-second shot to win their first-round NCAA game, but then lost in two overtimes to Utah, 85-84, to finish 19-11.

It had been a forgettable year, comparatively speaking. Smith was great, but anyone could see that a player on his way to the NBA—after bypassing the draft play his senior year—was taking care not to mess up a long, prosperous pro career by doing something physically silly during his NBA-preview season.

"Hey, Steve," Heathcote had said to Smith at one point during the Big

Ten schedule, "how about leading the team in rebounding some game?"

"Yeah, OK, Coach," Smith nodded. "That's what I'm going to do."

"Well, do it soon."

A few months later, Pat Williams, the Miami Heat general manager, called Heathcote to ask about Smith ahead of June's NBA draft. Miami had the first round's fifth pick and was thinking about Smith.

"Uh, Jud, he's not a soft player, is he?" Williams asked. "I saw him a couple of times and it looked like he was hanging back."

"Oh, no," Heathcote assured, happy he wasn't testifying under oath.

Miami took Smith, who went on to play fourteen sterling seasons in the NBA.

SOMEWHAT BETTER WAS MSU's 1991-92 EFFORT, which featured Respert's arrival as a gunslinger guard and scorer. Michigan State won its first ten games and twelve of its first thirteen to make it into the Top 10. MSU's Big Ten season was less of a thrill: 11-7, a second consecutive tie for third place.

After dusting Southwest Missouri State in the NCAA's first round, the Spartans lost to a team they had beaten by a point in December: Cincinnati beat them, 77-65, at Dayton.

Michigan State was in transition after the 1992 season, but in reverse fashion from where the Spartans had been three years earlier when Smith was blossoming into a star player and a fresh crop of talented kids was arriving.

Smith, though, had departed a year earlier. Steigenga and Montgomery had finished their careers in the NCAA tourney loss to Cincinnati. That left a couple of mainframe seniors in Peplowski and Stephens, as well as a sophomore sharpshooter in Respert, as State bored into the '92-93 schedule.

The rest of State's cast was graded incomplete as far as skills suited to turning a retooled team into a Big Ten contender. Kris Weshinskey could help off the bench. Eric Snow was an astoundingly talented guard, provided you could look past his shooting challenges. Then came a fleet of younger players: Daimon Bethea, Quinton Brooks, Anthony Miller, Jon Garavaglia and Jamie Feick.

The Spartans were going to seriously miss Montgomery's skills, especially his speed. He had arrived out of Southgate Aquinas as a point-
guard prototype of immediate service in East Lansing. Even as a freshman
he played with such understanding and command of the game that many
of his teammates suspected he was headed for a coaching career. Take
care of the basketball, distribute the ball, run the offense. When
Montgomery was on the court, MSU's most important backcourt element
was signed, sealed and delivered.

There was now an element of flux to Michigan State basketball heading into the 1992-93 season, Heathcote's seventeenth in East Lansing. The
Spartans promptly performed as if all the pre-season doubts were prophe-
cies waiting for fulfillment.

From the get-go it was not developing as the happiest of seasons.
Respert was on his way to another big year, of course; Peplowski was taking care of issues down low. But the need for two people to get the ball
was a basic inside-outside juggling act. Most often, it worked to MSU's
advantage, even as it created moments of frustration for Peplowski as he
rumbled along the baseline, aching for the basketball.

Heathcote had never coached a player quite like Peplowski. Here was
a certified lover of the low post, content to hang around the basket and
not be lured into the perimeter. Peplowski's belief was that he could wear
a saddle on any given night and have the Spartans ride along. His jump-
hook was standard procedure when he got the ball. If it wasn't there, he
was up and under. Predictable, reliable.

Younger teammates were going to miss Peplowski for reasons beyond
his back-to-the-basket skills. Peplowski was the team's court jester, a bru-
tally honest free-spirit who loved life, loved basketball, loved a laugh. He
had the usual bag of locker-room tricks. He could slather a teammate's
shorts with Ben-Gay. He might be seen sprinting naked through the training room. He could agitate a locker-room cohort with towels and squirts
of water. And then there was his reputation for slovenly domestic upkeep:
Early in Peplowski's time at MSU, his dorm room had been in such
appalling squalor that his mother shed tears.

As for Peplowski's down-low effectiveness, Respert and others felt as if his shooting was vital to any effort there. That is, unless Peplowski enjoyed the challenge of scoring against double-team and triple-team defense.

Respert's consistency during a dazzling four-year stint (he had played only one game his redshirt season) at MSU explained why his number, 24, would one day hang from the rafters at Breslin Center.

He scored 2,531 points, the most ever by a MSU player through MSU's 2005-06 season. His shooting percentages were in amazing harmony for his career, whether in overall field goals (48, 48, 47, 48), three-point shots (45, 43, 45, 47), or free throws (87, 86, 84, 87).

In retrospect, he had been a transcendent player at a stage when MSU basketball desperately needed a backcourt luminary as a bridge between the Steve Smith-Mateen Cleaves eras.

Respert's efforts notwithstanding, there was a kind of melancholy air to MSU basketball in the winter months of 1993, which not even Peplowski and his life-of-the-party antics could offset. What might have been a big season steadily slipped away. The Spartans lost eight games by a combined 32 points (two of the losses were by 12 points total in overtime), finished tied for eighth in the Big Ten (6-12), and were left with a 15-13 record, as well as a not-so-inviting trip to the National Invitation Tournament.

MSU players voted, reluctantly, to play. They came to appreciate the dividend from a supposedly second-tier tournament. Michigan State beat Kent State, Wichita State and Villanova to make it to the NIT Final Four at Madison Square Garden. There the run ended with a semifinal loss to St. Louis, followed by a mop-up overtime defeat against Alabama-Birmingham in the consolation game.

The Spartans learned that tournament competition against good basketball teams was always worthwhile. The NIT was a national-stage event. It meant a welcome trip to New York City. It was a chance to compete on a basketball court and at a celebrated sports facility where, for generations, history had been made.

Another advantage could hardly be understood with any sense of clairvoyance in March of 1993. The Spartans needed tournament experience as a warm-up act for what would increasingly become longer, deeper one-and-done tests in the NCAA tournament. Those post-season runs were just over the horizon, as was the head-coaching tenure of a man about to be promoted by Michigan State, an assistant coach named Tom Izzo.

CHAPTER 13

TULSA TWO STEP

OPTIONS WERE CLEAR-CUT in 1986 for a graduate-assistant basketball coach making $7,000 a year. You could own a car, although it would be something on the level of an old, weather-beaten Oldsmobile. You ate fast food at night, or threw some bargain-priced frozen entree from the grocery store into your cart ahead of its final destination in a microwave oven.

You hoped there would be a couple of functions or invitations coming your way that week. An event at Kellogg Center was always welcome, as was an invitation from Michigan State friends, where in either case you could count on digging into a full-course, salad-and-steak dinner, replete with a twice-baked potato, or maybe some of that terrific risotto that had become so fashionable, all of it accompanied by fresh vegetables and rolls and, as a grand finale, maybe by a scoop of ice cream splashed with chocolate sauce for dessert.

Tom Izzo was trying to justify the quality of life at Michigan State as a graduate assistant under head coach Jud Heathcote. It was not easy when you were always broke, often hungry, and wondering just what in blazes you were doing at age thirty-one working for, literally, starvation wages.

He had his degree in education from Northern Michigan University. He had the ability and freedom to work a gainful job. And yet, here he was, hanging around a Big Ten basketball team, making less than minimum wage, turning down chances at one coaching job after another.

Michigan Tech: He almost took a job at Houghton in the Upper

Peninsula, Izzo's homeland, during his second year under Heathcote. It was the wrong place at the wrong time.

Northern Michigan: His alma mater and Tom Izzo could have gone back as head coach—for $20,000 a year. When he balked, even his mother was angry with him for saying no to a job that would at least have moved him up a rung from poverty to the ranks of America's economically stressed.

YEARS LATER, DEEPER INTO IZZO'S COACHING CAREER, bigger opportunities, openings, or invitations would come his way: Western Michigan ... Eastern Michigan ... Central Michigan ... Northwestern ... Wisconsin. Some of them were good, some were within reach, some were a stretch. Wanting them would always be Izzo's problem. He preferred to be at Michigan State, the place that for a young bachelor whose passion was coaching, was Utopia minus the paychecks.

An Upper Peninsula native could kid about the difference in culture: How nice it was to go to the mall or to a movie theater in East Lansing and see more than one title playing.

Heathcote was sensitive to his part-time coach's struggles. He knew all about Tom Izzo's energy, his emerging coaching skills and his decency. Heathcote was in the process of working out with Doug Weaver, MSU's athletic director, an arrangement in April 1986 by which Izzo could legally (NCAA rules governing paid assistants were rigid) make $20,000 annually.

"If we can get that done," Izzo assured his boss, "I'm staying."

Heathcote responded in his familiar, cut-to-the-chase voice:

"We can get it done. But you're not staying. You're going with J.D. Barnett at Tulsa. You can go down there and be in charge of recruiting. If Mike Deane (Heathcote's top assistant) is gone from here in three or four years, we can talk about you coming back. So, you're out of here."

J.D. Barnett and Heathcote were old friends from a trusted coaching fraternity. The network was important to head coaches in need of capable staffers and to assistants who looked to head coaches as placement directors. If he had to leave East Lansing—and the thought was killing him— at least he was going to a place Jud knew would be good for him. At least he was going to have a few bucks in his wallet.

Tom Izzo's first paycheck, which showed up two weeks after he began work at Tulsa, was for a comparative king's ransom: $438. That was a month of take-home pay in his old job. He decided to celebrate. The next morning, Saturday, he went to a Tulsa mall and engaged in what was, for him, a reckless spending spree: He bought pants. He bought a couple of shirts. He went out to lunch. On a summer Saturday in Oklahoma, life for a young basketball coach was sweet.

It was not as if he were being overpaid or under-worked. Barnett drove a hard office. He wanted his staffers in their offices at 7 a.m. and preferred that they work through the evening, preferably until midnight or later. Nothing pleased J.D. Barnett more than to bring influential alums by the basketball offices well into an evening and display to them how hard his assistants were laboring.

Izzo had been in Oklahoma for eight weeks when the phone rang, on a Tuesday, a few days into June 1986.

"What are you doing?" asked the caller, a head coach by the name of Jud Heathcote.

"Just sitting here."

"Buy a house yet?"

"Nope."

"You haven't bought a house yet?"

"No. I just got settled into an apartment."

"Well, hang on," Heathcote said. "Mike Deane is interviewing at Siena College. If he gets it, that opens up his slot and I want you back here in it."

Thoughts spun in Izzo's mind throughout that day and night and into the next day. He was on the verge of getting the job he most wanted, in the town he most loved. He would live Michigan State basketball 24/7 as Jud Heathcote's top assistant. Each time the phone rang, Izzo picked it up, hoping he would hear Heathcote's voice.

But there was no call Wednesday. Nor on Thursday. He decided to phone Heathcote for a status report.

"Bad news," Heathcote said. "Mike's not taking the job."

One half of Izzo wanted to dissolve. Disappointment on this level was crushing, particularly when you had spent forty-eight hours knocking at heaven's door. The other half was relieved. He did not look forward to a farewell conversation with J.D. Barnett. It would not be well received and, conceivably, might be damaging to his career.

Izzo focused on happier thoughts, such as the next morning's breakfast. He and Barnett were meeting in the morning with a local car dealer, Ken Tate, a Tulsa booster who would hand Izzo the keys to a gorgeous new car. It was one of the legal perks an assistant coach on Izzo's level could expect at a place like Tulsa.

Early the next morning, a half hour before they were to leave for breakfast and for the new assistant coach's first drive in his new wheels, the phone rang in Izzo's office.

It was Heathcote.

"You're not going to believe this, but Mike wants the Siena job back."

"Is he taking it?"

"I don't know. Hang on."

Twenty minutes later, another call.

Heathcote: "They offered Mike the job."

Izzo barely heard the words as Barnett began yelling from the corridor: "Tom, c'mon, we've got to meet Ken."

Izzo was in a bind he could never have imagined.

"Jud," he said, in a desperate whisper, "what am I gonna do?"

Heathcote decided to table discussions for the time being.

"I'll get back to you," he said.

Tate, the Import Motors mogul, was a convivial gent, delighted to be placing in a new coach's hands the keys to a Datsun 300ZX. Cars carried a particular status in Oklahoma. It was the sort of favor friends of Tulsa's athletics wanted to confer upon loyal coaches—emphasis on loyal.

Izzo was soon tooling through Tulsa in his new wheels, so absorbed by the pure bliss of driving a hot new automobile he could manage only one thought: "If my friends back home in Iron Mountain could see me now."

His spirit was simultaneously sinking. He might be giving back the car that very night, at least if he survived Barnett's reaction when Izzo told him he was leaving for East Lansing.

Breakfast moved into lunchtime and beyond and still there had been no follow-up from Heathcote.

At 11 p.m., Izzo's phone rang.

"I've got it all worked out," Heathcote said. "I'll call J.D."

Izzo thought for a moment. Doing the decent thing trumped doing the easier, uncomfortable thing.

"No," he said. "I'll call him."

Izzo's roommate during his first weeks at Tulsa was a graduate assistant coach named Ron Jirsa, who years later would become an assistant at Georgia under Tubby Smith and next the head coach at Marshall. Jirsa had been around when assistant coach Kevin O'Neill—he was destined to become head coach at Northwestern in 1997—left Tulsa in similarly spontaneous fashion for Arizona earlier that year.

"You better hold onto your ass," Jirsa said when Izzo gave him the news late that night. "He wouldn't even let O'Neill clean out his desk."

At 8:15 the next morning, Izzo's phone rang.

"Tom," Barnett said, a crackle in his voice, "what's going on?"

Tulsa had that week interviewed former University of Minnesota assistant coach Flip Saunders, who was going to take a restricted-pay job on Barnett's staff (in step with NCAA rules on staff numbers and compensation).

Saunders was friends with Mike Deane, whose appointment at Siena had appeared that day in the Minneapolis newspaper. Saunders called Barnett to ask the logical question:

"Is Tom going back to Michigan State?"

Barnett in turn called Izzo, saying: "Flip's looking for you. He wants to talk with you."

Barnett paused and said: "Did Jud call you?"

For moments that seemed like minutes, Izzo was silent.

"Yeah …"

"Are you taking the goddam job?" Barnett roared.

"I'll be honest, J.D.," Izzo answered, "I'd like to."

Barnett followed with a barrage of blue language and expletives.

After the first salvo, he barely caught his breath before he hit Izzo with more thunder.

"Turn that car in immediately! And get out of that office! I want that car in twenty minutes!"

Izzo by now had ceased being embarrassed. He was mad. He had done nothing wrong except agree to join an old boss who had stuck to an earlier commitment and now wanted him back after Deane had departed for Siena. If Barnett wanted to come down on someone, blame Siena for hiring Deane.

Now without transportation, Izzo called Jirsa for a ride. The car keys he had owned for twenty-four hours were back in the custody of Import Motors.

"I'm not allowed to pick you up," Jirsa said, embarrassed that Barnett had given screw-him orders to a fellow assistant coach.

Izzo said he understood. He called a cab from the car dealership and was dropped off at the basketball office, where he planned to clean out his desk as an ugly exit unfurled.

It wasn't necessary. Barnett had already purged Izzo's office of anything remotely attached to an assistant who had been on the job for all of eight weeks.

It was now 4 p.m. Izzo had not heard a word from Barnett. No final orders, no calmed-down farewell, nothing. He decided to call his best friend, Steve Mariucci, who was now on the staff at Southern Cal.

"Just get out of there," Mariucci said, disgusted at how a young man's career obligation—to say nothing of his freedom—had caused a head coach to come so unglued.

Izzo headed to the airport, two duffel bags in tow, and caught a 5:30 p.m. connector to Lansing. Tulsa was in his rearview mirror. East Lansing, here comes Tom Izzo, carrying a few bruises from Barnett's verbal artillery but relieved to be going back to the place he knew he was supposed to be.

Izzo understood what he would be doing when he rejoined his old boss, Heathcote. He would be recruiting—happily so. He was now Heathcote's right-hand assistant and top talent scout. Finally Tom Izzo could get on with a personal goal of making the state of Michigan the Spartans' private recruiting province. It was Nirvana for a thirty-one year-old man who was hungry and determined to bring in kids who for too long had been finding excuses to go to Michigan, Syracuse, or anywhere but East Lansing.

Izzo had no idea where, or how, his career might evolve at Michigan State as he settled in as top assistant to a head coach who had not yet turned sixty. It was a little early to think about inheriting Heathcote's job. It was equally early to think of becoming a head coach anywhere on a major Division I level until he put a bit more muscle on his resume.

Six years would pass rapidly for Izzo at Michigan State. The landscape was changing. Heathcote, heading into the 1992-93 season, was sixty-five years old and thinking about playing golf whenever he wanted, quite possibly at the end of this season if Michigan State went out on a sufficiently high note. Would he retire in March, for sure? Would he stay on for an additional year? Heathcote wasn't sure and saw no reason why he had to commit.

It was autumn when he decided to have a chat with his boss, athletic director Merrily Dean Baker.

"I'd like Tom named head coach when I retire," Heathcote said, making clear he might want to coach another year.

Baker nodded.

"I like Tom," she said. "I'll look into that."

Heathcote had for some time been building his case for Izzo becoming Michigan State's next head basketball coach. He knew he would need the right trustees behind him, and he had them in Bob Weiss and Joel Ferguson. He knew he needed the backing of MSU's president, which he believed he had from interim president Gordon Guyer. He would rely on Weiss and Ferguson to work the internal politics with Guyer and avoid a national search that could make a mess of everyone's plans for Izzo.

Ferguson had been won over early on by Izzo when Ferguson's son, David, attended Michigan State basketball camp. Ferguson saw that Izzo worked not only with the better players, but that he worked with every

Jud Heathcote (left) with a young Tom Izzo in a game at Jenison Field House. In those days, Izzo made $7,000 a year as a graduate assistant. Today, he makes that much in a couple days.

kid in equal fashion. He was moved, as well, by how white and black players seemed to have a comfort level with MSU's young assistant.

Bypassing a national search was going to be a dramatic, even dangerous, step for a school that needed to get this appointment right. Privately, one trustee or administrator after another cornered Heathcote.

"Is Tom ready?" Weiss asked.

"Can he do this job?" asked Roger Wilkinson, the vice president over-seeing athletics.

Heathcote was adamant: yes, and double-yes. This wasn't specula-tion. Heathcote understood Izzo's skills better than anyone. They were all-encompassing. Hire him or regret it later.

Associate AD Clarence Underwood was not so sure. In fact, in February 1994, he was not sure about any aspect of MSU basketball. Heathcote, he believed, was no asset as head coach. Underwood was of the belief Heathcote had been presiding for too long over a so-so program doomed in most years to under-achievement, especially in recruiting.

The two men had never been close, a relationship more Heathcote's fault than Underwood's. Heathcote considered Underwood to be, on occasion, an obstructionist. It was an unfair label given the need for nailed-down rules compliance that had to withstand potential NCAA scrutiny. Heathcote had embarrassed Underwood a time or two in group settings, such as the basketball banquet where Heathcote had Underwood stand up as he told the audience it was Underwood's fault that several players could not receive a particular award the coach had picked out. In that instance, the problem was cost. The awards exceeded NCAA limits on expenditures. Underwood was obliged to report the infraction. With its history of past probations, Michigan State was not a school that could become cavalier about NCAA rules on any level, especially with president Peter McPherson running things.

As for Izzo, Underwood suspected that the young assistant needed seasoning. Underwood believed Michigan State's responsibility was to go national with a search. Better to take advantage of a marketplace in which good young basketball coaches were piled high and select one who would be a precise fit for MSU's needs and personality.

By February 1994, the Spartans were well on their way to a season Underwood believed was far too typical of Heathcote's teams. Michigan State was middle-of-the-pack (14-10 overall, 5-7 in the Big Ten) and Heathcote had yet to say whether he was retiring this year or in 1994.

Why, Underwood wondered, should MSU treat Heathcote so indul-gently when State's basketball program needed to name a successor and get on with life under Izzo? After all, Izzo was dubbed Heathcote's successor in 1993, pending Jud's departure. Underwood had a good relationship with McPherson and thought it was time to get the president involved and settle down the MSU basketball program.

Adding to his certitude was the reality that several executives, including McPherson, were just as uneasy with Heathcote's foot-dragging, to say nothing of fans that were getting edgier by the season.

Underwood wrote a memo to McPherson, taking care to keep it from his boss, Merrily Dean Baker, with whom he had an uneasy relationship. Better, he thought, to write it and hand-deliver it to one of the president's assistants in the Administration Building. The memo was dynamite and Underwood didn't want to ignite it.

That afternoon, February 17, 1994, McPherson called Underwood after reading the memo. He was not happy about a chain-of-command exclusion of Baker. Get the memo to her, McPherson said so the chief executives—McPherson, Wilkinson, Baker and Underwood—could hash out a plan if necessary.

Underwood sensed trouble. A discussion with the president would have been safe and of no consequence. A memo was another matter altogether. It was documentation, if not a declaration, and when it dealt with the removal of a high-profile university figure that was dangerous terrain.

Ten days later, on February 27, Underwood and Heathcote each received a phone call from *State News* reporter Kyle Melinn. It struck Heathcote as a peculiar time and place to get a call from a college newspaper reporter. The reporter's question was also strange.

"How do you get along with Clarence Underwood?" Melinn asked Heathcote when he phoned his home that evening.

"I get along with Clarence very well," said Heathcote, who was more inclined than Underwood to think of their dealings as sugar and spice. "We've had a long and good relationship."

"Are you aware of the memorandum he wrote?" Melinn asked.

"No."

Melinn read it over the phone to Heathcote.

MEMO

February 17, 1994

TO: President McPherson
FROM: Clarence Underwood, Jr.
RE: Head Men's Basketball Coach

As you know, both our men's and women's basketball programs are performing less than satisfactorily this season. However, since my responsibilities are with the men's basketball program, I will confine my comments there.

Based on the men's basketball team's wins-and-loss record over the past 10 years, and recognizing the need for immediate improvement in our recruitment strategies to elevate our team's Big Ten final standing higher than its fifth-place average, I wish to make the following recommendations:

(1) That I be authorized to approach Jud Heathcote and tell him that the university would like for him to retire from the men's basketball program, effective at the close of the present season. This will provide him the opportunity to announce his retirement gracefully. If he does not accept this option, then I recommend No. 2.

(2) That Jud Heathcote be terminated from the men's basketball program, effective March 31, 1994, without interruption of his base MSU salary through June 30, 1995. This date is essential to coincide with the close of the regular basketball season. It would allow head coach-elect Tom Izzo the opportunity to recruit and hire a top-notch assistant coach from a nationally ranked team when such coaches are usually available. It also would permit Izzo adequate time to plan an effective recruitment initiative for his staff to contact prospective student-athletes participating in summer camp programs.

(3) That Michigan State University provides Heathcote a farewell reception where his family, friends, boosters, and university representatives are invited.

Furthermore, I recommend that head coach-elect Tom Izzo be given a four-year contract with the university retaining the option to renew the contract after completion of the third year. His salary is yet to be determined.

I request the opportunity to meet with you at your convenience concerning the above recommendations.

Sincerely,

Clarence Underwood, Jr.
Senior Associate Athletics Director

There was a long silence. Heathcote was devastated. He had been the target of a backdoor ouster—by an athletic department colleague. A man who was ultra-sensitive to his status as a man and as a coach was emotional rubble. There had been an attempted coup against the head basketball coach orchestrated by an associate athletic director, a fellow Michigan State staffer.

Underwood was doing no better. He received a call from Melinn early that evening asking for a response to the memo. Underwood had asked how Melinn got hold of it. When there was no explanation, Underwood hung up. He had been confused by Melinn's motives during an interview four days earlier when Melinn showed up to speak with Underwood about a Black History Month feature.

In fact, Melinn was in possession of the memo even before he approached Underwood for what was a legitimate story assignment. The two issues were separate and unrelated. Melinn never believed the memo's contents would see print ahead of Black History Month's cessation on February 28.

Melinn's editor, Suzette Hackney, had a different appraisal when she learned about the memo on February 27. This was serious and explosive news. It was going into the newspaper, pronto. As for how Melinn obtained the memo, he and his editor knew the particulars. There was no theft, no dishonest or fraudulent methods involved. The memo had not been taken from Underwood's office.

The story of a head basketball coach betrayed by an associate AD became national news when the story broke on February 28. Clarence Underwood's memo, in fact, had made a mess of everything for everybody. Heathcote felt personally and professionally betrayed. McPherson was furious about a flap that had been totally unnecessary. Bob Weiss, a trustee who had no great regard for Underwood, wanted him fired, as did AD Merrily Baker, who was rushing back from NCAA meetings in Arizona to assume her place in another inimitable MSU battle royal.

Underwood was still at a loss to explain how the memo had been leaked. He had taken care to prevent it from being seen by anyone but McPherson, right down to deleting it from his personal computer. He had hand-carried the memo to McPherson's office.

It hardly mattered. Reaction in East Lansing was clear: Heathcote had a right to feel double-crossed. Plenty of critics, aggrieved fans included, were now sending the head coach their sympathy.

Underwood and others were smart enough to know Heathcote was going to use this moment resourcefully. He would stay on another year as head basketball coach, absolutely, just as he would revel in the reality that Underwood had made for himself a most uncomfortable bed.

Izzo meanwhile was aware of a new reality—his boss was staying on for another long year.

Izzo had a fine relationship with Heathcote, the boss whose support had set him up as his successor. At the same time, understandably he wanted to get on with his new life overseeing Michigan State's basketball team. Instead, he now foresaw another year of working for an assistant's salary doing an assistant's tasks.

Fortunately, he did those chores skillfully for the next year. And he coped with a financial situation that—like his relationship with Heathcote—was difficult at times, challenging always, but invariably nothing over which he had supreme control.

Izzo and Heathcote had shared MSU's good and bad times. Izzo had known recruiting disappointments and had taken them, many times, more personally than did Heathcote.

A prime example was Chris Webber. The super-sized, super-talented youngster from Southfield was in the eighth grade when he announced during a Sunday night WDIV-TV feature clip that he was going to Michigan State University when he finished high school (which was destined to be at Detroit Country Day).

The thirteen-year-old's college commitment was humorous enough to have earned a grin from those watching TV. A more serious side to WDIV's scoop was that Webber already had extraordinary talent, size, and potential. Within twenty-four hours, Izzo had heard from a Detroit-area alum about the budding basketball superstar who sounded as if he wanted to come out early—not for the NBA, but for Michigan State.

Izzo got a tape of WDIV's feature from Tim Staudt, sports director at Lansing's WILX-TV. He went from the tape to watching Webber play in a junior-high game. Soon after he invited the school's principal, basketball coach, and Webber's family for an unofficial introduction to Michigan State.

Izzo had no doubt Webber was going to be spectacular. Here he was, three years from getting a driver's license and already the owner of hands so big he held a basketball as if it were a grape. Webber had all the size and athleticism and passion for basketball that could be wrapped within a boy who looked, and played, more like a man.

The relationship gained strength by weeks and by months. Izzo and Webber's parents were tight. Izzo had rapport with the men who coached Webber at Country Day and during summer AAU leagues. Throughout Chris Webber's freshman, sophomore and junior years it was apparent he was headed to the school he had said as an eighth-grader he would attend: Michigan State.

Izzo was at Webber's games repeatedly. High school, AAU or wherever Webber was playing, Izzo was sitting. It was at a national AAU tournament in Jacksonville, Florida, where Webber and many of the nation's hotshots were playing during a month-long competition, that Izzo got acquainted with a young assistant coach from Duke named Tommy Amaker.

They would bump into each other at poolside every day. They talked. They had a friendship—as friendships went among college coaches.

"See you tonight at the game," one of them would say as the poolside break came to an end.

Michigan State was going to get Chris Webber. Eight weeks into the senior year of Michigan's most luminous high school athlete, a month before early commitments could be signed, Izzo regarded Webber as an 80 percent lock.

In the span of a few weeks those odds began to change. Mike Boyd, who was an assistant to Steve Fisher at the University of Michigan, had left in September of 1990 for the head-coaching job at Cleveland State. The loss of an eleven-year assistant coach figured to be tough on Fisher's recruiting rhythms during a particularly sensitive time. Michigan, though, was beginning to make inroads with Webber. The Wolverines were getting help from a hands-on U-M basketball booster named Ed Martin, a high roller who had a way of getting close to designated athletes.

Michigan was not only moving on Webber, it was also closing in on a potentially sensational freshman class. Most inspiring for Michigan was that Webber had suddenly and seriously entered the picture. Juwan Howard, a marvelous big man from Chicago, was on his way to Ann Arbor, as were a pair of Texas stars, Jimmy King and Ray Jackson.

Fisher badly wanted Detroit Southwestern High star guard Jalen Rose. By landing Rose the Wolverines could help entice Webber, and vice versa. Although the two players went to different high schools, they were friends the way regional stars often are. They had grown up as high-profile Detroit prep phenoms and already had played in local and national events together. If Webber had attended public and not private school, it would have been Rose's Southwestern.

Fisher decided a perfect choice for his vacant assistant's job would be Perry Watson, Southwestern's well-regarded head coach. Although it was nothing Fisher was going to trumpet, bringing on an accomplished high-school coach of Watson's skill and reputation carried significant strategic value. It might have the clinching impact on Rose's thoughts toward Michigan. Webber could then enjoy the kick from becoming part of Michigan's mounting recruiting momentum and national buzz over all the incoming talent.

The dots connected. From seventy-five miles away Izzo could see it, not to mention the irony in Watson joining a college-basketball program for which he had no particular love. High on Watson's grievance list was the way two heralded Southwestern prep stars from the 1980s, Antoine Joubert and Leslie Rockymore, had not flourished to Watson's expectations at Michigan.

Another incident helped explain why Michigan State and Webber were drifting apart. During a recruiting visit to Minnesota, which that weekend happened to be playing the Spartans in football, Underwood spotted Webber sitting in the Gophers press box, a violation of NCAA policy.

He asked Vickie Weiss, wife of trustee Bob Weiss, to take photographs of Webber in the press box as evidence in case it became a NCAA matter. Vickie Weiss had gotten a field pass from George Perles permitting her to take sideline photographs during the game.

"Why would you want to turn in a high-school player visiting Minnesota?" Vickie Weiss asked.

"Because," said Underwood, who thought infractions were infractions no matter where they occurred, "it's a violation of NCAA rules."

Weiss never appreciated that his wife had been dragged into the fray, particularly when it infuriated his friend, Heathcote. The coach in turn blamed Underwood for creating an incident that, Heathcote maintained, was damaging Webber's chances of signing with MSU.

In fact, Webber was distancing himself from East Lansing and cozying up steadily to Ann Arbor for reasons quite detached from the Minnesota flap. Many forces were at work, some of which would not be made public for years. Some of which would help place Michigan's basketball program on probation.

Heathcote's staffers—Izzo, Stan Joplin and Jim Boylen—were beginning to conclude Webber was headed to Michigan. Whatever his motive, he was blowing off MSU after a lengthy early-stage relationship and was now in U-M's corner. Also apparent was that Jalen Rose, who had not planned on visiting Michigan, had changed his disposition now that Perry Watson was headed to Ann Arbor. Now he was on *his* way to U-M.

Relationships between the two coaching staffs were civil but chilly, especially when Joplin, Izzo and Boylen would run into Brian Dutcher, Jay Smith, and later Watson. Michigan State's assistants were both jealous and resentful that the Detroit-area stars seemed ticketed for Ann Arbor.

Michigan's camp might have countered with two words: Magic Johnson. He was ready to sign with Michigan in 1977 until a strong-armed, one-on-one session in the Lansing Everett High School library with Spartans assistant coach Vern Payne—aided and abetted by Johnson's friend and agent, Dr. Charles Tucker—put his name on a MSU tender.

Michigan State's staffers would have offered a rebuttal: Johnson had not been seduced with the help of "loans" from a well-heeled booster named Ed Martin. Part of the frustration, MSU coaches would always say, stemmed from knowing bad stuff was happening and having no way to document it. MSU's assistant coaches were well familiar with basketball's surface and subterranean worlds—like assistant coaches everywhere, they beat the streets, hung out at the gyms, and knew everyone who mattered within a particular recruit's circle.

HEATHCOTE MEANWHILE PREPARED FOR HIS FINAL SEASON at Michigan State. The winter of 1994-95 would be remembered by his players years later not only as Heathcote's grand finale, but as the Spartans' endless winter. Or, rather, it seemed that way by the time Heathcote's troops had stood and waited through nearly a dozen going-away celebrations. The Farewell to Jud Tour was marked by pre-game rituals, rather remarkable for their humor and warmth, at all the opposing Big Ten arenas.

A simple explanation was that enemy schools liked Heathcote. Coaches appreciated him—Purdue's Gene Keady and Indiana's Bob Knight, in particular. They knew he played it straight in the recruiting and retention of basketball players. They loved his jokes and his no-frills style.

Opposing fans enjoyed him because he was entertaining. No one in basketball had Jud's expressions or animation. He stomped. He stooped as he shuffled in front of the MSU bench. He pumped his hands and arms like pistons on a camshaft. He slapped his forehead. He bellowed indictments of players that could be heard in the rafters.

And, yes, he and his team sustained enough losses at those opposing gyms during nineteen years to keep an opposing crowd from being resentful.

Heathcote's exit was nicely scripted: a 9-1 start (blemished only by an overtime loss at Nebraska); a seven-game Big Ten winning streak that pushed State's record to 16-2; second place in the Big Ten (a late shot at Iowa on March 8 clipped the Spartans, 79-78, and cost them a shot at a Big Ten co-championship) to go with a 22-5 overall record. That set up the Spartans' first-round NCAA tournament game against Weber State at Tallahassee, Florida.

MSU had been tearing up the competition all winter with its blow-torch backcourt of Eric Snow and Shawn Respert. One guard, Respert, was a Fourth of July show with his outside shooting. The other half of Fire and Ice, as they were known, was Snow, the one-time brick-laying offensive player who had settled down at the free-throw line (his previous troubles had been torture not only for himself but for anyone with an ounce of compassion) and who ran a basketball team from his point-guard spot the way General Patton ran an army division.

Teammates considered Snow about the toughest player they had ever seen on a basketball court. They remembered how it had been in earlier seasons, when his trips to the free-throw line were anguished, traumatic ordeals. He was having a difficult time hitting iron or even hitting the backboard.

After one particularly miserable effort his sophomore year, Snow broke down in the locker room, crying in absolute frustration and despair. Teammates watched him pick up the emotional pieces and become steadily stronger and more reliable at the line and with his overall offense. They saw him begin to ascend as a prime-time basketball player who, in contrast to any conceivable thoughts from earlier in his MSU years, was on his way to a long NBA career. In fact, his floating runner through the lane at the buzzer was good enough to shock Iowa in a late-season Big Ten game.

Heathcote's long coaching run was going to end at some point during the 1995 NCAA tournament. MSU was seeded third in the South Regional and was getting the fourteenth-seeded Weber State Wildcats,

Eric Snow's buzzer-beater sent the Spartans to a stunning win against Iowa in 1995, Coach Jud Heathcote's final season. Snow, who began his MSU career with a shocking inability to make free throws, continues a long and successful NBA career.

a Big Sky Conference tenant, and their wisecracking coach, Ron Abegglen. It was a dangerous team in the vein of all deeper-seeded NCAA tourney teams that enter a sixty-four-school contest with at least a shot at knocking off some of the fat cats, thanks in great part to a volatile line known as the three-point arc. Heathcote had coached enough Big Sky basketball at Montana before coming to East Lansing to understand these sorts of match-ups were ambushes waiting to happen.

The Spartans played well enough in their first-round game to grab a 47-36 halftime lead, not that Heathcote was impressed or reassured.

"Unless we play a better second half," the coach said during his intermission address, "we have no chance to win."

Heathcote meant it. Weber State had out-hustled and out-rebounded MSU, which owed its big lead to some fiery shooting. Percentages dictated that MSU's scoring was likely to ease off in the second half while Weber State's ferocity would continue and its shooting become more accurate.

Heathcote was right. The Wildcats pummeled MSU with a 42-26 second-half blitz to win, 79-72. Jud Heathcote's twenty-five-year head coaching career had ended on a Friday night in Tallahassee. His record: 420-273 overall, 340-220 during two decades at Michigan State.

Jud Heathcote's final farewell to East Lansing was going to take a while longer, perhaps, than Tom Izzo would have preferred. The new head coach paced and fretted and itched to get into his new office and begin working twenty-four hours a day as the unquestioned director of Michigan State basketball.

Heathcote's formal goodbye party was a not-so-intimate gathering of ex-players, ex-assistants, coaching friends, boosters, fans, media, etc., at Breslin Center. His bon voyage gift: a new Oldsmobile Aurora and a parting quip from the program committee: "OK, Jud, now get out of town."

TOM IZZO GOT TO WORK, which for him meant daily overtime shifts that were invariably closer to twenty hours than ten. He had his staff—Tom Crean, Stan Joplin and Brian Gregory—ready to unleash on a recruiting blitzkrieg. He had a strategy he had spent years formulating and honing, particularly during the two interminable years after he had been named Heathcote's successor. Every conceivable plan of attack, every possible preparation had been catalogued into the mind of a forty-year-old man whose energy and soul were about to be welded to a basketball program at Michigan State University.

The blueprint was ambitious, but also pragmatic. Izzo had the same goal as every other Division I coach in America: win the NCAA championship. That, however, could not be the creed by which you constructed a basketball team. The Spartans instead would recruit and coach to win the Big Ten. Play well enough to win the conference in any given season, and the NCAA tournament would take care of itself.

Changing the nature of MSU's recruiting was going to be the first item on the agenda. The University of Michigan had, for too many years, been assimilating into its program most of the state's premier high-school hotshots. U-M was a natural first inclination for in-state thoroughbreds.

One immediate recruiting question that had to be answered as Izzo settled into Heathcote's old office was whether to take a shot at Terrence Roberson, a 6-foot-7, 215-pound front-liner from Saginaw Buena Vista High, who was not on Michigan's wish list. Roberson had a bad-boy rap and academic challenges that were not necessarily impossible to overcome if MSU wanted him badly enough. It was up to Izzo. The coach ultimately decided not to pursue Roberson. He had to begin with kids who fit his definition of character or nothing was going to work in the years ahead, if there were to be years ahead.

Distance from the player's home to East Lansing was helpful, but didn't matter in Roberson's case. Izzo wanted players whose homes were within driving distance of East Lansing. He had come to a prevailing point of view during his years as an assistant: The farther from campus you recruited, the more problems a coach could expect. You needed geographical intimacy to keep tabs on a kid and to keep his family involved. Do that, and the dividends would be immense. Stray from your principles to bring on a kid who was a three-hour plane ride from campus and you could expect challenges in proportion to your frequent-flier points. Roberson was close enough to fit Izzo's criteria, but because of character concerns, Izzo decided to pass.

There was one immediate hang-up as Izzo gathered steam for his first full recruiting summer as MSU head coach. Only one coach could be on the road recruiting, the consequences of secondary NCAA violations from the early 1990s that included a summer-job infraction relating to a no-show player receiving a full paycheck.

The July recruiting season is for coaches a non-stop series of camps, clinics and summer competition. Izzo for the most part functioned as MSU's lone recruiting coach during that summer's twenty-five-day window, a period when he was gone from East Lansing twenty-one of those twenty-five days.

Izzo determined he could do the job of two or three coaches, and on some days he did just that. He was going wherever the players were, not only those he was hoping would commit that year, or the next spring, but players a full year or two away from decisions. The in-state and regional group was up for grabs, at least as far as Izzo was concerned: Mateen Cleaves, Shane Battier, Charlie Bell, Dugan Fife, DuJuan Wiley, as well as Ohio kids such as Andre Hutson and A.J. Granger.

Izzo's days typically began from 4:30 to 5 a.m. and often included four stops within the next twenty-four hours. He might begin with a flight to Peoria, Illinois, to see forward Brandon Cole (he would sign with Xavier) before flying to Toledo and grabbing a rental car to catch A.J. Granger in a scrimmage at Findlay, Ohio. Izzo would fly from Toledo to Flint to see Bell and Mike Chappelle (he chose Duke but later transferred to State) play in an AAU game that evening before shooting back to Detroit to watch Southfield superstar Shane Battier play at Detroit Country Day.

The next day, which for Izzo was five or six hours away, brought on a fresh recruiting cavalcade. Izzo's staffers came to relish his fatigue. When he most complained about exhaustion was when the Spartans seemed to make their greatest inroads. Izzo, they came to understand, had an uncanny knack for locking in on a recruit or an objective—and seeing it through—when he was most worn out.

It was manifested in different ways. Word may have filtered back that

Cleaves was taking Michigan State seriously. A high-school coach might have mentioned that MSU was in the hunt for a particular kid. These were signals that had not always come at the same intervals in previous years.

It helped that NCAA rules were different. There were few restrictions on mailings or on phone calls. Izzo and his staff thrived.

It was common for Izzo to call the office at 10 p.m. from a basketball camp or AAU tournament somewhere in the country and tell one of his assistants that a particular player's team just won by ten points. The assistant would send an immediate fax to the player's hotel congratulating him on winning and on scoring however many points. It was the kind of instantaneous feedback you had to provide if a kid was to know you were serious.

By late summer of 1995, everyone in college basketball realized the new guy in East Lansing was serious. Recruits, included. Michigan State had a different style and energy. MSU was everywhere, relentless, saying the right things, showing up at the right times.

Much of the motivation came from seventy-five miles away. Michigan was king. The only way U-M's stranglehold on state preps could be pried loose would be if Michigan State somehow exceeded the Wolverines in building relationships and selling a new coaching staff and its ideas on how basketball could be experienced in East Lansing.

But Izzo's competition was not only the University of Michigan. College basketball's ruthless recruiting meant there would always be many contenders for a franchise player, as there were for Battier, the Country Day superstar player and a model citizen Izzo dreamed of making a centerpiece at MSU.

Battier, however, was being romanced hard by Duke and by head coach Mike Kryszewski, an overwhelming 1-2 punch for Izzo to withstand. Battier ultimately headed for Durham, North Carolina, for an All-American career with the Blue Devils.

Izzo had no idea where a first-year coach's team or its recruiting base was headed when he gathered players for his first formal practice as MSU head coach on October 15, 1995. What he understood more clearly than anyone in East Lansing, even more deeply than did his staff, was that it all had to change, and in a hurry. The players he greeted in the autumn of 1995 were not going to win a Big Ten championship. The players he needed to make any such notions possible were still in high school. Even as he concentrated on the former, his and his team's future lay clearly with the latter.

CHAPTER 14

REFUSE TO LOSE

DURING WINTERS IN IRON MOUNTAIN AND MARQUETTE, when snowfalls would reach as high as a backboard, Tom Izzo was studying, as much as playing, the game of basketball. He was in his second home—any Upper Peninsula gymnasium where he competed during high school and college.

A basketball-coaching career was in its formative stage. It was the next step, apprenticeship, that would-be basketball coaches realized separated the passionate from the enthusiastic, the career coaches from the short-timers. Years of working slavish hours as a graduate assistant and assistant coach were the base price for some day—maybe—getting a legitimate head-coaching job.

Izzo's personal apprenticeship extended for fifteen years. It began as a graduate assistant coach at his alma mater, Northern Michigan University, and continued in an identical role at Michigan State, where in 1986 he was promoted to fulltime assistant, albeit not before he had taken an eight-week detour to the University of Tulsa in one of the clumsier short-term career moves any coach had ever made.

Tom Izzo had no doubt in 1995 he could coach college basketball on an elite level. All those years of impassioned sweat and study had crafted a solid basketball teacher and tactician. Whether base coaching skills would translate into winning seasons and a long tenure at Michigan State was the issue, as it always was for any coach at any new job.

His old boss, Jud Heathcote, understood better than even Izzo in the summer of 1995 that Michigan State's new man had anything, and every-thing, a Big Ten school could have ordered up in a new chief executive for men's basketball.

Izzo's problem, Heathcote realized, would be one of timing. The very point fans and media would be most suspicious about a young coach stood to be the period when he and his team would be most taxed.

Izzo was taking over a decidedly so-so MSU squad. In that sense, he had gotten the job a year too late. Had his old boss retired at the end of 1994 (as might have been the case before an infamous memo from then-assistant athletic director Clarence Underwood raised holy hell and spurred Heathcote to stay on an extra year), Izzo's first team would have been a top-tier Big Ten contender primed for a nice run in the NCAA tournament.

Heathcote, instead, stayed on as wagon-master over a group that did well enough: 22-6 record, a runner-up finish in the Big Ten, but a one-and-done showing in the NCAA tourney at the hands of mid-major Weber State University

At that point it was good night and good luck. Izzo was inheriting a team that had just sent both of its starting guards, Shawn Respert and Eric Snow, to the NBA. Izzo could get busy forging the remnants (Jamie Feick, Quinton Brooks, Ray Weathers, Jon Garavaglia, Thomas Kelley and Daimon Beathea), into whatever representation of Big Ten basketball prowess he could make of them during the winter of 1995-96, his rookie season as head basketball coach at Michigan State.

Heathcote knew that Izzo had the right stuff for running practices and for teaching a sophisticated game reliant on precision skills. Bench mechanics and on-the-fly decisions a head coach made during a game would require an adjustment, but the transition figured to be smooth for a guy as bright and as buttoned-down as Izzo.

Heathcote was proud of the fact he gave his assistants leeway to coach. The boss was no practice-session ringmaster. An assistant could coach and teach as much as he cared. He had the right to stop practice and talk to a kid at whatever point it seemed appropriate. Izzo would practice much the same philosophy when it was his turn to head MSU's staff.

He had added an assistant earlier that year, Tom Crean, an old friend who had worked with him as an MSU graduate assistant coach. Crean, from Mount Pleasant, Michigan, was brought back to East Lansing from the University of Pittsburgh, along with Stan Joplin and Brian Gregory. These three were disciples of the new guy's fire and resolve as Izzo's 1995 debut season drew near. They were about to disperse the same scorched-court heat generated by their boss on recruiting, practices, meetings, drills, off-season programs.

They were committed to blanket the territorial perimeter within and outside of Michigan in trying to nab as many program-building kids as possible. That meant working harder on relationships. They had to get more potential recruits on campus for informal weekend game visits. It required getting more high school coaches into Breslin Center during MSU practices.

The goal was to pound Michigan State basketball into the heads of basketball's in-crowd. The elite coaches had to know MSU was going to be a contender for the best kids in Michigan and within a five-state radius. If the men who coached high schools and AAU teams and who had ties with premier recruits were truly watching out for a prep star's interests,

Few, if any, college basketball coaches have sent as many assistants on to head-coaching jobs as Tom Izzo. Shown here are three of them. From the left, Stan Joplin (Toledo), Izzo, Tom Crean (Marquette) and Brian Gregory (Dayton). Others who have gone on to top jobs include Stan Heath (Kent State and Arkansas), Mike Garland (Cleveland State) and Doug Wojcik (Tulsa).

they were going to take the new crew in East Lansing seriously.

An essential ally was going to be Raymond Jones, the Flint (Michigan) AAU coach who ran a respected, high-profile summer team annually loaded with prime-time prep talent. Joplin was working hard in Flint and heard Jones say early that the key for Michigan State was to sign the big bruising power forward from Flint Northern, Antonio Smith. Joplin, Izzo and Gregory needed no sales pitch. Izzo had been recruiting Smith since he was a sophomore in high school—two years before Izzo's first season as head coach.

"But the guy you're really missing the boat on," Jones said to Joplin, referring to a forward from Flint Northwestern, "is Morris Peterson. He's going to be a player. If you get Antonio, and then Morris, you'll get Mateen."

Mateen was Flint Northern guard Mateen Cleaves. He was your basic prep football-basketball thoroughbred who was going to be a star basketball point guard for whatever college nabbed him. Michigan State had been scouting Cleaves since he was a freshman. Michigan State's bad fortune was that Cleaves, the summer between his junior and senior year, had lighted up the Nike all-star camp with an awesome open-court fireworks show. Various schools were going to make a desperate pitch for him, Michigan included. Cleaves was going to have his mind ransacked by eleventh-hour shoppers in the coming months as anyone who knew how recruiting worked in the winter of 1995-96 understood. Izzo and his staff, the supposed new tough kids on the block, would have to deal with it.

Florida State was becoming a major contender for Cleaves, and not only because of Cleaves' basketball skills. Bobby Bowden, the Seminoles' football coach who had was more like a deity in Tallahassee, made many trips to Flint in a bid to sell FSU as a two-sport choice for Cleaves. Izzo likewise had kept open a two-sport option for Cleaves if Mateen were to insist on giving both sports a shot.

Those wrinkles had yet to be ironed out. For now, working crazy hours and practically living in high-school gyms was the only strategy that made sense as Izzo and Co. scrambled to gain a recruiting beachhead. Friday nights were perfect examples for how the new coaching team and approach worked.

Already deep into their own first season of practices in the late autumn of 1995, the coaches and players would wrap up by 6 p.m., at which point Izzo, Joplin, Crean and Gregory would be off to catch high school games, often in Flint. They would reconvene at 11 p.m. or later for a meeting they otherwise would have had after practice.

The climate had changed for college basketball's head coaches, particularly within Michigan. It had been shifting since Bill Frieder took over at the University of Michigan in 1980. Frieder was a 24-hour-a-day coach and recruiter. He pushed to outwork his assistants in getting to high school games, eyeballing talent, and being a conspicuous presence. On Saturdays, after an afternoon game for his Wolverines, he would catch a night high-school game somewhere in the region. What Frieder loved about recruiting was that it differed entirely from practices. There were no time constraints that came with having to conform to kids and to their student schedules. His freedom to recruit was essentially unlimited. Frieder lived for it.

Heathcote had no such appetite. He loved coaching and loved having some semblance of a personal life. Recruiting got in the way. He would let his assistants do the bulk of the talent hunting.

Izzo was going to be more like Frieder, and at least as dogged as Frieder's successor, Steve Fisher, who had ushered into Ann Arbor a steady stream of billboard recruits, notably the early '90s Fab Five fleet headed by Chris Webber and Jalen Rose. It was a talent haul that incensed the Spartans' coaching staff because of suspicions about Webber's inducement, as well as Rose's eventual commitment ahead of Fisher's appointment of Detroit Southwestern High Coach Perry Watson—Rose's high-school coach—as a U-M assistant.

In the winter of 1995-96, the Wolverines were hotly pursuing Cleaves. It was the latest example of how Fisher and his gang created ongoing angst for Izzo and Co. The MSU staff had been through this before with Webber. Now another player who had been headed for East Lansing—in Webber's case, for four years—was abruptly shopping in Ann Arbor. What was going on? And what, by chance, did Ed Martin, the booster who was known by MSU's staff to be an aggressive soldier on behalf of the Wolverines, have to do with it?

Izzo's staff had ideas long before a federal grand jury and U-M internal investigation turned up evidence of $616,000 in "loans" from Martin to players, which in Webber's case came to $280,000.

The fear and ire intensified on February 17, 1996, a Saturday, as Izzo's team got ready for a game against Northwestern. Cleaves had been injured at 4:50 that morning in a rollover accident along M-14 between Detroit and Ann Arbor. Michigan star Maurice Taylor had been driving his Ford Explorer, loaded with U-M players, when it rolled into the median, injuring Taylor and four Wolverine teammates (Robert Traylor, Louis Bullock, Willie Mitchell and Ron Oliver), as well as Cleaves, who hurt his back.

Izzo got the news at 7:30 a.m in his hotel room. A few minutes later Gregory walked into Izzo's room.

"This ain't good," Izzo said, relaying the Cleaves news.

Izzo's initial reaction was that the accident would bind Cleaves to Michigan State. His mother, family and friends would decide Ann Arbor was no place for Mateen when teammates were out carousing until five in the morning. But the more he thought about it, the more he believed the mishap could have the opposite effect, making Cleaves feel closer to Michigan and to the players who, along with him, had survived a bad accident. There would be sympathy and the very best medical care extended and Cleaves would now be part of the family.

Izzo decided on a high-road response.

"The most important thing is that you're fine," he later told Cleaves. "Michigan State is still the place for you. Michigan is a great school. What happened was an accident. Just do what's best for your life and career."

The weekend of the accident had been a big weekend for revelry for Mateen Cleaves. Friday night's recruiting agenda included a stop at Martin's home in Detroit's Palmer Woods neighborhood, followed by a late session at a hotel near the Millender Center, across from Detroit's Renaissance Center, where strippers had been part of the night's private entertainment.

It was pure luck that no one was killed when the Explorer flipped and somehow landed on its wheels. Injuries were minimal, the most serious being Traylor's broken arm and Cleaves' injured back.

Izzo and his staff knew the M-14 incident meant double trouble for Michigan State. Cleaves was a risk to make Michigan his new lead horse.

He was also dealing with a back problem that could lead to complications down the road, even if the early prognosis was encouraging.

Five weeks later everyone in East Lansing was feeling better, as was Cleaves, who had been vowing that his sore back would be no hassle, for whichever school he played. He made his announcement March 25—it was Crean's birthday, the coach would forever remember—at Flint Northern amid an atmosphere of equal parts pageantry and secrecy.

In a conference room inside Breslin Center, a speaker phone was placed on a long table as an overflow crowd gathered. The sound was scratchy, almost inaudible, except for the only words that mattered in East Lansing: "Michigan State."

Cleaves' decision was viewed then, and years later, as the most important recruiting commitment Michigan State basketball had received since the April 1977 blockbuster—also kept secret to most until the last moment—when Magic Johnson held everyone breathless at Lansing Everett High as he announced he was choosing Michigan State over Michigan.

Nineteen years later, MSU's response was almost as raucous. In the Spartans' coaching offices, champagne poured. Secretaries and staffers cried. Izzo had been on the job for a single, tough year. A coaching staff's work schedules had been overloaded past the level of exhaustion. They had, at this moment, their first glee, an initial sign that things might go their way, after all.

Crean barely heard Cleaves' words before he pranced into his office to make two calls to Toronto: to Jamal Magloire, a superstar center who ultimately headed to Kentucky, and to David Thomas, a guard from Canada that MSU thought could be a solid Big Ten player.

TOM IZZO'S FIRST SEASON AS HEAD COACH had been so-so: 16-16 overall record, 9-9 in the Big Ten. The last game, an 80-70 loss to Fresno State, had ended State's visit to college basketball's second-tier tournament exercise, the NIT.

Everyone had tried mightily to make it work under a new coach with a rebuilt backcourt not half as scary as it had been when Respert and

Snow were around. Feick, Brooks, Weathers, Garavaglia, Beathea, Kelley, and the rest had bought more or less into the new coach's ways—not ideal commitment from Izzo's standpoint. Much of it had to do with trading in his old role for the new perch. Back when Heathcote had been barking and ripping into players, it was often up to Izzo to be the good cop, dispensing just the right measure of reassurance to keep a kid from getting down on himself or Jud.

Now it was Izzo's turn to play the heavy. Coaching psychology was never meant to be dispensed from opposite poles by the same person. You had to set up shop on one end or the other. As the 1995-96 inaugural ended, it was one more reason why Izzo needed not only talented players but also his own players that he could shape and influence from the day they walked onto campus.

He saw progress, hope and inspiration in MSU's one-by-one recruiting gains. Antonio Smith became the bedrock commitment—he had opted for Michigan State over Minnesota in November of 1994 (Jason Klein, a talented athlete from Grosse Ile, Michigan, also came aboard in the autumn of '94), four months before Izzo would formally and officially move into the head coach's office. It represented a leap of faith for a player such as Smith—trusting in the new coach and his program—and it became a tone-setter for the intensifying bid to get Cleaves, as well as Peterson, whom Izzo was inclined to sign after a long talk with Peterson's parents.

Peterson was a handful, all right. First on his list of favorite things to do was shoot a basketball. Somewhere beyond last was hitting the books. Izzo was going to bring Peterson to East Lansing with his parents' blessing, as well as with their urging that the head coach straighten out a young man of considerable potential, personally and athletically.

Taking in Peterson and maintaining Cleaves' favor was going to be a nifty balancing act for Izzo. The head coach knew precisely what Peterson needed his first year at Michigan State: a redshirt season. He had to get Peterson acclimated to academics and exposed to the realities of Big Ten basketball—both would require more sacrifice and commitment than the free-wheeling Peterson cared to apply. That much became apparent in the initial months of Peterson's MSU experience.

He showed up, at eighteen years old, with a paunch worthy of a fifty-five-year-old barfly. Teammates quickly considered him lazy and could see why Izzo was about to redshirt him. They wondered if he should be anywhere near a team committed to changing its competitive nature and winning. One concern was how Cleaves would react to Peterson's impromptu redshirt season. It could make for a rude surprise when Cleaves got to East Lansing. Cleaves, though, had enough confidence in his own ability, as well as sufficient knowledge of how Peterson and, say, Antonio Smith, differed, to understand the coach had a pretty good read on people and players.

A couple of solid prospects from Ohio named Andre Hutson and A.J. Granger had added to Izzo's fresh recruiting crop in 1995, his first full autumn as head coach. In the fall of 1996 came one more MSU pledge from Flint: Charlie Bell, a skilled, uncommonly debonair high school guard from Flint Southwestern Academy. Bell was another of the prep prodigies who would lead to Izzo's core cast to become known, naturally and nationally, as "The Flintstones."

Rarely would a player be more the product of an assistant coach's efforts than Granger, a 6-foot-8 (he would reach 6-foot-9 in college) front-line horse out of Liberty-Benton High School in Findlay, Ohio. Granger had been a favorite of Tom Crean when Crean was an assistant at Western Kentucky and at Pitt.

Granger warmed to Crean in part because his first choice, Ohio State, was having its share of internal issues and off-the-court incidents during the Randy Ayers coaching era, which made Granger leery. Cincinnati and its coach, Bob Huggins, were on Granger's list, as was Miami (Ohio), Ohio University, and Pitt.

Granger had gotten a phone call from Crean—not an unusual occurrence—late during a midweek afternoon the summer before his junior year, when Crean was still at Pitt.

"What's up?" asked the coach, in shoot-the-breeze fashion.

"Just going to play in the open gym tonight," answered Granger, who on some evenings would play late-night pick-up games with the University of Findlay's players.

Crean, who was in Pittsburgh, drove five and a half hours to watch a pick-up game—just to make sure a player he considered a serious prospect understood how badly Crean and Pitt wanted him.

Izzo himself had seen enough of Granger to put him on MSU's shopping list. Granger had insisted on playing within driving distance for his parents and the lure of a Big Ten school, within a three-hour drive of East Lansing, was enough to seal the deal. Granger, though, would always believe he had been Crean's, not Izzo's, recruit—that state of mind would make for a tense relationship with his head coach in years ahead.

Ever since he had decided in 1995 that Saginaw star and occasional bad-boy Terrence Roberson was not a fit for his new team, Izzo had been affirming with each recruit that Michigan State's program would be built according to his blueprint and philosophy.

If Izzo was dealing with an omnipresent state of anxiety in his early years as MSU head coach, it surprised no one who knew him or understood his makeup. He believed in—and thrived upon—his personal approach to taking on a challenge. It was, for him, a matter of assembling and integrating honorable component parts. You recruited talent, you coached that talent, you instilled in those skilled players know-how as well as intangible qualities that would make them champions, provided they bought into the ethic and paid a prescribed price.

That was the basketball side of Izzo's equation. He understood every bit as much that he had to meld with the University's disparate parts and personalities to make it all work and, just as important, to buy time at the outset when the team's fortunes would be tense.

MSU's 1996-97 SEASON BEGAN with a team structurally comparable to his first-year squad, even though Izzo knew he needed more muscle on the floor.

The eagerly awaited arrival of Mateen Cleaves turned to be disappointing, even disillusioning. Cleaves was at least twenty pounds overweight when he showed up for his freshman year. Worse, he wore a back brace everywhere but in the shower as a result of his March accident.

Some nights, the pain was so great he had to leave practice and head for a stationary bike to try and loosen up the knotted, inflamed muscles that caused such pain. Any thoughts he would make a splash as a freshman were absurd. The staff watched him maneuver in and out of that back brace and wondered about his future on and off the court.

Antonio Smith was settling in as a policeman down low. He was a character player and presence, if not a particularly gifted scorer. Izzo liked what he was seeing there—the first mingling of a basketball team's brick and mortar. Smith was already in the process of taking charge not so much voluntarily, but by virtue of his blast-furnace soul and spirit.

Jon Garavaglia was a player whose occasional soft efforts could infuriate coaches as well as teammates. Smith had seen enough during one particular practice part-way into the '96-97 season.

Antonio Smith may have been a force in the paint and the bedrock of Tom Izzo's basketball program, but he could also handle the ball when he needed to.

"You may not want to win," he shouted at Garavaglia, throwing him against a locker in the Spartans' dressing room, "but I do."

Izzo's second season began with some zest—seven victories in the Spartans' first eight games, the only loss a triple-overtime tumble at Calihan Hall against the University of Detroit. The Spartans won their next four games, and later had an early-season four-game Big Ten winning streak going until a five-game slide from January 22 through February 8 blew away any realistic shot at cracking the NCAA tournament.

MSU finished 17-12 overall and tied for sixth in the Big Ten at 9-9, ending up with a two-game cameo in the NIT tourney that simply doubled Izzo's personal reservoir of self-imposed pressure. It also made him recruit even harder.

AS HIS THIRD SEASON GOT GOING IN OCTOBER OF 1998, fans were beginning to wonder if the young guy from Iron Mountain was in over his head. No matter how much East Lansing wanted to believe Tom Izzo was going to build a showcase basketball program at Michigan State, a healthy skepticism was a natural fan response to a young coach. Doubts and fears were deep-seated at a university that had been trying for decades to find a football coach who would win regularly and stick with his job once he did begin winning.

In December, it got rough. The month had started well, as Jason Klein tipped in a shot to beat Gonzaga, 70-68, to win the Spartan Classic on November 29. That seemed to signal that things were getting better in Year Three of the Izzo era. But five days later the Spartans lost to Temple, 56-54, at Breslin Center. Nine days later came the killer: a 68-65 spill at Breslin against the University of Detroit. That made three losses to U-D by a total of seven points in three years under Izzo.

Heathcote had been back in town for a few days and had caught a couple of games, as well as talk-radio flak aimed both at Izzo and at Heathcote for having named Izzo his successor. Some fans concluded the new guy had to go. He had clearly gotten his job because of Heathcote's patronage and was demonstrably no better equipped to turn this program into a consistent winner than Heathcote had been during his long and fairly choppy reign. It looked like Clarence Underwood's 1994 memo was dead on.

State won its remaining three non-conference games to sit at 7-3 heading into the worst possible spot to begin a Big Ten season: West Lafayette, Indiana, against Purdue. Miserable place to play, vicious team to draw for a conference opener. Heathcote had talked plenty with Izzo through his first three seasons, and just as much through the 1997-98 schedule's early weeks.

The gist of the discussions was non-basketball. Keep your head up, Heathcote would tell him. The lumps were bound to come and they were going to come in these early years. Be patient. You're doing everything right. Give this process time.

He had considered calling Izzo prior to MSU's suicide mission at

Purdue. No, he thought—better to phone him after the shellacking, when Izzo would need a boost.

Instead, Michigan State ripped the Boilermakers, 74-57. It was an utter demolition job against a Gene Keady-coached team that in any year was tough enough to beat in East Lansing, let alone at a place that was more like a haunted house for visitors.

A week later, in East Lansing, the Spartans crushed Wisconsin, 63-40. They were on their way to winning 11 of their first 12 Big Ten games (the lone loss: 79-69 at Michigan) as Izzo and everyone else in a venerable basketball conference began to see that the pieces were fitting.

Smith was now a junior; Cleaves, Klein, Hutson and Granger were sophomores; Peterson (redshirted the previous year) and Bell were freshmen. Young as they were, they had skills, cohesion and toughness. They crashed the offensive boards and played scalding defense under the direction of their low-post lieutenant, Smith. They took good shots and distributed the ball democratically, thanks to the steadily strengthening point guard Cleaves.

They scored practically every time they inbounded off a timeout, the product of Izzo's endless inventory of designed plays that approached two hundred schemes.

They were beating teams for another reason. They were in better shape than their opponents. Izzo's work regimen had been Parris Island-tough. Players in early season would head to the MSU track and run six 440-yard sprints, followed by a string of 220s and 100s. They could then look forward to a two-hour (or longer) meat-grinding practice.

Sucking for air, forcing your body and mind to assume a subconscious response when things got past the point of agony, this was the part of college basketball fans scarcely imagined. Players accepted that they were seen in a far loftier light. It was not the fans' responsibility to know about year-round conditioning, or weight-room rigors, or two-hour study tables, or the endless meetings, tapings, medical treatments and practices, all sandwiched around a full load of classes. If a player left his room or apartment at 7:30 in the morning and got home at 10:30 at night, that was a MSU basketball player's life. It was also a college experience for which most students would have opted, given the full-ride scholarship and added perks that went with an athlete's territory.

During the season, games were considered by the players to be a breather from all those miserable practices and another evening of killer meetings that could last two hours. Izzo would stand with his video clicker and analyze film on an upcoming opponent, or dissect over and over the previous night's game.

It was all part of Izzo's passion for preparation as well as a manifestation of his evolving coaching persona that featured a particular strength. He was like a West Point military scientist in arranging defensive schemes and tactics Michigan State would use against opposing offenses. He was thorough, detailed and all-encompassing in breaking down the opposition and stylizing an attack against it.

Players would leave the locker room at 11 p.m. following an 8 p.m. game and arrive back at Breslin Center at 10 a.m. the next day for meetings.

"Hey, Coach," a player would say to a red-eyed Crean, "you look like you had two hours of sleep."

"That's because I did," Crean would say after a long night of breaking down film.

The payoff in March of 1998 was a co-Big Ten championship (shared with Illinois) that would have been an outright title had the Spartans not perished on the road against Illinois (84-63), or had they been able to win their regular-season finale at Breslin Center against Purdue, which went down as a 99-96 overtime loss.

What mattered was that Michigan State had won its first NCAA tourney ticket since Heathcote's 1995 team lost in his final game as head coach.

Spartans fans needed this morale boost. Football was still on the comeback trail under Nick Saban. Basketball had been on sabbatical for three long years. Now there was a sense that basketball was bringing MSU fresh energy and national respect.

The NCAA tournament confirmed it.

MSU rolled over Eastern Michigan and Earl Boykins, 83-71, in its first-round East Regional game at Hartford, Connecticut, and then whipped Princeton, 63-56. MSU had made the NCAA Sweet Sixteen for the first time since Georgia Tech had shot down the Spartans in overtime in their infamous 1990 regional game at New Orleans. Spartan loyalists ruefully recalled that Kenny Anderson's last-second shot that sent the game into OT was later proved to have been an after-the-horn basket.

The bad part about making the 1998 regional was drawing top-seeded North Carolina in the first game. MSU shot barely 30 percent against Vince Carter, Antawn Jamison and Co. and got what all the analysts pretty well expected: a 73-58 eviction from the tournament.

What might have been viewed as a breakthrough year for a young head coach and his still-tender team instead left Izzo unimpressed. He was almost glum as he talked with his players after the North Carolina rubout.

"We're gonna go back," he said, speaking of East Lansing, "and go to work."

NOT ONLY PLAYERS, BUT PERSONALITIES were being reconstructed. Peterson was a prime example. There was the day during mid-season when he showed up at the coaching office with tears in his eyes. He had gotten a "D" on an exam he was sure he had aced. This, from a player who had been redshirted because he began college as an academic dog, who had been forced to get out of bed for 6:30 a.m. study hall ahead of his 8 o'clock class as part of an ongoing crusade to pump self-discipline into a player who had arrived in East Lansing as an eighteen-year-old project.

Crean saw Peterson's wet eyes and initially thought a family member had died. After hearing about the distressing exam grade, Crean rolled into Izzo's office and slapped the head coach with a high-five.

"We got him," Crean chirped. "He gets it now."

Some of the challenges were more technical, more basketball-oriented. Cleaves and Granger, for example, each needed to re-do their jump shots. Mike Garland was now the overseer there as the coaching staff attempted to rid Cleaves of his funky-chicken, side-saddle jumper that needed a more streamlined release.

Cleaves bought into a new shooting alignment with his usual appetite for anything basketball-related. He restructured the shot, straightened his release, and then went to work shooting thousands upon thousands of jumpers, many evenings walking into Breslin Center with a teammate in tow, or with a team manager (Steve Finamore, perhaps) for a two-hour shooting spree.

Granger learned the same lesson when he paraded into East Lansing with a jump shot in need of re-tooling. Granger was an athlete. Athletes could always survive on strength, on basic hand-eye coordination, on extraordinary physical tools that assured them of a certain competency at any level. Big Ten basketball players, however—if they were to flourish—needed more of an edge.

Granger had an NCAA-Division 1 jumper because of an exceptional right wrist and finish that allowed him to knock down shots. Hitting that same shot with a skilled Big Ten defender in your face was a bigger challenge. That

Tom Izzo (left) lectures his "quarterback on the court," Mateen Cleaves. Cleaves rode all the criticism to a national title and became the first round draft pick of the Detroit Pistons in 2000.

meant being quicker, more refined and efficient with no wasted motion.

Izzo could see it the way a garage mechanic would diagnose car trouble. Granger's shot had to be seamless. He had to receive the ball to his left, maybe to his right, or even in his natural shooting slot—where he grabbed it was immaterial—and produce a repeating, uninterrupted catapult of the ball to the basket. Izzo had adopted the same methodology when he played. He, too, had been schooled to remove all unnecessary motion. It was 1-2-3: plant your lead foot, swing the ball into shooting position, put it up and in the basket.

It was a routine similar to that coached by Izzo's sharp-shooting predecessor, Heathcote, an acknowledged master at jump-shot physics. It was Izzo's style, as well. As he schooled his players in precise mechanics, working his way around the three-point line, Izzo could knock down shot after shot. He wasted no motion. He had a mechanically sound delivery system even if his shot was not particularly glamorous.

The one-dimensional Granger could bury a jump shot, frequently from three-point range. But scoring off a dribble, getting creative on a drive to the basket, embarrassing a baseline defender with a highlight levitation act—that was never going to be Granger. He would live or die by way of his jumper.

Looking at Michigan State's 1998-99 team, all told, Izzo was on the verge of something good, something special. Forget their youth. The Spartans had immense talent. You could make a case for a young team with Michigan State's skills—Smith, Peterson, Cleaves, Hutson, Bell, Klein, DeJuan Wiley, Granger—making nights miserable over a long winter schedule for a somewhat-jaded Big Ten.

Three games into the season, beating the big boys was still a challenge as Michigan State lost at Temple, 60-59. MSU was 5-1 when the Spartans lost consecutively at Duke (73-67) and at Connecticut (82-68)— rough games on the road, all of them. A critic might have had two reactions to MSU going 0-3 against three name-brand teams within a couple of weeks: (a) MSU was still a brick shy of a load when it came to matching up with the heavyweights; (b) Playing teams of this caliber, on the road, and hanging with them as well as the Spartans managed could pay off deeper into the season.

Izzo had sold his recruits on the quest for a national championship. Every coach on a major level talked about going to Final Fours, but Izzo understood Michigan State should be in the hunt there as well as for a Big Ten championship. The two objectives were one and the same when you thought about the competitive quality of Big Ten basketball.

The conference opener, at Wisconsin, was not reassuring. A game against Dick Bennett's Badgers was like changing from your game uniform into a straitjacket. Wisconsin 61, MSU 56, and now the Spartans were 10-4 overall and 0-1 in the Big Ten.

Not many would have believed on a cold night in Madison, Wisconsin, that Michigan State would have lost for the last time in the regular season. Not many of college basketball's rational thinkers would have banked on a Big Ten team playing for nearly three months minus a defeat. Not many who had seen Michigan State wobble in November, December, and in the first week of January would have been inclined to predict a twenty-two-game winning streak that would push the Spartans all the way to the Final Four.

It all happened because a team with sufficient skill had the right component parts. More, though, than how Cleaves ran the offense, or how Antonio Smith provided the down-low defensive presence of a Sherman tank, or how Morris Peterson off the bench was a textbook complement to Andre Hutson and Jason Klein, there was cohesion to the 1998-99 Spartans. It was alchemy, in some respects, the blending of various alloys into a solid mass of basketball prowess.

Charlie Bell was in the backcourt with Cleaves and became an embodiment of MSU's trademark knack for rebounding under Izzo. Thomas Kelley and Doug Davis could spell either Cleaves or Bell and present no serious falloff, particularly in the case of Kelley. A.J. Granger could bounce off the bench and knock down a three-pointer. If foul trouble struck, Lorenzo Guess could make a cameo and do enough constructive things to help put away a game.

The winning streak was turning into a national story: big victories

Tom Izzo (left) and assistant Tom Crean on the bench during the wildly successful Mateen Cleaves era. Crean eventually left to become head coach of Marquette, where he recruited star Dwyane Wade and made it to the Sweet Sixteen with the Warriors.

over Illinois, including a two-pointer at Champaign; 14- and 15-point drubbings of Michigan; a 56-51 payback against Wisconsin at Breslin Center; two-point victories on the road against Penn State and Minnesota.

SMITH NEEDED NO COAXING. He was like an aircraft carrier along the baseline: imposing, impregnable, a consolidation of defensive might and offensive capability. He would practice wearing gym shoes but no socks and run as if he had an oxygen bottle strapped to his jersey. In his four unparalleled years at Michigan State, coaches never saw him have a bad practice.

Crean, who tended to be the team's motivational psychologist—as well as Izzo's cohort in good cop/bad cop governance—knew MSU's resident papa bear needed to be particularly aggressive against a difficult Northwestern team, coached deftly by Izzo's friend, Kevin O'Neill.

Evan Eschmeyer, the Wildcat center who could be a load offensively or on the boards, had a shot at making a mess of MSU's winning streak unless Smith somehow neutralized him.

Crean, as usual, had an idea. He pasted Eschmeyer's picture on a paper plate and taped it to Smith's locker. On it he inscribed:

"Evan Eschmeyer, Leading Big Ten in Rebounding."

Beneath the bold top line, Crean wrote:

"Antonio, are you going to let Evan Eschmeyer eat you for dinner tonight?"

After Smith approached his locker and saw the signage, he ripped down the plate, crumpled it into a ball with one hand and threw it on the floor.

That night, as the Spartans slammed the Wildcats, 65-48, Northwestern got zero—*zero*—offensive rebounds. Smith tied Eschmeyer in knots as the other Wildcats skedaddled for their end of the court every time they missed a shot, fearing that MSU's fast break would vaporize them.

A winter-long basketball blitzkrieg by the Spartans had delivered MSU's first conference championship in nine years. The Big Ten tournament followed script. First, a scary two-point escape against Northwestern. Then, Wisconsin was flattened, 56-41, ahead of a 67-50 rubout of

Illinois in the tournament championship game.

Those early-season stumbles against good national teams on the road seemed as if they had happened during a different era, to a different Michigan State team, as MSU headed into the NCAA tournament with a 29-4 record and a top seed in the Midwest Region.

Michigan State no longer had any hang-ups about playing anybody. Ranked second in the nation and esteemed by the analysts—the Spartans' days of becoming anxious about a particular team on the schedule had vanished. There was a new bravado that showed in the tournament's opening rounds, at Milwaukee, as the Spartans dusted off Mount St. Mary's, 76-53, followed by a 74-66 dispatch of Number 9 seed Mississippi.

There were no soft spots, no deep blemishes marring the Spartans as Izzo's team headed to St. Louis for a Midwest Regional showcasing MSU, Kentucky, Oklahoma and Miami (Ohio). Michigan State was healthy and deep, which meant the Spartans could open up the throttle and see if their best stuff was good enough to get Michigan State to a Final Four for the first time in twenty years.

The media and college basketball junkies were curious about MSU. They especially wanted to know more about the point guard with the one-of-a-kind name: Mateen Cleaves.

Fans were right to be curious. No basketball player since Magic Johnson—not Steve Smith, not Scott Skiles—had so personified his MSU team or been so critical to its court performance. Cleaves had settled in as on- and off-the-court Spartan leader. He was State's quarterback, its policeman, its bouncer, its ram-rod, its heart, if not necessarily its soul, which might have been the province of Antonio Smith.

Their sidekicks were no slackers. Hutson, a one-time prep quarter-back from Trotwood, Ohio, had abundant skill and tremendous drive. He was a physically tough, 6-foot-8 forward who could play just as effective-ly whether he was or feeling 100 percent.

Bell, the "silent assassin" as his teammates referred to him, was an awesome amalgam of defensive prowess and endurance (like Smith, he seemed never to tire) who was capable of shooting and scoring assorted ways. He said little, although what he said always seemed to be meaningful in still-waters-run-deep fashion. His considerable personal polish was only slightly countered by the fact he was a certified pack rat. Each month, Nike would forward a pair of shoes to the players as part of MSU's endorsement contract. The shoes invariably would pile up in Bell's locker along with all other items from the Bell archives: empty deodorant bottles, shampoo containers, clothing, knick-knacks, mail.

Other players were factoring into a dream season for MSU.

Jason Klein, the Grosse Ile forward, had athleticism, as well as a fine shot that sometimes failed to show up.

Peterson was growing each week into one of the best college basketball sophomores in the land—a personal evolution that would not have been everyone's forecast when Izzo ticketed him for exile as a redshirt freshman.

Charlie Bell scores over Marcus Fizer of Iowa State in the thrilling 2000 regional final at the Palace of Auburn Hills.

St. Louis stood to be the formal unveiling for what Izzo had built, as well as for what could be expected, during his era of Michigan State basketball. The Midwest Regional was about to go down as the Spartans' coming-out party, the debut for a rising national power.

MSU's first test at St. Louis was going to be Oklahoma State, a team less fearsome than State's likely match in the finals—if the Spartans could get there—Kentucky. The Spartans displayed nothing spectacular in taking a 26-25 halftime lead against the Cowboys. They did keep dangerous Eduardo Najera from doing any serious damage (two-for-eight shooting, seven points total), and won the game, 54-46, to draw Kentucky, as expected, after the Wildcats polished off Miami.

Throughout East Lansing and MSU's sports galaxy, the hours leading into a Sunday regional final game had become a witch's brew of anxiety, excitement, hope, fear, superstition, paranoia and foreboding. That was balanced somewhat by a belief that Michigan State was playing too well, in too many dimensions of the game, to ultimately lose. What worried the Spartans' camp was that the opponent was Kentucky, a team of stature, experience, tradition and tournament savvy. Those were the very components that had helped Kentucky beat MSU in the 1978 regional finals at Dayton in Magic Johnson's freshman year, thanks to the uncanny foul-shooting of Kyle Macy.

Michigan State's fans had been through too much anguish over the years to not experience flashbacks—losing to Kansas and Georgia during star-crossed regionals in 1986 and 1990, respectively—ahead of the showdown with Kentucky. The players had their own battle against nerves, which was apparent as quickly as the first half began with a 17-4 run for the Wildcats.

State was out of rhythm, out of whack, and out of its game until jitters eased. But by halftime, the quicker, more athletic Spartans cut Kentucky's lead to a point, 26-25. State slowly, methodically, took control in the second half and watched as two of the Flintstones—Bell with a three-point dagger from the left wing in the waning minutes, and Peterson, who made six consecutive free throws in the game's final 30 seconds—finished off Tubby Smith's Wildcats (including future Detroit Piston star Tayshaun Prince), beating a premier national team for its twenty-second consecutive victory since the January 6 loss at Wisconsin.

Michigan State was off to St. Petersburg, Florida and the Final Four. Also coming to town were Duke, Connecticut, and the Final Four surprise team, Ohio State. OSU had been a fourth seed (behind Auburn, Maryland and St. John's) in the South Region, but grabbed a ticket to St. Petersburg with a regional-final takedown of St. John's.

Izzo was about to be discovered—fully—by national media that until St. Petersburg knew him mostly as a fourth-year head coach who had done nice things in a relative hurry at East Lansing. What the national coverage soon conveyed was that Izzo was winning friends and influencing critics who liked his style.

He was not intimidated by the national scene, no matter how far removed Iron Mountain, Michigan, may have seemed to others who were just learning about a geographical extension of Michigan known as the Upper Peninsula.

He came across as likeable, as substantial, as a guy who might be showing up at this four-team basketball prom in future years.

MSU's problem, if one was developing during a dream week for the Spartans' community, was Saturday's opponent: Duke. The Blue Devils had their usual glittering record and their usual cavalcade of stars: Shane Battier, Izzo's old recruiting target who had turned into a dynamite collegiate star; Elton Brand, Trajan Langdon, Corey Maggette, Chris Carrawell and William Avery.

Of course they also had coach Mike Kryszewski, who went to Final Fours the way some coaches stopped for coffee at a convenience store. They had muscle and firepower and poise.

And they had a 32-30 lead over State at halftime of a Final Four semifinal game in which MSU never felt comfortable. It had been a reversal from their experience throughout the week, when practices, and shoot-arounds, and even press conferences, had all gone smoothly, as if the Spartans had been doing this sort of thing for years.

Saturday's semifinal was from the netherworld. Michigan State had managed to stay within two at intermission but the Spartans inwardly knew this game was a realm removed from anything they had confronted during this season, or seasons before. They could hardly breathe going into the halftime dressing room.

A superbly conditioned team was having trouble catching its wind. The air seemed heavy and dense. It was so humid the basketball felt slippery to touch. Nothing about this game seemed like college basketball, some would say years later. It was too surreal to be college basketball. It was more like a weird dream, its details quickly forgotten.

The Spartans never got untracked. They shot feebly (26-for-70 from the floor), failed to penetrate on a par with Duke's knack for crashing the basket (the Blue Devils had 27 foul shots to 11 for the Spartans), and were even out-rebounded (44-40).

Duke was doing just enough, well enough, to cruise by State, 68-62, before dumping Connecticut for the national championship. MSU students took the outcome badly, and in some cases, dishonorably enough to get arrested. A frightful Saturday night riot broke out in East Lansing. Fires, malicious destruction, ugly exchanges with police, arrests—it was a black eye for Michigan State at the climax of a glorious week, a glorious season. It also incensed a basketball coach who told rowdy MSU students he wanted no part of them, or their zeal, if losing a basketball game was going to result in disorder so disgraceful to Michigan State.

For the Spartans, for Izzo ahead of anyone, the pain of losing a shot at the national title was no tougher to swallow than would be the farewell to Antonio Smith, the team's founding father. He had led the Flint parade to East Lansing. His physical and spiritual impact was incalculable.

Now he was gone. That was the bad news. The good news for Izzo and for a team that rather enjoyed this Final Four business is that it could be reached again if a few things were to go right the following season. Cleaves was coming back, right along with Peterson, Hutson, Bell, Granger and David Thomas.

There were some interesting freshmen on their way, Jason Richardson and Aloysius Anagonye, notably, as well as a transfer from, of all places, Duke: Mike Chappell, the one-time Southfield Lathrup High star who had a chance to help significantly on the perimeter and off the bench.

Richardson was a world-class prep star out of Saginaw Arthur Hill. He was 6-foot-6, 190 pounds, a one-time hockey player who gravitated toward a sport where his ceiling-touching vertical jump might be better appreciated.

Anagonye, out of Detroit St. Martin dePorres High, was another version of Antonio Smith: big, tough, a definitive power forward who would police the baseline and boards and put teeth on top of muscle into MSU's lineup.

AT THE START OF HIS FIFTH SEASON, Izzo's program was settling into a kind of factory-like rhythm. There was an automated facet to the process that in no way detracted from a coach's knack for keeping people happy and involved, which was his secret. Team managers, office assistants, video technicians, sports information personnel—everyone was made to feel as if he or she directly contributed, all because they did, and moreover, because the head coach recognized it and acknowledged every effort, individually.

Izzo's enterprise was clicking heading into the 1999-2000 season because he and his staff understood the fundamentals of outstanding recruiting. The coaches and their allies kept kids eligible and on track, academically. On other essential fronts, the head coach made his alumni golf outings and entered into a string of community-service projects and charitable efforts.

He somehow found time—minimal time, he realized—for his wife Lupe, and daughter, Raquel. It was a collective effort that required more hours than were in a day. Izzo squeezed time as if hours were toothpaste tubes.

He was also scheduling tough teams. Izzo was taking a calculated risk in putting the likes of Duke, Connecticut, Kentucky, Arizona, North Carolina and Florida on his pre-conference schedules. Playing billboard teams cut both ways: It was good for your squad's development and for a team's national profile. It was also risky business. .

Lose a player like Cleaves to a drive down the lane against some of the muscle-bound Sequoias routinely featured by college basketball's upper echelon teams and you could say goodbye to the Final Four three months before brackets were announced.

In the span of three weeks in December of 1999, with all the world wondering if Y2K bugs were about to create computer chaos heading into a new millennium, the Spartans had their unsettling moments. They hit a string of three losses: at Arizona (78-69), at Kentucky (60-58 in a payback for March's regional final), and then, inexplicably, at Wright State, which slapped the Spartans, 53-49. The Wright State defeat came the night before the football team would win the Citrus Bowl in Bobby Williams' debut. Izzo, of course, was in attendance in Orlando, ugly loss and all, chatting with fans at the game and at the airport as if all was right with his world.

Izzo was no less irked after the Wright State meltdown than Cleaves, who had influence over his team, on a relative scale, that surpassed anything possible for a coach. The Spartans returned to East Lansing from Wright State (Dayton, Ohio) and got busy watching film and preparing blast-furnace practices ahead of the Big Ten opener against Penn State.

Three games later, they were 3-0 after Peterson hit an improbable jumper to send MSU into overtime against Indiana, at Breslin Center, which ended up as a 77-71 victory for the Spartans. But nine days later, at Ohio State, it was December all over again: Ohio State 78, MSU 67.

On the charter flight back to Lansing, Izzo watched a DVD replay of the game. Four times he went over it, each time becoming more furious. Schoonie Penn and the Buckeyes had just made Michigan State look silly. Mental errors, bad plays, careless judgment, it was an overall appalling display of basketball in the eyes of a coach whose team was less than ten months removed from the Final Four. Worse, an Izzo team had failed to play tough basketball. To not play with indifference to cuts and contusions and concussions was, in Izzo's basketball values system, a moral offense.

When the team got back to Breslin Center for its customary post-flight meeting, Izzo was so worked up he ceased speaking—rather screaming— and turned the remainder of a midnight powwow over to Gregory. The Spartans were due back in seven hours for practice. Enjoy your nap, boys, the coach exhorted, because Izzo wasn't about to sleep this game off.

This had never happened, Izzo realized, when Antonio Smith was around, absorbing punishment, dishing it out in volumes, beating up on Hutson in a way Hutson and all his teammates understood must be part of an evolving champion's spirit. The Spartans' basketball culture had to return to yesteryear.

Players arrived at dark the next morning half-expecting Izzo to be brandishing a bullwhip. After stretching and loosening up, they noticed MSU equipment manager Dave Pruder pushing a cart onto the floor loaded with football equipment. No basketballs were in sight. The players were told to get busy putting on helmets and shoulder pads. Breslin Center was about to transform into Spartan Stadium.

Many of the players—Cleaves and Hutson were good examples—had been standout football players in high school, often quarterbacks. To rediscover, even for an hour or two, an old passion, was a sweet break from basketball's rigors even if it was being done for essentially punitive reasons.

The players were positioned in one-on-one gladiator standoffs, urged to belt away. Some of them were uneasy, even intimidated, at first. Within minutes, though, Breslin sounded like a high-decibel popcorn machine. Helmets and plastic slapped and clacked. Players had gotten into the spirit of coaching-monitored mayhem.

Izzo called off the hand-to-hand combat and ordered his team, still wearing its pads, to assemble for the infamous War Drill. Five players would convene in the paint directly around the basket; five players would take position outside the lane. Izzo or an assistant would throw a ball against the backboard glass, intentionally keeping it out of the basket. It was up to the warriors below to determine who got the prize.

Wearing pads was an invitation to turn the War Drill into a blood bath. Izzo was delighted at the prospect. A half-hour after the Battle of Breslin began, it was over. Pads came off. Players loved the energy and the sheer disorder of Izzo's brainchild drill. They proceeded to put together what might have been their best pure basketball practice of the season.

The Spartans lost only two more games leading up to the NCAA tournament: 70-67 at Purdue, and 81-79, in overtime, at Indiana on a flukey put-back of an airball at the buzzer. The Spartans headed into the tourney with a 28-7 record and the top seed in the Midwest Region, which, State fans had happily noted, included regional games at The Palace of Auburn Hills.

That kingpin seeding in the Midwest likely never would have been MSU's had not a terrible stroke of bad luck walloped Cincinnati just as MSU was heading to the Big Ten tournament in Chicago. Kenyon Martin, Cincy's fabulous All-American and front-line superstar, broke his leg and was out of the tournament. Michigan State had just climbed a spot in the seedings at the same time a powerhouse team was being sawed in two.

First up for State was sixteenth-seeded Valparaiso, which perished, 65-38, in a first-round game at Cleveland. Two days later, the Spartans marched out of Cleveland and into the Sweet 16 bracket with a 73-61 dispatch of Utah, which had knocked MSU out of the tournament in 1991.

Joining the Spartans at Auburn Hills would be Syracuse, Iowa State and UCLA. MSU was ticketed for fourth-seeded Syracuse in the Thursday night match-up.

Jim Boeheim's Orangemen were going to be a handful, every bit as much as Iowa State stood to be, if the Cyclones cleaned up on UCLA, which was expected. Syracuse made a living out of NCAA tournament games, even if Boeheim had yet to win a national championship.

Michigan State understood the heft and experience carried by Syracuse and Iowa State meant MSU would be playing a pair of Final Four-caliber games—if the Spartans survived Thursday night.

By halftime, the Spartans looked as if they were twenty basketball minutes away from the toughest homeward-bound bus ride of their lives. Syracuse led, 34-24, at intermission and had made a mess of MSU's attack with a savage zone defense. So much for backyard advantages, which the Spartans had counted on having as a mostly MSU crowd breathed verbal lava onto The Palace's floor.

Cleaves was apoplectic as MSU shuffled into the dressing room, stunned, discouraged, frustrated. He had turned down a shot at the NBA the previous spring to win a national championship and raise his stock ahead of June's 2000 NBA draft. Even before the coaching staff arrived in the dressing room, it was Cleaves, MSU's point guard and resident fire chief, who tore into his teammates.

"I'm not going out as a senior like this," he screamed, at Peterson, who had played especially poorly in the first half. "You're not playing your game. I'm not going out like this."

As the second half got underway, the Spartans began ripping into Syracuse's zone. They gradually tightened the game, then tied it, then ran away on a 37-9 strafing that included a closeout-run of 17 consecutive points and a 75-58 victory that sent MSU's Palace camp into delirium.

It was the brand of shock-and-awe basketball MSU had been capable of producing in its follow-up act to the 1999 Final Four. Now the Spartans had to figure out a way to do it all over again in Saturday's regional final against Iowa State.

The Cyclones were nasty. Marcus Fizer was a load down low, and Jamaal Tinsley was a brilliant guard on the floor. But he had spouted off during regional week about ISU's might and muscle—that made MSU's disposition all the more surly heading into a Final Four showdown.

The Palace set a record for crowd noise on that Saturday evening, March 25, 2000. No one officially measured it, but anyone there testified to it years later, including Palace president Tom Wilson who said his arena hadn't been that noisy since the Bad Boys era of 1988-90. Players who by then had been accustomed to their share of sellout crowds and raucous arenas, never again experienced anything to match the crowd roar during what became an MSU epic. Players had begun to use hand signals rather than waste their time yelling directives or orders. By the time MSU had

Morris Peterson lets fly with his signature three-pointer against Wisconsin in the 2000 Final Four semifinal. Even with a cast on his arm as a sophomore, Peterson was often the best player on the court for either side. His alley-oop jam from Mateen Cleaves at the end of the regional final against Iowa State remains one of the most famous plays in MSU hoop history.

begun climbing back from a nine-point, second-half hole—there were scarcely five minutes remaining—The Palace was shaking.

MSU was up by one late in the game when Cleaves threw a perfect alley-oop pass to Peterson, who rammed home the climactic bucket. For Spartan fans, past teases and torments vanished. MSU was heading to the Final Four. This time they were going after the grand prize.

THE GAME ENDED WITH ANOTHER MSU RUN OF 23-5. The spurt included free throws that were part of a second technical foul—and automatic ejection—against Iowa State coach Larry Eustachy, who had a meltdown in the face of officials' calls.

Coaches and players understood how improbable had been their victory, down nine points with five minutes and change to play to what many considered the toughest team left in the tournament.

Many factors contributed: The football-pad practice ... Cleaves' fiery oratory during halftime of the Syracuse game ... the contributions of bench players David Thomas, Richardson, Anagonye, and red-headed Adam Ballinger. Each element was crucial in an astonishing regional that brought a ticket to Indianapolis. MSU was about to get reacquainted with old friend Wisconsin in the semifinals, while Florida got ready for North Carolina.

IT WAS SAFE TO SAY, as Final Four week began to boil in Indianapolis, that the at-large basketball nation would have preferred something other than Michigan State-Wisconsin as a semifinal game. There was nothing personal against either school. It was simply that the two Big Ten bruisers had already played each other three times and MSU had won all three games.

Another factor was that basketball connoisseurs understood this would be battlefield basketball: a slow and methodical offensive effort drawn off defensive strength. It was going to be a basketball war of attrition. All anyone had to do was look at the scores of MSU's three victories over Dick Bennett's Badgers: 61-44, 59-54, 55-46. In the NBA, these were halftime scores. Folks glued to their TV sets across the land could expect to settle in Saturday for basketball's version of sumo wrestling.

Michigan State's concern was that you could not expect to beat a good Big Ten team forever. The odds against stumbling got longer the more games you played and won.

On the team bus to the RCA Dome, ESPN radio was airing an interview with Saint Joseph's coach Phil Martelli, who had been asked about the chances of beating a Final Four-grade team four times in a season.

Martelli was to the point.

"Michigan State beat them three times, which means one thing," Martelli said. "They're a better team. I'd expect them to win this one also."

By halftime of the Spartans-Badgers tough-man contest, no one was sure there would be a winner. The score was 19-17. MSU had a lead, if it could be called such. It was a score ripe for ridicule, but also a measure of what Wisconsin did to teams in dictating tempo and in playing paralyzing defense.

Then, Peterson and Cleaves put the game out of its misery. Peterson had 10 points during a 13-2 second-half spree that unclogged the game temporarily and put the Spartans in control. Cleaves' contribution was to get inside enough to get fouled. He made only 1 of 7 field-goal attempts but was 9-for-11 from the free-throw line as MSU extricated itself from another Badgers-manufactured tar-pit, winning 53-41.

The game statistics were a joke. MSU was 16-for-46 from the field (Peterson was a comparative shooting star with 7-for-15), while Wisconsin was 15-for-43. MSU had four assists for the day, Wisconsin eight. A national audience seemed to agree with CBS-TV basketball savant Billy Packer who implied that the best part about the game was that it ended.

Florida took care of Bill Guthridge's North Carolina team, 71-59, in the other semifinal, which was enough to make national media wonder if Michigan State could shake Florida's press in the championship game. Billy Donovan's team had beaten Illinois, Oklahoma State, Duke and the Tar Heels on their way to the grand finale. How would State, especially after the toe-to-toe slugfest against Wisconsin, handle a team with Florida's court-length fury?

Easily, as it turned out. The Spartans had analyzed Florida's alleged super-press and had concluded it was nothing special. Regardless, they were sticking with their game plan. Take it to the Gators offensively, play barbed-wire defense, rebound, be careful with the ball.

Izzo had helped forge a unity among his players by virtue of his own cussedness. In a perfectly human way, the players many times during a season wanted to beat the living snot out of him. They hated those hard practices. They hated after a three-hour workout having to be back at Breslin in 90 minutes for a meeting or film session. They despised getting chewed out during a practice, or in the middle of a game, or during a film session. They wanted freedom to be screw-offs, to be out late, to go to class when they chose to go to class, and to do what other kids did at the end of the day: go to a bar, play video games, work a couple hours on a paper and then, maybe, watch TV the rest of the evening.

They had no such lives. They were major-college basketball players. They were hostage to a rigid schedule. But they also aspired to win. And that meant you paid the price, you many times hated your coach, and yes, you also came to love your teammates. It had no bearing on what you thought of them as players. You were a band of brothers, sometimes united by your absolute contempt for your coach, the guy who at a particular moment could make your life hell.

There were so many times breaking from a timeout when Hutson, for example, might say to Granger: "I'm going to set a pick for you. Knock down the shot." Granger would answer: "You bet." The pick would be set. The shot would drop. It was the way in which a supremely cohesive group responded because of the culture Izzo had molded. For a head coach whose job was part symphony conductor, it was all a matter of striking the ultimate competitive chord.

The Spartans thought about such things while standing on the RCA Dome court that Monday, April 3, 2000, as a nation tuned into a NCAA national championship game. The Spartans were astonished by what they saw in the Gators after Michigan State took a 10-point lead. There was, on the NCAA championship court, a stunning stream of you-did-this, you-did-that bickering among Florida players who were disintegrating at the moment when team unity was a moral imperative.

Izzo's team knew that MSU would win even after Cleaves left the court with an ankle sprain after getting tripped up on a fast break by Florida's Teddy Dupay. Cleaves' exit came just as Michigan State prepared to take command in a NCAA championship game it could now easily lose, a game that now had the makings of a standard-issue MSU basketball tragedy. Memories flashed for Spartans fans—the clock at Kemper Arena, the Kenny Anderson shot at New Orleans.

This time, however, character was about to be revealed. There was Mike Chappell, the Duke transfer who had struggled for most of the season, his

Mateen Cleaves quarterbacked Tom Izzo's offense all the way to a national title victory against Florida in 2000.

first at Michigan State. He made the shift worthwhile for himself and for his new team when he poured in five quick points to keep MSU from melting down.

There was Cleaves, four and-a-half minutes after hobbling to the dressing room, marching back from the locker room a la Rocky Balboa entering the fight arena. It was reminiscent of that Thursday night in 1979 when Magic Johnson had limped from the locker room to the court after injuring his ankle in a game against Ohio State, a critical game MSU won in overtime, in part because of the reassurance that flowed from Johnson's dramatic entrance.

There were contributors galore as Michigan State beat the Gators, 89-76. Cleaves was named the Final Four's Most Outstanding Player. Izzo had a national championship five years after he had taken the reins as head coach. Michigan State had its first national basketball title in twenty-one years. And East Lansing had all the excuse it needed for a night of revelry.

Izzo was among those who had been shaped by the years with Cleaves and the Flintstones. He had experienced purity in their spirit, a fire to their competitiveness, which he was not likely to encounter ever again. It was why he would name his son Stephen Thomas Mateen Izzo.

The coach was going to enjoy himself, the parades, the parties, the celebrations—for a few days, anyway. Then he would get back to work nailing together a framework for coming seasons. Izzo was losing Cleaves, Peterson and Granger. He was picking up a pair of awesome freshmen.

Of primary importance was Marcus Taylor, the super guard from Lansing Waverly, who was coming to Michigan State as the best home-grown talent since Sam Vincent. Taylor looked to be close in potential impact to a 1977 Lansing Everett product by the last name of Johnson. Also coming aboard was a massive power forward from Marion, Indiana, Zach Randolph, who had his share of legal baggage stemming from an earlier firearms possession flap. The problem had been satisfied with local courts and Randolph had put together an impressive senior year, in the classroom and on the court, further convincing Izzo to give a basically good kid a carefully considered chance in East Lansing

Even in losing senior talent as irreplaceable as Cleaves and Peterson, there were reasons to think that next season's team would be explosive. Richardson was going to be a sophomore and had already shown that he could dazzle in, sky-scraping, All-American fashion. Bell was back at guard, along with the under-appreciated David Thomas, with Taylor set to join them. Hutson was going to provide some essential Flintstones character and toughness. Anagonye was growing into his anointed role as successor to Antonio Smith. Bench strength was going to be significant in Chappell, Adam Ballinger and Adam Wolfe.

Yes, there was a lot of work to do, but work, like a heartbeat, had become for Izzo an involuntary act.

CHAPTER 15

GOODBYE AND GOOD LUCK

A MONTH AFTER THE NATIONAL CHAMPIONSHIP commotion, Izzo was ready for a long-deferred vacation with Lupe and Raquel, who was now five years old. It was going to be a Disney World-sponsored trip with an initial stop in Orlando ahead of a Caribbean cruise. If only he could board that boat with a clear mind.

He could not. Izzo had gotten a call a couple of weeks earlier. It was Pete Babcock, general manager for the Atlanta Hawks. He was in the market for a new coach now that Lenny Wilkens had been let go one year into a reconstruction program, a dismissal that didn't seem fair to a coach of Wilkens' stature.

Babcock had been following Izzo. He had seen the way Izzo's teams defended, the manner in which they attacked a game. Babcock liked how Michigan State's players seemed to respond to a coach who was simultaneously able to push and inspire a team. The Hawks' GM saw in Izzo precisely what Atlanta needed as it sought to turn young players fresh from college into a newer, ultimately more playoff-tough bunch than the 50-victories group that had been blown up a year earlier following a second-round loss to the New York Knicks.

Izzo knew Babcock superficially from past meetings and conversations at places like the Great Eight Tournament. Once they began talking in late April, the two men clicked quickly enough so that Izzo asked Babcock a ton of questions on every facet of NBA basketball and how it played out in Atlanta. At first blush, he was cool to the NBA. It was not the kind of move he cared to make at forty-five years of age, five years into his MSU stint, a month after State's national championship.

The Hawks' GM urged him to accept a no-risk option: Think it over. Consider all those advantages: big money, the freedom from recruiting, a fresh challenge, perks he could never command in a college job. Izzo might be more ready than he realized for a step into basketball's glitz-and-glamour stratosphere.

A week later, Babcock called and suggested that the two meet again to talk, perhaps in San Antonio, where Izzo was headed for a speaking engagement. That made sense to Izzo. Babcock, who, by now, was going to unveil a GM's version of the full-court press, knew he had a chance to land Izzo.

The conversation in San Antonio was nothing short of a conversion for Izzo. Babcock's conviction was that a coach of Izzo's particular talent, a coach who had extraordinary skill at grooming and commanding respect from young basketball players—the very kind he would be inheriting with the Hawks—would be in perfect position to repeat his MSU experience in the NBA. None other than Magic Johnson had told Babcock the same thing.

"What you have in Izzo is the next Pat Riley," Magic said, a reference to his old Los Angeles Lakers coach who was now in Miami.

Izzo had become warmer to the idea for a simple reason. Babcock pointed to the fact more and more players were leaving college early for the NBA draft. In a league where even kids fresh from high school were "coming out," there was no longer a continental divide between college and NBA players, or even between high school and pro, if you cared to consider Moses Malone, Kevin Garnett and Kobe Bryant, to name three.

Izzo was heading back to East Lansing for more thought. Emotionally, there was no way he was leaving Michigan State in May of 2000 for the Atlanta Hawks or any other NBA job. Babcock had merely given him a different, rather tantalizing, perspective.

Izzo quietly informed Peter McPherson, the MSU president, of Atlanta's interest, and his decision to at least talk. The two agreed to keep the matter quiet. There was no point in broadcasting a job overture Izzo had no urge to accept.

The coach, though, was conflicted. He kept hearing Babcock's selling pitch. The GM's points were sound, thrilling even, for a man who had been diving into challenges, personal and professional, for so many years.

What he, Lupe, and Raquel needed was time together on that cruise ship in the Caribbean. Everything was going to be clearer when they got back.

Perhaps. Except that everything was now becoming more complicated by the hour. Word had leaked to various media that Atlanta was chasing Izzo. In the balmy May air, East Lansing was suddenly shivering at the thought that MSU's basketball savior was on his way out of town. It was six months after Nick Saban bolted for LSU, and now—a month removed from its shining moment at the NCAA tournament, Michigan State was staring at the possible departure of another kingpin coach.

The Izzo family was a few hours from boarding a cruise ship when Lupe decided a placid vacation on the Caribbean was fantasy. There was too much unease and commotion. The lack of resolution, she realized, would haunt her, her husband, and Michigan State, for the next week.

"We can't do this," she said. "We can't do this to the University. Let's just head back and get this thing settled. You're going to have to make a decision."

Izzo called Babcock, who suggested that it might help if everyone came to Atlanta for a day or two. Lupe could get a feel for the town and residential neighborhoods as Tom got a better grasp on the Hawks. A private jet was arranged to fly them from Orlando to Atlanta late that night.

The next morning, Izzo toured Philips Center and was impressed by the NBA team's swank facilities. The group, which included Stan Kasten, soon moved to Babcock's home. There they were joined by Atlanta Braves general manager John Schuerholz, an associate of Kasten, the two-sport executive who had also worked as Braves president before joining the Hawks.

Schuerholz assured Izzo that there would be rounds of golf at Augusta National Golf Club—just a sampling of the good life enjoyed by an Atlanta Hawks head coach. Schuerholz also brought Braves pitcher—and Lansing Waverly High School alum—John Smoltz as one more member of a select group organized to recruit Izzo. The fraternity was headed by Magic Johnson, who was on the speakerphone in an adjoining room urging Izzo to take control of a young NBA team and bring his Pat Riley-style presence from East Lansing to Atlanta.

Izzo was getting excited. The Hawks had six players twenty-five years of age or under and were looking at ten million dollars in available salary-cap cash with which to pursue free agents. As for the coach's compensation package, it was through the roof: close to sixteen million dollars for five years, about three times the salary he was making in his new contract with Michigan State. Izzo could not believe the perks: automobiles, credit cards, gasoline cards, lavish per diems.

With that national championship in his hip pocket, maybe it was time to think about taking a next step. Izzo gave the go-ahead for his agent, John Caponigro, of Bloomfield Hills, Michigan, to fly to Atlanta for dinner with Babcock. They would hash out the business details before Izzo would make a final decision.

As Thursday turned into Friday, word of Izzo's serious romance with Atlanta was by now raging across East Lansing, and throughout all of basketball, as Thursday turned into Friday. Kasten and Babcock were pushing for Izzo to sign immediately. If they failed to get the deal done in Atlanta, both men realized odds would lengthen once Izzo got back to Michigan State.

The coach understood he had to go home first. He needed to talk, to think, to make sure that what he was about to do—and it was becoming clear to him that Atlanta would be the choice—was absolutely the correct career move for him and for his family. Even though Izzo was leaving for home, Babcock was convinced as he drove the Izzos to the airport they would return to Atlanta to stay.

The coach, whose job status was by now national news, arrived at Detroit Metro Airport that afternoon. He was met by assistant coach Brian Gregory, who was in charge of driving everyone home and helping avoid a media crowd that had the terminal staked out.

Izzo knew he had to act quickly. He needed to talk with Peter McPherson; he needed to talk with his staff and with players; he sooner or later had to say something to the media and to an MSU community that was on edge. There were conversations late that day and into the evening with McPherson, as well as with Joel Ferguson, the all-sports, all-the-time trustee who was not about to be distanced from an issue as monumental as Izzo's fate. Clarence Underwood, who had been named athletic director the previous year, was there to talk and to listen.

Izzo needed to see his players. The responsibility he felt to them was second only to his family. They met that evening at Breslin Center—Izzo, his staffers, and a quorum of team members who were no longer sure who would be their head coach when they began formal practices in five months.

Izzo explained the opportunity and his torn feelings. They were basketball players, all of whom dreamed of playing in the NBA, a few of whom would. They could relate to his invitation: the NBA's grand stage, the money, the prestige, the adventure.

Izzo told them that there had been one primary consideration keeping him from the Hawks. He had recruited every one of his players. He had brought them to East Lansing, and had deep misgivings about leaving them, especially after all they had gone through in winning a national championship.

Al Anagonye, who so many times reminded Izzo of Antonio Smith, his program's founding father, spoke up.

"Coach, you can go take that job and we'll still love you and be behind you one hundred percent," Anagonye said. "You told us to follow the dream. You follow the dream."

Izzo's heart melted. Leaving a young man like Anagonye, who embodied a team's human goodness as much as its basketball skill, was going to require from a sentimental Italian coach an uncommonly bloodless decision. It was a verdict he needed to reach by the next day, Saturday. It had been his pledge to McPherson as MSU paced the floor and waited for another marquee head coach to decide on East Lansing or on job relocation to the Deep South.

Financially, there was little to consider. Michigan State had already given Izzo a new, long-term contract worth just over one million dollars per season. MSU could sweeten the deal a smidgen, but if he were to stay in East Lansing, Izzo might as well figure on leaving two million dollars per year on the table.

It was a lot of money, to say nothing of the NBA allure he had tasted during his two days in Atlanta. From a straight business and professional vantage point, the Hawks were probably his better bet. He could justify it, as well, by what all that cash could do for the Izzo clan, not to mention for Lupe's eleven siblings and their children.

Izzo needed to talk with someone who knew, who really knew, the business; who had perspective from a national mountaintop; who could tell him whether he was nuts to leave, or crazy to stay.

It came by way of a phone conversation that night with CBS-TV analyst Bill Raftery, himself an ex-college coach. Raftery immediately calmed a man who felt as if he were choosing between life and death. Relax, Raftery told him. You'll be fine, either way, because a good coach always will be a good coach. In other words, Izzo could expect high-profile jobs in proportion to his exceptional coaching skills.

Raftery, though, wanted Izzo to think especially hard about the present. He was six weeks from having won an NCAA championship. It looked to Raftery, to anyone who knew college basketball, as if MSU's back-to-back trips to the Final Four might be a mere warm-up for Izzo and the Spartans.

The NBA jobs will always be there, Raftery said. The money will only get better. There was no reason to feel as if Izzo had to jump today at the NBA's first serious offer.

Raftery's words provided Izzo with exactly what he had been seeking: a measure of clarity.

It was getting late. He and Lupe talked until past midnight, at which point his wife, who had an early-morning commitment, went to sleep, leaving her husband some essential private time.

It was mid-May, and just mild enough to sit on a back deck and allow the night's sounds, stars and solitude to wash over him. The setting, as well as the sense of peace steadily enveloping him, struck a man who seldom had such time to himself as nothing less than spiritual.

He was still sitting on the deck at 3 a.m. when he realized there was nothing left to consider. He, Lupe and Raquel were staying in East Lansing. He was simply not ready to leave his team or Michigan State, much less a mission he had undertaken a mere five years earlier.

He called Babcock later Saturday morning to tell the Hawks' GM he was staying at Michigan State. Babcock was gracious, disappointed, but not entirely surprised Izzo had decided on sticking in East Lansing.

"Understand completely," said Babcock, who was aware the Hawks had just put Izzo through an ordeal as career choices went. "I'll call Stan."

"No, Pete," Izzo said, appreciatively, "I'll go ahead and tell him."

Izzo phoned Kasten and knew he would be in for a different kind of conversation. Kasten was a flamboyant New York City guy who was as funny as he was brilliant.

Kasten feigned disbelief—incredulity that Izzo and his wife were turning down a king's ransom to stay at MSU. Kasten, of course, knew perfectly well why Izzo was staying. He understood completely how difficult it would be for someone like Izzo to say goodbye to Michigan State at age forty-five, six weeks after winning a NCAA championship. It was why he wanted Michigan State's basketball coach to sign the Hawks' contract before he ever left Atlanta the day before.

"Tell you what," Kasten said, having some fun with his own assertiveness, "you leave a piece of paper on the kitchen table with the dollar figure on it and let your wife walk past it all weekend. Then call me Monday morning and say you're taking the job."

Izzo cracked up. Kasten had a few moments more of fun with a coach he very much liked. The Hawks' president thanked him genuinely for taking Atlanta's offer as seriously as he did, and wished a skyrocketing college basketball coach all the best.

That afternoon, at a media conference, the wavering and emotion in Izzo's voice told best why he was staying.

"We've got a great bunch of guys," he said, making clear his players had been the difference. "I'm going to put the bull's-eye on their backs.

We're going to go into the year thinking we can win another national championship."

MANY OBSERVERS WHO SIZED UP college basketball's elite heading into the 2000-01 season gave the Spartans a good shot at back-to-back championships.

Although Tom Izzo had lost heavily from his 2000 team (notably Cleaves, Peterson and Granger), he was bringing in immense talent in the persons of Zach Randolph and Marcus Taylor. Randolph, at 6-foot-8, was dominating every high school all-star game in the country and stood as the top recruit in the country. Taylor was a top-five national recruit as well, a point guard with shooting skills that exceeded those of Cleaves, although no one was suggesting he could bring Cleaves' floor spirit, toughness and leadership.

Two high-school players had made Michigan State's incoming recruiting class a national story, not only because of their talent, but also because of Randolph's unsettling past. He was a poor kid from Marion, Indiana, blessed with a mother who could do only so much in bringing a boy through adolescence unscathed. Randolph's felony charge for weapons possession was the kind of misdeed that would either foreshadow a life marked by trouble, or it would be regarded as a young teenager's stupid mistake and be viewed as such by people, beginning with a circuit judge.

The latter point prevailed, and not only because Randolph was staring at a potentially prosperous basketball career. The incident occurred when

Zach Randolph spent only one year in East Lansing before joining the Portland Trailblazers. But during that season—which ended in Minneapolis with a Final Four semifinal loss to eventual champion Arizona—he became regarded by many as the best inside scorer in MSU history.

Randolph was barely sixteen. Those who knew him at Marion High, beginning with his coach, Moe Smedley, understood that Randolph was no incorrigible, no habitual bad boy, a point Smedley hammered at Izzo and assistant coach Brian Gregory, who had been working on Randolph for some time.

Randolph was ready to commit to Michigan State during the spring of his junior year. It was an announcement that otherwise would have been national news when Randolph was already regarded as a franchise player, the kind of recruit who could by himself elevate a college program.

Randolph's hang-up was that it took two to tango. Izzo had gotten sufficient assurance on the legal problems—their origin, their severity, the likelihood there would be no repeat acts—but was less certain if Randolph would get his grades in good enough shape to qualify for entrance to MSU.

"You're going to have to prove to us that you'll make some changes in order to come here," Izzo told Randolph. "We'll keep recruiting you and keep doing everything we've been doing. But we won't make a decision until the end of your (junior) school year."

Smedley was blown away. He could not believe that a college coach would have drawn such a gutsy line between himself and a superstar recruit. There was no wiggle room, Smedley said. Izzo was prepared to slam the door on a kid so talented that Michigan State could just about count on an annual trip to the Final Four.

Gregory and assistant coach Stan Heath went to Marion High in April of 1999 to personally work with academic counselors on arranging an academic plan that would enable Randolph to become a NCAA qualifier.

For the next twenty-four months, extending from his senior year at Marion High through his freshman year at Michigan State, Randolph met every prescribed guideline.

Randolph's talented Spartan co-recruit, Taylor, was an entirely different person and player. Also different was his situation and challenge heading into the 2000-01 season. Hometown college athletes are invariably more demanding projects for coaches because they never separate from their culture, which can include family, friends, and abundant degrees of home-cooked hero-worship, as well as the community's urgent expectations.

Taylor was going to be influenced by every element, including his father, James, who was very much an involved dad. Izzo had no difficulty understanding that Marcus Taylor entered MSU with a hometown star's built-in entourage. It came with the territory.

For all the talent that had danced off to professional basketball after the NCAA championship, there was little sense that the Spartans had turned into have-nots as a new season began. Izzo's team ran over its first twelve opponents, including North Carolina, old friend Florida, as well as Kentucky, before getting nipped, 59-58, at Indiana.

The Spartans lost only two more regular-season games—at Ohio State, 64-55, and at Illinois, 77-66, where Bill Self was now coaching after Lon Kruger had taken the Atlanta job Izzo turned down. Bell and Hutson provided the senior sass to go with all the talent beneath them: Richardson, the dunk-meister who was simply a spectacular basketball talent; Anagonye, who down low was like an aircraft carrier's anchor; Thomas, an experienced, capable guard who made Taylor's transition easier; and Randolph, who was a gifted mass of offensive talent and in the process of shedding twenty-one pounds his freshman year.

If only he played a sliver of defense.

Randolph hated any of basketball's distasteful chores: defense, practice and conditioning. He liked to score, and what a touch he had underneath as he slipped and slid and angled and, with his soft hands, improvised a lovely shot that usually found twine.

Gregory, who had coached under Jud Heathcote in his waning years before spending a year on Izzo's staff, had returned to MSU in 1999 after working for Stan Joplin at Toledo and Kevin O'Neill at Northwestern. Izzo told Gregory he would be in charge of low-post players.

Gregory apprised Izzo of his strategy for coaching Randolph as the kid from Marion arrived.

"Zach," Gregory playfully quoted himself as saying to State's prized freshman, "you just go ahead and do whatever you want down there."

Everyone in the basketball world, beginning with State's coaching staff and players, understood that Randolph's single mission in life was to play in the NBA. The coach could live with a player and his NBA dream when it meant he would play with focus and with drive in his bid to join basketball's elite.

One thing everyone knew about Randolph was that he would make the NBA by way of his game exploits, and in spite of his practice habits, which by themselves would have made him a stretch to play in the Continental Basketball Association.

Randolph, though, was getting better by the week as his freshman season evolved. It helped that MSU's existing muscle and experience— Hutson, Anagonye, Richardson, Bell—enabled a phase-in that deep into the Big Ten season had made Randolph a miserable young man for opposing teams to defense or constrain.

State's winning streaks during the 2000-01 season (twelve games, four games, six games) were no longer gee-whiz news in East Lansing. Izzo's teams, with back-to-back Final Fours on their dossier, had settled into an exquisite rhythm all because of what the head coach and his staff had wrought in six years. The Spartans were an elite college basketball program, and along the way had developed a killer instinct.

A BAD BUMP, RARE DURING A YEAR when MSU closed its regular season at 24-3, came in the Big Ten tournament when State acted as if it were in a hurry to get on with the NCAA carnival. The Spartans lost in the first round to Penn State, 65-63.

State fans worried about omens ahead of the NCAA pairings could relax. Izzo's team, again getting a Number I seed (it made three in a row), was headed for another Final Four. First victim: Alabama State, crushed, 69-35, in a first-round game at Memphis. Next up: Fresno State, ripped, 81-65, which sent the Spartans to Atlanta for the South Regional.

Gonzaga was going to be up next, and the Bulldogs were going to be tough. They, like the Spartans, were headed to the Sweet Sixteen for a third consecutive year. They had Dan Dickau and Casey Calvary and plenty of tournament-seasoned snipers who could make a mess of things for MSU, which looked possible after State's five-point halftime lead melted in the second half. Gonzaga was on top briefly before Bell heated up, finishing with 21 points, as the Spartans ran away to win, 77-62.

That meant Temple in the regional finals. John Chaney's team had all the luster and substance typical of Final Four teams. It had a tough Philadelphia pedigree. It had pizzazz.

It also had an impossible task catching Michigan State. By the time a high-scorer as unlikely as David Thomas had tossed in 19 points (8-for-10 from the field), State had held off the Owls, 69-62, to win a trip to Minneapolis for what had become MSU's annual Final Four journey.

Michigan State had accumulated cachet during the Izzo years. Everyone recognized and respected the Spartans two years after State had crashed past Kentucky to begin its Final Four string. Media were familiar with Izzo and with his teams.

The Spartans were also welcome at the 2001 Final Four because they were entertaining. In that facet of MSU's makeup, Richardson was king. The sophomore from Saginaw seemed to be in the air more than he ever resided on the hardcourt. His dunks could be heard as much as they were seen. He was grand theater, and not a bad reason to buy a ticket to any game in which Richardson's aerial act stood to be showcased.

No one could match the thunder and lightning of a Richardson dunk. They were soaring, gravity-defying slammers as creative as they were powerful. Often times they were the practice's last act before players hit the showers. Richardson was simply a dynamic basketball player who awed even his teammates. How many times during a practice scrimmage had Spartan players tried to box him out on a rebound, only to see—and feel—Superman bound over them to snatch the rebound and slam down a put-back dunk. Teammates could appreciate that Richardson not only beat teams, but that he demoralized them.

Bell was another of the Spartans' celebrities as Michigan State pulled into Minneapolis. He was suave and polished, which the public found attractive in a college basketball player they had come to know through his regular Final Four appearances. On the court, Bell was the same player, albeit tougher. He ran and defended with equal zeal. It was Bell who had a defensive move named after him, just as Hollywood celebrities have their names permanently attached to Wilshire Boulevard deli sandwiches.

"The Charlie Bell move" was an uncanny fast step over a high screen, enabling him to stay with his man in an amazing act of skill and dexterity.

What neither Bell, nor Richardson, nor their MSU cohorts could figure out in the NCAA semifinals was how to handle an Arizona team that had its own phalanx of stars. The menacing Richard Jefferson was going to be a bad piece of business for the Spartans, as was Gilbert Arenas, Michael Wright, Loren Woods and Jason Gardner.

The Spartans were where they wanted to be at halftime, within a basket, as Arizona led, 32-30. The second half was Arizona's, entirely. State went cold and the final stats told the story: Bell was 1-for-10 from the floor, Richardson 2-for-11; MSU was 2-for-14 on three-pointers compared with Arizona's 7-for-14 and lost in a Final Four blowout, 80-61. That sent Arizona into the finals against Duke, which had come from behind to knock out Maryland.

There were few tears after this one, in the locker room, or in East Lansing, all because of what a team had accomplished a year after three-fifths of its lead horses had run out of eligibility. The Spartans had experienced the equivalent of a rebuilding year and come within a game of playing for a second consecutive NCAA championship.

They could get busy thinking about throwing together a Final Four grand slam if they could take their existing talent and keep it on track for 2002, the loss of Bell and Hutson notwithstanding. The remaining cast could consist of Jason Richardson, Randolph, Taylor, Anagonye, to say nothing of State's bench depth: Ballinger, Adam Wolfe, Jason Andreas, to go with another gaudy batch of freshmen: Kelvin Torbert, Alan Anderson and Chris Hill.

But how many of the hotshots were actually coming back was another issue. Richardson had offered assurances, albeit easily retracted assurances, that he was coming back for his junior year. The Spartans' coaching staff was among those who had their doubts. As for Randolph, he was going to be NBA-bound just as fast as the NBA scouts made it known he would be an early first-round pick. Message received. Richardson was becoming more aware by the minute that the June draft would likely treat

Jason Richardson may not have been good enough to start for MSU in 2000, but he also led them to the 2001 Final Four before leaving to begin a tremendous NBA career.

him and his NBA dream lavishly.

Richardson was first to declare, on April 10, as Michigan State's increasingly populous basketball nation somberly resigned itself to a fact of life: If you were going to run with the big boys in NCAA basketball, be prepared to wave goodbye to your share of short-timers, just as Duke and North Carolina had done in recent years.

By the time Randolph announced, Michigan State had been gutted. Izzo fulfilled a promise by showing up at Randolph's press conference in Marion—an appearance that, for Izzo, was like being asked to attend a dinner honoring Steve Fisher. The Spartans were losing more talent and heft in 2001 than had departed the previous year in Cleaves, Peterson and Granger.

A rock-solid Spartan basketball program had just experienced a seismic shift in talent and experience, the very components that won conference championships and kept Spartan teams busy in the NCAA brackets.

IN 2001-02, CLEARLY, A LOT WAS GOING TO DEPEND on the freshmen. Based upon their recruiting profiles, they had a chance to be very good even as Big Ten rookies.

Kelvin Torbert was a muscular, 6-foot-4 jumping jack out of Flint Northwestern High who was good enough to have given a serious thought to entering the NBA draft. Alan Anderson was another perimeter player, 6-foot-6 out of Minneapolis.

Chris Hill was not a jaw-dropper. He was a 6-foot-3 guard from Lawrence North High in Indianapolis and had come within a whisker of playing instead for Marquette, where ex-Izzo lieutenant Tom Crean was now head coach. The Spartans' staff had seen him play a couple of times ahead of his senior year. He was good, but Michigan State had been looking for more in a point guard than for the shooter Hill figured to be.

Gregory had even told Crean to take a look, which Crean was happy to do as he became interested in a backcourt that was going to be welcoming a young man from Chicago named Dwyane Wade. Hill's team was playing in an AAU tournament in Orlando.

Gregory was floored by Hill's shooting finesse. He had never seen a better-looking jumper. Hill handled the ball as well as he carried himself. Gregory realized Izzo, who had seen him play only once, would need a second look.

Gregory called Hill on August 2 and again on August 3, each time leaving a phone message and a request that Hill call back.

He heard nothing. Gregory was one day from never phoning again when the call came: Hill had gone home to Indianapolis to begin two-a-day workouts for football. His parents were not home. Messages had not been received. Yes, he was interested, very interested, in a Michigan State team that had just wrapped up its third straight Final Four.

Izzo and Gregory flew to Indianapolis a month later to watch Hill during a 45-minute basketball workout. They were not sure as they went through his performance afterward if he had missed a single shot. They wanted him badly, as did Crean. Izzo, the patriarch of a MSU coaching staff that had suddenly spawned a handful of national head coaches, got dibs on Hill, who was heading for East Lansing.

Gearing up for October's first practice of 2001-02, Izzo had not dealt with a team so limited since his pioneer days as Spartan head coach. He had stacked talent deeply enough through the Flintstones years and, seemingly, beyond, to ensure he had a solid starting five each winter, and at least a couple of blue-chippers off the bench.

The exits of Richardson and Randolph had changed everything. The backcourt was suddenly young.

In 2001-02, Michigan State was about to finish 19-12 and 10-6 in the Big Ten, just good enough to get a NCAA invitation. The NCAA spot was consolation, at least, following a season that had not been easy.

Taylor was one problem. He seemed never to enjoy anything about basketball that was not personal to him. His old high-school coach, Phil Odle, had noticed how unemotional Taylor had been when Lansing Waverly won the state's high school basketball championship. When Taylor's energy level was negative it dragged down teammates and turned what should have been a buoyant experience and culture into something quite diminished.

He and Izzo had their differences over Taylor's role. The coach preferred that Taylor think about point-guard responsibilities and less about scoring. Taylor had an opposing viewpoint, one closer to that of his father, who could often be heard critiquing Izzo's coaching from the stands. Plenty of times, the coach heard it. Plenty of times, a man's Italian blood would boil.

Just as often, friends, associates and other coaches would tell Izzo to forget the sniping and concentrate on a job he did better than anyone else who would have been sitting on that Michigan State bench.

PROBABLY FIVE MINUTES AFTER NORTH CAROLINA STATE finished off State's return-to-earth 2001-02 season with a 69-58 victory at Washington, D.C., Izzo was ready to convene practice for 2002-03 and reacquaint himself with the sensation of having a team deep enough, talented enough, experienced enough, to compete for a Big Ten championship and for a lengthier ride in the NCAA tourney.

The program was beginning to resemble its old self, anyway. Three potentially excellent recruits were about to be initiated: Paul Davis, the 6-foot-11 Sequoia from Rochester High who had a shooting touch to go with his size and who looked as if he might be hanging around East Lansing for two years, maximum, before traipsing off to the NBA.

MSU had fought off some sinister (in State's mind) recruiting efforts on the part of Missouri and head coach Quinn Snyder to hold onto Detroit Crockett guard Maurice Ager, who had a chance to be extraordinary if

Izzo knew anything about talent and upside.

And then there was the new guy whose name no one could pronounce: Erazem Lorbek, from Ljubljana, Slovenia, which was one way for a coach known for minding his backyard to expand Michigan State's recruiting base.

Izzo had become acquainted with Lorbek by way of the MSU coach's rising stature. He was now a part of the international basketball circle, as had been the case in the summer of 2001 when he was an assistant coach on the United States team at the Goodwill Games.

Lorbek's father was general manager for a European professional basketball team and had wanted to see his 6-foot-10 son play college basketball in the United States. Gregory had seen enough video to know the kid could play. The concern was whether he had clandestinely performed as a professional, which was always the fear when you dealt with players of his size and skill, and with their proximity to the sometimes murky world of Eastern European pro ball.

Izzo and Gregory came to realize the senior Lorbek knew NCAA rules and had been careful to keep his son's amateur status untainted. Izzo and Gregory decided there was no choice but to take their longest-ever recruiting visit: to Ljubljana, Slovenia.

They departed Detroit at 10 a.m. on a fall day in 2001 and arrived in Ljubljana about ten hours later to meet early the next morning with Lorbek and his parents. An hour later they were headed for the airport and were back in Detroit twenty-four hours after they had departed.

The trip had been worth it. They knew Lorbek was going to be a good player. They needed to know more what they were getting in Lorbek, the person. They had to get a bead on his family. Everything clicked during their in-and-out trip. Lorbek committed in the spring of 2002.

If only he were a point guard. The Spartans suddenly were in need of one. Taylor had seemed for most of his sophomore year to be following a perfectly scripted storyline. He was getting better by the week, better by the game, finishing the year as one of only two Big Ten players in history to lead the league in scoring (17.7) and assists (5.0) per game. He was going to lock down point guard for the Spartans and become one of college basketball's prime-time players.

Taylor had been reading from another script. He announced on March 27, twelve days after State's NCAA tournament ended, that he was going to test June's NBA draft. By not hiring an agent, he could get a bead on his market value and retain an option to return to school.

Anybody who knew Taylor in the spring of 2002 knew there would be an agent. Taylor was going to the NBA, no matter how many scouting reports, advisers, talent evaluators or NBA general managers told him to stay in school, improve his considerable skills, and be a guaranteed first-round choice later in his career. He was anything but a sure bet for the first round in 2002, a fact subsequently confirmed when Minnesota made him its second-round choice (fifty-second player selected) in June after Taylor had decided he was putting Michigan State in his past and getting on with NBA life.

It was not the kind of loss Izzo could sustain anymore than he could have planned for Taylor's exit with recruiting contingencies. You had too few scholarships to offer in a given year to stockpile talent in case someone ran off to the NBA. Professional teams have the option to trade for, or sign, emergency help if a key player goes down or is suddenly lost to free agency.

Izzo's team had no choice but to prepare for a season with Hill moving from his natural shooting-guard role to the point, which was not ideal in either party's mind. About the only reason for State's faithful to shake off Taylor's departure was that the rest of the team had talent in excess of its youth.

Anagonye, Adam Wolfe and Ballinger were forlorn seniors amid a sea of underclassmen. Anderson, Hill and Torbert were sophomores. Davis, Ager and Lorbek were freshmen. A couple of reserves, Jason Andreas and Rashi Johnson, were the lone juniors.

The younger players quickly learned the routine, Four hours before the game the team would have its pre-game meal: spaghetti, chicken, something healthy with ample carbohydrates. No dessert. Players could grab a cookie from the media room if they were really craving something sweet.

There would be a two-hour break before the team was obliged to be back at Breslin Center at least 90 minutes before tip-off. Players would get their ankles taped and get dressed. They would head to the court for a warm-up. The coaching staff would reconvene players 55 minutes before each game started. Izzo would come into the locker room 5 minutes later, sharp. That night's game plan would be gone over again. The key areas of concentration would be reviewed for 20 minutes. Players would return to the court for a warm-up before heading back to the dressing room exactly 11 minutes before tip-off.

Final instructions consisted of each player being told whom he was guarding. Izzo's pre-game speeches tended to be short and to the point. Then, everyone headed down the tunnel and onto the court for showtime.

The newer talent was beginning to define Izzo's 2002-03 team. Hill was not better off, personally, at point guard but he was giving MSU stability there. Anderson was a sophomore who played, most of the time, like an upper classman. Torbert was not yet blossoming into the vintage Flint superstar some had forecasted him to be, but he was helping off the bench, all as Davis, Ager and Lorbek got steadily better.

The Spartans lost four games by a total of eight points to finish the regular season 18-11, and in a third-place conference tie at 10-6. Fans in East Lansing wondered throughout the winter where Michigan State might have been with Taylor, much less with Richardson and Randolph. Then again, they knew. The Spartans would likely have been the nation's top team, counting down the weeks until State jetted off to another Final Four, perhaps to another NCAA championship.

Paul Davis surprised many when he decided to play four years at MSU, improving significantly with each passing season.

What they were likely to do in the 2003 NCAA tournament was anyone's guess. The team was too young and had lost too many tense games for any grandiose thoughts about ripping through a regional bracket. Then came a couple of surprisingly easy MSU wins in the early-round games at Tampa against Colorado (79-64) and Florida (68-46)—even in a rebuilding year, a seventh-seeded Michigan State team could breeze into the Sweet Sixteen.

The Spartans missed Taylor in the backcourt, but had enough frontline super-structure to make things difficult for teams that lacked MSU's size and athleticism. Facing Anagonye was like going against a semi-truck down low. His only hang-up was a unique capacity to pick up two fouls in the game's first two minutes, not always cheap ones. Anagonye was sometimes too strong for his own good. A quick move, a hand extended at the right angle, could send an opposing player skidding across the floor.

Davis and Lorbek were coming on as MSU's big-man game-changers. The two were each a fingernail beneath seven feet tall, and needed only to play with a tad more muscle and savvy for State to do damage at the South regional in San Antonio, an ambitious order when sixth-seed Maryland—defending national champion—was next up, led by savvy point guard Steve Blake from the title team.

MSU was on top, 29-24, at halftime but trailed late in the game until Davis—who seemed to be growing up by the minute—scored MSU's last six points, including a dunk to tie it, and a bank-shot off the glass with 4.7 seconds remaining to beat the Terrapins, 60-58, and send Izzo's team on to the regional finals against Texas.

State's joyride ended against Texas in the regional finals, 85-76. The score seemed to be a fair measure of the gap in talent and experience between two teams, as well as a reminder to Michigan State that hitting a wall at the regional finals had not been the worst way to end a season compromised from the outset by Taylor's ill-fated defection to the NBA draft.

IN 2003-04, EVERYONE WAS COMING BACK. Izzo's team, absolutely, was going to bounce back to its old Big Ten-contending, NCAA tournament-bashing ways.

There was the tall timber up front: Davis, who could be up and down, in and out from game to game, but who looked as if he might break loose as a sophomore. And there was Lorbek, who in the Texas game had been 6-for-11 from the floor on his way to 14 points to go with nine rebounds.

The backcourt was going to be getting a new freshman ace in Shannon Brown, a superb talent MSU had courted and signed out of Proviso East High in Maywood, Illinois. Everyone else returned: Anderson, Davis, Ager, Torbert and Hill, the three-point shooting machine who would have led the Spartans in Boy Scout medals and GQ style points had such numbers been kept.

Andy Katz, the college basketball guru for *ESPN.com*, wrote a day after the 2003 NCAA championship game that Michigan State would be Final Four-bound again in 2004.

"The Spartans didn't lean on their seniors much and still got to the Elite Eight – a step further than UConn," Katz wrote. "Michigan State had one of the top recruiting classes in the nation coming in this season, and Paul Davis, Maurice Ager and Erazem Lorbek each got better as the season got longer."

There was only one problem with Katz's clairvoyance. He did not see Lorbek declaring on May 10 that he was heading home to Europe to turn pro.

Izzo was becoming unbearably adept at taking the high road after losing one player after another to pro basketball, whether they were ready or not (Taylor was not), or whether they wanted to or not (it was suspected deeply that Lorbek's father had pressed his son to turn pro against the youngster's wishes).

Izzo's stock congratulatory speech invariably contained the words "follow" and "dream" as he waved goodbye to a player who had been counted on to be a bulwark during MSU's coming season. An occasional loss to the NBA was part of the territory, he realized. The Richardsons and Randolphs of the Spartans' basketball world were going to be short-stay players from the day they walked onto campus.

Losing Taylor had been a different experience altogether. He was not ready. He had nothing to gain and everything to lose by fleeing Michigan State for a futile run at the NBA. Now Lorbek, who stood to benefit in so many ways by continuing at Michigan State, was boarding a plane and leaving for a professional basketball experience that would happily have waited for him.

Izzo would have been in much sturdier shape with Lorbek to attack a tough, early-season schedule entering the 2003-04 season, a stretch of games that would include Kansas, Duke, Oklahoma and Kentucky at Ford Field in front of the largest crowd ever to watch a basketball game, pro or college. Most coaches subscribed to the notion that you scheduled fairly easily in November and December, mixing in an occasional toughie to make sure a team could take a punch ahead of its conference schedule.

Izzo had OD'd on heavyweights. Had his not-ready-for-prime-time players stayed clear of the NBA the previous two springs, things might have gone differently for a Spartan team that was about to go 0-and-4 against those four marquee schools. Adding in losses at Syracuse and UCLA, that made the Spartans 0-for-6 against the powerhouse gauntlet.

As Izzo approach his ninth season in East Lansing, he found himself with a surreal kind of status. For so many years—decades, really—he had been within a conference ruled by tribal chiefs: Heathcote, Bobby Knight at Indiana, Gene Keady at Purdue, Tom Davis at Iowa. Now they were all moving on or nearing retirement. Izzo was behind only Keady in Big Ten seniority.

His relationships with other coaches reflected his new status as Big Ten old-timer and three-time veteran of the NCAA Final Four. Although he had not been particularly close with Steve Alford at Iowa, Izzo one day in Iowa City found himself counseling Alford, who had come to him wondering how Michigan State's commander in chief did it, how he managed to absorb the pressure and maintain such consistency in his team's performance and in his coaching demeanor.

Izzo was touched. This was a new role for him, offering an opponent coach solace, particularly when the opponent coach looked at him with such obvious regard.

Izzo got along with most of his colleagues. He was never going to be as close with Keady as Heathcote had been for fifteen years, but the two coaches liked each other immensely and had known each other, seemingly forever. Izzo had shared mutual respect and good feelings with Tommy Amaker at Michigan since their early days as assistants, staking out Chris Webber at the Nike camp.

He and Bill Self at Illinois were absolute buddies compared with the old cold-war relationship that had enveloped Heathcote and Illini coach Lou Henson, although Heathcote had nothing on Knight when it came to contempt for Henson.

Izzo's least likely choice for a cordial dinner with another Big Ten basketball coach was Bo Ryan at Wisconsin. There were a couple of problems with Ryan. His teams tended to beat Michigan State way too often, particularly in Madison. And they did not always win with the same degree of grace Izzo insisted on seeing in his team.

The blood got particularly hot during a bad night at Wisconsin on February 11, 2003, when the Badgers broke open a close game in the waning minutes and rubbed a loss in State's faces when Alando Tucker and Devon Harris slammed home gratuitous, encore dunks as time melted away in a 64-53 victory.

"We'll never forget this," Izzo told Ryan as they met for one of the shortest handshakes in NCAA basketball history en route to their locker rooms.

The feud lasted all of two years, a veritable era in Izzo's annals. After the Spartans whipped Wisconsin, 77-64, at Breslin Center in February of 2005, the two coaches passed each other as one departed the podium used for post-game press conferences and one arrived.

"Whatever I can do for you, buddy," Izzo said, waving at Ryan as if the two were fraternity brothers catching up after a few years apart. "Go get 'em, buddy."

Michigan State's hopes for getting anywhere in the Big Ten in 2003-04 rested on how far Anderson, Davis, Hill, Torbert, Brown and Ager, were going to take a team after its four early-season losses to the box-office big boys.

The conference season was pleasing enough: 12-4, including an overtime loss at Purdue, and, of course, another bad trip to Wisconsin. Izzo's scheduling had essentially kept State from a 20-win campaign (18-11 regular season), although the dividend for taking on non-conference bruisers was a tougher team down the stretch and into the NCAA tournament.

Seventh-seeded Michigan State drew tenth-seeded Nevada in the West Regional first-round game at Seattle. Playing all those November-December desperadoes, then the tough Big Ten schedule, should put MSU in shape for one of its typical first-round massacres.

No one doubted it would be just that as the Spartans opened up a 16-point lead that was still nine points, 43-34, at halftime.

Then came the second half. In the final 20 minutes, Michigan State scored 23 points. MSU totaled seven points in the game's final 9 minutes, 51 seconds. The final: Nevada 72, Michigan State 66. This would not go down as one of MSU's better NCAA tournament hours.

MSU's BASKETBALL FRAMEWORK IN OCTOBER of 2004 was automatically going to be stronger for the obvious reason good and seasoned players were returning. There had been, for a pleasant change, no pro basketball defectors. The returning crew was exceptionally talented. Drew Neitzel, a sparkling point guard from Grand Rapids Wyoming Park High, was expected to help.

Whether it was offense or defense, Shannon Brown was a dependable clutch performer during an MSU career that began in 2003.

The Spartans were deep enough, skilled enough, muscular enough (Matt Trannon was coming aboard upon completion of football season), and hungry enough after their short stay in the 2004 NCAA tourney to bring back a little of that old

Izzo-induced Final Four savoir-faire that had recently gone missing.

Opponents could pick their poison: Davis, provided he was having one of his good nights, could make a mess of another team on both ends of the court. Anderson was Anderson: a graceful perimeter player. Hill was no Mateen Cleaves in the fire-and-fury mold of backcourt leaders Izzo craved, but he was a lustrous shooter. Ager was developing into a star, Shannon Brown was a budding All-American. Torbert was money off the bench.

Michigan State was primed to make another Final Four run as the autumn of 2004-05 arrived. There was enough skill and depth to make it plausible. With a little luck Michigan State might be running in the four-horse race for a national title when the season convened at St. Louis.

The Spartans had their customary pre-season dip when they lost back-to-back road games to Duke and George Washington, but that was the last loss until January 16, when MSU endured its annual defeat at Wisconsin, although this one was beyond bitter. State had been up by eight points with just over two minutes to play only to watch it all dissolve in a 62-59 loss.

Izzo's team dropped only one of its next ten games—a bad 81-68 home defeat to super guard Dee Brown and Illinois before welding together another six-game winning streak ahead of an overtime loss at Indiana. One more less-than-stirring appearance at the fatiguing Big Ten tournament (a 71-69 loss to Iowa) seemed, again, to have little effect on a State team that was 22-6 and ranked fifteenth nationally heading into the NCAA tournament.

Two tough opening-round games at Worcester, Massachusetts, went to Michigan State (fifth seed) as the Spartans whipped Old Dominion, 89-81 (56 percent shooting by MSU, 39 percent by Old Dominion), and Vermont, 72-61, (Ager with 19 points, Vermont with 31 percent shooting from the field), to win a promotion to the South Regional at Austin, Texas.

Michigan State was accustomed to using ten players in a typical slug-it-out contest against good competition. Tim Bograkos provided great value off the bench, while Drew Naymick also helped. Trannon was the guy who could shake things up, pull down a huge defensive board, and ensure that any fouls called against him would not be of the pitty-pat variety.

Teammates marveled at how Trannon would shift within a day or so from Spartan Stadium to the basketball court and never seem as if there was any required adjustment period. He was an excellent athlete with a zest for basketball. Trannon seemed to play as if basketball were a lovely bonus and not a continuation of the tough hours, meetings, practices, study tables, and demands that he signed on for from one season to the next.

In Michigan State's regional opener against Duke, Trannon had a typical contribution (two points, three rebounds, two fouls). This was the same top-seeded band of Blue Devils that had thumped MSU, 81-74, back in November at Cameron Indoor Stadium. In March, Michigan State was simply the better team, winning 78-68, as Davis scored 20 points to go with 17 from Anderson and 14 by Ager. One premier seeded team down, another to go as Kentucky (seeded second in the South bracket) got ready for yet another regional final against the guys from East Lansing.

From the pure perspective of a white-knuckle college basketball fan, this was going to be the best of the MSU-Kentucky NCAA regional showdowns that had been staged between the two schools since the 1950s.

The Spartans were down, 37-33, at halftime but surged ahead, 70-62, late in the second half, courtesy of a sizzling stretch of shooting (15 of 18 from the floor). Then Kentucky threw together a 13-5 run that tied it, 75-75 with the last three points coming on a wild three-pointer by Patrick Sparks that bounced several times before it dropped through the net. The question was whether Sparks' foot had grazed the three-point line ahead of his shot. Replay after replay was shown, analyzed, debated, and argued both ways. Officials decided the three-point shot stood. Game tied.

Michigan State was set to lose by a basket of any flavor as the first overtime wound down with Kentucky in possession. Rajon Rondo helped the Spartans by dribbling in place for eight or so seconds before dishing off to Kelenna Azubuike, who promptly retreated to the right corner and never got off a shot before the buzzer sounded. It was 81-81, second overtime on the way.

Michigan State had by this time seen enough of overtime and Kentucky. The Spartans nailed six free throws in the final 12 seconds to win, 94-88, and grab for Izzo his fourth Final Four in seven seasons. It was a flag-planting moment for Michigan State, which showed that the 1999-2001 string of consecutive Final Fours had not been all a product of the Flintstones. The frequency of MSU's visits, rather, was clear proof that Izzo had constructed an extraordinary basketball machine in East Lansing.

Fitting, perhaps, that the semifinal match-up would pit Michigan State against a national college basketball dynasty, North Carolina, which had the kind of reputation Izzo yet hoped to acquire at Michigan State. The Tar Heels, of course, had spent decades building their ivory-tower basketball presence, a fact not lost on Izzo as he and the Spartans pulled into St. Louis.

They were to be joined by Illinois and by Louisville, which had the obvious potential of creating an all-Big Ten championship game. Michigan State had the more difficult assignment, at least in the eyes of anyone out-side of Louisville. Bruce Weber's Illini had crushed Michigan State, 81-68, at Breslin Center, the only time they met during the Big Ten season, and were likely to be too much for Louisville.

The same was being said about North Carolina. With their custom-ary corps of NBA-bound thorough-breds (Rashad McCants, Jawad Williams, Sean May and Raymond Felton, among others), the Tar Heels were an elegant NCAA bas-ketball team.

Michigan State was acquiring a bit of Hollywood itself as Izzo's team got ready for a night of unfath-omable pre-game nervousness—but that was what playing on the Final Four stage, with its ability to grip a nation, was all about.

Matt Trannon, after sitting out as a Pro-position 48 athlete in 2002, became a multi-sport star as a wide receiver in football and forward in basketball.

The Spartans showed no particular jitters in the first half and went to the dressing room with a reassuring 38-33 lead, which was not the way North Carolina intended for the final 20 minutes to be played. After the Tar Heels had knotted it, 49-49, Roy Williams' team went on a 12-0 spurt that grew into an 87-71 blowout. Though it was not made public prior to the game, MSU's Alan Anderson had injured a knee against Kentucky and was scoreless during the loss to North Carolina.

Two nights later, North Carolina put away Illinois for the national championship.

That night Izzo understood something that night few Spartans fans could appreciate after the four-in-seven-years Final Four spree. It was not likely to be a regular event in the ensuing years. Conditions that had helped Michigan State to an abnormal number of appearances for any team were going to be tough to duplicate. Recruiting was more competitive, the Flintstones had been an aberration, new coaches with stratospheric energy levels had come to his conference, and NBA ball was taking more and more players earlier in their college careers, if not right out of high school.

"We're not Duke, we're not North Carolina," Izzo said, in a hallway outside the Spartan locker room after the Tar Heels game. "We're Michigan State, and it's not easy replenishing these guys."

Izzo's basketball life would become even more taxing.

IN THE 2005-06 SEASON, the Spartans broke even in the Big Ten, going 8-8, splitting with Michigan among others. They were 20-10 during the regular season, including an epic early-season, three-overtime chiller against Gonzaga and Adam Morrison, which saw Gonzaga escape, 109-106. The Spartans had lost in one of the universally recognized great college basketball games in recent years.

Four months later they lost their only game in the Big Ten tournament to Iowa, 53-48. Then they lost their season finale, in the first round of the NCAA tournament, helping George Mason become the nation's Cinderella saga.

Later that month, in April of 2006, they were told Shannon Brown was going to "explore" the NBA draft, an exploratory mission that ended on June 8 when he announced formally that he had retained an agent and was headed for the NBA. He was picked twenty-fifth by the Cleveland Cavaliers.

Izzo's reaction was no different than it had been all the times earlier when a talented athlete was leaving his coach, leaving his team, leaving his school, for a career dream.

"It's a very good decision that was thought out, acted out, and involved the right people," Izzo said, stoically, "and, for that, I hope Michigan State people applaud that it was done the best way it could be done."

He might have been speaking for how he wanted his own self-engineered basketball program to be viewed some future day, long after he left East Lansing. Unlike some of his NBA-bound players, Izzo's problem was that he was never quite sure when that would be.

CHAPTER 16

LIFE AFTER A LEGEND

ON WEEKEND WINTER NIGHTS IN THE LATE 1980s, Munn Arena was still the vogue place to be on Michigan State's snow-covered campus. Not quite fifteen years old, Munn Arena was everything a Michigan winter was not—a hockey palace that was warm, inviting, exciting, intimate, special in all the ways a single facility can be during a raw season in East Lansing.

How much that crackling atmosphere had to do with the quality of hockey players was a fair question. Michigan State's players were premier amateur North American hockey talents. They wore shimmering green-and-white uniforms that sparkled beneath the arena lights and, as they skated, *en masse*, during their graceful warm-up circles, people stepped to their seats prepared for a pulse-pounding night of entertainment. A Michigan State hockey ticket was special.

You had to have a season ticket, or know somebody who did, if marquee teams were coming to East Lansing. On many evenings it hardly mattered who was helping to provide that night's entertainment. What mattered was being on hand for a Michigan State hockey game that had become something of a status symbol in East Lansing as Ron Mason continued to sculpt one of the nation's certifiably elite college sports programs.

What the fans wanted, of course, was another national championship, emphasis on another. Mason had already taken care of the first with his first national title—MSU's second—in his seventh season as Spartans head coach. There was no reason to think national titles in the plural would not follow when Mason annually pumped another half-dozen star recruits onto his carefully constructed, precisely calibrated hockey roster.

He had been building a showcase program from the day he arrived in April 1979 as head coach to reconstitute a hockey team that had all but dissolved during Amo Bessone's latter years. Recruiting files at the time consisted of a manila folder in a file cabinet. As with all rebuilt college programs—football, basketball, hockey, whatever sport—the new structure was going to be built with Grade A recruits, an effort that, within only a few seasons, began to re-establish Michigan State's hockey muscle.

Within three years, Mason had MSU back in the NCAA tournament. On came the cavalcade of stars and superstars: Craig Simpson, Kelly Miller, Harvey Smyl, Mike Donnelly, Gord Flegel, Lyle Phair, Mitch Messier, Jeff Parker, Don McSween, Kevin Miller, Bill Shibicky, Joe Murphy, Bobby Reynolds, Rod Brind'Amour, Bob Essensa. By 1985-86, Michigan State was ready for its first NCAA championship since 1966, which came in a marvelous 6-5 victory over Harvard in Providence, Rhode Island, on a goal by Donnelly.

Mason, though, was crashing headlong into a problem that a basketball coach by the name of Tom Izzo would deal with fifteen and twenty years later. Keeping the kind of talent on the ice that won NCAA championships until their eligibility expired could be a difficult assignment.

Players wanted to play in the National Hockey League if they had the skills, which a good many of Mason's recruits were already buffing and polishing when they stepped for the first time onto Munn's ice. Murphy left after his freshman year, weeks after MSU had won its 1986 national championship, when Detroit made him the 1986 NHL draft's first overall pick. Simpson had gone a year earlier, drafted second overall by Pittsburgh. Brind'Amour was ninth overall in 1988, goaltender Jason Muzzatti twenty-first overall in the same draft.

The Spartans should have won the title in 1989, and would forever believe as much. It was a winter of supreme hockey talent in East Lansing: Brind'Amour, Reynolds, Kip Miller, Danton Cole, Jason Woolley, Shawn Heaphy, Peter White, Pat Murray, Steve Beadle, Brad Hamilton, Jim Cummins and Don Gibson.

It was the year when Michigan State took a 38-6-1 record into the Frozen Four at St. Paul, Minnesota. It was the year, as well, when Muzzatti's goaltending broke down at the most crushing of moments for a Michigan State team that would never quite forgive itself for losing to Harvard, 6-3, in the semifinals.

Upsets, they are called—those moments in sports when a decidedly better team is surprised, stunned, outplayed, outworked, and, in any event, finally beaten by a lesser team that was able to exceed its physical limitations. Harvard had upset a Michigan State team favored to win in 1989.

In 1990, fans wondered if it was about to happen again, just twelve months later, as the 34-5-3 Spartans prepared to meet Boston University in a three-game quarterfinal series at East Lansing. Michigan State had partied in the opener, 6-3, and was posed to wrap up its third consecutive Frozen Four ticket as early as the next evening in a best two-of-three qualifier. Instead, BU won the second and third games, each by a 5-3 score.

Of little consolation was Kip Miller's incredible season. He became only the second Spartan in history to score a hundred or more points (101 on 48 goals and 53 assists; Tom Ross had 105 in 1975-76) and became the first Michigan State player to win the Hobey Baker Memorial Award given each season to college hockey's premier player.

Boston University spoiled the party. The back-to-back losses to the Terriers were excruciating defeats for a coach and for a Michigan State hockey camp that wanted the gratification of national championships on a par with MSU's national hockey prominence. One reality beginning to settle into East Lansing's collective hockey consciousness ten years into Mason's stint at MSU was that this gray-haired hockey mentor, who wore a matching platinum moustache, was on his way to becoming college hockey's all-time winningest coach.

It would not happen as rapidly as Michigan State preferred. Recruiting was no longer a bonanza for Mason as the 1990s arrived. Getting those waves of brilliant forwards was becoming more difficult, in part because there were so many other programs on the rise, including one in Ann Arbor, where Red Berenson was thriving as coach at Michigan.

Bringing to East Lansing a pair of game-changing defensemen each season was not the regular exercise it had been through the 1980s. Results were predictable. Seasons when thirty to thirty-five victories had testified to Michigan State's national clout on the ice, and in the homes of elite recruits, were giving way to less inspiring winters: 17-18-5 in 1990-91, when it was up to Jason Woolley, Shawn Heaphy, Dwayne Norris, Kerry Russell, Peter White and Bryan Smolinski to make the most of a mediocre product.

There was a rebound in 1991-92, which included State's first Frozen Four trip in three years. It ended with a 4-2 loss to Lake Superior State (where Mason began his head-coaching career) in the semifinals, although a 26-10-8 record had been behavior more associated with a Mason team as Norris, White, Smolinski, Steve Suk, Rem Murray, Rob Woodward and Joby Messier took care of the Spartans' essential business, which that winter was offense.

What the Spartans could not have realized, and would not have accepted, in April of 1992, was any suggestion Michigan State had seen its last Frozen Four for seven long seasons. The Spartans were about to go into a deep freeze of their own, winning only about two dozen games most years without once advancing to hockey's post-season ball. That kept the likes of a NHL-bound Anson Carter from stepping even once onto college hockey's grand stage.

Anson Carter starred at MSU from 1992-96 before becoming a productive player in the NHL. He amassed 106 goals and 72 assists at State.

Mason would have more enjoyed his own personal accomplishment had the mid-1990s winters been kinder to his team. On March 18, 1994, the Spartans had spotted Bowling Green a 2-0 lead before Steve Guolla broke loose for three goals, sending State to a 3-2 victory and giving Mason more victories (698) than any college hockey coach in history. (Mason had been BG's head coach before coming to East Lansing.)

But for years March had been a particularly nettlesome month for the Spartans.

State's 1997-98 near miss had been especially brutal, leaving fans and a hockey team anguished over a season that had seemed, to so many in East Lansing, as if it would end with an NCAA championship.

The Spartans had lost only five games as they got ready for Ohio State at the NCAA West Regional at Yost Arena in Ann Arbor. They had beaten the Buckeyes in three of four games, and their last victory, a week before the NCAA regional re-match, had been a classic. It was a 3-2, double-overtime victory for Michigan State in the Central Collegiate Hockey Association championship game at Joe Louis Arena, settled when Shawn Horcoff scored two minutes and 30 seconds into the second extra period.

That goal followed by three weeks another history-maker for the Spartans when Chad Alban, State's exceptional senior goaltender, became the fourth college hockey goalie in history to score a goal when he ripped a shot from behind, and right, of his own net dead into Ferris State's goal in a 6-3 victory at Munn Arena.

Michigan State's record belied the fact State was by no means overwhelming in 1997-98. There were quality forwards in Mike York, Sean Berens and Rustyn Dolyny, but it was Alban's goaltending (1.57 goals-against average, and .926 save percentage) that helped achieve State's glitzy record.

But in the regional decider, it was Ohio State's turn to win an overtime game, 3-2, knocking out Michigan State. State's fans were further embittered when Michigan won the NCAA championship. MSU had beaten the Wolverines all three times they played in 1997-98.

The heartbreak seemed to have had some sway with hockey's gods a year later. On March 28, 1999, when, with less than two minutes to play,

Michigan State got a pair of goals 32 seconds apart (Adam Hall and Andrew Hutchinson) to beat Colorado College, 4-3, and end its seven-winter exile from the Frozen Four. The run ended with a 5-3 loss to New Hampshire in the semifinals.

Hockey at Michigan State had been one of the University's Big Three sports for decades, enjoying a kind of cult following during lean football and basketball years. The icers had been a consistent winner during Mason's years and had steadily become a box-office smash, all the while exposing Munn Arena's 25-year-old limitations (it had been

Adam Hall led State to four NCAA appearances from 1998-2002, scoring 79 goals and adding 47 assists during a stellar career.

build to accommodate about 6,500 when many thought it should be constructed to hold 8,000).

Expansion was a must. Luxury suites were essential. Refurbishing was a necessary project for a university that had any sense of stewardship over a resource as valuable as Michigan State hockey. Club seats, luxury suites, as well as a new press box, were inaugurated on January 7, 2000, just as another new addition, a goaltender named Ryan Miller, was settling in at Munn Arena.

Miller was another of the descendants of Elwood (Butch) Miller and his brother Lyle, the ex-Spartans who had helped steer so many from his family to Michigan State: Kelly, Kevin, Kip and now Ryan.

The Spartans were getting in Ryan Miller a goaltender that elite college hockey teams were lucky to see in a generation. He was gifted, and ready to play as a freshman. It helped that he had a sterling supporting cast (Mike Weaver, Brad Fast and John-Michael Liles on defense; Shawn Horcoff, Adam Hall, Rustyn Dolyny, and Brian Maloney up front).

The bad news for Miller and MSU was that another kick to the gut awaited in March, this time in a 6-5 overtime loss to Boston College at the NCAA West Regional.

Miller was going to be better as a sophomore, which meant Michigan State had a sterling chance to be the same, as the Spartans were in making the Frozen Four (32-4-4), in big part due to Miller's 1.32 goals-against average. What Miller could not do was score. Michigan State dropped yet another Frozen Four semifinal game, this time to North Dakota, 2-0.

The Frozen Four visits were proving to be routinely disappointing, but Michigan State was more than happy with hockey's ongoing prestige and ability to lock in a constituency that was unfailingly loyal to Mason's program. The hockey team's base was so deep and devoted that Michigan State's athletic department, which was increasingly attempting to be imaginative in an era that mandated creativity, could begin to think big, very big, with respect to hockey.

It began with a startlingly big idea from an assistant coach at a sponsor's party at Munn Arena in January of 2001. Assistant hockey coach Dave McAuliffe suggested somewhat wildly that a hockey game at Spartan Stadium would be a nifty event, if somehow ice could be created on the field. Mark Hollis, the associate athletic director whose duties centered on marketing initiatives, heard McAuliffe's suggestion and grinned along with everyone else. Then he thought about it more deeply. He began checking with companies that installed ice surfaces. The idea took root, growing until Mason, athletic director Clarence Underwood, and another associate athletic director, Greg Ianni, made a formal presentation to MSU president Peter McPherson and vice president Fred Poston in April of 2001.

The executives bought it. Tickets were going to go on sale in late June for an October 6 game at Spartan Stadium between Michigan and Michigan State, aptly named The Cold War. It had a chance to make Michigan State home to the largest crowd ever to watch a single hockey game.

Hollis was on vacation when ticket manager Wendy Brown called an hour after Cold War seats went on sale.

"Thanks a lot," she said, with mock sarcasm. "They're (ticket-buyers) out the door."

Pulling off an outdoor hockey game in a football stadium, in any month, would have been a Hollywood-grade production. Staging it the first Saturday of October, when weather in Michigan could be anywhere on the meteorological spectrum, was a challenge all its own.

Michigan State got its lesson there as a temporary rink was set up early in the week, melted and flooded amid Indian Summer temperatures. Sun and wind more in keeping with May made engineers wonder how they could ever get the ice surface level enough for skaters. By Wednesday, seventy-two hours before face-off, there were actual waves splashing against the boards.

Mason could see a disaster on the horizon.

"Let's not do it," he said.

The forecast, though, was for cooler air to arrive by the weekend. Things were settling down everywhere but at the box office.

The game was going to be a sellout: 74,554. National and international television snippets would be immense for a novelty game that had about it no silliness; not when two blood-serious college hockey rivals on the scale of Michigan and Michigan State were playing.

There was going to be a Roman Coliseum air to the game with the players entering amid swirling smoke; laser and fireworks shows between periods; a country singer, Shannon Brown, performing; and Gordie Howe, wearing a Team USA jersey, dropping the first puck.

Howe had been a late addition. Earlier negotiations had dis-

Goalie Ryan Miller set the NCAA record for shutouts with 26 during his three-year career at MSU. The only thing State didn't manage to win during that time was an NCAA title.

solved when his negotiating team wanted a warehouse full of Gordie Howe bobblehead dolls to be part of the night's commerce. MSU balked. At the eleventh hour, Howe's agent called to say Gordie was in, sans bobbleheads.

An evening that had, from the outset, almost as much capacity for disaster as for success, was a smash hit in terms of the crowd (sellout), TV exposure (ESPN cut to the game at regular intervals on a peak college football night), and in revenue (about $500,000) for Michigan State's coffers. The game itself was appropriately dramatic. Jim Slater, a Spartan freshman, scored with 47 seconds remaining in regulation to tie it, 3-3, and send an amazing evening of sports entertainment into overtime, during which neither team scored.

Two weeks later, Mason reached one more uncharted place on college hockey's frontier: 900 victories.

He was also within nine months of taking a new job. MSU was looking for a successor to retiring athletic director Clarence Underwood. Mason was part of an intimate group of coaches and associates tabbed to draw up a wish-list of qualities, credentials and traits they wanted in MSU's new AD.

Conversation eventually led Mason to decide the person they wanted was MSU's hockey coach. Michigan State executives agreed. By mid-season, word was out that Ron Mason, North America's all-time leader in college hockey victories, was on his way to the AD's office.

East Lansing's prevailing mystery now was who would end up behind the bench overseeing Spartan hockey. This was not a conventional act to follow, succeeding Mason, the John Wooden of college hockey.

On top of the list was George Gwozdecky, the University of Denver head coach who had been an assistant under Mason when State won the 1986 national championship. Gwozdecky, though, had a happy situation at Denver, and felt no need to uproot.

Mason's choice became more and more obvious: It was going to be his one-time player and assistant coach at Lake Superior State, Rick Comley, head coach at Northern Michigan, who had already been talking with Mason about a move to East Lansing, although not as hockey coach.

Mason wanted Comley as an associate athletic director. Now that

Comley was fifty-five, and had put in twenty-six years as Northern Michigan's head coach, Michigan State's invitation was intriguing. Comley also bought Mason's thought that Gwozdecky would be perfect in East Lansing.

Only after it became apparent Gwozdecky would stick in Denver did the next move become clear to the two men: Comley was coming to East Lansing, but as hockey coach.

Mason's last game, on March 22, 2002, was a 2-0 loss to Colorado in the NCAA West Regional at Yost Arena. His amazing career ended with a record of 924-380-83, more victories than any one coach had amassed in the history of college hockey.

What he was leaving Comley from a team that had finished 27-9-2 was excellent top-tier talent, although MSU's one-of-a-kind goalie, Ryan Miller, had won the 2002 Hobey Baker Award and had foregone his senior year of eligibility to join the NHL.

John-Michael Liles, Brad Fast, Jim Slater—there was a typical nucleus of Mason-crafted talent to haul much of the load in Comley's first year, if the adjustment to a new coach and culture could be made. Depth was going to be Comley's and Michigan State's problem.

Comley was going to face his own adjustments moving from Marquette to East Lansing. Gone was the small-town intimacy, the absence of scrutiny, he had known in the Upper Peninsula. Lansing/East Lansing was by no means New York or Philadelphia, but talk radio was big and kept the heat on a coach who was never going to be viewed as favorably as the giant he replaced.

East Lansing's suspicions about anyone stepping in for Mason would have been overwhelming, Gwozdecky, perhaps, as an exception. The fans simply did not know what to make of Comley. His team sputtered during his first winter in East Lansing, although those who were getting to know him came to like him for his dimension and substance. It followed that a person of Comley's intellect and apparent character must be the right man, particularly for Mason to have entrusted to him Munn Arena's keys.

Comley was conversant with respect to just about any subject. He had an impressive knowledge of other sports and teams; he was up on current events and issues; he loved going to the theater with his wife, Diane, with whom he had a relationship others found quite touching, the way a man of his age might be seen walking with his wife and holding her hand as if they were high school sweethearts.

He simply had to win more. For any new coach it was generally a matter of getting his own program, players and environment established. Comley was going to play a more wide-open offensive game than Mason had found fashionable. Comley was a different conductor at the helm of a different and diverse symphony that was going to require time if MSU hockey were to become more cohesive and return to the upper echelon.

A player who was about to blossom was John-Michael Liles, a defenseman by trade who was going to be frenetically involved in Michigan State's blue-line offense and its harder-charging pushes up the ice. He would lead the team in scoring during Comley's first season, which ended in a 7-5 loss to Comley's old team, Northern Michigan, in the CCHA tournament at Joe Louis Arena.

Nothing was going to change for the better, or change quickly, for Comley as the Spartans teeter-tottered through his first three seasons (23-14-2, 23-17-2, 20-17-4) before a season-closing blitz in 2005-06 (two losses in their final 16 games) put Michigan State into an NCAA Regional game against Maine, which the Black Bears won, 5-4, to leave Comley's team at 25-12-8, and convince most of the wait-and-see throngs that something akin to Mason's consistency was now governing Comley's program.

Getting the crowds back loomed as another issue. They had fallen off at Munn Arena as the Mason years gave

Rick Comley from Northern Michigan was AD Ron Mason's choice to replace himself. It took four years for Comley to produce positive results, reaching the NCAA Regional Finals in 2006.

way to Comley's administration, in part, it was believed, because tickets for MSU football and basketball had become a serious budget item (seat-license fees were now in vogue at Michigan State as had been the rage in college and professional sports). The discretionary dollars once slapped down for a Munn Arena season-ticket package were fewer as Michigan's overall economy had its effects on East Lansing's hockey market. Money, however, had rarely been an issue within a Michigan State sports community that tended to find adequate cash when Spartan icers were winning and providing the sort of excitement and entertainment that had been commonplace for decades at stately Munn Arena.

In March of 2006, Rick Comley was looking ahead to future winters after Michigan State had missed by a goal or two against Maine of heading deeper into a NCAA tournament. Comley had been around East Lansing for only a few seasons, but a man who knew history the way he had command of so many subjects, understood twenty years was long enough for Michigan State to have gone without one more NCAA hockey championship.

CHAPTER 17

BELLES HAVE A BALL

HOW MANY MORE AIRPORTS, flight connections, rental cars and recruiting letters she could endure was the lingering question for Karen Langeland in December of 1999. She had been coaching at Michigan State since 1976. She was fifty-one years old. At some point there needed to be a life filled with experiences that coaching a Big Ten women's basketball team was not about to accommodate as a new millennium dawned.

Karen Langeland had been a watershed coach in Michigan State's hundred-year-plus sports saga. She arrived in East Lansing, a woman still in her twenties, fresh from high-school teaching and coaching. Then she was handed a task that transcended sports and engaged the far more daunting realm of making American intercollegiate athletics more embracing and less condescending toward society's women.

The job description said something quite different, of course. Langeland understood the social mission for equality in women's athletics was simply going to be an innate part of where Michigan State, and all American universities, would be traveling in the years to come.

In December of 1999, much had been accomplished in that regard, certainly more than Langeland and her contemporaries might have envisioned nearly twenty-five years earlier. No longer were women basketball players competing in a national tournament obliged to stay four to a hotel room, two to a bed, as had been the case in 1977. That was Langeland's first year as head coach, when Michigan State qualified for what then passed as the NCAA championship: the National Association of Intercollegiate Athletics for Women tournament in Minneapolis.

By 1999 the women had the same equipment, facilities, road accommodations, meals, and appropriately compensated coaches as did the men. None of that was Langeland's issue as Christmas drew near and Michigan State's campus settled down after the previous month's commotion, when football coach Nick Saban suddenly departed for LSU and Bobby Williams was plugged in as his successor.

Langeland had two years left on her contract and too little left in her personal gas tank. She was tired of it all. She needed what so many people in their respective occupations seek after too many years doing the same thing, no matter how fulfilling it might, at times, be. She needed fresh scenery.

A phone call was made to Clarence Underwood, whose status as interim athletic director had been changed to full-time with formal appointment as Michigan State's newest AD. Could she meet with him at an out-of-the-way spot to talk business?

They agreed on a chat at the MSU International Center, which had likewise quieted down now that students had completed exams and were on their way home for the holidays. Underwood had no clear idea why Langeland wanted to meet, except that it made sense given his promotion and the obvious reality that he would be governing MSU athletics for the next two-and-a-half years.

"Clarence, I think I need to retire," she told Underwood, whom at first thought she was joking.

Langeland explained her fatigue, her frustration with trying to relate to a new generation of students and athletes. They seemed so dead-set on blaming everyone for whatever strife existed in their lives and were so disinclined to accept personal accountability.

Langeland also had an idea for Underwood to consider. She loved administration. She was organized. It was the part of her coaching job that she most enjoyed, being buttoned-down, prepared and comprehensive in her planning and paperwork. Other coaches hated those duties. She thrived on them.

"I don't know if you need help with anything," Langeland said to Underwood, "but I'd like to work with coaches as opposed to, say, working with facilities, or academic support, or compliance."

Underwood realized she was dead serious. He also knew enough about Langeland's skills set to understand she might be onto something.

"Let me give some thought to what you've just said," he told her. "You've had a lot of years here. You've been very loyal to Michigan State. That means a lot to everyone here."

Langeland had only one other request: Would her boss keep this discussion confidential? She feared that her team, or incoming recruits, might be unsettled if any speculation or any hint of her departure leaked prematurely. Underwood assured her the conversation was between them.

He also had other matters to consider a week before Christmas, specifically Michigan State's journey to Orlando, Florida, for the Citrus Bowl game against Florida, which was to be Williams' debut as Spartans head coach. In between functions, meetings, and getting a splash of sun ahead of the return to East Lansing and winter, Underwood was buttonholed by an associate AD named Tracy Ellis-Ward, who supervised ten sports and was involved in MSU events management.

Ellis-Ward informed Underwood that she would be leaving for a front-office job with the Women's National Basketball Association.. Underwood was about to follow up Williams' appointment with another unanticipated hire.

It was going to be Langeland. She would be overseeing the ten sports that had been under Ellis-Ward. She would also be placed in charge of MSU summer sports camps that annually hosted between eight thousand and nine thousand teens.

It was exactly the kind of position she had ideally seen herself filling when the first serious thoughts about leaving coaching cropped up. She and Underwood agreed that word of her move to Jenison Fieldhouse would remain a secret until after her ongoing basketball season had wrapped up in March.

There was one problem threatening their airtight agreement. Underwood was being quizzed regularly about Ellis-Ward's job. Why was he not acting to fill her position? Was the job going to be posted?

Underwood met with Langeland.

"Would you help me out here?" he asked. "Would you allow us to announce that you're retiring?"

Langeland understood. It had been naïve, perhaps, to think a staff shift of this nature was going to remain quiet for the next three months. She arranged to tell her players ahead of MSU's formal announcement that Langeland would be moving from the Breslin Student Events Center to Jenison as an associate athletic director.

Langeland could look back on two decades at Michigan State and reflect on moments too emotional to easily categorize as good or bad:

There had been the awful 1997 NCAA second-round loss to North Carolina, at Chapel Hill, when the Spartans messed up against a screen and allowed a three-point shot at the buzzer that sent the game into overtime, which the Tar Heels won, 81-71. That loss kept the Spartans from their first NCAA regional. It was a game, and a moment, that would create nightmares for Langeland in years to come.

There was the announcement from Nicole Cushing in March of 1996 as Langeland and her players prepared to board a flight home from Hartford, Connecticut, after losing a NCAA second-round game to Connecticut.

Cushing had just been named Big Ten freshman of the year. She was a budding All-American. She was going to be a franchise player for the Spartans spanning her next three years in East Lansing.

"I'm getting married," Cushing told Langeland.

So much for that mini-dynasty as Cushing departed a year before the MSU-North Carolina nightmare played out.

There was the gutsy, laudable effort mounted in the late 1970s by Jill Prudden, Carol Hutchins and Kathy DeBoer, who hired an attorney and filed a class-action suit against the discriminatory travel budgets, a clear violation of Title IX, which led to those demeaning two-to-a-bed accommodations.

Now it was someone else's turn to take a shot at making Michigan State's basketball women a team of excellence. It was up to Underwood and his team, primarily senior associate athletic director Shelley Appelbaum, to determine whom that person might be.

Appelbaum's scouting had taken her to a young coach in Maine who had been steadily building a winner, and an impressive fan following at the University of Maine: Joanne P. McCallie, a one-time Big Ten player at Northwestern in the 1980s when she was known as Joanne Palombo.

McCallie had grown up, by her own admission, as a "Navy brat" who had lived everywhere from Monterey, California, to Corpus Christi, Texas, to Bermuda, to Brunswick, Maine, where she became a hot basketball recruit for Duke and Northwestern.

Joanne P. McCallie is often calm in the huddle, but can blister her team when the situation calls for it—as she did before it rallied against Tennessee in the Final Four semifinal in 2005.

A recruiting trip to Evanston, Illinois, settled that issue, after which she found a place on Northwestern's all-time career assists list (she was still seventh in 2006) and made All-Big Ten honorable mention.

Her interests were omnivorous: radio and television, political science, film, law, and business. She had interned in a downtown Chicago law firm during her undergrad days and decided the legal profession was too isolated and research-driven to make it her career. She would instead opt for graduate school and seek an MBA, which took her to Auburn and to a job as a graduate assistant coaching the Auburn women's basketball team.

She had never for a moment thought seriously about coaching beyond her pragmatic stint as a grad assistant. But by her second season, as Auburn began showing up at NCAA Final Four tournaments and McCallie came more and more to appreciate her role as a mentor, to understand that coaching (she was made a fulltime assistant after two years as a graduate assistant) offered an extraordinary opportunity to nurture and enrich people.

Coaching steadily was revealing to Joanne Palombo that there was something decidedly vocational about working in such a way with young women, in a sport she loved, in the same sport that had already provided such a pronounced influence on her own life.

At age twenty-six, she was being courted by her home-state college, the University of Maine, to become head coach of the Black Bears. She was now married to John McCallie, an economics professor whom she had met at Auburn when he was working on his PhD and she was completing her MBA.

The difficulty in accepting a job at Maine was that John was on a tenured track at the University of Alabama-Birmingham, not the kind of professor's seat you blithely abandoned. They decided on Maine, a move that was going to change the McCallies' life as much as it transformed the Black Bears' basketball women.

Crowds at Maine soared from a thousand a game to five thousand as a team that finished 9-20 in McCallie's first year ascended in a hurry, to 20, 24, 27 victories a season, and six times made the NCAA tournament.

McCallie was dynamic and charismatic. She could recruit and she could coach. She had an intuitive skill for knowing how to get on someone and when to back off. The community fell in love with her, including those two well-recognized Black Bears fans, Stephen and Tabatha King.

She had also turned down her share of jobs or interview requests ahead of Appelbaum's call in the winter of 2000: Florida State, Nebraska, Wake Forest, Washington, Long Beach State among them.

The difference when Appelbaum called was that Michigan State wanted to bring her husband on board, as well, as a professor. It was an invitation McCallie could think seriously about. What she would not do is subject herself to a conflict of interest. Appelbaum was told that McCallie would not contact Michigan State; any communication must originate from East Lansing, and all conversations must be confined to her one day a week when she was off work.

Appelbaum followed orders. Each week, religiously, Appelbaum would call on McCallie's off-day to discuss a range of issues that would need to be agreed upon before any decisions could be made.

When Maine's 1999-2000 season ended (20-11, NCAA tournament berth), the way was cleared to talk in earnest with a Big Ten school she had known only superficially from her Northwestern playing days. Michigan State also needed to be aware of another matter: she was nine months pregnant. Any interviews needed to be conducted in Maine.

Michigan State chartered a plane owned by ex-Spartan star Kirk Gibson and flew a ten-person contingent to Portland, Maine, two hours from Maine's campus. Underwood and Appelbaum were joined by vice presidents Fred Poston and Kathy Lindahl, by associate athletic director Mark Hollis, and others who needed to talk directly with Michigan State's only serious candidate to replace Langeland.

Joanne and John McCallie had decided in advance of their Portland interviews that nothing would be done ahead of their own concerted discussions, which meant Michigan State was going to be waiting for a day or two, at least, before any agreements were made.

Michigan State was just as determined to return to East Lansing with Joanne P. McCallie's name on a contract. Underwood presided over the meeting, leading discussion that, for the athletic department personnel, quickly focused on McCallie, basketball and Michigan State. Poston, meanwhile, was engaged in a discussion about an economics appointment with her husband John. MSU's double-team was being applied in a manner the Maine coach had to appreciate.

Twenty minutes into their conversation, Underwood requested that he and Poston be allowed to speak, alone, with the McCallies. After the rest of the party left, final matters were resolved, paperwork was presented, contracts were signed, and Michigan State had not only a new coach, but also a new university family that would carry a multi-dimensional influence.

There was still much that McCallie did not know, including the specifics of her responsibilities and where she would be living. The visits to East Lansing during her playing days were in-and-out blurs that provided no sense for anything other than locker rooms and Jenison Fieldhouse's gym. She assumed East Lansing was much like Ann Arbor, or Madison, Wisconsin. It was no doubt one of those campuses intertwined with the urban setting. Fine, as university environments went, but nothing spectacular from an aesthetic standpoint.

When she made it to East Lansing shortly after her son, Jack, was born (the McCallies already had a daughter, Madeline), what Joanne P. McCallie saw left her awed. She had no sense for how beautiful were Michigan State's campus and grounds, for the marvelous way in which it was self-contained, separated from a quaint town just across Grand River Avenue.

What she knew about the basketball situation in East Lansing was less of a mystery. It was destined to be what other schools and teams were like when a new coach arrived. There were going to be new methods of recruiting, of coaching, of competing. She was going to attempt to instill in them all the floor-diving, go-for-it aggression she wanted to see in a basketball team, which was, for her, something of an extension of an Italian woman whose passion for basketball had always been full-throttle.

She was going to get help from her coaching counterparts, Tom Izzo, and his assistants, Brian Gregory and Mike Garland. They knew a little about taking over a team where a coach had no choice but to make an impression quickly and to begin forging a product in line with that coach's convictions and methodology.

Izzo over and over used the phrase "changing the culture" during his visits with McCallie. He and Gregory made sure the new coach understood she was hardly the only newcomer who had dealt with precisely the issues she was now confronting at Michigan State.

"What's wrong?" Izzo would ask as he passed by McCallie's office and saw the stress in her face.

McCallie would tell him that she preferred not to talk about it.

"Yeah, you're gonna talk about it," he would say. "I've been where you are and I know."

Recruiting was going to be a first, necessary step, which for McCallie meant she had to become quickly familiarized with new geography and with the talent inside of MSU's essential recruiting radius.

Everyone in Ingham County had been on McCallie to get going on a sharpshooter out of Dansville High School by the name of Lindsay Bowen.

"You've got to sign this kid, you've got to sign her," one local after another told the new Spartans' coach, urgency in their voices.

"Could you let me see her play first?" McCallie would answer, half-laughing.

Another local star, Kristin Haynie, from Mason High School, would stop by the office to talk with McCallie, but said scarcely a word. Her shyness was appealing. She was being recruited hard by all the Big Ten schools, although McCallie was on the fence.

"Could you give me time just to go through the natural order of things?" McCallie asked Haynie following her junior year of high school.

Haynie had boiled it down to Michigan and Michigan State. She was trying to decide, as was McCallie. By the end of July, McCallie had agreed Haynie was a player MSU wanted. Haynie, though, waited two-and-a-half more months before committing to MSU. She told McCallie later it was the interlude that had sold her; that understanding a head coach wanted to get to know her had ultimately made the difference.

Michigan State's talent bin as McCallie arrived was not sufficient to win a Big Ten championship, nor, most likely, to win any invitations to the NCAA tournament. She focused on defense and on implementing the Joanne P. basketball ethic, which was going to not necessarily win friends, but it would influence people.

The Spartans were 10-18 in 2000-01, but climbed to 19-13 the following season to get a spot in the Women's National Invitation Tournament, where

Kristen Haynie was a key recruit in helping Joanne P. McCallie turn women's basketball around at Michigan State.

the Spartans made it to the semifinals.

A year later, in 2002-03, the Spartans were 17-12, but moved to 10-6 in the Big Ten, good for a fourth-place tie (MSU had been ninth the previous season) and a first trip to the NCAA tournament for a Spartans team coached by McCallie.

It was another 10-6 season in the Big Ten for Michigan State in 2003-04, and this time the NCAA tournament run was a game longer as McCallie's team beat Arizona before losing to Texas and finishing the season a strong 22-9.

McCallie's recruiting had steadily picked up as Michigan State began to climb in profile and, as had happened at Maine, in box-office receipts. The Spartans had made an earnest marketing effort toward getting a community to embrace a team that was skilled, that had appealing students and athletes who were bound to be more approachable than their male counterparts, who would pose for photographs with a small child, who could endear a populace that had been conditioned to a much more distant relationship with its male basketball heroes at Breslin Center. It was all a product of tradition, of gender, of incessant attention to which one cast of players had long been exposed versus a group of women who had a higher appreciation for crowds and for those rooting for them.

Kelli Roehrig and Liz Shimek were two more stars McCallie had brought to East Lansing as MSU began assembling in October for the 2004-05 season. They were about to join Haynie, Bowen, Rene Haynes, Victoria Lucas-Perry, and others for what was going to be a Hollywood basketball story, whether the women realized it or not.

The Spartans were 28-3 as the 2005 NCAA tournament got rolling. They had gone 14-2 in the Big Ten to finish as co-champion, and anyone handicapping the NCAA women's basketball tournament in 2005 would not have been surprised if Michigan State had a meaningful experience at an NCAA Regional.

The Spartans first mowed down Alcorn State before slipping past Southern Cal, 61-59, in a second-round game at Minneapolis. The Spartans were back in the Sweet Sixteen for the first time in eight years, playing at the Midwest Regional at Kansas City.

First up, and first down, was Vanderbilt, which was dispatched, 76-64. And then came Stanford, the nation's top-ranked team. The Cardinal fell to the Spartans, 76-69, as all the basketball fever that had engulfed East Lansing during Izzo's Final Four runs now swept over a women's team that, amazingly, was joining Izzo's troops in side-by-side Final Four appearances. The women left for Indianapolis as the men headed for St. Louis.

Michigan State had only to beat the biggest, baddest wolf in any NCAA women's tournament: Tennessee, the dynastic team coached by Pat Head. The Lady Volunteers and Head had intimidated more than one opponent through the years that might otherwise have had a shot at beating them.

The Spartans held their poise early, trailing by six at the half, 31-25, but fell apart in the first five minutes of the second half. They were down, 49-33, and about to go the way of other teams Tennessee had, through the years, chewed up and spit onto the hardcourt.

McCallie thought otherwise as Michigan State called time out with 14:30 on the clock.

"You have to be kidding me," she squealed. "We've come all this way and we're gonna pull this crap?"

McCallie basically let it be known she was not attaching herself to an effort as timid as MSU was turning in at its showcase moment. She had never been angrier as a coach.

Her words fueled a comeback, as Roehrig, Lucas-Perry and Shimek went to work and Bowen knocked down a pair of big three-pointers. The ensuing timeouts were more civil.

"They're going to choke," McCallie yelled, trying to make her players understand that knocking off the giant was within their power. "They're going to buckle. When one of them does miss a shot, you'll see it."

McCallie knew she had gotten to Bowen and Haynie. She could always get to Bowen and Haynie.

The comeback was now certified storybook stuff. Lucas-Perry sank two free throws with 1:20 on the clock to tie the game, 62-62. Haynie's steal and lay-up put Michigan State on top for the first time since the game's opening minutes. Roehrig's basket with 35 seconds left kept MSU on top as Tennessee missed three consecutive shots, setting up Lucas-Perry for a lay-up that finished off the biggest comeback ever by a NCAA Final Four women's team.

The Spartans had outscored Tennessee, 35-15, to shoot down Goliath and leave Head with a numbed expression as she hurriedly, and briefly, shook hands with McCallie.

"Good game," Head said.

It was, indeed, one of the greatest games in the history of the MSU women's basketball program.

But MSU's magic was spent. The title game was an 84-62 blowout loss to Baylor that simply reminded a coach, a team, and a community, that they were in good company—Izzo's team had gone to a Final Four once, and lost, before a second time produced a national championship trophy.

Joanne McCallie (right) gives instruction to Lindsay Bowen, who ended her career as MSU's second-leading scorer behind Liz Shimek.

One was coming, McCallie had to believe, as she and her players headed back to East Lansing and to a basketball-crazy town that now knew it had more than one team to love.

THAT CHAMPIONSHIP TROPHY DID NOT COME in 2006, although the endlessly repeated word by which college sports teams and their status are sized up—"program"—earned a bit more luster when MSU made it to the NCAA Sweet 16 for the second consecutive season. It was evident both in State's record (24-10 against a brutal schedule), and in the Breslin Center turnouts (6,787 on average, tenth in the nation in attendance). This story had been building since McCallie arrived to do exactly what she had done at Maine: make women's basketball a box-office smash, taking crowds that averaged just over a thousand at both schools and boosting attendance 500 percent.

The Spartans in 2005-06 played twelve games against ranked teams, including three of the eventual Final Four schools. Eight of State's defeats came against teams ranked in the top ten.

MSU managed to finish in a third-place tie in the Big Ten and, because of the schedule, to pull a fourth seed at the NCAA tournament. The Spartans behaved in a way their men friends at Breslin Center would have appreciated, cleaning up on Wisconsin-Milwaukee (65-46), and rallying to beat Kentucky (67-63), which put McCallie's team into the East Regional at Bridgeport, Connecticut, against top-seed Duke.

Duke had its customary clout in 2006, and ran over the Spartans, 86-61, not that it diminished much of what had happened the past two seasons as McCallie's basketball stage production became a season-long hit. The Spartans ran their two-year record to 57-14, won twenty-three consecutive games at home (a streak snapped on a shot at the horn against Ohio State on January 22), and finished the year with a 27-1 home record spanning the 2004-05 and 2005-06 seasons.

Their sterling seniors, Shimek and Bowen, went out magnificently, finishing as the top two scorers in MSU history, 41 points apart (Shimek, 1,780; Bowen 1,739). Underclassmen Lucas-Perry and Rene Haynes had breakthrough years. McCallie, six years into a program that was maturing into a national model, could feel good as she prepared for a spring and a summer getting reacquainted with her family. She could enjoy an off-season of work, and reflection on the good fortune that had come her way that day when she and husband John sat with the folks at Michigan State and said "yes,"—when they had never planned to do any such thing.

The only entity that had the McCallies bested on the good-fortune scale was Michigan State. Not all of the University's coaching selections spanning recent years and decades had worked out. This one did, and best of all from Michigan State's perspective was sensing the possibilities and the good times that lay ahead.

ACKNOWLEDGMENTS

One thing about a book project on the scale of Spartan Seasons II is that the author does not write the story as much as others tell it. It is an effort that is greatly dependent upon the input, and assistance, of those who either were directly involved in a particular segment of Michigan State sports history, or those who in one manner or another assist in researching MSU's sports past.

Not many of the names listed here had any particular gain in speaking at length about their experience at Michigan State. They all assisted, nonetheless, and most of them donated time far in excess of that which was initially requested.

I am grateful.

Specific thank-you notes begin with my friend of thirty-four years, Stan Stein, whose passion for Michigan State sports gave birth to the original *Spartan Seasons*, as well as to its sequel, *Spartan Seasons II*. No one has a deeper love for Michigan State than Stan Stein. He was the person who first conceived a need for an in-depth book on MSU sports that would take readers to a new level of understanding about a unique sports galaxy. It was his drive, determination, investment, and patience that led to publication of both books. He managed along the way to research, edit, arrange, schedule, and communicate (many times during one of his energy-sapping flights to and from Asia) as he came to embody this book's necessary work ethic.

Deep thanks, as well to this book's publisher, Bill Haney, who devoted incredible energy toward a project that was particularly challenging because of the time necessary to put together a manuscript so comprehensive. Bill Haney is a marvelous professional, a writer's editor, a skilled writer himself, and a good friend. I, as well as the *Spartan Seasons II* audience, could not have benefited more from a publisher's devotion to professionalism.

John Lewandowski, the associate athletic director who heads up MSU's sports information effort, assisted in everything from scheduling interviews to answering important trivia questions. His assistant, Paulette Martis, was spectacular in handling endless questions and correspondence. Lewandowski's sports information colleagues—Jamie Weir, Matt Larson, Ben Phlegar—and interns such as Branden Gerraud Wilson, bailed us out time and time again with assistance that spanned the spectrum.

A considerable amount of travel became part of this book's interview regimen. Whether it was Nick Saban in Baton Rouge, Louisiana, or Peter McPherson in Washington, D.C., or assistant coaches such as Charlie Baggett in Mobile, Alabama, all gave lavishly of time they did not have to spare.

There were other publications that also assisted mightily in tracking chronology and facts-checking as we put together a book that is, of course, an effort in sports history.

George Perles and his co-author Vahe Gregorian gave an important account of the Perles years in *The Ride of a Lifetime.* Clarence Underwood's book, *Greener Pastures*, was of immense help, as well, in keeping MSU's sports timeline in order.

Media friends were also helpful in providing insight and accuracy. None of them shared more graciously than Steve Grinczel of Booth Newspapers, and Neil Koepke of the *Lansing State Journal*.

Attempting to cite each individual is impossible. A collective expression of appreciation is offered to those below, realizing, painfully, that some good folks are no doubt being overlooked:

Shelley Appelbaum, Pete Babcock, Charlie Baggett, Merrily Dean Baker, Tim Bograkos, Bill Burke, Rick Comley, Jim Comparoni, Tom

Crean, John DiBiaggio, Terry Denbow, Tico Duckett, Dave Dye, Lisa Eberhardt, Jack Ebling, Dan Enos, Jim Epolito, Brad Fast, Joel Ferguson, Steve Finamore, Gus Ganakas, Fred Girard, A.J. Granger, Vahe Gregorian, Brian Gregory, Steve Grinczel, Adam Hall, Paul Harker, Herb Haygood, Jud Heathcote, Pam Henning, Jemele Hill, Mark Hollis, Greg Ianni, Tom Izzo, Stan Joplin, Michael Kasavana, Stan Kasten, Neil Koepke, Karen Langeland, Matt Larson, John Lewandowski, Paulette Martis, Ron Mason, Charlie McBride, Joanne P. McCallie, Kyle Melinn, Tom Newton, Julie Pagel, Tara Paternoster, Ben Phlegar, Peter McPherson, Reggie Mitchell, Merritt Norvell, Tom Nowland, Mike Peplowski, George Perles, Shawn Respert, Nick Saban, Terry Saban, Linda Selby, Jack Shingleton, Zena Simmons, John L. Smith, Tim Staudt, Matt Steigenga, Jason Strayhorn, Joe Tate, Milt Tenopir, Sylvia Thompson, Clarence Underwood, Morris Watts, Jamie Weir, Bob Weiss, Roger Wilkinson, Bobby Williams, Branden Gerraud Wilson, Adam Wolfe, Pat Zacharias.

I had to reach around the country—and beyond—for help in this venture. Jacinta Calcut took her composition and design equipment—as well as her energy and talents—to Jamaica to continue her tireless efforts to give the book its final look. Her husband, Ken, brought forward the design concept for the book's cover.

To help get word of the existence of *Spartan Seasons II* to a wider community, Allie McCafferty designed and set up a new website for the publisher, Sports Seasons Publishing.

I have been the beneficiary, but not the only one, of your contributions. Michigan State University and its sports community are also enriched by your willingness to share so freely.

LH

Now for the rest of the story...

The Michigan State sports saga had its origin decades ago.
In his original *Spartan Seasons*, published in 1987, Lynn Henning
captured the inside stories about Magic...Gibby...Duffy...
Muddy...Mason...and countless other MSU legends. In that
acclaimed, definitive book on Spartan sports, Henning
illuminates the dark corners and solves the behind-the-scenes
mysteries that have always made the MSU sports scene so
fascinating and controversial.

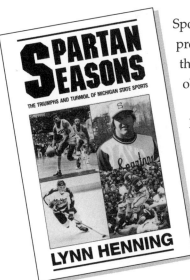

Sports Seasons Publishing has
produced a new, limited edition of
that classic, a must-have for the fan or
observer of Michigan State sports.

For your own sports bookshelf or
as the perfect gift for the Michigan
State alum or sports fan, order
your copy today. Personally
inscribed by the author on
request at no extra charge:

Sports Seasons Publishing
1947 Long Lake Shores
Bloomfield Hills, MI 48302

Hard cover: $13.95
293 pages; photographs
Order direct from: sportsseasonspublishing@comcast.net
or by phone (credit cards only): 248 478-9235